# *All on* C

## *Ken Pugh*

**Scott, Foresman/Little, Brown Higher Education**
*A Division of Scott, Foresman and Company*
*Glenview, Illinois   London, England*

Cover photo: Fran Heyl Associates

Library of Congress Cataloging-in-Publication Data
Pugh, Kenneth.
  All on C / Kenneth Pugh
    p.  cm.
  Bibliography: p.
  Includes index
  ISBN 0-673-18603-2
  1. C (Computer program language)  I. Title.
QA76.73.C15P82  1989
005.13'3—dc20                                           89-061570
                                                            CIP

Library of Congress Catalog Card No. 89-061570
ISBN 0-673-18603-2

    2  3  4  5  6—KPF—94  93  92  91  90

Printed in the United States of America.

Scott, Foresman and Company
Glenview, Illinois  London, England

Trademark Acknowledgments

MS-DOS is a registered trademark of Microsoft Corporation.
OS/2 is a trademark of International Business Machines.
UNIX is a registered trademark of AT&T.
VAX/VMS is a trademark of Digital Equipment Corporation.

# Table of Contents

# Preface

C is a computer language whose use has been rapidly increasing over the past few years. Although C is commonly associated with the UNIX operating system, it is becoming widespread on microcomputers running MS-DOS and OS/2. The language is easy to implement on different computers due to its simplicity and portability. However, its rich set of operators enables the programmer to implement algorithms efficiently.

## APPROACH

The language can be taught from many different approaches. One could teach "Classic C," using the constructs in the language to their fullest extent. This would include embedding assignment statements in places that other languages do not allow, and creating a concise program, as opposed to a maintainable or explainable one. Classic C is described in this book in only a few examples so you can understand code other programmers have written. It is shown also for those few times when code execution must be very fast, but still kept in a higher-level language than assembly language.

Another approach is to teach C as alternative procedural language to FORTRAN or Pascal. C routines can be written to look similar to those in other languages. The constructs that make C unique can then be applied to make these routines more efficient or effective. For example, FORTRAN lacks a record or structure data construct for passing sets of heterogeneous data to subroutines. Pascal does not let you manipulate bits in memory with as much freedom as C does.

The latter approach is taken in this book. The first goal is to make a program work. An emphasis is placed on writing functions and programs that are readable and maintainable. The idiomatic expressions seen in many programs are introduced only after the basic material has been covered. Good programming style is taught by example. All the examples in this book follow the guidelines outlined in boxes on style and in a review chapter on style. Programmers learn by initially imitating examples, rather than reading an explicit list of guidelines. For example, variable names in the sample programs are not simply s or r, but sum and result.

The material is covered in an approach similar to beginning books for other languages. Summaries at the end of each chapter enable a student who has had some programming experience to quickly cover the salient points without reading through the explanatory material. A full program is given at the end of each chapter that demonstrates the material covered in the chapter.

The first portion of this book covers basic language concepts, so you can program exercises of sufficient complexity to get a good understanding of the use of C. The remainder of the features are then outlined. With the notable exceptions of the increment and decrement operators, the #define, and the address operator (for scanf), the opening chapters should present concepts familiar to anyone who has programmed in another language. Next, the facets of C not found in many other languages, such as pointers, are explained. After an examination of the remaining features of the language, more complex data structures, such as lists and trees, are discussed. Finally, the structured use of packages with C is explored in a case study of a simple database with an emphasis on modular code.

## ANSI C AND THIS BOOK'S CODE

The C covered is the ANSI standard C (ANSI C), as adopted in September 1988. Differences between this standard of the language and that described in the Kernighan and Ritchie original implementation of C are summarized in Appendix C. Suggestions for modifications of the sample routines so they can work with older compilers are in Appendix B.

The only major difference between the C code shown in this book and the ANSI standard is the form of the function header. The standard includes an alternative function header in which the parameter descriptions are embedded in the calling sequence. The code in this book follows the current style, as it is prevalent throughout most current C programs. This is a problem in showing examples in a book relying on a standard not yet fully implemented. Appendix J shows some programs written with the new header form.

## BACKGROUND

I assume throughout the book that you have some background in computers. You should be familiar with text editing and have had an introduction to a computer language, such as BASIC, FORTRAN, or Pascal in a semester-length course or equivalent. You should be aware of the concepts of variables, assignment, expressions, conditional execution, loops, functions, and arrays.

# ACKNOWLEDGMENTS

My appreciation to Leslie Killeen, my wife, for enduring the amount of time it took to write this book, and for taking care of many of the mechanical facets of its publication. To Stuart Trask for his attention to the details. To Daniel Turney for his comments and corrections on everything from the grammatically trivial to the logical bug. To Peter Leed for his editorial comments. To my other reviewers for their numerous suggestions and corrections on organization, style, and content. They are Harry Lewis of Harvard University, Gary Fostel of North Carolina State University, Steve Allen of Utah State University, Furzsina Veresh and Marek Holynski of Boston University, Jim Hugens of Florida State University, and also Mike Michaelson and Seth Aaronson. To B. A. for sunny days in which to write outside.

Kenneth Pugh

# Suggested Schedule for a 14-Week Course

# Chapter One

# Introduction to ANSI C

C is a versatile language for writing programs ranging from simple applications to complex operating systems. The organization of this book parallels this diversity. After a brief historical note, a simple program introduces the process of compiling, linking, and executing a C program. Then more involved programs demonstrate many of the features of C and some of the pitfalls.

## HISTORY OF C

Although the explosion in its use is recent, the C language has a long history. Its ancestor, Basic Combined Programming Language (BCPL), was developed by Martin Richards in 1967. Ken Thompson refined it into a system with the succinct name B. Dennis Ritchie started with B, added features to (''enhanced'') it, and created the original implementation of C in 1972. It was first implemented on a DEC PDP-11 computer. From this early background, C developed as a high-level language with close ties to assembly language. Many of its instructions represented one or two machine instructions on the PDP-11. It was designed with hardware independence in mind. The compiler was rapidly ported to diverse machines, such as the IBM 370 and the Honeywell 6000.

The original C had many traits that were remnants of its original heritage. C's use expanded as the UNIX operating system developed. Until then, most operating systems had been written in assembly language. UNIX was written mostly in C, with only a small kernel in assembly language. When personal computers arrived on the scene, many programs were written in assembly and other languages, such as Pascal. C proved to be an excellent language to develop programs on personal computers: its speed approaches assembly language, and its portability makes code transfer easily to the myriad variations of PC architectures. Thus, C rapidly has become the PC programming language of choice today.

In 1983 a small group of C developers formed the X3J11 committee of the American National Standards Institute (ANSI). The purpose of this committee was to standardize the C language. The original definition for C was Appendix A of *The C Programming Language* by Brian Kernighan and Dennis Ritchie (K&R). That description served as a de facto standard, with most compiler manufacturers describing their products in terms of deviations from it. The changes from the description in K&R to the ANSI standard are listed in Appendix C of this text.

## THE FIRST PROGRAM

The best way to start learning C is to try a program. A simple C program is

**Listing 1.1 Hi Everybody**

```
#include <stdio.h>

main()
    {
    printf("\n Hi everybody");
    }
```

### Entering the Program

You can try out the program development process with this example.[1] The first operation is to enter this program into your computer. You can use the word processor or text editor that you use for other languages. On personal computers, you can use any word processing program that can produce a pure ASCII file (one that contains no special formatting characters). On a mainframe IBM, you might use kedit or with UNIX, vi or ed. Save this program as hello.c.

### Compiling the Program

Once the program has been entered, you compile it by invoking the compiler. On almost all systems, the name of the compiler is cc. You simply type the name of

---

[1] If you are running the programs under a UNIX environment, you may wish to add printf("\n"); to this program, to return the cursor to the next line. The program should read:

```
main()
    {
    printf("\n Hi everybody");
    printf("\n");
    }
```

On some systems, you may need to switch the position of the \n character, so the quoted string will appear as "Hi everybody \n". If so, you will need to make this change on all quoted strings used with printf in this book.

the program to be compiled after the cc, so to compile the sample program, simply type **cc hello.c**. Most compilers automatically append the .c, so you can simply type **cc hello**.

The compiler translates this program file (called the *source file*) and creates a machine language file that represents the program in the native instructions of the computer on which you are working. This is the object file that is usually named by using the first part of the name of the source file and appending .o or .obj. Thus the object file for the hello program would be named hello.o. For many compilers, the translation is a two-stage process. The source file is first translated into an assembly language file and then the assembler translates this file into the machine instructions.

If the compiler cannot translate your program, it will report one or more errors. If you get compiler errors with the hello program, either it was entered incorrectly or your word processor added formatting characters to the source file that the compiler does not understand. Your compiler may display an error something like Cannot find include file. You may have typed the line #include <stdio.h> improperly or the file stdio.h that was supplied with your compiler may not reside in the proper disk directory.

**Linking the Program**

The next step is to link this object file with the library. The library contains routines that help in starting and ending this program and in performing input and output. Each operating system has its own linker. The UNIX linker is automatically invoked by the C compiler. On other systems, you run it manually. Simply specify the name of the object file and the name of the library at the operating system prompt.

The linker combines the object file and the necessary routines in the library and produces an executable file. The executable file (or simply, *executable*) is customarily named using the first part of the object file name and appending .exe or .com. So the test program's .exe file would be called hello.exe. On UNIX systems, it is called a.out.[2] Figure 1.1 illustrates the compile/link process. Table 1.1 summarizes linker commands for popular operating systems.

printf is a function in the standard C library. Functions are described in detail in Chapter 4. The printf function in the library outputs the data you give it to

**Table 1.1 Linker Commands for Various Systems**

| MS/DOS | link hello | |
|--------|------------|--|
| UNIX | cc hello.c | (linker called implicitly) |
| VMS | link hello | |

---

[2] You can use the compiler option -o to give a different name to the file. The line cc -o hello hello.c produces an executable file called hello.

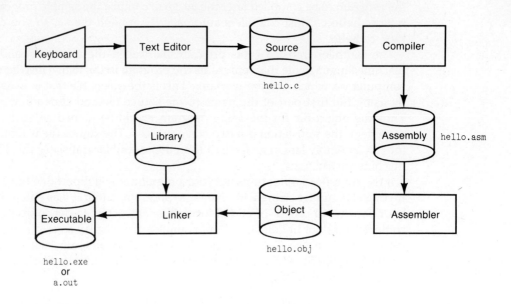

**Figure 1.1 The Process of Compiling and Linking**

the terminal.[3] If you get an error from the linker similar to print undefined, you probably misspelled printf in the program or typed it using uppercase letters. You should go back to the editor, correct the error, and recompile and try linking again.

### Running the Program

You then run the program by typing the name of the executable file at the operating system prompt, such as **hello**, or **a.out**. The program will be loaded and run, and you should see

Hi everybody

appear on your terminal.

## A GUESSING PROGRAM

Now that the basics of editing, compiling, and linking have been mastered, a more complex program is in order. The following program has the computer guessing a number that the user has thought of. Each feature of the program is explained briefly after the listing. Subsequent chapters explain each feature in detail.

---

[3]This assumes you have not redirected the output, a technique shown in Chapter 5.

**The Code**

Listing 1.2 guesses a number you are thinking of. Its logic is based on a binary search technique. In each round you respond to its "guess" with an indication of whether the guessed number is higher or lower than your number. Its next guess is then in the middle of the remaining possible values.

**Listing 1.2 Guessing Game**

```c
#include <stdio.h>
int main()
    {
    int number;

    /* Initial output */
    printf("\n Think of a number between 1 and 127");
    printf("\n I am going to guess your number");

    /* Guess the number */
    number = guess_number();

    /* Output the answer */
    printf("\n Your number is %d", number);

    exit(0);
    }

int guess_number()
/* Guesses a number between 1 and 127 */
    {
    int guess;                /* Current guess */
    int answer;               /* What the user answers */
    int difference;           /* How much to change the guess by */

    /* Initialize the values */
    difference = 32;
    guess = 64;

    while (difference > 0)
        {
        /* Print current guess */

        printf("\n My guess is %d", guess);
        printf("\n Type 0 if this is your number");
        printf("\n Type 1 if this is higher than your number");
        printf("\n Type -1 if this is lower than your number");
```

```
/* Get an answer */
printf("\n Your answer is:");
scanf("%d", &answer);

if (answer == 0)
    {
    /* Guessed it */
    difference = 0;
    }
else if (answer == -1)
    {
    /* Guess was low */
    guess = guess + difference;
    difference = difference / 2;
    }
else if (answer == 1)
    {
    /* Guess was high */
    guess = guess - difference;
    difference = difference / 2;
    }
else
    /* Invalid response */
    printf("\n Enter 0, -1, or 1");
}
return guess;
}
```

---

### Style Tip

If you are running the programs under a UNIX environment, you may wish to add printf("\n"); to each program just before the call to exit, to return the cursor to the next line. On some systems, you may need to switch the position of the "\n" character in strings passed to printf from the first to the last.

---

This program employs two functions: main and guess_number. The main function is always the first one executed, regardless of where it may appear in the source file. After the opening curly brace ({), a variable is declared—number. This holds the value the user guessed. The printf function is called twice to print messages on the terminal. The guess_number function is then called, and it returns a value that is assigned to number. printf is called again to output the number. Then a call to the exit function ends the program. The closing curly brace (}) completes the definition of main. If the call to exit had been left out, the compiler would assume there should be one at the end of the main function.

The guess_number function contains three variables: guess, answer, and difference. The values for guess and difference are assigned initial values. The major portion of the function is the while loop. As long as the condition difference > 0 is true, the statements from the opening curly brace to the matching closing brace just before the return statement are executed over and over. The first statements in this loop call printf to output messages on the screen. The scanf function is called to "scan" the terminal keyboard for a value. The function is passed two items: an indication of the type of value expected and a place to put the input value. The "%d" tells scanf to input an integer value. The &answer tells scanf where to put the value that has been input.

Following the scanf are a series of if statements that test the value of answer. If the value is 0, the number has been guessed and difference is assigned a value of 0. When the test is made at the beginning of the while loop, it will be false, and the next statement executed is the return statement. This statement ends the guess_number function and the value of guess passes back to the calling function, main.

The #include <stdio.h> line includes some additional source code that does not appear in the listing. The statements in this code tell the compiler about use of the printf and scanf functions. This code would compile on most compilers even if this statement were omitted. However, it is a good practice to include it.

If the value of answer is −1 or 1, the value of guess is altered by the value of difference. If the user does not ever answer 0, eventually the value of difference becomes 1. The next value to be assigned to difference would be ½. A fraction cannot be represented as an integer value, so the result of the division is 0. This value is assigned to difference, and the loop ends.

If the user enters any number other than 0, 1, or –1, the function prints a message and does not make any changes to the values of difference and guess.

Listing 1.2 shows many features of C you will master in forthcoming chapters. You may wish to enter the program in your computer and run it to see how it works. If you run into errors in the compilation phase, correct the source file and be sure it matches the example exactly. If you have XXX undefined errors in the link phase, check that printf, scanf, and guess_number are all spelled correctly in the source file. Figure 1.2 represents the binary search process performed by Listing 1.2. The dotted line represents the path followed by the sample output.

**Program Output**

When you execute the program, the following should display on your terminal:

```
Think of a number between 1 and 127
I am going to guess your number
My guess is 64
Type 0 if this is your number
Type 1 if this is higher than your number
```

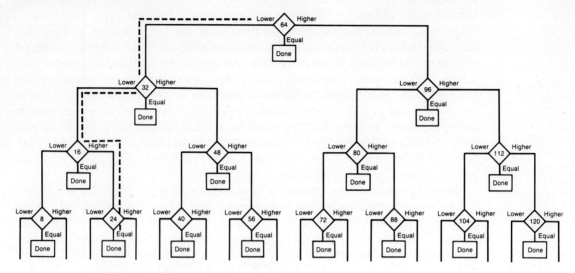

**Figure 1.2 Binary Search Branching**

```
Type -1 if this is lower than your number
Your answer is:
```

Type –1, **0**, or **1** and press **Enter**. A sample session in which the user's number is 24 looks like the following. The user's responses are shown in this typeface.

```
Think of a number between 1 and 127
I am going to guess your number
My guess is 64
Type 0 if this is your number
Type 1 if this is higher than your number
Type -1 if this is lower than your number
Your answer is: 1

My guess is 32
Type 0 if this is your number
Type 1 if this is higher than your number
Type -1 if this is lower than your number
Your answer is: 1

My guess is 16
Type 0 if this is your number
Type 1 if this is higher than your number
Type -1 if this is lower than your number
Your answer is: -1
```

```
My guess is 24
Type 0 if this is your number
Type 1 if this is higher than your number
Type -1 if this is lower than your number
Your answer is: 0

Your number is 24
```

Possibly your program compiled and linked without any errors but the program did not run as just shown or it came out with the wrong answer. You should carefully proof your source file against Listing 1.2.

## YOUR MISTAKES AND PROGRAM ERRORS

We all can learn a lot by making mistakes. When you have successfully run Listing 1.2, you can try it unsuccessfully in different ways to note its reactions. The first technique is simply to run the program, and when it asks for a number, type some "garbage characters" such as **XYZ**. The program will respond in one of several ways. Either it will respond that your number is 64 or 1 or 127, or it will go into an endless loop, prompting you to input –1, 0, or 1. The input routine scanf was told to expect an integer number. It read your keystrokes and did not find characters it could interpret to be a number. So the routine did not insert any value into answer. If no value is entered in answer, whatever value was previously in the variable is still there. If no value is ever put into a variable, its value remains as whatever happened to be in its memory location when the program started. This is usually a "garbage value" (a value that is unknown and causes a program to produce incorrect output or "garbage").

If the value in answer happened to be 0, –1, or 1, the program would react as if you had typed that number in response to each of its requests. The program would determine that the number is 64, 127, or 1, respectively. If the value in answer is anything else, the program asks for the value again and again.

Another error-causing approach is to "lie" to the program about whether the guess was higher or lower. This causes the program to display the wrong answer. There is very little you as a programmer can do to prevent this type of error from occurring. Certain errors you can make do not cause the compiler to display an error message, but they cause the program either to give incorrect answers or to "hang up" or freeze the display. In the latter case, the only way to continue is to restart the entire computer system. You might wish to make a copy of your source file and try compiling it with one or more of these errors:

1. Leave out the & before answer in the call to scanf.
2. Leave out the ,number in the printf call in main.
3. Leave out the ,guess in the printf call in guess_number.

The causes for each type of error will be explained in the appropriate chapter.

## SUMMARY

- The program development process for C is to create a C source file using a word processor or text editor, compile the program, link it, and run it.
- A C program consists of one or more functions. The function named main is the first function executed.
- A program may compile and run, but may contain errors not detected by the compiler.

## SELF-TEST

1. How do you create a C program?
2. What is the first function to be executed?
3. What possible errors may occur when compiling and running a program?
4. What are the purposes of printf and scanf?

## ANSWERS

1. You create a source file with a text editor. The compiler is then run to transform this source code into object code. You then run the linker to create an executable file, which is what you run as an operational program.
2. The main function.
3. Errors reported by the compiler; errors reported by the linker (such as misspelled function names); and input errors made by the user.
4. These functions output and input values to an executing program.

## PROBLEMS

1. Using Listing 1.1 as a guide, write a program that outputs your name, address, and telephone number.
2. Alter Listing 1.2 so it guesses numbers between 1 and 32767.
3. Write a program that fills the screen of your computer with the numbers from 1 to 9, the letters a to z, or both. The program should not force the screen to scroll. In other words, output from the program should stop at exactly the end of the screen. Include with your program a discussion of the various means that could be used to accomplish this task.

4. Write a program that accepts the amounts of various U.S. coins, computes their value in dollars, and converts the result to Japanese yen. The program should prompt for the current value of dollar to the yen. Yen results should be rounded to the nearest yen.

5. Write a program that accepts seconds and converts the amount to hours, minutes, and seconds. After the conversion is completed, the program should prompt for the current time or obtain the current time from the system clock. The converted time should then be added to the current time, and the new time should be output. The program should then determine if that time is night or day.

6. Write a program that draws the letter E on the screen using series of the character X. The letter should be centered, and the height of the letter should be user-selected from a range of 5 to 23 characters. For example, for a height of 5 characters, the program might draw on the screen:

```
XXXXX
X
XXX
X
XXXXX
```

7. Write a program that accepts a user's age in years and displays 1 of 10 fortune cookie-type sayings. The fortune displayed can be selected by some formula related to the user's age. For example, users aged 0 to 5 years get fortune 1, users aged 5 to 10 years get fortune 2, and so on.

# Chapter Two

# Data Types, Variables, and Simple Operations

C has a wide variety of data types that can hold everything from a binary value to a long floating point number. Selecting an appropriate type helps your program run efficiently. Three basic data types of variables and constants are int, double, and char. Assigning values to variables and performing arithmetic operations are then discussed. After a look at expressions, comments, and #defines, a few examples demonstrate how all these features combine into a program.

## DATA TYPES

The most common data type is the integer or int. An integer can contain only whole numbers, usually from $-32767$ to $+32767$.[1]

The floating point data type (double) holds noninteger numbers. It contains numbers whose absolute value is as small as $10^{-38}$ to as large as $10^{+38}$ with at least 10 decimal digits of significance.

The character data type (char) is used for individual characters. It can contain values that represent the character set on a computer. Depending on the machine, this can be the ASCII set, the EBCDIC set (of IBM), or another set. ASCII values, the most common, are shown in Appendix F. Unlike its treatment in most other

---

[1]The range given for each data type is the minimum range according to the ANSI C standard. Some computers and compilers have larger ranges. You should check the manual for your compiler for its particular limits. Chapter 9 has a table on limits for all types of variables. This book assumes two byte integers. Four byte integers are common on large computers.

Two byte integer numbers are stored in sixteen bits. There are $2^{16}$ combinations of bits. $2^{15-1}$ combinations are used for positive numbers, $2^{15-1}$ combinations are used for negative numbers, and one combination is used for 0. The remaining combination is usually used to represent a negative number, so on most computers, the lower limit is $-32768$. However, there are a few machines on which this last combination is used for other purposes.

languages, the `char` is not treated as a special type but simply as a short form of an integer.

Each data type has a corresponding constant and variable syntax, described next.

### Constants

*Constants* represent values that cannot be altered when a program executes. Each data type has its own form of constants. The integer constant is simply an integer number, such as 55, −3, or 32458. The double constant is a number with a decimal place, such as 55., 55.55, or −3.3. The double constant can also be represented using scientific notation, such as 55E0, 5555E−2, and −.33E1.

The character constant is represented using single quotes. For example `'A'` represents the letter A encoded in the particular character set for a computer.[2] Multiple characters are represented by a string constant, which uses double quotes, as `"AB"`. Strings in C are somewhat different from strings in most other languages. A full discussion will be postponed until Chapter 6, which deals with arrays in depth. For now, merely note that the character constant `'A'` is not the same as the string constant `"A"`.

### Variables

*Variables* are names of memory locations for storing values that vary. To name a memory location, you need to declare a name as a particular data type. This is coded by the following:

```
data-type name-of-variable;
```

For example,

| Declaration | Meaning |
|---|---|
| `int number;` | number is an integer variable |
| `double answer;` | answer is a double variable |
| `char chr;` | chr is a character variable |

Certain terms cannot be variable names. These *reserved words* (so called because the language "reserves" the right to use them), or keywords, are shown in Table 2.1.

Names can be any combination of letters (upper and lowercase), digits, and underscores. The name must begin with either a letter or an underscore. The ANSI standard suggests that names beginning with an underscore may become reserved words in the future, so you should limit names to those beginning with just a letter. By convention, names of variables are in lowercase characters.

---

[2] The ASCII character values are shown in Appendix F.

## Table 2.1 List of Keywords

| Keywords | Usage |
|---|---|
| auto | storage type |
| break | control flow (in for, while, do-while, switch) |
| case | control flow (in switch) |
| char | data type |
| const | data type modifier |
| continue | control flow (in for, while, do-while) |
| default | control flow (in switch) |
| do | control flow |
| double | data type |
| else | control flow (with if) |
| enum | data type |
| extern | storage type |
| float | data type |
| for | control flow |
| goto | control flow |
| if | control flow |
| int | data type |
| long | data type modifier |
| register | storage type |
| return | control flow (in function) |
| short | data type modifier |
| signed | data type modifier |
| sizeof | built-in operator |
| static | storage type |
| struct | aggregate data type |
| switch | control flow |
| typedef | data type declarator |
| union | aggregate data type |
| unsigned | data type modifier |
| void | data type |
| volatile | data type modifier |
| while | control flow |

All variables must be declared before they can be used to store values. Many languages, like BASIC and FORTRAN, allow the use of a variable in a routine without a declaration. Its presence signifies the programmer wants memory set aside for that variable. C is stringent in this regard. In addition, it does not allow two variables of the same name within the same function. There are exceptions to this rule to be discussed in Chapter 9.

Names can be up to 31 characters long. The compiler accepts longer names, but the extra characters may be ignored. Names that are spelled the same way but have letters in different cases are treated as two different names. For example,

```
int number;
int Number;
```

declare two different variables. If you tried referring in your program to a name, say, NUMBER, the compiler would report that it was undeclared or undefined. Two declarations as:

```
int
a_very_long_variable_name_greater_than_32_characters;
double
a_very_long_variable_name_greater_than_32_characters_a;
```

would produce a message that you had redeclared the variable

```
a_very_long_variable_name_greate.
```

You should make up meaningful variable names that take advantage of the sizable length allowed. For example,

| Declaration of Variable | Comment |
| --- | --- |
| int c; | a bit short |
| int cnt; | a little better |
| int count; | about right |
| int count_of_how_many_times; | a bit wordy |

Longer names help to make your program readable. However, if names are too long, they may interfere with readability.

You can declare more than one variable by giving a list separated by commas.

```
int i, j, k;
```

declares i, j, and k to be ints. Because it is good programming practice to put a comment on the declaration line describing the variable, this form appears only rarely in this book.

---

### Style Tip

Use meaningful variable names. They are one key ingredient in writing a readable program.

---

## STORAGE CLASSES AND INITIALIZATION

The storage for a variable can be managed in two ways. The memory location it uses can be fixed and never changed while the program is executing. Or the location can be given to the variable (allocated) when the function is called and taken away (deallocated) when the function is finished. By default, variables that appear declared in a function are of the latter type. These are called *automatic variables* (auto), because storage is automatically allocated and deallocated for them. When a function is called, the values in these variables are whatever happened to be residing in the memory locations. These values are not useful, so you should initialize the variables when you declare them. You can do so by following the form:

*data type variable-name = value;*

For example, compare the declarations here.

| **Declaration** | **Meaning** |
|---|---|
| int number = 7; | number is an integer variable initialized to 7 |
| double guess = 99.5 | guess is a double variable initialized to 99.5 |
| double answer = 3.3E1; | answer is a double variable initialized to 3.3E1 or 33 |
| char chr = 'A'; | chr is a character variable initialized to 'A' |

A static variable is allocated a memory location when the program starts executing. It is deallocated only when the entire program is finished. This type of variable is useful for those instances when a function needs to keep a value between successive calls. The static variable can be given an initial value, but it is only assigned that value once, when the program starts to execute. To declare a variable as static, simply place the word static before the declaration. If you don't explicitly initialize a static variable, it is set to 0.

| **Declaration** | **Meaning** |
|---|---|
| static int num; | declares num to be a static variable initialized to 0 by default |
| static double temp = 5.5; | declares temp to be a double variable that is initialized to 5.5 |

---

## ASSIGNMENT

The simplest operation to perform with variables is assigning their values. The value can be a constant, another variable, or the result of an operation. For example,

| **Declaration** | **Meaning** |
|---|---|
| int number; | declares number to be an integer variable |
| int new_number; | declares new_number to be an integer variable |
| number = 5; | puts the value 5 into number |
| new_number = number; | puts the value that is in number (5) into new_number |

The left hand of an assignment operator (=) must represent a memory location where a value can be stored. This is called an *lvalue* (short for left value). A constant does not represent a memory location, so 5 = number; gives a compiler error. Nor does an expression, so number + 1 = 5; will also give an error.

If the data type on the right-hand side of an assignment does not agree with the data type on the left-hand side, then an arithmetic conversion is performed, according to the following table:[3]

---

[3]A full table is in Chapter 9.

| Left-hand Side | Right-hand Side | Conversion |
|---|---|---|
| int | double | fractional part discarded; integral number part is converted to integer representation |
| double | int | converted to floating point representation |

As will be further described in Chapter 9, the assignment operator has a few more properties that are unlike any other language. The assignment operator has a value, which is that being assigned. This value can be used in an expression. For example, a_number = (number = 3) * 5 puts the value 3 into number. Then it takes that value (3), multiplies it by 5, and puts the result (15) into a_number.

Although these properties can be useful, they can also cause many errors for the novice C programmer. In the beginning, you should try not to use them. Throughout most of this book, the assignment operator appears by itself. It is followed by a semicolon to make it a statement, which is the equivalent of the assignment statement in other languages.

## ARITHMETIC OPERATORS

The arithmetic operators perform the standard arithmetic operations. They are addition (+), subtraction (−), multiplication (*) and division (/). These binary operators require two values to operate on. The two unary operators, the minus (or negation) operator (−) and the unary plus (+), only require a single value. The result of all these operators is a value usable in other operations. There is also a modulus operator (%) that can only be applied to integer values. The value of x % y is the remainder when x is divided by y. For example:

| Expression | Meaning |
|---|---|
| 2 * 3 | has a value of 6 |
| 2 * 3 + 7 | has a value of 13 |
| 7 % 2 | has a value of 1 |
| 7 % 4 | has a value of 3 |

### Precedence and Associativity

When an expression involves multiple mathematical operations, such as 2 * 3 + 7, the compiler must evaluate it to determine what operation to perform first. The compiler uses rules to decide the order, called *precedence rules*. An operation with higher precedence than another is performed first. Operations of equal precedence are performed in an order that depends on their associativity. Multiplication, division, and modulus have equal precedence. They have higher precedence than addition and subtraction, which are of equal precedence. They are all left to right associative. *Associativity* determines how a sequence of operators of the same precedence group values. For example, with a + b + c and left-to-right associativity, the addition of a and b is performed before c is added. For the arithmetic operators, these rules work just like those in algebra.

With 2 * 3 + 7, the multiplication 2 * 3 is performed first, then the addition. Note that the actual order of terms in the expression is not significant—it would not matter if this was written as 7 + 2 * 3. The multiplication would still be performed first.

You can alter the order of precedence by using parentheses. The operation inside a set of parentheses is always performed before an operation outside, so 2 * (3 + 7) will be calculated as 3 + 7, or 10, times 2, totaling 20. Some more examples are

| Expression | Evaluated as |
| --- | --- |
| 2 * 6 + 9 / 3 | 2 * 6 is 12, 9 / 3 is 3 , 12 + 3 is 15 |
| 2 * (6 + 9 / 3) | 9 / 3 is 3, 6 + 3 is 9, 2 * 9 is 18 |
| (2 * 6 + 9) / 3 | 2 * 6 is 12, 12 + 9 is 21, 21 / 3 is 7 |

## CONVERSION

If the arithmetic types on either side of an arithmetic operator are different, the compiler automatically converts one so the types match. C does an implicit conversion with the char data types. All char values are converted to integers (int) The ramifications of arithmetic on character values are covered in Chapter 9. For the types covered so far, these conversions would work as

```
int i;
int j;
char c;
double d;
```

| Expression | Meaning |
| --- | --- |
| i + j | two ints, addition is in integer arithmetic. |
| d + i | int and a double, the value of i is converted to a double and the addition is in floating point. |
| c + i | c is promoted to an integer, the addition is performed in integer arithmetic. |

You might wonder if there is a reason not to make all values doubles so you would not have to worry about integers at all. Doing arithmetic in floating point can take 10 to 100 times longer than doing it as integers. A program running a few seconds with integers might run minutes with doubles. Floating point should only be used if the program requires noninteger numbers.

## EXPRESSIONS AND STATEMENTS

An *expression* in C is any valid combination of operators, variables, constants, and function calls. A call to a function, whether it be part of the compiler or one included in the source code, can produce a value usable in an expression. The guess_number function in Chapter 1 is an example of such a function. Examples of expressions are

| Expression | Meaning |
|---|---|
| 2 * 4 + 7 | is a valid expression |
| 2 * * 4 + 5 | is not valid |
| guess_number() | is a valid expression |
| guess_number() + 7 | is a valid expression |

The value of an expression can be assigned to a variable, passed to a function, or used to build a more complex expression.

A *statement* is an expression followed by a semicolon, such as

| Expression | Statement |
|---|---|
| 2 * 4 + 7 | 2 * 4 + 7; |
| guess_number() | guess_number(); |
| guess_number() + 7 | guess_number() + 7; |

The null statement is just a semicolon (;). It is a place holder where a statement is required, but you do not want to do anything. An example of a null statement occurs in Chapter 3 with the if statement.

## COMMENTS AND WHITE SPACE

*Comments* are portions of the program that help someone who reads the actual program code to figure out what the program is supposed to do or how it works. The compiler ignores comments when it translates the program. A comment is any block of text surrounded by /* and */. For example,

```
/* This is a comment */
```

Although they are not needed by the compiler, comments should be included in every program you write. Even if no one else reads your program, it is a way of indicating to yourself why you coded something a certain way. These notes can be written on a slip of paper, but those slips have a way of disappearing. Including them with the code itself ensures that the explanation will always be there.

At a minimum, the purpose of each variable and each function in a program should be explained with a short comment. These can appear on the same line as the declaration. Each section of code that performs an operation should be commented. The comments in Listing 1.2 and the example functions give an indication of how frequent your comments should be. Overcommenting code hardly ever is a problem. Undercommenting it usually is.

White space consists of characters that are usually ignored by the compiler. You insert white space with characters such as the space, tab (horizontal and vertical), form feed, and new-line characters. Blank comments insert space, too. This makes C free form. You can write the statement

```
function(5.1,1)+7
```

as:

```
function   (   5.1 ,   1   )   + 7;
```

or

```
function
    (
    5.1
    ,
    1
    )
    +
    7
    ;
```

Keep a standard spacing convention, such as one line to a statement; otherwise, your programs may become unreadable. Blank lines can separate portions of code, even if comments are not appropriate. Keywords, names, and constants must be separated by white space from each other. For example,

```
double x;                cannot be written as doublex;
int i;                   cannot be written as inti;
```

| *Style Tip* |
| --- |
| Use blank space to break up programs. It graphically helps in understanding the program. Use comments to explain the code, not repeat it. |

## THE printf AND scanf FUNCTIONS

The functions `printf` and `scanf` input and output information from a program. They are covered in detail in Chapter 5 and Appendix G. A brief description of these functions is given here, so you can get values into and out of your program. The forms in this book for calling these functions are[4]

```
printf("format-string",one-or-more-values...);
scanf("format-string",address of a variable);
```

The `printf` function simply prints the characters in the *format-string* unless it is one of these format specifiers:

| Specifier | Data Type |
|-----------|-----------|
| %lf | double |
| %d | integer |
| %c | character |

Then it outputs the value with which you call it. The data type should agree with the type you specify in the format string. The character '\n' in the format string forces a new line on the terminal.

For scanf, the format string should contain one of the specifiers. The data type of the variable whose address is given should agree with that of the specifier. The & operator (address operator) should appear on all simple variables (ones that are not arrays) in scanf calls. This operator will be explained in detail in Chapter 8. If you had the following declarations, printf and scanf would produce the results shown.

```
int a = 5;
int b = 8;
double d = 13.;
char c = 'Z';
```

| Call | Output |
|------|--------|
| `printf(" Hi there");` | Hi there |
| `printf("\n Hi\n there");` | Hi |
| | there |
| `printf("\n A is %d", a);` | A is 5 |
| `printf("\n A is %d B is %d", a, b);` | A is 5 B is 8 |
| `printf("\n C is %c", c);` | C is Z |
| `printf("\n D is %lf", d);` | D is 13.000000 |

| Call | Notes |
|------|-------|
| `scanf("%d", &a);` | input integer value to a |
| `scanf("%c",&c);` | input character to c |
| `scanf("%lf",&d);` | input floating point value to d |

---

[4] You can input multiple values with scanf, as is shown in Chapter 5.

Whenever you use `printf` or `scanf` in a file, you should have this line at the top of the file:

```
#include <stdio.h>
```

This statement tells the compiler to read a file named `stdio.h` and place the contents in your file before the compiler compiles it. Your current compiler may not require this, but it is a good practice to get into. Chapter 11 covers the `#include` command in more detail.

---

| *Debug Hint* |
| --- |
| Check all `scanf` calls for the address operator on simple variables. Omitting it may cause your program to bomb. |

---

## THE #define COMMAND

C provides a way of giving a name to a constant value using the `#define` command. The form is simply

```
#define NAME value
```

The name can be in any case (uppercase, lowercase, or mixed). After this line is inserted, wherever the name appears in your program, C substitutes the value given for it. It works like a search and replace command in your word processor. For example, if you code

```
#define INCHES_IN_METER 39.37
```

then you can write

```
inches = INCHES_IN_METER * meters;
```

and it will be just as if you had written

```
inches = 39.37 * meters;
```

The `#define` has many other uses, as will be shown in Chapter 11. One note of caution: The exact value as you type it will replace the name everywhere. If you enter

```
#define INCHES_IN_METER 39.37 ;
```

the compiler will interpret the statement as

```
inches = 39.37 ; * meters;
```

and the compiler will have given you an error.

---

### Debug Hint

Do not use a #define with the same name as a variable. For example,

```
#define a 5
int a;
```

will give a compiler error as it will look to the compiler like:

```
int 5;
```

---

You can write programs without using #defines, but they make your program a bit more readable and more maintainable.

---

### Style Tip

Within reason, all constants in a program should be #defined. A standard convention is to use uppercase letters for the name of the #define.

---

## SAMPLE PROGRAMS

Here are a few programs demonstrating some of the basic operations that have been described.

Listing 2.1 converts a length in meters to a length in inches. The input value is placed in meters. It is used in the expression meters * INCHES_IN_METERS and the value of the expression is assigned to inches. The values of both variables are then printed.

**Listing 2.1 Meters to Inches**

```
#define INCHES_IN_METERS 39.37

#include <stdio.h>

int main()
/* Converts meters to inches */
    {
        double inches;              /* Length in inches */
        double meters;              /* Length in meters */
```

```
/* Get a measure in meters*/
printf("\n Input a length in meters: ");
scanf("%lf", &meters);

/* Convert it to inches */
inches = meters * INCHES_IN_METERS;
printf("\n %lf meters is %lf inches", meters, inches);

exit(0);
}
```

This one converts a temperature in Celsius to one in Fahrenheit. Note that SCALE is specified as a division. This constant is actually computed by the compiler. It is much clearer than using .55555555555555.

Listing 2.2 follows the same pattern as Listing 2.1.

**Listing 2.2 Celsius to Fahrenheit**

```
#define OFFSET 32.              /* Zero degree offset */
#define SCALE (5./9.)           /* Scale factor for degrees */

#include <stdio.h>

int main()
/* Converts Fahrenheit to Celsius */
    {
    double celsius;            /* Temperature in Celsius */
    double fahrenheit;         /* Temperature in Fahrenheit */

    /* Input a temperature */
    printf("\n Input a temperature in Fahrenheit: ");
    scanf("%lf", &fahrenheit);

    /* Convert it */
    celsius = (fahrenheit - OFFSET) * SCALE;
    printf("\n Temperature in Celsius is %lf", celsius);

    exit(0);
    }
```

This program is adapted from *101 BASIC Computer Games* by Digital Equipment Corporation (1975). It is based on *Arithmetica* of Nicomachus, who died in 120 A.D. You are to think of a number between 1 and 100 and divide it by 3, 5, and 7. The program asks for the remainders and places them in remain_3, remain_5, and remain_7. It then computes answer using the formula that was created by Nicomachus and prints it out.

**Listing 2.3 Nicomachus's Guessing Game**

```
#include <stdio.h>

int main()
/* Nicomachus's game */
    {
        int remain_3          /* Remainder of division by 3 */
        int remain_5;         /* Remainder of division by 5 */
        int remain_7;         /* Remainder of division by 7 */
        int answer;           /* Answer */

        printf("\n Think of a number between 1 and 100");
        printf("\n What is the remainder when your number is divided by 3? ");
        scanf("%d", &remain_3);
        printf("\n What is remainder when divided by 5? ");
        scanf("%d", &remain_5);
        printf("\n What is remainder when divided by 7? ");
        scanf("%d", &remain_7);

        answer = 70 * remain_3 + 21 * remain_5 + 15 * remain_7;
        answer = answer % 105;
        printf("\n Your number was %d", answer);
        printf("\n If you don't agree, check your arithmetic");

        exit(0);
    }
```

## SUMMARY

- Three data types for variables and constants are integer (int), floating point (double), and character (char).
- All variables must be declared before they are used. They can be initialized in the declaration.
- Automatic variables are allocated storage only when a function is executing. Static variables are always allocated storage.
- Expressions are combinations of operators, constants, variables, and function calls.
- Precedence and associativity rules determine how an expression is interpreted.
- The assignment operator assigns the value of an expression to a variable.
- The #define is a symbolic substitute for constants.

## SELF-TEST

1. What will be the values of i and d after this code is executed?

```
double i = 3.5;
int d = 5;
d = 3 * i;
i = d * 2;
```

2. What is the value of c after this code is executed (if using ASCII codes)?

```
char c = 'A';
c = c + 10;
```

3. What are the values of a, b, and c after each of the three assignment statements?

```
main()
    {
    int a;
    int b;
    static int c = 5;
    b = a;
    a = c;
    b = c * a;
    }
```

4. What will be printed after the following is executed?

```
int a;
int b = 8;
a = b % 5;
printf("\n a is %d \n b is %d", a, b);
```

5. What are the values of c, d, and e?

```
int c;
double d;
int e;
c = 7 / 4 + 7 * 2;
d = 7. / 4. + 7. * 2.;
e = d + .26;
```

6. What are values of a, b, and c, if the input in each case is 12.3?

```
int a;
scanf("%d",&a);
```

```
char b;
scanf("%c",&b);

double c;
scanf("%lf",&c);
```

## ANSWERS

1. d will have value of 10. i will have value of 20.

2. c will have the value 'K'.

3. The values are

   | a | b | c |
   |---|---|---|
   | garbage | garbage | 5 |
   | 5 | garbage | 5 |
   | 5 | 25 | 5 |

4. The printed values are

   a is 3
   b is 8

5. The values are

   | | |
   |---|---|
   | c is 15 | 7 / 4 is 1, 7 * 2 is 14, 1 + 4 is 15 |
   | d is 15.75 | 7 / 4 is 1.75, 7. * 2. is 14., 1.75 + 14. is 15.75 |
   | e is 16 | 15.75 + .26 is 16.01, which truncates to 16 |

6. The values are

   | | |
   |---|---|
   | a is 12 | scanf stops at the ., because that cannot be part of an integer. |
   | b is '1' | (ASCII value 49) |
   | c is 12.3 | scanf stops at the space, because that cannot be part of a floating point number. |

## PROBLEMS

1. Rewrite the meter program (Listing 2.1) to accept inches and return meters.

2. Try changing the %lf to %d or vice versa in the sample programs. See what answers your program gives.

3. If these variables are declared as

```
int i = 7;
int j = 9;
double f = 3.3;
double g = 5.3;
```

What are the values of

```
i + j * f
(i + j) * f
f * i + g * j
(f + g) * (i + j)
```

4. Write a program that inputs a weight in pounds and outputs the weight in kilograms.

5. Newton's formula is

$$\text{Force} = \text{mass} * \text{acceleration}$$

Write a program that inputs a mass and acceleration and outputs the force.

6. Write a program that inputs an integer (assume less than 1000) and writes out the digits, one to a line.

7. Write a program that computes the area of a triangle. The formula is

$$\text{Area} = \text{sqrt}(s(s - a)(s - b)(s - c))$$

where a, b, c are the lengths of the sides and s is the semiperimeter,

$$s = (a+b+c)/2$$

and sqrt is a compiler-supplied function that returns a double. You will need a line that reads #include <math.h> at the beginning of your program.

8. Write a program that computes the miles per gallon for an automobile. You will need to input a starting mileage, an ending mileage, and a number of gallons.

9. Alter Listing 1.2 so it guesses floating point numbers between 1 and 127. You should test difference against a very small number (say .00001), rather than against 0.0.

10. Try typing in numbers such as 65535, 65536, 2147483647, and 2147483648 as answers for Listing 1.2. See what the program guesses as your number. Why do you think this happens?

11. The `sizeof` operator gives the size of a data type in bytes. `sizeof(int)` will have a value of 2 if the length of an `int` is two bytes or 4 if it is four bytes. Write a program to determine the size of a `double`.

*Chapter Three*

# Control Flow

In the programs in Chapter 2, the execution flowed from the beginning of `main` to the end. Every time the program runs, all the instructions execute from top to bottom. Without a way to change to the order of execution, a program would only be good for calculating, not computing. C provides many ways for altering this flow of execution, or control flow. These techniques include selection of alternative statements to execute (`if`) and repeating a series of statements (`while`, `do-while`, and `for`).

## THE if STATEMENT

The `if` construct provides that a statement will be executed only if a certain condition or test expression is true. The `if` has the form

```
if (test-expression)
    statement
```

If `test-expression` is true, the statement is executed; otherwise, it is skipped. The test expression[1] is usually a comparison of two values, using the relational and equality operators.

### Relational and Equality Operators

The relational and equality operators compare two values. The result of this comparison is a value that is true or false. If the first value compared to the second value agrees with the test, the result is true. There are six different tests, and so six different operators.

[1]These test expressions are termed *conditions* or *predicate expressions* in some texts.

30

| Relational Tests | Operator Symbol |
|---|---|
| greater than | > |
| less than | < |
| greater than or equal to | >= |
| less than or equal to | <= |

| Equality Tests | Operator Symbol |
|---|---|
| not equal to | != |
| equal to | == |

Using these operators, you can write tests as

| Expression | Result |
|---|---|
| 3 > 6 | false |
| 6 > 3 | true |
| 6 < 3 | false |
| i >= j | true if i has a value greater than or equal to the value of j; otherwise, false |

These tests can be the condition for the if statement, as in

```
if (number < 0)
    number = -number;
if (j >= 5)
    j = 3;
```

The values of true and false that are the result of the relational operators are actually the integer values 1 and 0, respectively. The condition in the if statement actually tests for a zero or a nonzero value. If the value of the condition is non-zero, it is treated as true. Sometimes you can take advantage of this. You might use a variable to hold only a true or false value. For example, suppose you had

```
#define TRUE 1
#define FALSE 0
int done = FALSE;
```

then you might use

```
if (done)
```

instead of

```
if (done == TRUE)
```

This is common coding practice for variables that have only true and false values. These are referred to as *boolean* variables or *flags*. On the other hand, the fact that the condition is simply a value is a significant reason why some programs do not work. If the code were

```
if (a_number == 0)
    b_number = 5;
```

the value of a_number is tested against 0. If it is 0, the relation is true and b_number will be assigned the value of 5. However, if you mistyped it and it was coded

```
if (a_number = 0)
    b_number = 5;
```

a_number will be assigned the value of 0. This 0 value is the value of the condition and is always false. b_number will never be assigned a value.

### The if-else Statement

Another form of the if is the if-else. With this form, one alternative is executed if the condition is true. The other alternative is performed if the condition is false. The form is

```
if (test expression)
    statement-if-true
else
    statement-if-false
```

Figure 3.1 gives two ways in which the if-else is shown graphically. An example of the if-else is

```
if (a_number > 5)
    b_number = 7;
else
    b_number = 3;
```

Here if a_number is greater than 5, b_number = 7 will be executed; otherwise, b_number = 3 will be.

## COMPOUND STATEMENTS

You may want to perform two statements if a certain condition is true. The if form only allows one. You can combine multiple statements into a single statement using

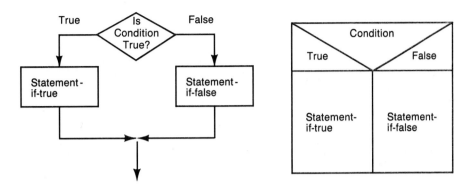

**Figure 3.1 Diagram of the if-else Statement**

braces ({}). These are placed before and after the statements to be combined, as in

```
if (a_number > 5)
    {
    b_number = 7;
    c_number = 3;
    }
else
    b_number = 3;
```

The first two assignments are performed if a_number is greater than 5; otherwise, the third assignment is executed. One or more statements surrounded by braces is called a *compound statement* or *block*. You can use compound statements anywhere you use a single statement. If you try to write a compound statement without the braces, as in

```
if (a_number > 5)
    b_number = 7;
    c_number = 3;
else
    b_number = 3;
```

you get a compiler error. You have two statements after the if condition, and there can only be one between it and the else.

The statement following an if can be an if itself, such as

```
if (a_number > 5)
    if (b_number > 3)
        d_number = 14;
```

---

***Style Tip***

---

Decide on a style of indentation (Chapter 14 gives some alternatives) and stick with it. Be consistent in your placement of braces. This book uses two lines for `if` statements, with the second line indented.

```
if (test-expression)
    statement
```

For compound statements, the book shows braces on separate lines and indents them. It uses braces lined up with the statements inside the compound statement.

```
if (test-expression)
    {
    statements
    }
```

---

If a_number > 5 is true, the condition b_number > 3 will be tested. If the second condition is true, d_number will be assigned 4. Suppose the example were

```
if (a_number > 12)
    if (b_number > 15)
        d_number = 17;
else
    d_number = 19;
```

This might be interpreted as "if (a_number > 12) is false, then d_number = 19." However, the else is always paired with the most recent unpaired if. So d_number = 19 is only executed if a_number > 12 is true and b_number > 15 is false. If you really want the other way, then you need to use a compound statement, such as

```
if (a_number > 12)
    {
    if (b_number > 15)
        d_number = 17;
    }
else
    d_number = 19;
```

The braces enclose the inner if, so it is interpreted as a simple if. The else is then matched with the outer if. You can also write this as

```
if (a_number > 12)
   if (b_number > 15)
       d_number = 17;
   else
       ;                            /* Null statement */
else
   d_number = 19;
```

The semicolon (;) is the null statement fulfilling the requirement that a statement follow the else.

If two relations need to be tested, you could code

```
if (a_number > 7)
   if (b_number > 8)
       d_number = 9;
```

However, you can more easily use the logical operators to combine these tests.

## LOGICAL OPERATORS

Two logical operators combine true or false values in a single value. They are the AND operator and the OR operator. A third logical operator, NOT, simply negates a true or false value. The symbols for the operators are

| Logical Operation | C Operator |
|---|---|
| AND | && |
| OR | \|\| |
| NOT | ! |

The single symbols & and | have a different meaning in C, as Chapter 9 explains, so be sure to use the correct symbols. The vertical bar (ASCII value 124) appears on many keyboards as a split vertical bar ( ¦ ). The logical AND operator has a result of true if both values are true. Table 3.1 summarizes the results of AND operations.

The logical OR operator has a result of true (a value of 1) if either is true. This is shown in Table 3.2.

### Table 3.1 Results of the AND Operation

| Left Value | Right Value | Result of Left AND Right |
|---|---|---|
| false (zero) | false (zero) | false (zero) |
| false (zero) | true (nonzero) | false (zero) |
| true (nonzero) | false (zero) | false (zero) |
| true (nonzero) | true (nonzero) | true (one) |

**Table 3.2 Results of the OR Operation**

| Left Value | Right Value | Result of Left OR Right |
|---|---|---|
| false (zero) | false (zero) | false (zero) |
| false (zero) | true (nonzero) | true (one) |
| true (nonzero) | false (zero) | true (one) |
| true (nonzero) | true (nonzero) | true (one) |

The logical NOT has a value of true (one) if the value it operates on is false (zero) and a value of false (zero) if the value is true (nonzero). Here is a summary of the results of the NOT operator.

| Value | Result of NOT Value |
|---|---|
| false (zero) | true (one) |
| true (nonzero) | false (zero) |

Using logical operators, you could write the previous example as

```
if ( (a_number > 7) && (b_number > 8) )
   d_number = 9;
```

With flag variables, you could write conditions as

```
if (!done && (a_number > 3) )
```

The AND and OR operators are always evaluated from left to right. If the left side for an AND is false, the right side is not performed. If the left side for an OR is true, the right side is not calculated. With the previous test, if a_number is less than or equal to 7, the comparison of b_number to 8 is not executed.

---

## PRECEDENCE

The examples have more sets of parentheses than the rules require. Relational operators have a greater precedence than logical operators, so they need not be separated by parentheses. Both have lower precedence than arithmetic operators. The precedence of the operators so far is summarized in Table 3.3.

This if (!done && a_number > 3) would be interpreted as shown earlier. In these examples, using parentheses is only for the reader's sake, not for the compiler's. It is far better to over-parenthesize (within limits) than to under-parenthesize. This will become more apparent when the remaining operators are covered in Chapter 9.

**Table 3.3 Precedence of Operators**

| Symbol | Definition |
|--------|------------|
| ! | logical negation |
| – | unary minus |
| + | unary plus |
| | |
| * | multiplication |
| / | division |
| % | modulus |
| | |
| + | addition |
| – | subtraction |
| | |
| < | less than |
| <= | less than or equal to |
| > | greater than |
| >= | greater than or equal to |
| | |
| == | equality |
| != | inequality |
| | |
| && | logical AND |
| | |
| \| \| | logical OR |
| | |
| = | assignment |

## SAMPLE PROGRAMS

Here are a few examples of programs using the `if` statement. These programs are repeated in several forms throughout the book, so you can get an idea of approaching the same problem many different ways.

### Date Check

This program asks the user for a month, day, and year. It then checks to see whether the date is a valid date. The program simply requires a two-digit year. The code assumes it represents a year between 1901 and 2000. As an exercise, you could modify the program so it works for dates outside of this range.

The program inputs the date into `month`, `day`, and `year`. It then checks `day` for being less than 1. Next, it performs multiple tests on `month` to determine the maximum number of days in the month. If `year` is evenly divisible by 4, it is a leap year, so the February test is for 29 rather than 28.

**Listing 3.1 Date Check**

```
#include <stdio.h>
#define TRUE 1
```

```
#define FALSE 0
/* Months of the year */
#define JAN 1
#define FEB 2
#define MAR 3
#define APR 4
#define MAY 5
#define JUN 6
#define JUL 7
#define AUG 8
#define SEP 9
#define OCT 10
#define NOV 11
#define DEC 12

int main()
/* This program inputs a date and checks for its validity */
    {
    int month;              /* Month to check */
    int day;                /* Day to check */
    int year;               /* Year to check */
    int valid;              /* Flag for valid date */

    /* Input date */
    printf("\n This program checks for a valid date");
    printf("\n Enter the month: ");
    scanf("%d", &month);
    printf("\n Enter the day: ");
    scanf("%d", &day);
    printf("\n Enter the year: ");
    scanf("%d", &year);

    /* Assume date is good until proven otherwise */
    valid = TRUE;
    /* Check low end of the day value */
    if (day < = 0)
        valid = FALSE;

    /* Check for February */
    if (month == FEB)
        {
        /* Month is February, check for leap year */
        if (year % 4 == 0)
            {
            if (day > 29)
                valid = FALSE;
            }
```

```
      else if (day > 28)
              valid = FALSE;
        }
   else
        {
        if ((month == JAN) || (month == MAR)
              || (month == MAY) || (month == JUL)
              || (month == AUG) || (month == OCT)
              || (month == DEC)
              {
              /* Month is 31-day month */
              if (day > 31)
                 valid = FALSE;
              }
        else
              {
              if ((month == APR) || (month == JUN)
                 || (month == SEP) || (month == NOV))
                 {
                 /* Month is 30-day month */
                 if (day > 30)
                    valid = FALSE;
                 }
              else
              /* Month was not one of the twelve */
                 valid = FALSE;
              }
        }

   /* Print result */
   if (valid)
        printf("\n Day is valid");
   else
        printf("\n Day is invalid");

   exit(0);
   }
```

Notice that the braces are not needed for every statement belonging to each else. Without them, the code would look like the following and execute exactly the same.

```
else if ((month == JAN) || (month == MAR)
      || (month == MAY) || (month == JUL)
      || (month == AUG) || (month == OCT)
      || (month == DEC))
```

```
        {
        /* Month is 31-day month */
        if (day > 31)
            valid = FALSE;
        }
    else if ((month == APR) || (month == JUN)
        || (month == SEP) || (month == NOV))
        {
        /* Month is 30-day month */
        if (day > 30)
            valid = FALSE;
        }
        else
        /* Month was not one of the twelve */
        valid = FALSE;
```

## Root of a Quadratic

A quadratic equation has the form $ax^2 + bx + c = y$. The roots of a quadratic equation are those values of x for which y has a value of zero. The quadratic formula gives the method for solving for the roots. It is:

$$root = (-b \pm sqrt(b^2 - 4ac))/(2a)$$

A solution for both roots appears in Chapter 10. This program only gives the root for the addition of the square root term, not the subtraction of the term. The input values are placed in a, b, and c. Two tests are required. If the value of a is zero, then a divide-by-zero error occurs. If so, the equation is not a quadratic one and the formula does not apply. If b * b - 4 * a * c is less than zero, the square root is imaginary. If neither of these cases applies, the root is printed out.

**Listing 3.2 Root of a Quadratic**

```c
#include <stdio.h>
#include <math.h>

int main()
/* This computes the quadratic root (one value only) */
    {
    double a;       /* Coefficient for x**2 */
    double b;       /* Coefficient for x**1 */
    double c;       /* Coefficient for x**0 */
    double result;  /* Root */
    double temp;    /* For temporary value */

    /* Input values */
    printf("\n a is : ");
```

```
scanf("%lf", &a);
printf("\n b is : ");
scanf("%lf", &b);
printf("\n c is : ");
scanf("%lf", &c);

/* Do computation, if a is nonzero */
if (a != 0.0)
    {
    temp = b * b - 4.0 * a * c;

    /* Check for negative, as cannot take square root of a negative value */
        if (temp >= 0.0)
        {
        result = (-b + sqrt(temp)) / (2 * a);
        printf("\n Result is %lf", result);
        }
    else
        printf("\n Imaginary root");
    }
else
    printf("\n Not a quadratic equation");

    exit(0);
    }
```

The line #include <math.h> is necessary so the compiler will know that sqrt returns a double. This concept is covered fully in Chapter 4.

## THE while LOOP

In many instances the same set of statements is executed more than once. The statements are executed while a condition is true. This is the reason for a looping construct like the while. The while loop takes the form

```
while (test-expression)
    statement
```

If text-expression is true, the statement is executed; it is checked again. If the expression is still true, the statement will be executed again. Figure 3.2 graphically displays the while loop. Unless something in the statement makes the condition false, the loop repeats endlessly. In almost all cases, at least two actions occur in the body of the while (that is, the statement that the while controls) and thus it usually appears as

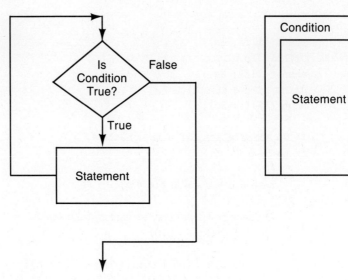

**Figure 3.2 Diagram of the while Statement**

```
while (test-expression)
    {
    statement
    statement
    ...
    }
```

Recall that a compound statement can be substituted wherever a single statement can appear. This book uses the braced compound statement form throughout, even if a single statement is enclosed in the braces.

To sum numbers 1 to 5, you could use the while construct as

```
sum=0;
i=1;
while (i<=5)
    {
    sum = sum + i;
    i = i + 1;
    }
```

If your programs seem to hang up, try placing a call to printf inside of any while loops. Then you can see whether you are exiting a loop.

| *Debug Tip* |
|---|
| Always use braces on while loops. Then you can easily insert a debug statement in the loop to see why you might not be exiting the loop or why you are exiting it before you want to. |

## SAMPLE PROGRAMS

Here are two examples of programs using a while loop. The first computes a factorial of a number, and the second computes the average of a series of numbers.

### Factorial

This program computes the product of the numbers from 1 to an input number. This product is called the factorial of the number. The number for which you are computing the factorial is input to end_number. The values of number and product are then set to 1, and the while loop is repeated until number is greater than end_number. In each repetition of the loop, the value of number is incremented by 1. If you omit this statement, the loop would never terminate.

### Listing 3.3 Factorial

```
#include <stdio.h>

int main()
/* This program computes the factorial of the input number */
    {
    int product;        /* product */
    int end_number;     /* number to end on */
    int number;         /* number to increment */

    /* Input numbers */
    printf("\n Input the ending number: ");
    scanf("%d", &end_number);

    /* Initialize for loop */
    number = 1;
    product = 1;

    /* Loop until ending number is exceeded */
    while (number <= end_number)
        {
        product = product * number;
        number = number + 1;
        }

    printf("\n Factorial is %d", product);

    exit(0);
    }
```

### Averaging Program

The second sample program here sums a series of numbers and calculates the average. The program prompts the user for input until a zero value is entered. It then computes the average and outputs it. The values of sum and count are set to 0 and done, the flag that controls the loop, is set TRUE. Then the program repeatedly asks for a number from the user. The value is placed in number. If number is 0.0, then the value of done is set to FALSE, the loop terminates, and the average is computed.[2]

**Listing 3.4 Averaging Program**

```
#include <stdio.h>

#define TRUE 1
#define FALSE 0

int main()
/* This program averages input values until a 0 is entered */
    {
    int count;              /* How many numbers */
    double sum;             /* Running sum */
    double number;          /* Input number */
    double average;         /* Computed average */
    int done;               /* Loop termination flag */

    /* Initialize values */
    sum = 0.0;
    count = 0;
    done = FALSE;

    /* Get input values */
    while (!done)
        {
        printf("\n Input a number to average (0 to exit): ");
        scanf("%lf", &number);
        if (number == 0.0)
            done = TRUE;
        else
            {
            /* Add to sum and increment count */
            sum = sum + number;
            count = count + 1;
            }
        }
```

[2]You could use a variable called done and test for !done or use not_done, setting it to TRUE and then to FALSE. Just be consistent.

```
/* Compute average */
if (count > 0)
      average = sum / count;
else
      average = 0.0;

/* Output results */
printf("\n Sum of #%d numbers is %lf", count, sum);
printf("\n Average of these numbers is %lf ", average);

exit(0);
}
```

## THE do-while LOOP

The body of a while loop is not executed if the test expression is false the first time. Certain programming situations require the loop to execute at least once. For these instances the do-while is useful. Its form is

```
do
      statement
      while (test-expression);
```

The semicolon following *test-expression* is required by the syntax. Figure 3.3 graphically depicts the do-while loop. Notice that the test is performed after the statement is executed.

Using the do-while, the factorial program in Listing 3.3 could be written as in Listing 3.5.

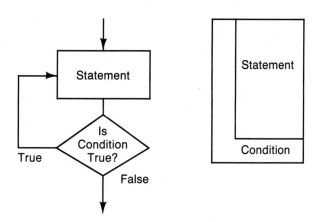

**Figure 3.3 Diagram of the do-while Statement**

**Listing 3.5 Factorial with do-while**

```c
#include <stdio.h>

int main()
/* This program computes product of numbers from 1 to input number */
    {
    double product;              /* product */
    int end_number;              /* number to end on */
    int number;                  /* number to increment */

    /* Input numbers */
    printf("\n Input the ending number: ");
    scanf("%d", &end_number);

    /* Initialize values */
    number = 1;
    product = 1.0;

    /* Loop until done */
    do
        {
        product = product * number;
        number = number + 1;
        }
    while (number <= end_number);

    printf("\n Factorial is %lf", product);

    exit(0);
    }
```

In Listing 3.3, when end_number was zero, the loop would not execute at all. In Listing 3.5, it does execute one time. You can always use a while loop in place of a do-while loop by initializing the variable in the loop test.

---

## THE break STATEMENT

The break statement exits a loop before the condition becomes false. The next statement executed is the one immediately following the loop, that is, the one to be executed when the loop terminates.

Suppose you wanted to sum numbers 1 to 5 but to stop if the sum exceeded 9.

```c
sum = 0;
i = 1;
while (i <= 5)
```

```
    {
sum = sum + i;
if ( sum > 9)
        break;
i = i + 1;
    }
```

This could have been written as

```
#define TRUE 1
#define FALSE 0
sum = 0;
i = 1;
over_sum = FALSE;
while ( (i <= 5) && (!over_sum) )
        {
    sum = sum + i;
    if ( sum > 9)
            over_sum = TRUE;
    else
            i = i + 1;
        }
```

The style you select is a matter of taste. Some programming schools prefer the latter style, because it is helpful to list all conditions for exiting the loop at the beginning. However, for short loops the former is perhaps clearer, because it does not introduce another variable. Any loop with a break can be written without one. Depending on the process involved, the break sometimes is clearer. Using the break, the averaging program might be written as follows. The test condition for the loop is FOREVER (the value of 1), so the only way the loop will terminate is to execute a break. This occurs when the input number is 0.0.

**Listing 3.6 Averaging Program with break**

```
#define FOREVER 1
#include <stdio.h>

int main()
/* This program averages input values until a 0 is entered */
        {
        int count;              /* How many numbers */
        double sum;             /* Running sum */
        double number;          /* Input number */
        double average;         /* Computed average */
```

```
/* Initialize values */
sum = 0.0;
count = 0;

/* Input numbers until 0 entered */
while (FOREVER)
    {
    printf("\n Input a number to average (0 to exit): ");
    scanf("%lf", &number);
    if (number == 0.0)
        break;
    sum = sum + number;
    count = count + 1;
    }

/* Compute average */
if (count > 0)
    average = sum / count;
else
    average = 0.0;

printf("\n Average of %d numbers is %lf", count, average);

exit(0);
}
```

## THE for STATEMENT

Many while loops follow a common structure. The flow is to initialize a variable, test a condition based on the variable, do something, then increment the variable and go back to the test. This statement takes the form

```
initialization
while (test-expression)
    {
    statement
    incrementing
    }
```

In the example to sum the numbers 1 to 5, the parts of this statement are

```
sum = 0;
i = 1;                                  /* initialize i */
while (i <= 5)                          /* test condition based on i */
    {
```

```
    sum = sum + i;              /* do something
    i = i + 1;                  /* increment i */
    }
```

The `for` construct is a common way of coding this type of logical flow. Its basic form is

```
for (initialization; test-expression; incrementing)
    statement
```

Figure 3.4 shows graphically the flow of the `for` statement. Using the `for`, the loop would look like

```
sum= 0.0;
for (i = 1; i <= 5; i = i + 1)
    {
    sum = sum + i;
    }
```

The braces can be omitted, because the body of this `for` loop is only a single statement. However, as mentioned for `while`, braces almost always appear in the examples.

The `for` loop can decrement the variable as well as increment it. The summing loop could look like

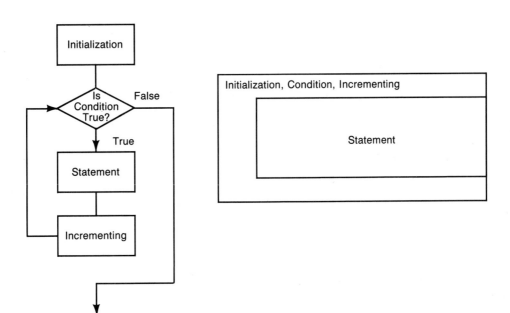

**Figure 3.4 Diagram of the for Statement**

```
sum = 0.0;
for (i = 5; i >= 1; i = i - 1)
    {
    sum = sum + i;
    }
```

Chapter 10 shows other ways to write a `for` statement. Normally, the `for` loop should be used simply as a way of writing this common type of `while` loop.

---

### Debug Tip

---

Frequently errors are caused by going around loops once too few or once too many times. Add a `printf` to the body of the loop to check the number of repetitions.

---

## INCREMENT AND DECREMENT OPERATORS

Adding one to or subtracting one from a number is so common in programs that C has a special set of operators to do this. They are the *increment* and *decrement operators,* and their symbols are ++ and --. The two characters must be contiguous (contain no spaces). They can only be applied to variables, not to constants. Instead of coding

```
i = i + 1;
```

you can write

```
i++;
```

or

```
++i;
```

The distinction between these two forms will be covered in Chapter 8. If you only use increment and decrement as the sole operators in an expression, you will not have to worry about the difference in coding style. Usually a `for` loop like the first one introduced would be coded as:

```
sum = 0;
for (i = 1; i <= 5; i++)
    {
    sum = sum + i;
    }
```

The decrement loop would be coded as

```
sum = 0;
for (i = 5; i >= 1; i--)
    {
    sum = sum + i;
    }
```

The factorial program could be written with a for loop as follows. The for statement makes it readily apparent the loop will run for values of number from 0 to end_number.


**Listing 3.7 Factorial with for**

```
#include <stdio.h>

int main()
/* This program computes the product of numbers from 1 to the input number */
    {
    int product;           /* product */
    int end_number;        /* number to end on */
    int number;            /* number to increment */

    /* Input numbers */
    printf("\n Input the ending number: ");
    scanf("%d", &end_number);

    /* Initialize value */
    product = 1;

    /* Loop until done */
    for (number = 1; number <= end_number; number++)
        {
        product = product * number;
        }

    printf("\n Factorial is %d", product);

    exit(0);
    }
```

| *Style Tip* |
|---|
| Use i++ in preference to i = i + 1. Not only is the former shorter to write, but once you get used to the style, its meaning is clearer. |

## A COMPLEMENTARY GUESSING PROGRAM

The following program is complementary to the original guessing program introduced in Listing 1.2 using the constructs in this chapter. In this program, the user is asked to input values for minutes and seconds to get a random answer for the computer. The two values are combined to get answer. The loop repeats until done is set TRUE. This occurs either when the user gives up by guessing a zero or negative number or the guess is correct. The box shows the pseudocode for this program. *Pseudocode* is a form of describing the operation of a program with a mixture of logical code structure and text descriptions.

---

### *Pseudocode for the Complementary Guessing Program*

Determine a number
While not done
  Check guess
  Output answer based on guess
  If guessed or given up
    Then done

---

**Listing 3.8 Guessing Game in Inverse**

```
#define FALSE 0
#define TRUE 1
#define MAX_NUMBER 200
#include <stdio.h>

int main()
/* Guessing game */
    {
    int done;            /* When done with guessing */
    int answer;          /* The computer's answer */
    int guess;           /* The user's guess */
    int minutes;         /* Time in minutes */
    int seconds;         /* Time in seconds */

    /* Initialize--get number */
    done = FALSE;

    /* Get some numbers to compose guess */
    printf("\n How many minutes past the hour is it? ");
    scanf("%d", &minutes);
    printf("\n How many seconds past the minute is it? ");
```

```
scanf("%d", &seconds);
answer = (minutes * seconds + seconds) % MAX_NUMBER + 1;

printf("\n I'm thinking of a number between 1 and %d", MAX_NUMBER);
printf("\n You can enter 0 or a negative number to give up");
/* Loop until correct guess or guess less than 1 */
while (!done)
    {
    printf("\n What is your guess? ");
    scanf("%d", &guess);

    if (guess < 1)
        {
        /* User is giving up */
        printf("\n You giving up? ");
        printf("\n The answer was %d", answer);
        done = TRUE;
        }
    else if (guess > MAX_NUMBER)
        /* Guess was too big */
        printf("\n That's too too big");
    else if (guess == answer)
        {
        /* Guess was correct */
        done = TRUE;
        printf("\n That's it--good guessing");
        }
    else if (guess < answer)
    /* Guess was too small */
        printf("\n Too low");
    else if (guess > answer)
    /* Guess was too big */
        printf("\n Too big");
    }           /* End of while loop on done */

exit(0);
}
```

## SUMMARY

- The `if` statement executes a statement if a condition is true.
- The `if-else` statement executes one of two statements, depending on whether a condition is true or false.
- The `while` loop executes a statement repeatedly while a condition is true.

- The do-while loop executes a statement repeatedly until a condition is false. The statement will be executed at least once.
- The for statement is a generalization of the while loop, combining an initialization part, a test part, and an increment part.
- Relational and equality operators compare two values and have a true (one) or false (zero) result.
- Logical operators combine true (nonzero) and false (zero) values and have a true (one) or false (zero) result.

## SELF-TEST

1. What is the value of j after the following code is executed?

```
j=0;
while (j<5);
    j++;
```

2. If the value of year is 5 and day is 29, what is the value of valid after this code is executed?

```
valid = TRUE;
if (year % 4 == 0)
    if (day > 29)
        valid = FALSE;
else if (day > 28)
    valid = FALSE;
```

3. How many times will this loop execute?

```
for (i = 0; i < 5; i++)
    {
    i++;
    }
```

4. What is the value of the following if the value of a is 03?

```
! (a != 0) || a > -7 && !5
```

5. What is the value of 5++?

6. If you execute a loop that looks like

```
sum = 0;
i = 1;
while (i <= 5)
```

```
sum = sum + i;
i = i + 1;
```

what do you think happens?

---

## ANSWERS

1. The loop will never exit, because the semicolon following (j<5) is the body of the loop. j is never incremented.
2. It is TRUE. The else is paired with if (day > 29).
3. Three times. The values of i tested by i < 5 are 0, 2, and 4.
4. The value is 1. Based on precedence, this is interpreted as

```
(! (a != 0) || ( (a > -7) && (!5) )
! 0           || (   1    && 0 )
1             ||     0
1
```

5. There is no value. The compiler reports an error, because the increment operator can only be applied to simple variables.
6. The while would never exit, as the body of the loop is just the statement sum = sum + i. The value of i never changes.

---

## PROBLEMS

1. Produce a table showing values of x, $x^2$, and $x^3$ for values of x from 1 to 50.
2. Write a program that inputs a number and outputs the sum of odd integers from 1 to the number.
3. Write a program that inputs two numbers and sums all integers (1 to the first number) that are multiples of the second number.
4. Write a program that computes the miles per gallon for an automobile. Input a starting mileage and an ending mileage. You should allow the user to input several values for gallons, which the program will sum.
5. Write a program that inputs a number and finds all the factors of the number. (Hint: If x % y == 0, then y is a factor of x).
6. Write a program that inputs a number and determines whether it is a prime number (a number with only 1 and itself as its factors). See the hint in Problem 5.
7. Let S be the sum of

$$\tfrac{1}{2}^2 - \tfrac{1}{4}^2 + \tfrac{1}{6}^2 - \tfrac{1}{8}^2 \ldots$$

Write a program that inputs a number and computes S using that number of terms.

8. Rewrite the equation in Problem 7 so it inputs a value and computes S using terms until the absolute value of the next term to be added is less than the input value.

9. Leibnitz's formula for pi is

$$PI = 4* (1 - 1/3 + 1/5 - 1/7 + ...)$$

Write a program that computes pi up to the limit of the accuracy for your computer.

10. Write a program that determines your checking account balance. You should input the starting balance, checks, and deposits and output the final balance.

11. Write a program that reads in several exam scores and prints the average score, and the number of scores in each grade category according to

| Score | Category |
|---|---|
| 90–100 | Excellent |
| 70–89 | Average |
| 0–69 | Below average |

12. Write a program that inputs an integer and writes out the digits, one to a line.

13. If an amount of principal is invested at some interest rate per period, the total amount after a number of periods is

$$total\_amount = principal (1 + rate)^{number\_periods}$$

Write a program that inputs a principal and rate and number of periods and prints out the total_amount.

14. The half-life of an isotope is the time required to decay to one-half its original mass. Write a program that inputs an original amount, year, and half-life, and outputs the remaining amount.

$$a = se^{(year/half\text{-}life)}$$

where a is the amount remaining, s is the starting amount, and e is 2.71828.

15. Alter Listing 3.2 so it accepts a four-digit year. A leap year is any year that is a multiple of 4, except for years that are multiples of 100 (ends of centuries). However, years that are multiples of 400 are leap years.

## Chapter Four

# Functions

You could write every program with only one function—main. Breaking a program up into separate functions, each of which performs a particular task, makes it easier to develop the program. The human mind can only deal with a limited number of details. Inside each individual function, you can concentrate only on the details of its operations. The more useful functions you develop, the easier it will be to write larger programs. Your C compiler manufacturer supplies many common functions in a library, so you do not need to reinvent them. This chapter covers writing functions, calling them, and retrieving their values.

## FUNCTION DEFINITION

A *function* is a set of statements that stands by itself. The set of statements has an identifier—the function name. The statements can be executed by using the name in a routine. This is termed "calling the function." A set of values known as *parameters* or *arguments* can be passed to the function. The called function can return a value to the calling program, which it may or may not use in an expression. The form of a function definition is

```
data-type function-name(parameter-list)
declarations-of-parameters
    {
    declaration-of-local-variables
    statements
    }
```

The `data-type`, which is optional, specifies the type that the function will return. If you omit `data-type`, C assumes it will return an int value. The `function-name` is the name with which it will be called. You cannot have more than one function in a program with the same name.

The *parameter-list* is a list of variable names in which the values from the calling program are placed. In the declarations of parameters, you specify what data types the parameters are supposed to be. If you forget to declare a parameter, the compiler will assume it is an int.

The opening brace starts the body of the function. Any local variables are then declared followed by executable statements. The closing brace ends the definition of the function.

The computation of a factorial in Listing 3.3 could be written as two functions. The main function could input the numbers, and another function, factorial, would do the computation. This would look like the code in Listing 4.1.

**Listing 4.1 factorial Function**

```
#include <stdio.h>

int main()
/* This program computes the factorial of the input number */
    {
    int product;            /* product */
    int end_number;         /* number to end on */
    int number;             /* number to increment */

    /* Input the numbers */
    printf("\n Input the ending number: ");
    scanf("%d", &end_number);

    product = factorial(end_number);

    printf("\n Factorial is %d", product);

    exit(0);
    }

int factorial(ending_number)
/* Computes the factorial of a number */
int ending_number;          /* Value for which to compute factorial */
                            /* Returns factorial */
    {
    int number;             /* Number to increment */
    int product;            /* Product */

    /* Initialize */
    product = 1;

    /* Loop until exceeded ending number */
    for (number = 1; number <= ending_number; number++)
        {
```

```
        product = product * number;
        }

    return product;
    }
```

The value of end_number is passed to factorial when the function is called. This value is placed in ending_number. When the function ends at the return statement, the value of product is passed back to main and assigned to result.

The parameter names may or may not be the same as the variable names with which the function is called. The parameters of a function are referred to as *formal parameters*. These are the variables that receive the values passed to the function. The values passed are referred to as the *actual arguments*. In this case, ending_number is the name of the formal parameter. The actual argument passed to factorial is the value of end_number. If the input number was 3, the actual argument has the value 3 and that number is passed to the function and placed in end_number. You could also make a call as factorial(5); in which case the actual argument is the value 5.

On a slightly more complex level, you could write a function to find the value of a number raised to a power, because there is no C operator to do this. This function is passed two values, a double and int. The values are placed in base and exponent. These values are then assigned to the local variables exp and number. If exp is negative, the reciprocal of number must be used, and exp is negated. Then the for loop repeats for exp number of times.

**Listing 4.2 main Function Calling power Function**

```
double power(base, exponent)
/* Computes the result of a base raised to an integer power */
double base;                        /* Value to be raised to a power */
int exponent;                       /* Power to which to raise base */
    {
    int exp;                        /* Exponent */
    double number;                  /* Number to raise to power */
    double result;                  /* Answer */
    int count;                      /* Counter for loop */

    /* Initialize */
    exp = exponent;

    /* If a negative power, then invert the base */
    if (exp < 0)
        {
        number = 1 / base;
        exp = -exp;
        }
    else if (exp > 0)
        number = base;
```

```
/* Do the computation */
result = 1.0;
for (count = 0; count < exp; count++)
    {
    result = result * number;
    }

return result;
}
```

The double on the first line declares that the function will return a double value. The name of the function is power. The parameter list (base,exponent) states it will have two values passed to it. The next two lines declare base will be double and exp will be an int. Then follows the body of the function. The next four lines declare local variables. Next are the executable statements. The next-to-last line is the return statement. It returns the value of result to the calling program. The calling program is free to use this value in whatever way it determines.

The main function that calls power inputs two values into root and exponent. These values are then passed to power.

**Listing 4.3 main Function Calling power Function**

```
#include <stdio.h>

int main()
/* This program computes a number raised to a power */
    {
    double root;            /* Root to raise to power */
    double answer;          /* Answer */
    int exponent;           /* Power to raise root */

    printf("\n This program computes the power of a number");
    printf(" raised to an integer power ");
    printf("\n Input a number: ");
    scanf("%lf", &root);
    printf("\n To what integer power do you wish");
    printf(" this number raised? ");
    scanf("%d", &exponent);

    answer = power(root, exponent);

    printf("\n The answer is %lf", answer);

    exit(0);
    }
```

The user might wish to raise 3 to the second power. When the program runs, the interaction on the terminal would look like the following. The user's responses are shown in this font.

```
This program computes the power of a number raised to an integer power
Input a number: 3
To what integer power do you wish this number raised? 2
The answer is 9.000000
```

---

### Style Tip

Comment your functions enough so a person reading your code can understand what they do, what parameters they expect, and what values they return.

Use #defines for error return values.

---

## NAMES OF FUNCTIONS

Names of functions follow the same rules as names of variables. You should use meaningful function names. However, you should not use a name of any function in the C library as these are reserved function names. These names are listed in Appendix G.

If you define two functions with the same name in the same file, the compiler gives you a DUPLICATE NAME XXX error or something similar. If the same name is defined in two different files, the linker will give you an equivalent error message. Unfortunately, some linkers only use the first six characters of the function name, without regard for upper- or lowercase. Thus, compute_number and COMPUTE_NUMBER and compute_average may represent the same name to the linker, even though you have three different functions.[1]

---

### Style Tip

Keep functions short—a page or two. If you write longer functions, try to break them into smaller modules.

---

## RETURN FROM FUNCTION

The return statement exits from a function. If a value follows the return statement, that value is what is passed back to the called program. If there is no value

---

[1]Although the examples in this book use long names, within each program there is no duplication of the first six characters in function names. If your linker has this limitation, you can use macros (see Chapter 9) to rename the functions without changing your code. This six-character limitation applies only to external references (function names and external variable names), not to local variable names.

after the `return`, nothing is passed back. If the calling program tries to use the value of the function, a meaningless or garbage value will be accessed. For example, a will be assigned garbage with this code:

```
bad_function()
    {
    return;
    }
...
a = bad_function();
```

The `return` statement does not need to appear at the end of the function. It can occur anywhere in the function. A function also can contain multiple `return` statements. Whichever one is executed first will end the function execution. If you forget to insert a `return` statement, the closing brace acts as an implicit return statement. The function executes as if a `return` with no value had been put there.

A good guideline is that each function has one and only one return statement that appears on the last line of the body of the function. The examples in this book will always follow this guideline. In some instances, multiple returns may make the code clearer. Some programmers follow a convention of using parentheses around the returned value. If you use expressions for return values, rather than a simple variable, the code will be clearer.

Functions usually return some value to indicate whether they were able to complete the operation they were designed to do. Try to avoid designing functions that simply stop when an error occurs. Sometimes it is possible for a function to return a specific value (such as −1) indicating an error. Other times two values need to be passed back because there is no unique value. Chapter 8 shows how to pass back two values. The factorial function should really be written like Listing 4.4. The value of `ending_number` is tested to see whether it is less than zero, because there is no definition of the factorial of a negative number. The value is tested against `LARGEST_NUMBER`, as the value of the factorial of a large number will exceed the limit that can be contained in an `int`. The value of `factorial(7)` is the largest factorial that will fit in a two-byte integer.

**Listing 4.4 factorial Function**

```
#define LARGEST_NUMBER 7

int factorial(ending_number)
/* Computes the factorial of a number */
int ending_number;                 /* Value for which to compute factorial */
                                   /* Returns factorial */
    {
    int number;                    /* Number to increment */
    int product;                   /* Product */

    if ((ending_number < 0) || (ending_number > LARGEST_NUMBER))
```

```
      product = -1;
   else
      {
      /* Initialize */
      product = 1;

      /* Loop until exceeded ending number */
      for (number = 1; number <= ending_number; number++)
         {
         product = product * number;
         }
      }
   return product;
   }
```

---

### Style Tip

Use a single return statement in most functions. With multiple returns, it is harder to determine which return the function executed.

---

## FUNCTION PROTOTYPES

Whenever C comes across an identifier followed by parentheses, it assumes it is the name of a function. If it has no more information, it also assumes the function returns an integer. With power and main above, if the power function comes before main in the source file, the compiler knows it returns a double.

Suppose power is defined after main. When the compiler comes to the call to power in main, it assumes it returns an int. As the compiler reaches the definition of power, it will find that this call really returns a double. The compiler reports an error, as the return types disagree. For the program to work correctly, a function prototype can be coded. This prototype simply declares what data type is returned by a function. In its simplest form a prototype looks like this:

```
data-type function-name();
```

This form tells the compiler to assume *function-name* returns a value of *data-type*. For the power function, you would use a prototype:

```
double power();
```

before the main function.

In some instances a function does not need to return a value. If you use a return statement with no value, garbage is returned. It would be a logical error if the calling function tried to use this value. The data type void was invented to take care of this case. A function can have a data type of void, which says it is not going to return a usable value. If the programmer attempts to use it, the compiler reports an error. For example,

```
void function();
...
a = function();
```

causes a compiler error. Expanded function prototypes are discussed in Chapter 10.

## PARAMETER AGREEMENT

The actual arguments in the calling function and the formal parameters in the called function must agree. There must be the same number, with the same data types, and in the same order.[2] If they are not, the program either produces wrong results or may not run at all (but it will compile and link). For example, if the call to power from main were

```
answer = power(exp);
```

```
answer = power(base);
```

```
answer = power(exp,base);
```

or if you called power with

```
answer = power( 2 , 5.0 );
```

```
answer = power( 2 , 5 );
```

```
answer = power( 2.0 , 5.0 );
```

you would receive the wrong answer. You can define a function in one source file and have a call to that function from another source file. When the two compiled files are linked together into a single program, the reference in the second file is matched with the definition in the first file. If the power function is defined in the same source file where it is called, the compiler can check that the parameters agree. If a function is defined in another source file, the compiler cannot check for agreement. Methods of linking and checking multiple source files are shown in Chapter 10. For now, it is important to check parameters on all functions that you use.

---

[2]printf and scanf are exceptions. They can have a varying number of arguments. Although there are ways of writing functions like these, they are tricky to use, as will be shown in Chapter 5 on scanf.

## LIBRARY FUNCTIONS

Every C compiler manufacturer supplies many functions in a *library*, which is simply a collection of functions. The functions are listed in Appendix G. Each function has an associated *include file*. Such files contain function prototypes for a related group of functions. These prototypes are usually of the expanded prototype form, to be discussed in Chapter 10, which gives information on the data types and number of parameters.

You should be sure to have one or more lines that read

```
# include <header.h>
```

at the beginning of any source file that uses library functions. The `header.h` should be the name of the corresponding source file. For example, if you call `sqrt`, you should have #include <math.h>.

## THE lint PROGRAM

If you forget to put in the corresponding header file for library functions, there is another way of checking parameter and return type agreement. Many systems provide a program called `lint`. This program checks the data types of the return values of functions and the data types and numbers of parameters. It will inform you of any mismatches in these areas. You execute `lint` by simply typing

```
lint source-file-name
```

Each `lint` program varies slightly in its syntax for checking the library functions, so you should check the manual for your particular computer's syntax. The program was named `lint` because it "picks out the fluff" in code. In addition to type checking it reports potential errors such as unused variables.

| *Debug Tip* |
|---|
| Run `lint` on all your programs. It may catch errors the compiler misses. |

## CALL BY VALUE

When variables are passed to a function, only the current value of the variable is passed. The function cannot affect the value of the variable in the calling program. The `power` function could have been written as shown in Listing 4.5.

**Listing 4.5 power Function**

```
double power(base, exponent)
/* Computes a power of base raised to a number */
double base;                    /* number to raise to a power */
int exponent;                   /* power to which to raise base */

    {
    double result;              /* the answer */
    int count;                  /* counter for loop */

    /* If a negative power, invert the base */
    if (exponent < 0)
        {
        base = 1 / base;
        exponent = -exponent;
        }

    /* Compute the answer */
    result = 1.0;
    for (count = 0; count < exponent; count++)
        {
        result = result * base;
        }

    return result;
    }
```

Even though power has changed the values of base and exponent, the values of root and exponent in the calling function main will not change.

## SAMPLE FUNCTION—date_check

Here is the code similar to Listing 3.1, which checked dates, using a function. The function is passed values for month, day, and year. It returns a value of TRUE or FALSE.

**Listing 4.6 date_check Function**

```
#define JAN 1
#define FEB 2
#define MAR 3
#define APR 4
#define MAY 5
#define JUN 6
#define JUL 7
#define AUG 8
```

```
#define SEP 9
#define OCT 10
#define NOV 11
#define DEC 12
#define TRUE 1
#define FALSE 0

int date_check(month, day, year)
/* Checks a date to see whether it is valid */
int month;                       /* month to check */
int day;                         /* day to check */
int year;                        /* year to check */
                                 /* returns TRUE if valid */
                                 /* FALSE if not valid */
    {
    int valid;                   /* Flag for valid date */

    /* Assume date is good until proven otherwise */
    valid = TRUE;

    if (day <= 0)
        valid = FALSE;
    if (month == FEB)
        /* Month is February, check for leap year */
        {
        if (year % 4 == 0)
            if (day > 29)
                valid = FALSE;
        else
            if (day > 28)
                valid = FALSE;
        }
    else if ((month == JAN) || (month == MAR) || (month == MAY)
        || (month == JUL) || (month == AUG) || (month == OCT)
        || (month == DEC))
        {
        /* Month is a 31-day month */
        if (day > 31)
            valid = FALSE;
        }
    else if ((month == APR) || (month == JUN) || (month == SEP)
        || (month == NOV))
        {
        /* Month is a 30-day month */
        if (day > 30)
            valid = FALSE;
        }
```

```
        else valid = FALSE;
        return valid;
        }
```

The function returns a value, rather than printing out the result. It is more flexible this way. The caller of the function can decide what to do if the date is invalid, which might be to print a message or to ask for another date. The date_check function is called by a main function that looks like the following. Note that you can change what is returned for invalid dates without changing the date_check function.

**Listing 4.7 main Function Calling date__check**

```
#include <stdio.h>

int main()
/* Checks a date for validity */
    {
    int month;              /* Month to check */
    int day;                /* Day to check */
    int year;               /* Year to check */
    int valid;              /* Valid date flag */

    /* Input the date */
    printf("\n This program checks for a valid date");
    printf("\n Enter the month: ");
    scanf("%d", &month);
    printf("\n Enter the day: ");
    scanf("%d", &day);
    printf("\n Enter the year: ");
    scanf("%d", &year);
    printf("\n Date is %d/%d/%d", month, day, year);

    /* Check the date and print the result */
    valid = date_check(month, day, year);
    if (valid)
        printf("\n Date is valid");
    else
        printf("\n Date is invalid");

    exit(0);
    }
```

## CALL BY REFERENCE

Some functions return more than one value. The return statement can only return one value to the calling routine. To pass back more values, use the parameter list to pass the addresses of the values. This is termed a call by reference. The called function can change the values of the variables at these addresses. A simple variable is passed by reference by using the & address operator on its name.[3]

The most common place this is found is with the scanf function. You can use scanf to return multiple values, although it has not been shown in this manner. The & operator actually passes the address of the variable. Once the input value is translated to the internal machine representation, scanf places it into this address. For example,

```
scanf("%d%d",&i,&j);
```

The scanf function returns two values from the keyboard input and places those values into i and j.

If you leave off the address operator on a parameter that is to be passed by reference, your program will not run correctly, if it runs at all. The value passed will be the value of the variable, not its address. The called routine will interpret that value as the address and put a value there. Call by reference can be a source of error, so the full description on how to create functions that use it will not occur until Chapter 8. However, arrays, which are covered in Chapter 6, are passed by reference.

## SCOPE OF NAMES AND EXTERNAL VARIABLES

The variables that have been used so far are only declared inside a function, either in the parameter list or as local variables. There are other variables, called *external variables*, that have a broader scope.

The *scope* of a name is the portion of the source file over which it will be recognized. Declarations of local variables and function prototypes are only recognized within the function they appear in. Your #define statements are recognized from their point of appearance in the source file to the end of the source file. For consistency's sake, function prototypes and #define statements are usually placed at the beginning of a source file.

### External Variables

Variables declared outside of functions are called *external variables*, or simply *externals*. There is also a variation of external, called *static external*, which is described in Chapter 10. These variables are recognized by any functions in the source file that follow their declaration. External variables can be initialized just like static

---

[3]An indirection * operator is required in the called function, as will be shown in Chapter 8.

variables. If you do not initialize an external, it will be set to zero. External variables are also called *global variables*, because they can be accessed by any function in the whole program.

For example,

```
int number;
a_function()
    {
    number=7;
    }
b_function()
    {
    number=9;
    }
```

Both a_function and b_function affect the value of the external variable number.

If you attempt to use an external variable before it is declared in the source file, the compiler reports an error. For example, you would get an error if you wrote

```
c_function()
    {
    another=7;
    }
int another;
```

The definition of an external declares the data-type of the variable and actually sets aside storage for it. The declaration of the extern simply states the data-type of an external variable, but does not set aside storage.[4] So you can use the keyword extern to declare the variable as an external, without defining it. For the previous code you can write

```
extern int another;
c_function()
    {
    another=5;
    }
int another = 9;
```

Normally you should define all external variables at the beginning of a source file or at least before any functions that use them, so extern would not be required. Chapter 10 covers the use of extern when you have multiple source files.

[4]The ANSI standard permits multiple definitions of the int number; form in a single source file, with only one having an initial value. The form shown here is suggested as a coding standard. An extern declaration can appear in the source file where the definition appears.

---

| ***Style Tip*** |
| :---: |
| Minimize the use of global variables. Values needed by functions should be passed through the parameter list. This eliminates the interdependence of the functions and simplifies debugging. |

### Sample Program—Averaging

This program performs the averaging of numbers in a slightly different manner. Three routines access the externals `sum` and `count`. These are placed after the `main` function, because `main` does not need to access them. The `start_average` function initializes the values, `add_to_average` adds values to them, and `compute_average` returns the average. These are reusable functions, which could be incorporated into other programs. Functions to compute means, standard deviations, and other statistical values could be written in a similar manner.

**Listing 4.8 Averaging Program with Externals**

```c
#include <stdio.h>
#define TRUE 1
#define FALSE 0
double compute_average();

int main()
/* Computes the average of input numbers */
    {
    int done;               /* Flag for done with input */
    int number;             /* Input number */
    double average;         /* For result */

    done = FALSE;
    start_average();
    printf("\n This program averages numbers till a zero is input");

    while (!done)
        {
        printf("\n Input a number, 0 to end ");
        scanf("%d", &number);
        /* If number is 0, then exit */
        if (number == 0)
            done = TRUE;
        else
            add_to_average(number);
        }
```

```
        average = compute_average();
        printf("\n Average is %lf", average);

        exit(0);
        }

double sum;                     /* Keeps current sum of numbers */
int count;                      /* Keeps current count of numbers */

void start_average()
/* Initializes the average */
    {

    sum = 0.0;
    count = 0;

    return;
    }

void add_to_average(number)
/* Adds a number to the average to be computed */
int number;                          /* Number to add */
    {

    sum = sum + number;
    count = count + 1;

    return;
    }

double compute_average()
/* Computes the average */
    {
    double result;

    if (count != 0)
        result = sum / count;
    else
        result = 0.0;

    return result;
    }
```

Notice the function prototype double compute_average(); at the beginning of the program. This declares that the function returns a double.

## REUSING VARIABLE NAMES

The same variable name cannot be reused in the same block or compound statement. For example,

```
function()
    {
    int number;
    int number;
    ...
    }
```

is an error, because it tries to declare two variables with the same name. However,
code such as

```
int number;
function()
    {
    int number;
    number=7;
    ...
    }
```

does not cause an error. The first number is an external variable number. The second is the local variable number. The assignment statement refers to the local variable. Reusing a name like this can lead to more time debugging the code. In large
programming projects, external variables are designated with a unique prefix or
suffix to ensure that a match with a local variable does not occur.

---

### *Style Tip*

Do not use global variables to pass values to functions. Use the parameter
list.

---

## THE main AND exit FUNCTIONS

You assign the name main to the first function executed when the program runs.
When a program starts, compiler-supplied startup code is executed, which then
calls this function. The operating system passes main two values. Chapter 12 covers
the use of these parameters.

The exit function ends the execution of the program. The function may be called
from anywhere in a program. Normally it is called only from the function main.

Just like `returns`, it is best to have only one call to `exit` in your entire program. If you forget to put one in, C assumes the closing brace of the function `main` represents a call to `exit`. The `main` function can be declared as returning either an `int` or a `void`.

The value passed to `exit` is returned to the operating system. Many systems have a provision for checking the value that an executed program returns. This can be tested in a batch (or exec or shell) file to control what program is run next. Check your operating system manual for further details.

## ALGORITHMS

An *algorithm* is a method for solving a problem. Algorithms usually are mathematical in nature but do not have to be. Algorithms can be judged on how efficient they are in execution speed, the amount of code and data storage required and the accuracy of the result that they produce. There are efficient algorithms and inefficient ones. Usually, the selection of an algorithm is more important to the efficiency of a program than using "tricky" code.

There are many ways of writing a program for a lunar lander game. All of them revolve around the basic equations of motion. These equations are

$$\text{new\_velocity} = \text{acceleration} * \text{time} + \text{old\_velocity}$$

$$\text{distance} = (\text{new\_velocity} + \text{old\_velocity}) * \text{time} / 2$$

$$\text{distance} = \text{old\_velocity} * \text{time} + \text{acceleration} * \text{time}^2 / 2$$

To play lunar lander, the user guesses how much fuel to use over a time period (that is, the burn rate). The burn rate times some fuel factor produces a force counteracting the acceleration of gravity. If the burn rate is such that the counter force equals gravity, the velocity is unchanged. If it is higher, then the lander slows down. If the rate is less, the lander speeds up.

The calculation can be simplified by making the time interval one second. The time factor then drops out of these equations until the last second.

If the distance to the moon goes negative, the lunar lander has reached the surface in the last second. The time for this last second needs to be recomputed to find out exactly when the lunar lander hit. The third equation (a quadratic equation) must be solved for the time.

The `while` loop repeats until `done` is set `TRUE` when the distance to the moon is less than or equal to zero. The `get_burn_rate` checks the remaining fuel and then inputs the burn rate. The `new_distance` is the distance remaining after `burn_rate` has been applied for one second. If this distance is less than zero, the quadratic equation is solved for the fraction of the second it took to make the distance equal to zero. Upon exiting the loop, `new_velocity` at touchdown is tested to see which message to print.

The following box describes the program in pseudocode.

```
┌─────────────────────────────────────────────────────────────────────┐
│              Pseudocode for the Lunar Lander Program                  │
├─────────────────────────────────────────────────────────────────────┤
│                                                                       │
│              Lunar lander                                             │
│                  Initialize                                           │
│                  While not done                                       │
│                      Get burn rate                                    │
│                      Compute new distance                             │
│                      If new distance less than zero                   │
│                              Compute fraction of a second             │
│                              Set done to TRUE                         │
│                                                                       │
└─────────────────────────────────────────────────────────────────────┘
```

**Listing 4.9 Lunar Lander Game**

```c
#include <math.h>
#include <stdio.h>

#define MOON_TO_EARTH 6.          /* Moon to earth gravity ratio */
#define GRAVITY (32.2/MOON_TO_EARTH)
                                  /* Acceleration due to gravity */
#define DEACCELERATION 1.1        /* Deacceleration per unit fuel */
#define START_DISTANCE (6440/MOON_TO_EARTH)
                                  /* Starting distance from ground*/
#define START_VELOCITY (644/MOON_TO_EARTH)
                                  /* Starting velocity */
#define START_FUEL 50.            /* Starting amount of fuel */
#define START_BURN_RATE 0         /* Starting burn rate */
#define MAX_BURN_RATE 5.          /* Maximum burn rate */
#define CRASH_VELOCITY (60./MOON_TO_EARTH)
                                  /* Crashing velocity */
#define TRUE 1
#define FALSE 0


double get_burn_rate();

/***************************** MAIN PROGRAM *****************************/

int main()
/* Lunar landing program */
    {
    double distance;            /* Distance to go to surface */
    double velocity;            /* Velocity at the start of second */
    double burn_rate;           /* Burn rate on the fuel */
    double fuel;                /* Amount of fuel left */
    double acceleration;        /* Acceleration over one second */
```

```
double traveled;          /* Distance traveled over a second */
double new_distance;      /* Distance remaining at end of a second */
double new_velocity;      /* Velocity at end of a second */
double seconds;           /* Time in decimal */
int time;                 /* Time in integer */
int done;                 /* Flag for done with landing */
double decimal_seconds;   /* Fraction of seconds of final second*/

/* Initialize the values */
distance = START_DISTANCE;
velocity = START_VELOCITY;
burn_rate = START_BURN_RATE;
fuel = START_FUEL;
time = 0;
done = FALSE;

/* Until landed, keep asking for burn rate */
printf("\n           Seconds  Feet to go  Velocity");
printf(" Fuel (lbs) Burn rate");
while (!done)
    {
    printf("\n %10d     %10.2lf %10.2lf %10.2lf ? ",
        time, distance, velocity, fuel);

    /* Get the burn rate */
    burn_rate = get_burn_rate(fuel);

    /* Go for 1 second and compute new velocity and new distance */
    acceleration = -burn_rate * (DEACCELERATION * GRAVITY) + GRAVITY;
    new_velocity = velocity + acceleration;
    traveled = .5 * (velocity + new_velocity);
    new_distance = distance - traveled;

    /* Check to see whether we have landed */
    If (new_distance <= 0.0)
        {
        /* Compute the fraction of a second when the landing occurred */
        if (acceleration == 0.0)
            /* Not a quadratic--use straight solution */
            seconds = distance / velocity;
        else
            /* Solve quadratic equation */
            seconds = (-velocity + sqrt(velocity * velocity +
                (distance * (2. * acceleration)))) 
                    / (acceleration);

        /* Compute the velocity at touchdown */
```

```
                    new_velocity = velocity + acceleration * seconds;
                    decimal_seconds = seconds + time;
                    new_distance = 0.0;
                    done = TRUE;
                    }
                else
                    seconds = 1.0;
                    /* Set remaining fuel */
                fuel -= burn_rate * seconds;

                /* Set time and velocity for next iteration */
                velocity = new_velocity;
                distance = new_distance;
                time++;
                }

        /* Landed !! */
        if (new_velocity > CRASH_VELOCITY)
            printf("\n You CRASHED !! Velocity %lf", new_velocity);
        else
            {
            printf("\n Good landing at %lf feet per second.", new_velocity);
            printf(" Time is %lf seconds", decimal_seconds);
            printf("\n %lf pounds of fuel left", fuel);
            }

        exit(0);
        }


/*************************** GET_BURN_RATE ****************************/

double get_burn_rate(fuel)
/* Gets the burn rate */
double fuel;                        /* Remaining fuel */
    {
    double burn_rate;               /* Burn rate to return */

    if (fuel < .001)
        {
        printf("\n Out of fuel");
        /* Fuel is out, burn rate to 0 */
        burn_rate = 0.0;
        }
    else
        {
        /* Get the burn rate */
        scanf("%lf", &burn_rate);
```

```
                    if (burn_rate < 0.0)
                        burn_rate = 0.0;
                    else if (burn_rate > MAX_BURN_RATE)
                        burn_rate = MAX_BURN_RATE;
                }

            if (fuel < burn_rate)
                burn_rate = fuel;

            return burn_rate;
            }
```

## DESIGN

You will notice that most of the functions presented in this book follow a common form. It looks abstractly like

1. Entry (declare parameters and local variables)
2. Initialize (set variables to starting values)
3. Process (do computation as required, perhaps in a loop)
4. Terminate (compute result)
5. Exit (return the result)

Each function is broken up graphically with white space between each of these sections. Chapter 15 has a discussion on more details of design, but you should be aware of it as you go through the examples.

---

### *Style Tip*

---

One way to start is with a description of the function in words. Then add comments around each line. Then add the actual code after each appropriate comment. This keeps your code commented.

---

## SUMMARY

- A function is the basic program module in C. It may be passed values as parameters and return a value.
- The parameters passed when a function is called should agree in type, number, and order with the parameters in the function definition.
- Variables declared within a function are only available to that function.
- External variables are available to all functions in a program.

**SELF-TEST**

1. What value does d have after this code executes?

```
double func(a,b,c)
int a;
int b;
int c;
    {
    int i;
    i = a + b - c;
    return i;
    }
...
double d;
d = func(2., 3., 4.);
```

2. What value does a have after this code executes?

```
int i = 7;
func1(k)
int k;
    {
    int i, j;
    j = i * 3;
    return j;
    }
...
int a;
a = func1(7);
```

3. What is printed out when you run this code?

```
main()
    {
    int a = 7;
    int b = 6;
    func2(a, b);
    printf("\n a is %d b is %d", a, b);
    }
func2(c, d)
int c;
int d;
    {
    int e;
    e = c * d;
```

```
        d = 7 * c;
        printf("\n c is %d d is %d e is %d", c, d, e);
        return;
        }
```

4. What is printed when this function executes?

```
double func3(a)
int a;
        {
        double ret;
        if (a < 0)
                ret = -.5;
        else if (a > 0)
                ret = .5;
        else
                ret = 0.;
        return ret;
        }
main()
        {
        int k = 12;
        k = func3(k) * 7;
        printf("\n k is %d", k);
        }
```

5. What is printed when this function executes?

```
main()
        {
        double k;
        k = sqrt(4.);
        printf("\n k is %lf", k);
        }
```

## ANSWERS

1. Garbage. The function func was called with floating point constants. The code was expecting ints.

2. Garbage again! The value 7 is passed to the function func1. It is multiplied by the value of the local variable i, not the global variable i. The local variable has not been initialized, so it has a garbage value. Garbage times anything is garbage.

3. c is 7 d is 49 e is 42

   a is 7 b is 6

   Even though the value of the parameter d is changed in the function func2, the value of 6 in the calling function does not change.

4. k is 3 is printed. 12 is passed to func. func returns .5. Then .5 * 7 is 3.5, which is truncated when it is assigned to k.

5. k is ???, where ??? is garbage. Because sqrt is not declared as returning a double, the compiler assumes it returns an int. If #include <math.h> or double sqrt(); is included, then k is 2.000000 would be printed.

---

**PROBLEMS**

1. Determine how many digits there are to the left of a decimal point in a number. (Try dividing the number by 10 until the result is less than 1.)

2. If your compiler does not have the srand() and rand() functions, then create them, as shown in Appendix B. Then write a function returning a random number that is in a specified range.

3. Write a program to play roulette using the rand() function. The player (user) bets which slot a ball will land in. The ball randomly lands in a slot between 1 and 36. If the player has guessed that slot, the payoff is 35 to 1. If not, the player loses the bet.

4. There are sequences, called *Taylor's Approximations*, which look like

$$\sin(x) = x - x^3/3! + x^5/5! - x^7/7!$$

   where x is an angle expressed in radians. Write a function returning the sine of an angle. Keep adding terms until the term being added is less than some small value.

5. The Taylor's Approximation for cos(x) looks much like the sin(x) in Problem 4. To avoid duplication, write a cosine function that calls the sine function.

6. Write a function that checks a time for validity on a 24-hour clock, such as:

   time_check(hour, minute, second)

7. Write a function that computes the area of a triangle. The formula is

$$AREA = sqrt(s(s - a)(s - b)(s - c))$$

   where a, b, c are the lengths of the sides and s is the semiperimeter:

   s = (a + b + c)/2

   and sqrt is a compiler-supplied function that returns a double.

8. Write a quad_root function that returns the root of a quadratic equation. Although a quadratic equation has two roots, only return the one that uses the positive value for the square root. See Listing 3.2. Alter Listing 4.9 to call this function to solve for seconds.

9. Rewrite Listing 3.8 to call a time function. (See Appendix G.) Use the value of time to determine the computer's answer.

10. Change the average functions (Listing 4.8) so they average doubles, rather than integers.

11. Write a set of functions (similar to Listing 4.8) to compute the highest and lowest values in a series of numbers passed to them.

12. Using a function you have written, extract just the comments. Ask several fellow students if they can tell how the function works.

# Chapter Five

# Input, Output, and Character Functions

Most other languages provide some input and output commands to communicate with the world outside of the computer's central processor. The C language does not have these commands. However, it does provide a standard set of functions to perform input and output. You can use these functions to communicate with the user executing your program and to read and write disk files. The basic routines covered here perform formatted input and output, as well as single character input and output.

## FORMATTED OUTPUT

As you have seen, `printf` is the standard output function. It outputs to the file `stdout`, which by default is the terminal screen. `printf` outputs strings of characters. It converts internal machine representation of numbers to characters for output. The form of `printf` is

```
printf(format,zero-or-more-values);
```

The format controls what will be output. Characters other than specifiers that appear in the format will be output just as they appear. Format specifiers are sets of characters that begin with the percent sign (%). They tell `printf` that a corresponding value will also be passed in the call and how the value should be converted.

Nonprinting characters that control how the output will appear on the screen may also be passed to `printf`. The most common is the new-line character, which appears as \n. This forces the next character to begin in the first column on the next line. `printf` simply continues to print characters on a line starting where it left off with the previous `printf`. If you don't insert any new-line characters, the output simply starts on a new line when it has reached the end of a line. The underline in the following examples shows where the next character to be output would be placed.

**Call to printf:**                                    **Output on screen:**

```
printf("This is output");
```
This is output_

```
printf("\n One line\n Next line");
```
One line
Next line_

```
printf("This is right next to");
```
This is right next
tothis_

```
printf("this");
```

The three format type specifiers introduced so far are %d, %lf, and %c. These correspond to the data types int, double, and char.[1] These have been shown as:

**Statements**                                         **Output**

```
int number = 77;
printf("\n Value is %d", number);
```
Value is 77

```
double real_number = 3.3;
printf("\n Value is %lf", real_number);
```
Value is 3.300000

```
printf("\n 2 + 2 is %d", 2 + 2);
```
2 + 2 is 4

```
printf("\n A is %c", 'a');
```
A is a

```
printf("\n A is %d", 'a');
```
A is 97

In the last two examples, the value output is the ASCII value of the letter *a*. The %c prints this as the character; the %d prints it as a decimal value. As each data type is examined, the formats for that type will be shown. A detailed listing of formats appears in Appendix G.

If you forget to insert a variable after the format and you have included a format specifier, your printout will include a garbage number. Similarly, if the data type specified in the format does not agree with the data type of the value you pass, you will get garbage. The output format is determined by the specifier, not by the data type of the value passed. Table 5.1 lists some of the possibilities. Unfortunately, neither the compiler nor most lint programs check for these errors.

You can print out multiple values with a single printf call, such as shown in this program line and its output:

---

[1]The format letter d stands for *decimal integer* and lf for *long float*. The term *long float* is an obsolete synonym for double. However, the format specifier is not.

```
printf("Values are %d and %lf",number,real_number);
```

Values are 77 and 3.3

Just ensure that the number and type of values agree with the number and types of the format specifiers.

Get in the habit of having the line #include <stdio.h> at the beginning of every file in which input or output functions are called, as mentioned in the previous chapter. Your compiler may not require it for the program to run correctly, but some compilers do.

## FORMAT SPECIFIERS

You can use several options with format specifiers. The most common are to specify a width to be printed out and to specify the number of decimal digits for float values.

A number between the % and the format letter gives the width to be printed. If the number of characters required to print the value is smaller than this width, additional spaces are printed on the left. The additional spaces can be added on the right (called *left justification*) by prefacing the number with a hyphen (-). If the number is larger than this value, printf will use as many characters as necessary to print the value.

For double values, a period and another number can follow the width. This second number tells how many digits following the decimal point to print. If you do not specify this precision, printf prints six digits.

You can print double values in scientific notation (E-notation) using a %le specifier. This prints numbers with a mantissa and an exponent. The mantissa has one digit to the left of the decimal point. A %% is an escape sequence to print the literal percent (%) character.

To demonstrate the options of format specifiers, the output of an integer value 17 and a double value of 36.5 appear in Table 5.2. The length is the number of characters that printf will output. The underline is where the next character will be printed.

### Table 5.1 Output Format Possibilities

| *Statements* | *Output* |
|---|---|
| `int number=77;`<br>`printf("Value is %lf", number);` | Value is ? |
| `double real_number=3.3;`<br>`printf("Value is %d", real_number);` | Value is ? |
| `printf("Value is %d");` | Value is ? |
| `printf("Value is %d", 3.3);` | Value is ? |

## Table 5.2 Format Specifier Options

| Specifier | Printout | Length |
|---|---|---|
| %d | 17_ | 2 |
| %4d | 17_ | 4 |
| %-4d | 17 _ | 4 |
| %lf | 36.500000_ | 9 |
| %10lf | 36.000000_ | 10 |
| %10.2lf | 36.50_ | 10 |
| %-10.2lf | 36.50 _ | 10 |
| %le | 3.650000e+01_ | 12 |
| %10le | 3.650000e+01_ | 12 |
| %10.2le | 3.65e+01_ | 10 |
| %-10.2le | 3.65e+01 _ | 10 |
| %% | %_ | 1 |

---

### Debug Tip

The format for printf is a string, not a character.
The line printf('a') produces garbage. Using printf("a") produces the letter *a* on the screen

---

Using the format specifiers, you could write a program to show how precise your compiler is. The value of 1/3 cannot be represented precisely with a single number. There will always be some error. The program prints the values of 1/3, 1/30, 1/300, and so forth, and the values of 3., 3.3, 3.33, and so on. The value 1/3 is precisely represented by an endless string of 3s.

### Listing 5.1 Precision Testing Program

```
#include <stdio.h>

int main()
/* Tests precision of compiler/computer */
    {
    double x;
    double y;
    int i;

    /* 1/3, 1/30, 1/300, and so on */
    x = 1.0 / 3.0;
```

```
printf("\n Here is 1/3 multiplied by powers of .1 ");
for (i = 0;  i < 50;  i++)
     {
     printf("\n x times -%d power of 10 is %30.20le", i, x);
     x = .1 * x;
     }

/* 3 + .3 + .03 + .003, and so on */
x = 3.0;
y = x;
printf("\n\n Here is x plus powers of .3");
for (i = 0;  i < 20;  i++)
     {
     printf("\n x plus 3. times -%d power of 10", i);
     printf(" is %30.20le", x);
     y = .1 * y;
     x = x + y;
     }

exit(0);
}
```

A portion of the printout follows. Double values have a limited precision. You can see from the printout that the computer on which this program was executed stores the equivalent of 14 decimal digits.

```
Here is 1/3 multiplied by powers of .1
x times -0 power of 10 is            3.33333333333332100000e-01
x times -1 power of 10 is            3.33333333333330900000e-02
x times -2 power of 10 is            3.33333333333329600000e-03
x times -10 power of 10 is           3.33333333333319800000e-11
x times -16 power of 10 is           3.33333333333312400000e-17
x times -17 power of 10 is           3.33333333333311100000e-18
x times -18 power of 10 is           3.33333333333310000000e-19
x times -19 power of 10 is           3.33333333333308800000e-20
x times -30 power of 10 is           3.33333333333295300000e-31
x times -49 power of 10 is           3.33333333333271900000e-50

Here is x plus powers of .3
x plus 3. times -0 power of 10 is        3.00000000000000000000e+00
x plus 3. times -1 power of 10 is        3.29999999999999900000e+00
x plus 3. times -2 power of 10 is        3.32999999999999800000e+00
x plus 3. times -3 power of 10 is        3.33299999999999800000e+00
x plus 3. times -4 power of 10 is        3.33329999999999800000e+00
x plus 3. times -10 power of 10 is       3.33333333329999700000e+00
x plus 3. times -19 power of 10 is       3.33333333333332800000e+00
```

With Listing 4.2, the power program, if you enter a large value for both the root (say 100000.) and the exponent (say 100), the program will not give the right answer. The result is 10 to the 500th power, which most computers cannot contain in a double variable. Similarly, if you enter 666666666666. to the second power, you do not get 444444444444444439556. as the answer.

## FORMATTED INPUT

The corresponding function for input is scanf. The scanf function reads the stdin file, which defaults to the keyboard, and converts the characters into internal machine representation. The form that has been shown is

```
scanf(format,&variable);
```

For example:

```
int number;
double real_number;
scanf("%d",&number);
scanf("%lf",&real_number);
```

The scanf function is not a forgiving input function. With printf, if you make an error in writing the call, you simply get garbage on the screen. If you make an error with scanf, your program may blow up. Be sure to include the ampersand on all simple variables (those that are not arrays) that you pass to scanf.

You can input multiple items with a single scanf, as with printf. Be sure that the number and types agree. You will not see scanf used often in this way in the examples.

```
scanf("%lf%d",&real_number,&number);
```

The scanf function returns a value you can test. It is the number of items that were converted. Appendix G lists additional specifiers and features for scanf.

scanf is not a ''user-friendly'' input function, as may be seen in Listing 5.2.

**Listing 5.2 scanf Function**

```
#include <stdio.h>
int main()
/* Demonstrates scanf function */
    {
    int number = 5;
    int second_number = 7;
```

```
        printf("\n Enter a number");
        scanf("%d", &number);
        printf("\n Number is %d", number);
    scanf("%d", &second_number);
    printf("\n Second number is %d", second_number);

    exit(0);
    }
```

Try running this program. When you enter the number in response to the prompt, type **310** (the digit 3 followed by the lowercase letter *l*, followed by the digit 0) and press Enter. You will see

```
Number is 3
Second number is 7
```

on the screen. This is because scanf stopped reading the input characters when it found the letter *l*. Because the letter is not a digit, the program simply converted what it found (the digit 3) to a number and displayed it after Number is. When scanf was called the second time, it started with the letter *l*. Because it was not a digit, conversion simply stopped at that point and nothing was placed in second_number.

Chapter 6 shows some additional features of scanf. Some functions that can be used in its place are described in Chapter 16. One basic use of scanf is to read a file that was produced by calls to printf. Then you may be more certain not to encounter as many problems.

---

## CHARACTER INPUT AND OUTPUT

Two functions read characters from the standard input and write them to the standard output: getchar and putchar.

The getchar function returns characters typed on the keyboard. If you type an end-of-file character (a Ctrl-D for UNIX, a Ctrl-Z for MS-DOS), the function returns the value defined as EOF in stdio.h.

The putchar function places the character it is passed on the screen. The terminal may not necessarily display the character, if it is part of a control sequence that performs such operations as positioning the cursor or changing the attributes of the characters.

---

### *Debug Hint*

Always use an `int` to receive the value returned by `getchar`, as in

```
int c;
c=getchar();
if (c==EOF)
    ...
```

If you declared `c` to be a `char`, the value of `EOF` may not fit into it.

---

This program just fills the screen with the character #.

**Listing 5.3 Fill Screen Program**

```
#include <stdio.h>
#define NUMBER_ROWS 24
#define NUMBER_COLS 80

int main()
/* Fills screen with characters */
    {
    int row;        /* Counter for number of rows to output */
    int col;        /* Counter for number of columns to output */

    /* Output a screen's worth of characters */
    for (row = 0; row < NUMBER_ROWS; row++)
        {
        for (col = 0; col < NUMBER_COLS; col++)
            {
            putchar('#');
            }
        putchar('\n');
        }

    exit(0);
    }
```

Listing 5.4 copies the keyboard input to the screen. It loops until the character returned by `getchar` is the end-of-file value. If you run this program and type in the letters **abc** and press Enter, you will see a second line on the screen that reads abc. On many systems, the keyboard input is buffered, so the response produced by this program may be unexpected. The `getchar` function echoes the input character to the screen, so the first line is produced by `getchar`. However, `getchar` does not return to the calling program any characters until a carriage return (that is, a new line) is entered. This enables the user to backspace over errors in typing. The getchar function stores the characters in its own buffer until the new line is entered.

When the carriage return is read, getchar returns each character in the sequence that was entered for each successive call. The second line of output is produced by putchar outputting each character returned by getchar.

**Listing 5.4 Copy Program**

```
#include <stdio.h>
#define TRUE 1
#define FALSE 0

int main()
/* Copies input to output */
    {
    int c;                      /* Current character */
    int eof;                    /* End of file flag */

    /* Initialize end of file */
    eof = FALSE;

    /* Output character till end of file */
    do
        {
        c = getchar();
        if (c == EOF)
            eof = TRUE;
        else
            putchar(c);
        }
    while (!eof);

    return;
    }
```

| *Debug Hint* |
|---|
| putchar requires a character, not a string.<br>putchar('A'); outputs the character *A* to the screen.<br>putchar("A"); outputs a garbage character to the screen. |

## STANDARD INPUT AND OUTPUT AND REDIRECTION

C assumes there is a standard input device and standard output device. The standard input is the terminal keyboard and the standard output is the terminal screen. Output from `printf` and `putchar` goes to the screen. Input from `scanf` and `getchar` comes from the keyboard.

On UNIX, MS-DOS, and OS/2 systems, you can redirect the input and output when you execute a program. You redirect simply by using the redirect input (<) and redirect output (>) symbols. These will cause the input to be read from the specified file and the output to be written to the specified file.

```
program-name < input-file > output-file
```

For example, the first program in this book could be run as

```
hello > hello.dat
```

"Hi everybody" would not appear on the screen, but a file would be created called `hello.dat`. If you examined it with your text editor, you would see `Hi everybody` in it.[2]

Using redirection Listing 5.4 could copy any file by executing it as (if `copyfile` was its name):

```
copyfile < infile > outfile
```

This redirection is depicted in Figure 5.1.

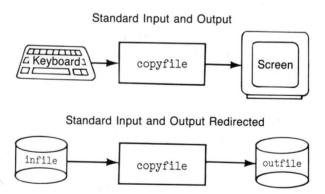

Standard Input and Output

Standard Input and Output Redirected

**Figure 5.1 Standard Input and Output**

[2] You would type **a.out > hello.dat** on UNIX systems if you did not use the -o option in compiling the program.

# CHARACTER VALUES

Characters are treated as integers for the most part. Because most systems represent characters in C using the ASCII code (see Appendix F), you might see many character functions assume the contiguous sequence of alphabetic character values. For example, because uppercase and lowercase characters do not have the same value in the ASCII code, there are several functions that test for case and convert from one to the other. A test function for ASCII values might look like the following listing.

**Listing 5.5 isupper Function**

```
int isupper(chr)
/* Tests if a character is uppercase (for ASCII only) */
int chr;                       /* Character to test */
                               /* Returns
                                     0 if not uppercase
                                     nonzero if uppercase
                               */
    {
    int ret;

    ret = ((chr >= 'A') && (chr <= 'Z'));

    return ret;
    }
```

A function that converts from lowercase to uppercase could also take advantage of the fact that the letters are contiguous. The lowercase characters start with *a*, which has a decimal value of 97. The uppercase characters start with *A*, which has a decimal value of 65. To convert a lowercase letter to uppercase, you need only subtract 32 (97 − 65). Instead of using the decimal number, this is shown as 'a' - 'A'. The function would look like this listing.

**Listing 5.6 toupper Function**

```
int toupper(chr)
/* Converts a character to uppercase (ASCII only)*/
int chr;                       /* Character to convert */
                               /* Returns
                                     character in uppercase, if lowercase
                                     character unchanged, otherwise
                               */
    {
    int sub;                   /* Amount to subtract */
    int ret;                   /* Return value */
```

```
    if ((chr >= 'a') && (chr <= 'z'))
        sub = 'a' - 'A';
    else
        sub = 0;
    ret = chr - sub;

    return ret;
    }
```

The character functions are documented in Appendix G. When you use them, be sure to insert a line that reads #include <ctype.h> at the beginning of the file. Although this is not necessary with some compilers, it is a good idea to make it standard practice.

---

### Style Tip

Do not use the decimal values of integers in your code.
if (c == 'C') is much clearer than if (c == 67).

---

A handy function is one that does not return until it gets a Yes or No answer. This function inputs characters until either a *Y* or an *N* is encountered. The toupper() function changes lowercase letters to uppercase letters.

**Listing 5.7 yes__no Function**

```
#include <stdio.h>
#include <ctype.h>

#define YES 1
#define NO 0
#define UNDEFINED -1

int yes_no()
/* Returns YES or NO */
    {
    int c;      /* Input character */
    int ret;    /* Return value */
                /* Returns YES if character is y or Y; NO if n or N */

    /* Loop till either yes or no */
    do
        {
        c = toupper(getchar());
        if (c == 'Y')
            ret = YES;
        else if (c == 'N')
```

```
            ret = NO;
        else
            ret = UNDEFINED;
        }
    while (ret == UNDEFINED);

    return ret;
    }
```

If you renamed the function called `main` in Listing 4.9 to `lunar`, then you could keep playing the game with this `main` function. You can use a similar routine to play many of the games over and over without rerunning the program.

**Listing 5.8 Repeat a Game Program**

```
#include <stdio.h>
#define YES 1
#define NO 0

int main()
/* Plays a game over and over */
    {
    int ret;        /* return value */

    /* Play the game until no more interest in playing */
    do
        {
        printf("\n Do you want to play this game?");
        ret = yes_no();
        if (ret == YES)
            lunar();
        }
    while (ret != NO);

    exit(0);
    }
```

The next program counts how many sentences there are in a file. It could be expanded to count words, determine number of words per sentence, and so forth, so you could tell how complex a document was. The `main` function loops until the character input is the end-of-file. For each character, it calls `is_endsent`. `is_endsent` returns `TRUE` if the character is a period, question mark, or exclamation point.

**Listing 5.9 Sentence Counting Program**

```
#define TRUE 1
#define FALSE 0
```

```
int is_endsent(c)
/* Determines whether c is a character that could end a sentence */
int c;                          /* Character to test */
                                /* Returns TRUE if end of sentence
                                     character
                                     FALSE if not */

    {
    int ret;                    /* Return value */

    if ((c == '.') || (c == '?') || (c == '!'))
         ret = TRUE;
    else
         ret = FALSE;

    return ret;
    }


#include <stdio.h>

int main()
/* Counts number of sentences in standard input */
    {
    int number_sent;          /* Number of sentences */
    int c;                     /* Current character */

    /* Initialize */
    number_sent = 0;

    do
        {
        /* Get character from file and test it */
        c = getchar();
        if (is_endsent(c))
             number_sent++;
        }
        while (c != EOF);

    printf("\n Count of sentences is %d", number_sent);
    }
```

## SUMMARY

- Input and output in C are provided by library functions.
- The printf function provides formatted output to the standard output, usually the terminal screen.

- The scanf function provides formatted input from the standard input, usually the keyboard. It is not a user-friendly input function.
- The getchar and putchar functions read and write a character at a time.
- The redirection operators on the command line switch the input and output to files other than the keyboard and the standard screen.

## SELF-TEST

1. What is printed when this code is run?

```
int a = 7;
char b = 'c';
printf(" a is %d", b);
```

2. What does this code do?

```
int c;
do
    {
    c = getchar();
    if (islower(c))
            c = toupper(c);
    putchar(c);
    }
    while (c != EOF);
```

3. What is printed when this code is run?

```
printf("\n Constant is %10.5lf", 32.33333333);
printf("\n Constant is %3.1lf", 32.33333333);
```

4. What is printed when you run this code?

```
double a = 7.2;
printf("\n a is %d", a);
```

5. Here is a program called prog:

```
main()
    {
    double e;
    scanf("%lf", &e);
    printf("%lf", e);
    }
```

What happens if it is run with these commands in sequence?

```
prog > outfile
prog < outfile
```

# ANSWERS

1. a is 99. The ASCII value of c is 99.
2. The program copies the input characters to the output with all lowercase letters converted to uppercase. It outputs the value of EOF at the end.
3. Constant is 32.33333
   Constant is 32.3
4. a is ???, where ??? is a garbage value, due to printing a double value using the integer format.
5. The value input from the keyboard will be written to outfile by the first execution. outfile will be read by the second execution and the value printed on the terminal screen.

# PROBLEMS

1. Try some of the following erroneous calls to scanf to see what your program does. Follow each with a printf to output number and real_number.

   ```
   int number;
   double real_number;
   scanf("%lf",&number);
   scanf("%d",&real_number);
   scanf("%d");
   scanf("%lf");
   scanf("%lf",real_number);
   scanf("%d",number);
   ```

2. Translate an input integer value into Roman numerals. The corresponding values are

   I = 1, V = 5, X = 10, L = 50, C = 100, D = 500, M = 1000

3. Translate input Roman numerals into integers. Test that your program handles the following:
   a. immediate end-of-file
   b. an invalid character (not I, V, X, L, C, D, or M)
   c. an illegal sequence (such as IVI)

4. Write a routine that returns the type of a character. Types can include ALPHABETIC, DIGIT, SPACE, and PUNCTUATION.

5. Write a program that reads an input file and writes it to an output file with multiple blank characters replaced by a single blank.

6. Write a program to count
   a. the number of digits in input file.
   b. the number of alphabetics in input file.
   c. the number of spaces in input file.

7. Write a program that counts the number of braces and checks whether they are paired. Do the same for parentheses.

8. Write a program that counts the number of lines in a file. Alter it so it outputs the lines preceded with the line number.

9. Write a program that translates multiple spaces into single characters.

10. With the power program (Listing 4.3) in Chapter 4, if you enter .1 to the 8th power, .000000 is printed, although .00000001 is the correct answer. The `printf` function has printed only the first six decimal digits of the answer. How would you fix this? Try raising .333333333333 to the third power.

11. Write a program that checks what division by 0 does on your system.

12. Read the full description of `scanf` in Appendix G. What does `scanf("*[^ \n]")` do? How could you use this to make inputting value more reliable?

13. Change the lunar lander program (Listing 4.9) so the user inputs a burn time as well as a burn rate. With this enhancement users would not have to type the same number over and over.

14. Write a program that determines the average length of words in a file.

15. Write a program that determines the average number of words per sentence in a file. You can assume a sentence ends in a period, a question mark, or an exclamation point. You can also assume there are no quotations (such as "What?" he asked) and no abbreviations (such as Mr.) to make the program simpler.

16. Change the `printf` call in Listing 4.3 to `%40.20lf` or `%le`. Run the program again. Try inputting values such as *.3333333333* to the third power and see what values are printed.

17. Floating point representations are never exact. Try writing a program to find the largest number that, when added to 1.0, does not change the value of 1.0.

18. Write a program that inputs a source file of C code and writes out the file with indentation as shown in the sample programs. You may already have such a program on your system. It may be called `pretty_print` or something similar.

# Arrays

Each of the simple variables discussed so far has a unique name that identifies a particular memory location. The array references a group of variables of the same data type that are stored in contiguous memory locations. A subscript or index selects one of the variables from the group. Arrays are used to hold tables of values.

## ARRAY DECLARATION

The declaration of an array looks like

```
data-type name-of-array[number-of-elements];
```

For example,

```
int grades[5];
```

declares grades to be an array of 5 integers and sets aside contiguous memory for these variables. Each individual variable in the array is called an *element*. The number of elements is also called the size of the array.

There are no built-in operations you can perform on an array as a whole. Each element in the array is the same as a variable of the equivalent type. To refer to an element, you use the name of the array with a *subscript*. A subscript is also called an *index*, and the terms are used interchangeably in this text. The form for using a subscript is

```
name-of-array[subscript-value]
```

The first element of the array has a subscript value of zero. The last element of the array has the subscript value of *number-of-elements* minus one. Thus, the elements in the above array run from grades[0] to grades[4]. To refer to an element, you can use any of the following: a constant, such as grades[3]; a variable, such as grades[i]; or an expression, such as grades[i*2+3]. To set all the elements in grades to zero, you can code

```
for (i=0; i < 5; i++)
    {
    grades[i] = 0;
    }
```

There is no checking for a subscript falling outside the range of zero to *number-of-elements* minus one. If you use one, your program either acts unpredictably or bombs out. This may occur particularly when you use a variable for the subscript. You should check the value before using it or ensure that your code prevents an incorrect value. For example, you might write

```
#define SIZE_GRADES 5
int grades[SIZE_GRADES];
int i;
if  ( (i >= 0) && (i < SIZE_GRADES) )
     grades[i] = 7;
else
     printf("\n Error in grades subscript %d",i);
```

If you are doing something with each element of an array, such as setting it to zero, your code should look like

```
for (i = 0; i < SIZE_GRADES; i++)
    {
    grades[i] = 0;
    }
```

## ARRAY INITIALIZATION

To initialize an array, you list the initial values inside braces, separated by commas. For example,

```
#define SIZE 5
int grades[SIZE] = {3, 4, 5, 8, 9};
```

defines grades as an array of five ints and places the initial values as in Figure 6.1.

| grades[0] | 3 |
|-----------|---|
| grades[1] | 4 |
| grades[2] | 5 |
| grades[3] | 8 |
| grades[4] | 9 |

**Figure 6.1 Array of Grades**

You can initialize any type of array—automatic, static, or external.[1] It is usually inefficient to initialize an automatic array, and you can usually arrange your functions so this is not necessary. If you do not initialize all the elements, the remaining elements are initialized according to their storage type (0 for externals and statics, garbage for automatics).

You do not need to specify the size of the array if you give the initial values. The compiler counts how many values there are and sets the size of the array to that count. For example, the following declares the same array as the previous code declared:

```
int grades[]={3,4,5,8,9};
```

If you declare an array in this manner, you can determine the number of elements using the sizeof operator. This gives the size of memory required by a data type or variable. For this array, the number of elements is sizeof(grades)/sizeof(int). Usually you have a #define looking like this:

```
#define S_GRADES (sizeof(grades)/sizeof(int))
```

| *Style Tip* |
|:---:|
| Always use a #define to represent the size of an array. |

## ARRAYS AS PARAMETERS

Passing an individual element of an array to a function follows the same process as passing a regular value of that type. The called function receives the current

---

[1]ANSI C compilers are required to support the initialization of automatic arrays. However, this feature is not included in many compilers that support most of the ANSI features. In this case you could simply use the following to perform the same operation:

```
static int grades_init[SIZE] = {3, 4, 5, 8, 9};
int grades[SIZE];
/* Copy the initial values into the automatic array */
memcpy(grades, grades_init, sizeof(grades));
```

value of the element. (Call by value was discussed in Chapter 4.) For example, if you had `grades` declared as shown earlier, you could call the `add_to_average` function in Listing 4.8 as

```
add_to_average(grades[i]);
```

You can use an array as a parameter when calling a function. The called function can use and modify the values of the elements in the array. This is a call by reference.[2] To pass an array, you simply use

```
function-name(name-of-array);
```

and in the called function:

```
function-name(parameter-name-for-array)
data-type parameter-name-for-array[];
```

---

### Debug Tip

A frequent error is exceeding the boundaries of an array. Check all the indices used with arrays against the range from 0 to one less than the size of the array.

---

The declaration of the array simply states the parameter is an array. The storage has been allocated in the calling function. The called function does not indicate the size of the array, as it has no knowledge of it. The parameter list simply indicates that it is receiving an array. Typically, the call includes a parameter whose value is the size of the array. The called routine can check that it does not use a subscript exceeding this array size. For example, a called and calling function might look like

Calling function:

```
#define SIZE_GRADES 5
int grades[SIZE_GRADES];
func(grades, SIZE_GRADES);
```

---

[2]The name of an array is actually the address where the array is stored. So you do not need the address operator for this call by reference, as shown in Chapter 4.

Called function:

```
func(array, size)
int array[];
int size;
```

The values in an array passed as a parameter can be altered. That is, assignments in the called function affect the values of the elements in the array that is passed. This is termed a call by reference. A common function is to zero the elements in an array. You could write a function zero_array to do this, such as

**Listing 6.1 zero_array Function**

```
void zero_array(array,size)
/* Zero the elements in an array */
int array[];              /* array to zero the elements in */
int size;                 /* number of elements in array */
    {
    int i;                /* index for array */

    /* Zero the elements in the array */
    for (i=0;i<size;i++)
        {
        array[i]=0;
        }

    return;
    }
```

If you called this function with

```
int some_array[5]={1,2,3,4,5};
...
zero_array(some_array,5);
```

then after the call, each element in some_array would be 0. However, if you called it as:

```
zero_array(some_array[0],5);
```

this would be an attempt to pass just an element as the entire array, and the program would not execute properly—it might not compile, it might bomb, or it might not produce the correct answers.

The data type of the array must agree with the data type of the array passed as a parameter. A different function would need to be written to zero an array of doubles. Its header would look like

```
zero_array_double(array,size)
double array[];
int size;
```

An array could pass the values for a date correcting function date_correct. This is similar to the date_check (Listing 4.9), but an invalid date will be changed to a valid one. You might use it in a program in which you want execution to continue, even if there is an input error.

The main function inputs the values into elements of the array date_array. It then passes the array to the date_check function. This function uses two arrays to store the number of days in each month, one for leap years and the other for nonleap years. Based on the value of the year, one of the two arrays is used to test the high end of the month. If any of the values in date cannot pass the test, the value is set to a valid one. Note that the test for the month must be done before using it as the index into the days_in_non_leap or days_in_leap arrays. If the index is outside the range 0 to 11, such as days_in_leap[12] then the day would be tested against a garbage value. Note how the use of arrays has simplified the test of the high range for the months over Listing 4.6.

**Listing 6.2 Date Correction Program**

```c
#include <stdio.h>
#define MONTH 0                 /* Index of month in array */
#define DAY 1                   /* Index of day in array */
#define YEAR 2                  /* Index of year in array */
#define SIZE_DATE 3             /* Size of array */

#define TRUE 1
#define FALSE 0

int main()
/* Checks and corrects a date */
    {
    int date_array[SIZE_DATE];      /* The date to correct */
    int result;                     /* Result of validity check */

    /* Input the date */
    printf("\n This program checks for a valid date");
    printf("\n    and corrects the date if it is invalid");
    printf("\n Enter the month: ");
    scanf("%d", &date_array[MONTH]);
    printf("\n Enter the day: ");
    scanf("%d", &date_array[DAY]);
    printf("\n Enter the year: ");
    scanf("%d", &date_array[YEAR]);
```

```
    /* Check the date */
    result = date_correct(date_array);
    if (result)
        printf("\n Date is valid");
    else
        {
        printf("\n Date is invalid");
        printf("\n Date corrected to %d/%d/%d",
            date_array[MONTH], date_array[DAY], date_array[YEAR]);
        }

    exit(0);
    }

int date_correct(date)
/* Checks a date for validity and corrects it if invalid */
int date[];                      /*Date to check */
    {
    int valid;                   /* Return value */
    static int days_in_non_leap[] =
        {31, 28, 31, 30, 31, 30, 31, 31, 30, 31, 30, 31};
            /* Number of days in month--nonleap year */
    static int days_in_leap[] =
        {31, 29, 31, 30, 31, 30, 31, 31, 30, 31, 30, 31};
            /* Number of days in month--leap year */

    /* Assume date is good until proven otherwise */
    valid = TRUE;

    /* Check the low end for day */
    if (date[DAY] <= 0)
        {
        valid = FALSE;
        date[DAY] = 1;
        }
    /* Check the month range */
    if (date[MONTH] < 1)
        {
        valid = FALSE;
        date[MONTH] = 1;
        }
    else if (date[MONTH] > 12)
        {
        valid = FALSE;
        date[MONTH] = 12;
        }
    /* Check the day in the month */
```

```
    if (date[YEAR] % 4 == 0)
        {
        /* A leap year */
        if (date[DAY] > days_in_leap[date[MONTH] - 1])
            {
            valid = FALSE;
            date[DAY] = days_in_leap[date[MONTH] - 1];
            }
        }
    else
        {
        /* A nonleap year */
        if (date[DAY] > days_in_non_leap[date[MONTH] - 1])
            {
            valid = FALSE;
            date[DAY] = days_in_non_leap[date[MONTH] - 1];
            }
        }

    return valid;
    }
```

Here is a different approach to the averaging program shown in Listing 4.8. The main program has an array called numbers. The values to be averaged are stored in this array by the input routine input_array. The array is then passed to the averaging routine average_array to compute the average. In both calling sequences, the size of the array (either the actual size or the number of elements that have input values) is passed as a parameter.

The advantage of this approach is once the values are in the array, you can call other functions to perform operations on it, such as finding the lowest or highest value. The disadvantage is the size of numbers is limited by memory, thus limiting the quantity of values you can average. The functions in Listing 4.8 have no limit on the number of values.

**Listing 6.3 Average Array Program**

```
#include <stdio.h>
#define TRUE 1
#define FALSE 0

double average_array(array, size)
/* Computes average of values in an array */
int array[];                    /* Array to average */
int size;                       /* Number of values in array */
    {
    double sum;                 /* To keep the sum */
    double result;              /* The answer */
    int i;                      /* Index for array */
```

```
        /* Initialize sum */
        sum = 0.0;

        /* Compute the total */
        for (i = 0;  i < size;  i++)
            {
            sum = sum + array[i];
            }

        /* Compute the average */
        if (size > 0)
            result = sum / size;
        else
            result = 0.0;

        return result;
        }


int input_array(array, max_size)
/* Input array of values */
int array[];                    /* Array of values returned */
int max_size;                   /* Size of array, maximum number of values to
                                        input */
                                /* Returns number of values input */

{
int done;                       /* Flag when input is done */
int count;                      /* Number of values */

done = FALSE;
count = 0;

/* Input numbers until maximum count or zero value is entered */
while (!done)
    {
    printf("\n Enter a number");
    scanf("%d", &array[count]);
    if (array[count] == 0)
        done = TRUE;
    else
        {
        count++;
        if (count == max_size)
            done = TRUE;
        }
    }
```

```
        return count;
        }

#define SIZE 50                  /* Maximum number of values to average */

int main()
/* Averages up to SIZE numbers */
        {
        int numbers[SIZE];        /* Values */
        int count;                /* Number of values */
        double result;            /* Average */

        printf("\n This program averages up to 50 numbers");

        /* Input numbers, average them, and print result */
        count = input_array(numbers, SIZE);
        result = average_array(numbers, count);
        printf("\n Average is %lf", result);

        exit(0);
        }
```

## CHARACTERS AND STRINGS

Many other languages have a separate data type that is a collection of characters
or string. C does not possess such a data type, but has created a convention to
handle strings. A string in C is an array, each element of which is a character and
that ends with '\0', the NUL character.[3] For example,

```
char a_string[5]={'A','B','C','D','\0'};
```

defines an array of characters as shown in Figure 6.2.

| | |
|---|---|
| a_string[0] | 'A' |
| a_string[1] | 'B' |
| a_string[2] | 'C' |
| a_string[3] | 'D' |
| a_string[4] | '\0' |

**Figure 6.2 Array of a_string**

---

[3]\0 has the same value as a decimal 0, but it is only the size of a character (a byte). '\0' is used when
you refer to the NUL character.

| Element | Value | |
|---|---|---|
| a_string[0] | 'A' | (ASCII value 65) |
| a_string[1] | 'B' | (ASCII value 66) |
| a_string[2] | 'C' | (ASCII value 67) |
| a_string[3] | 'D' | (ASCII value 68) |
| a_string[4] | '\0' | (ASCII value 0) |

Because there are no inherent array operations in C, there are no inherent operations on strings. All string manipulations are performed by a standard set of functions. The most basic of these is strlen. The strlen function determines the number of characters in a string. It is passed an array of characters. For example, strlen(a_string) returns 4, because the terminating '\0' is not counted. strlen might look like the code in Listing 6.4.

**Listing 6.4 strlen Function**

```
int strlen(in_string)
/* Computes the number of characters in a string */
char in_string[];              /* String to count characters in */
    {
    int count;                 /* Count of characters */

    count = 0;

    /* Increment count while character is not the NUL character */
    while (in_string[count] != '\0')
        {
        count++;
        }

    return count;
    }
```

If the array were defined as

```
char bad_string[5]={'A','B','C','D','E'};
```

then strlen(bad_string) would keep incrementing count until it found a memory location that contained a '\0'.
If the array were defined as

```
char one_string[5] = {'A', 'B', 'C', '\0', '\0'};
```

strlen would return 3 as the length of the string. Even though the array is longer, the NUL character in the fourth element terminates the string.

The string functions include the string copy function strcpy. This might be called with

```
char to_string[5];
char from_string[5]= {'A', 'B', 'C', 'D', '\0'};
strcpy(to_string, from_string);
```

strcpy copies the values in from_string to to_string one at a time, including the terminating '\0'. The to_string should be dimensioned big enough to hold all the values to be transferred. If it is not, the additional character values will still be copied, but into memory locations allocated to other variables. strcpy could be written as follows.[4] Note that do-while is an appropriate control structure, because the loop needs to be executed at least once.

**Listing 6.5 strcpy Function**

```
void strcpy(to, from)
/* Copies one string to another */
char to[];                      /* Where to copy to */
char from[];                    /* Where to copy from */
    {
    int index;                  /* Current character index */
    int c;                      /* Current character */

    /* Initialize */
    index = 0;

    /* Copy characters up to and including the terminating '\0' character */
    do
        {
        c = from[index];
        to[index] = c;
        index++;
        }
        while (c != '\0');

    return;
    }
```

Compiler-supplied functions operating on strings include: strlen to compute the length of a string; strcpy to copy strings; strcmp to compare two strings; strcat to concatenate two strings; and strchr to search for a character in a string. These functions are documented in Appendix G.

[4]The library version of strcpy returns a value that is the address of to. This form is covered in Chapter 8.

## STRING LITERALS

Often you will prefer to specify a string without having to list the characters individually, as in the previous example. The string literal is the form for doing this. You specify the characters surrounded by quotation marks, as "ABCD". This is equivalent to the list of characters with a terminating NUL character. This form is used in two different ways. First, you can use it as a constant string, which can be passed to functions. For example,

```
strcpy(to_string, "ABCD");
```

copies five characters (including the unseen terminating NUL) to to_string.

You can also use it to initialize an array of characters. The first example could be set as

```
char a_string[5] = "ABCD";
```

and the five values would be set as in that example. If you initialized it as

```
char a_string[5] = "ABCDE";
```

then the fifth element in the array would be an E and there would be no terminating '\0'. Thus, if you initialize an array with a string, you usually let the compiler do the counting, just as

```
char a_string[] = "ABCDE";
```

makes a_string an array of six elements with the NUL terminator.[5] Note that

```
char a_string[] = "";
```

makes a_string an array of one element, with the element being the NUL terminator. This is called the *null string*.

If a string constant must be broken over a line, it can be handled two ways. First, the line can end with a backslash (\) immediately followed by a new-line (carriage-return). The string continues in the first column of the next line. Second, two string literals next to each other or separated only by white space are concatenated. For example, with the first way,

```
"ABC\
DEF"
```

---

[5] You could include a '\0' character in a string literal. This would make strlen report the length up to that character instead of the ending '\0'.

DEF" must begin in the first column or there will be spaces in the string constant. This produces the same result as

```
"ABC"
"DEF"
```

Both of these are the same as

```
"ABCDEF"
```

## OUTPUT AND INPUT OF STRINGS

printf has a format specifier you can use to print the characters in a string. The "%s" specifier tells printf you are passing it the address of an array of characters. It will successively print the characters until it finds the NUL terminating character.

```
char string[5] = "ABCD";
printf("\n String is %s", string);
```

prints on the screen:

```
String is ABCD
```

The corresponding format specifier in scanf tells it to input characters until it finds white space (a space character, new line, or tab). The value passed to scanf is an address of a character array. The characters are put into this array and the NUL terminating character is added as the last value. The array must be big enough to hold all the expected characters plus the terminating one. You do not need the & on an array that is passed to scanf.

```
char in_array[10];
scanf("%s", in_array);
```

## SAMPLE FUNCTIONS

### The get_line Function

There are a couple of standard library functions that can read strings containing spaces. These are gets and fgets, which are documented in Appendix G. You might want to write your own functions for this purpose, ones that you could modify as desired. The function is passed an array and a size for the array. The input characters are placed into the array until either a new-line character or the end-of-file is read or the array has been filled with size characters.

**Listing 6.6 Get a Line Program**

```
#include <stdio.h>

#define TRUE 1
#define FALSE 0
#define END_COUNT 0           /* Function terminated on count */
#define END_EOF 1             /* Function terminated on end-of-file */
#define END_NEWLINE 2         /* Function terminated on new-line
                                   character */


int get_line(string, size)
/* Gets a string from the standard input up to a maximum size */
char string[];               /*Where to put the string */
int size;                    /* Size of string */
                             /* Returns
                                 END_COUNT if count is reached
                                 END_EOF if EOF was terminator for input
                                 END_NEWLINE if newline (carriage return)
                                 was terminator for input */
    {
    int count;               /* Count of how many characters have been
                                 placed */

    int done;                /* Flag for loop */
    int ret;                 /* Return value */
    int c;                   /* For input characters */

    /* Initialize values */
    count = 0;
    done = FALSE;
    ret = END_COUNT;

    /* Decrement size by 1 to leave room for terminating NUL */
    size--;

    if (size <= 0)
        done = TRUE;

    /* Loop until EOF, '\n', or size is reached */
    while (!done)
        {
        c = getchar();
        if (c == '\n')
```

```
                {
                done = TRUE;
                ret = END_NEWLINE;
                }
        else if (c == EOF)
                {
                done = TRUE;
                ret = END_EOF;
                }
        else
                {
                /* Add the character to the string */
                string[count] = c;
                count++;
                if (count == size)
                        {
                        done = TRUE;
                        ret = END_COUNT;
                        }

                }
        }

    /* Put on the terminating NUL */
    string[count] = '\0';

    return ret;
    }
```

### The word_count Function

This routine counts how many words a string contains. It uses a library routine called isspace to determine whether the character is a space. To use this function, you need to include the corresponding file, ctype.h. Each character function in Appendix G requires this header file.

**Listing 6.7 Word Count Program**

```
#include <ctype.h>                 /* Include for the isspace function */

int word_count(string)
/* Counts the number of words in a string */
char string[];                     /* String to count the word in */
                                   /* Returns number of words in the string */
    {
    int count = 0;                 /* Count of words */
    int index = 0;                 /* Current index into string */
```

```c
        while (string[index] != '\0')
            {
            /* Skip over multiple spaces */
            if (isspace(string[index]))
                    index++;
            else
                    {
                    /* Start of word, increment count */
                    count++;
                    index++;
                    /* Just increment index until end of word */
                    while (!isspace(string[index]) && string[index] != '\0')
                            {
                            index++;
                            }
                    }
            }

        return count;
        }

#include <stdio.h>

int main()
/* Demonstrates the word count function */
        {
        static char array[] = "The rain in spain";
        int ret;

        ret = word_count(array);

        printf("\n Number of words in :%s: is %d", ret);

        exit(0);
        }
```

## MULTIDIMENSIONAL ARRAYS

You can have multidimensional arrays. You declare the array using multiple brackets ([]). A two-dimensional array has a declaration of the form:

*data-type name-variable[number-second-dim][number-first-dim];*

You can have up to 12 dimensions for an array of simple data types, although you will seldom require more than 3. Each fully indexed element of a multidimensional array acts like a simple variable. For example, if you declared an array as

```
#define SIZE_1D 2
#define SIZE_2D 3
int array_2d[SIZE_2D][SIZE_1D];
```

array_2d[2][1] is an integer and can be used anywhere an int is used. You can initialize the double dimensioned array as[6]

```
int array_2d[SIZE_2D][SIZE_1D]={
    {1,2},
    {3,4},
    {5,6}
    };
```

This is laid out in memory as shown in Figure 6.3.

Just as you use initializers for single dimensioned arrays, you can leave off the size of the array, but only for one dimension. So the previous array could be initialized as

```
int array_2d[][SIZE_1D]={
    {1,2},
    {3,4},
    {5,6}
    };
```

If you reference a multidimensional array with less than the maximum number of dimensions, you are actually referencing an array. For example, array_2d[2] is actually the third array in array_2d. Whereas array_2d[2][1]/2 is a valid expression, array_2d[2]/2 is invalid. More information on multidimensional arrays and ways to pass them to subroutines is given in Chapter 12 on pointers. The sub-arrays of array_2d are shown in Figure 6.4.

A double dimensioned array is treated as an array of single dimensioned arrays. You could pass a single dimensioned element to a routine as zero_array (Listing 6.1). For example,

```
zero_array(array_2d[1], SIZE_1D);
```

would call the function and pass it the address of array_2d[1][0]. The function would zero the two ints at that address (array_2d[1][0] and array_2d[1][1]).

---

[6] This can also be coded as

```
int array_2d[SIZE_2D][SIZE_1D]={1,2,3,4,5,6};
```

However, the text version is clearer.

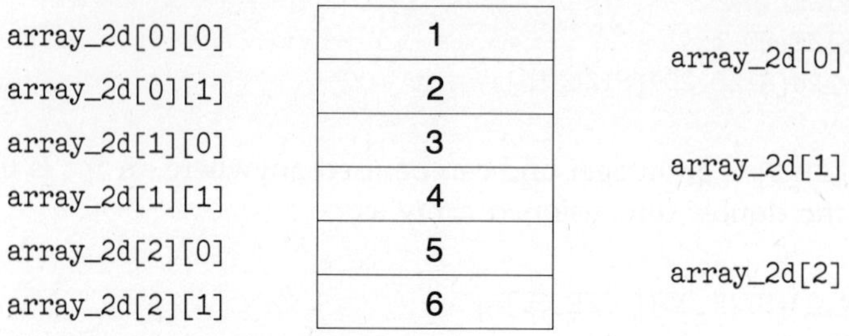

```
array_2d[0][0]  │      1      │
array_2d[0][1]  │      2      │      array_2d[0]
array_2d[1][0]  │      3      │
array_2d[1][1]  │      4      │      array_2d[1]
array_2d[2][0]  │      5      │
array_2d[2][1]  │      6      │      array_2d[2]
```

**Figure 6.3 Two-Dimensional Array**

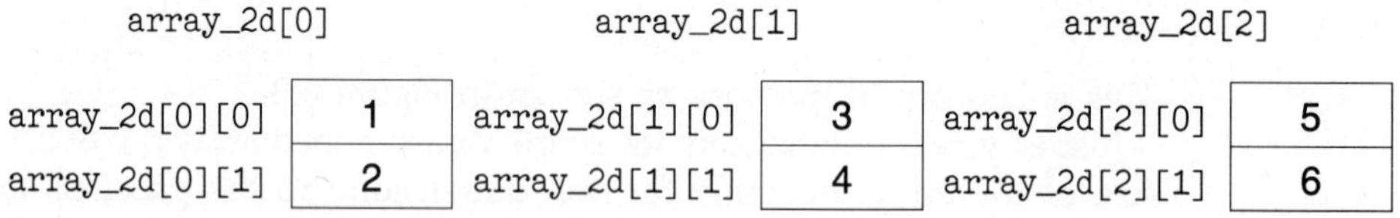

```
        array_2d[0]                array_2d[1]                array_2d[2]

array_2d[0][0] │  1  │   array_2d[1][0] │  3  │   array_2d[2][0] │  5  │
array_2d[0][1] │  2  │   array_2d[1][1] │  4  │   array_2d[2][1] │  6  │
```

**Figure 6.4 Subarrays in Two-Dimensional Array**

If you call a function and pass it a two-dimensional array that you wish to treat as a two-dimensional array, you must specify the second dimension in the called function. For example,

```
func(array_2d, SIZE_2D);        /* Call to function */
func(array, size)
int array[][SIZE_1D];
int size;
    {
    ...
    }
```

To illustrate two-dimensional arrays further, here is date_check, Listing 4.6, rewritten again. The days in each month are stored in a two-dimensional array. The first subarray days_in_month[0] contains the days for nonleap years. The second subarray days_in_month[1] contains the days for leap years. Notice how compact this code is compared to Listing 4.6. Using arrays as tables can dramatically decrease the code required to perform a particular function.

**Listing 6.8 date_check with Array**

```
#define TRUE 1
#define FALSE 0


int date_check(month, day, year)
/* Checks a date for validity */
int month;                              /* Month to check */
```

```
int day;                        /* Day to check */
int year;                       /* Year to check */
                                /* Returns TRUE if valid date
                                            FALSE if not valid */

    {
    int valid;                  /* Return value for day is valid */
    int leap;                   /* Index for type of year */

    static int days_in_month[2][12] =
        {
        {31, 28, 31, 30, 31, 30, 31, 31, 30, 31, 30, 31},
        {31, 29, 31, 30, 31, 30, 31, 31, 30, 31, 30, 31}
        };
                                /* Number of days in month */
                                /* days_in_month[0] for nonleap year */
                                /* days_in_month[1] for leap year */

    /* Assume date is good until proven otherwise */
    valid = TRUE;

    if (day <= 0)
        valid = FALSE;
    else if (month < 1 || month > 12)
        valid = FALSE;
    else
        {
        /* Set appropriate index for leap year */
        if (year % 4 == 0)
            leap = 1;
        else
            leap = 0;
        if (day > days_in_month[leap][month - 1])
            valid = FALSE;
        }

    return valid;
    }
```

## SAMPLE PROGRAM—HANGMAN

This game plays hangman, the old game that you play to guess letters until you have guessed correctly or you are "hung." It only has four words, but you can easily add more. The program uses a double dimensioned array to store the words.

The letter_guessed array keeps track of what letters have been guessed. It is indexed by the character value. The guess_so_far array has the letters that have been guessed in their proper place in the word. The body_parts array contains the strings for the parts that will be lost if a guess is wrong. The answers array has the potential answers.

The input for hours and minutes gives a pseudorandom number to use to pick out an answer. The guess_so_far is set to a string of underscores, and all elements in letter_guessed are set to FALSE.

The program calls get_guess to get a letter that has not yet been guessed. If the input letter has not been guessed, the element of letter_guessed indexed by that letter is set TRUE.

The got_one flag shows whether the letter is in the answer. number_right keeps track of how many letters in the answer have been found. If the letter is in the word, got_one is set TRUE, and number_right is incremented by the number of times it appears in the word. If got_one remains FALSE, number_wrong is incremented and a part of the body is lost.

---

### *Pseudocode for Hangman*

```
Hangman
       Initialize
       While not done
             Get a guess
             Check the guess
             If all right
                   set done true
             If too many wrong
                   set done true
```

---

**Listing 6.9 Hangman Game**

```c
#include <ctype.h>              /* For toupper and isalpha functions */
#include <stdio.h>

#define TRUE 1
#define FALSE 0

#define MAX_WRONG 6             /* Maximum number of wrong answers */
#define MAX_WORD 10             /* Maximum length for words */
#define NUMBER_ANSWERS 4        /* Number of answers */
#define NUM_CHAR 256            /* Maximum different character values */
#define MAX_ANSWER 20           /* Maximum size of answer */

int main()
/* Plays the game of hangman */
int length;                     /* Length of answer */
int answer_index;               /* Index of answer */
int number_wrong;               /* Wrong guesses so far */
char guess_so_far[MAX_ANSWER + 1];
```

```
                                        /* Letters guessed so far */
char letter_guessed[NUM_CHAR];
                                        /* Flags if letter was guessed */
int number_right;           /* Correct guesses */
int i;                      /* Index */
int done;                   /* Flag for finished */
char guess;                 /* Character that is guessed */
int got_one;                /* Flag if character is right */

static char body_parts[MAX_WRONG][MAX_WORD] =
    {"HEAD", "BODY", "LEFT ARM", "RIGHT ARM",
    "LEFT LEG", "RIGHT LEG"};
                                        /* Body parts to lose */
static char words[NUMBER_ANSWERS][MAX_WORD] =
    {"DATA", "FLOAT", "DOUBLE", "INTEGER"};
                                        /* Potential answers */


/* Initialize the answer */
printf("\n Welcome to Hangman");

/* Get an index to the word */
answer_index = randomize(NUMBER_ANSWERS);

/* Initialize the guessing counters */

length = strlen(words[answer_index]);
number_wrong = 0;
number_right = 0;
for (i = 0; i < NUM_CHAR; i++)
    {
    letter_guessed[i] = FALSE;
    }
for (i = 0; i < MAX_ANSWER; i++)
    {
    guess_so_far[i] = '_';
    }
guess_so_far[length] = '\0';

/* Start the game */
printf("\n I'm thinking of a word %d characters long", length);
done = FALSE;
/* Keep going until right or dead */
while (!done)
    {
    /* Get a letter that has not been used before */
    guess = get_guess(letter_guessed);
```

```
                got_one = FALSE;

                /* Check the guess */
                for (i = 0; i < length; i++)
                    {
                    /* If the correct character, record it */
                    if (words[answer_index][i] == guess)
                        {
                        guess_so_far[i] = guess;
                        number_right++;
                        got_one = TRUE;
                        }
                    }

                /* Test to see whether the guess was a good one */
                if (got_one)
                    printf("\n Good going, so far your guess is %s", guess_so_far);
                else
                    {
                    printf("\n You just lost your %s", body_parts[number_wrong]);
                    number_wrong++;
                    }

                /* If have guessed all the letters, then a winner */
                if (number_right == length)
                    {
                    done = TRUE;
                    printf("\n You guessed it");
                    }

                /* If too many wrong guesses, then a loser */
                else if (number_wrong == MAX_WRONG)
                    {
                    done = TRUE;
                    printf("\n You are dead");
                    printf("\n Word was %s", words[answer index]);
                    }
                }

        exit(0);
        }


/*********************** GET_GUESS ***********************/
int get_guess(letter_guessed)
/* Gets a guess, returns the character guessed */
/* Checks to see whether character has already been guessed */
char letter_guessed[];            /* Array of flags for letters already used */
```

```
    {
    int good_guess;              /* Flag when guess is good */
    char guess;                  /* Character that is guessed */

    guess = '\0';
    good_guess = FALSE;
    while (!good_guess)
        {
        /* Skip any extra newline characters */
        if (guess != '\n')
            printf("\n What is your guess? ");
        scanf("%c", &guess);

        guess = toupper(guess);

        if (isalpha(guess))
            {
            /* Check whether letter was already guessed */
            if (letter_guessed[guess - 'A'] == TRUE)
                printf("\n You guessed that");
            else
                {
                letter_guessed[guess - 'A'] = TRUE;
                good_guess = TRUE;
                }
            }
        }

    return guess;
    }

/***************************  RANDOMIZE  ************************/
int randomize(limit)
/* Returns a "random" number from 0 to limit - 1 */
int limit;                       /* Number should be less than this */
                                 /* Returns random number */
    {
    int minutes;                 /* For minutes */
    int seconds;                 /* For seconds */
    int answer;                  /* For answer */
    printf("\n How many minutes past the hour is it? ");
    scanf("%d", &minutes);
    printf("\n How many seconds past the minute is it?");
    scanf("%d", &seconds);
    answer = (minutes * seconds + seconds) % limit;
    return answer;
    }
```

## SUMMARY

- An array is a group of variables with a single name.
- An element of an array is referenced using the name and subscripts.
- Passing an array to a function permits the function to change the values in the array.
- Arrays can have multiple dimensions. To access an individual element, the number of subscripts must be equal to the number of dimensions.

## SELF-TEST

1. What will happen when you run this code?

```
#define LENGTH 10
char string[LENGTH];
int i;
for (i = 0; i <= LENGTH; i++)
    {
    string[i] = ' ';
    }
```

2. What will the value of sum be for this program segment?

```
#define ROW 2
#define COL 3
static int array[ROW][COL]={ {1,2,3}, {4,5,6} };
int i, j;
int sum = 0;
for (j = 0; j < ROW; j++)
    {
    for (i = 0; i < COL; i++)
        {
        sum = sum + array[i][j];
        }
    }
```

3. If you run the following, what prints out?

```
static char string_array[10];
printf("\n Initial string is :%s:", string_array);
for (i = 0; i < 5; i++)
    {
    string_array[i] = 'A';
    }
printf("\n Final string is :%s:", string_array);
```

4. Given these declarations:

```
int array_a[5];
static double array_b[5] = {1.,2.,3.,4.,5.};
```

what will happen with the following code?
a. `array_a = array_b;`
b. `array_a[1] = array_b[1];`

5. Given

```
int a[5];
```

What is the operation of the following code?
a. `scanf("%d", &a[1]);`
b. `scanf("%d", a);`
c. `printf("%d", a[1]);`
d. `printf("%d", a);`

---

## ANSWERS

1. The value of a space will be placed in all elements in string *and* in the memory location right after where string is stored.
2. Garbage. Values will be added from `array[2][0]` and `array[2][1]`, which are not part of the array. The reference to `array` should have read `array[j][i];`
3. `Initial string is :: Final string is :AAAAA:`
   Each element in `string_array` is initialized to zero, the NUL character, because it is a `static` array. The character *A* is placed in the first five elements. `string_array[5]` remains the NUL character, which is the terminating value for a string.
4. a. The compiler will give an error. You cannot assign an array to an array.
   b. `a[1]` will get the value 2.
5. a. Input value goes into `a[1]`.
   b. Input value goes into `a[0]`. The name of an array all by itself is the address of the first element. a is equal to `&a[0]`.
   c. Value in `a[1]` is printed out.
   d. The address of a is passed to `printf`. This value is printed out as if it were an `int`.

## PROBLEMS

1. Write a function to find the maximum and minimum of an array of numbers.
2. Write a function to find the standard deviation of an array of values.

$$\text{Standard deviation} = \text{sqrt (sum } (x - \text{mean})^2/(n - 1)$$

3. Write a function to find the day of the year for a date that is passed as a month, day, and year.
4. You can alternatively declare the array in date__check as

```
static char month_days[2][13]={
    {0,31,28,31,30,31,30,31,31,30,31,30,31},
    {0,31,29,31,30,31,30,31,31,30,31,30,31},
    };
```

What are the pros and cons of declaring the array this way?

5. For a double dimensioned array, the called function must know how big the second dimension is. Thus, if you write a function to add up all the elements in

```
int int_array[NUMBER_ROWS][NUMBER_COLS];
```

where NUMBER_ROWS and NUMBER_COLS have been #defined, the routine might look like

```
sum_array(array,number_rows)
int array[][NUMBER_COLS];
int number_rows;
    {
    int row;
    int col;
    double sum;
    sum=0.0;
    for (row=0;row < number_rows; row++)
        {
        for (col=0;col<NUMBER_COLS;col++)
            {
            sum = sum + array[row][col];
            }
        }
    return sum;
    }
```

Write a routine that returns the largest row average in a double dimensioned array.

6. Write a routine that computes the number of days from January 1, 1980, to the date supplied as a parameter.

7. Write a program to add together two strings that represent two numbers, for example, "1.2" and "3.2" should produce "4.4". First code your program assuming that both numbers have the same number of digits, then take away this assumption.

8. Count how many digraphs (combinations of two letters) there are in a file. (Hint: Use a double dimensioned array of count[26][26] with count[0][0] for *AA*, count[1][0] for *BA*, and so on.)

9. Write a routine to find the mode, the most frequently occurring value, in an array. For example, with

$$5, 7, 9, 3, 6, 5, 7, 7,$$

the mode is 7, because it occurs most often.

10. Write a routine to find the median (middle value) of an array. For example, with

$$3, 5, 7, 8, 9, 11, 15$$

the median is 8, because it is the middle element in the array. If the array has an even number of elements, you should average the two on either side of the middle.

11. Write a function that evaluates a polynomial of the type

$$coef[0]*x^0 + coef[1]*x^1...coef[n - 1]*x^{(n-1)}$$

The function header might look like

```
double eval_polynomial(coefficient,number_of_coef,x_value)
double coefficient[];
int number_of_coef;
double x_value;
```

12. Write a function to perform a substitution cipher. For each letter in a string, replace it with a letter in encoding array. The function might look like

```
subcode(string_out, string_in, encode)
char string_out[];
char string_in[];
char encode[];
```

13. Write a function to insert a string at a given index in another string. The new string increases by the size of the inserted string. Be sure that your function checks for possible errors, such as attempting to insert a string after the end of the present string.

14. Write a function that deletes characters in a string at a given index.

15. Write a function that converts an array of characters to an integer. The characters are in the range of 0 to 9. You might add error checking to ensure that the characters are in this range.

16. Write a function that prints a histogram. You could call it with

```
histogram(x_array,y_array,size)
double x_array[];              /* values for labels */
int y_array[];                /* number of times */
int size;
```

and have it display something like

```
3.2 ***
4.4 *****
```

17. Write a program that expands tabs into spaces. The program needs to keep track of what the current position on the line is. For example, if tabs were every eight spaces, showing tabs as the exclamation character

```
ABC!DEFGHI!J!K
```

would expand to:

```
01234567890123456789012345678 9 (column count)

ABC     DEFGHI  J       K
```

18. Exams are graded according to the following:

| Score | Grade |
| --- | --- |
| 90 and above | A |
| below 90 | B |
| below 80 | C |
| below 70 | D |
| below 60 | F |

Write a function that reads a series of scores and outputs the number in each grade and the average of each grade.

19. How could the letter_guessed array in hangman be made smaller?

20. Write a function that determines whether a string is contained in another string.

21. Write a game to play tic-tac-toe with two players. The computer simply keeps track of the moves and announces when one player has won. You might try the following alterations to the game:
    a. Allow more than two players.
    b. Let the number of rows and columns in the game be adjustable.
    c. Make the game three dimensional.

22. Write a program that performs the following. The user inputs a number and then enters a series of numbers from 1 to that number. Your program should

determine which number (or numbers) is missing or duplicated in the series, if any. For example, if the user entered 5 as the initial number and then entered the following sequences, the results should be as shown.

```
Input Sequence          Output
1 2 3 4 5               Nothing bad
```

However, if 7 were the high number, the user would see the results on the right for the following number entries:

```
1 3 2 4 5               Missing 6
                        Missing 7
```

And if 10 were the high number and the user entered the numbers shown on the left, note the list of missing and duplicate numbers:

```
1 2 4 7 4 4 5 10 8 2 6    Duplicate 2 (2 times)
                          Missing 3
                          Duplicate 4 (3 times)
                          Missing 9
```

The program should check the high number that the user inputs to ensure that it does not exceed the size of any array you might be using for storage.

23. Write a function to return the number of characters in a string, not counting contiguous spaces that come just before the terminating NUL.

24. Modify hangman to graphically print out the body parts that have been "hung."

# Chapter Seven

# Structures and Unions

In arrays, the elements are all one data type. A *structure* is a collection of variables that can be diverse types. The name of the structure refers to the entire group of variables. A member name selects a particular variable within a structure. Structures—similar to records in other languages—group data items relating to each other, such as the name and address of a person or an hour, minute, and second of time.

*Unions* are collections of variables sharing the same memory locations. They access the same memory multiple ways, such as with two different structures.

## STRUCTURE DEFINITION

*Structures* are objects whose variables can be of different types. Each variable in a structure is called a *member*. The advantage of structures is that several values can be treated as a single entity when they are passed to a function or assigned.

The simplest form to declare a variable to be a structure is

```
struct
     {
     declarations-of-members
     } name-of-structure-variable;
```

The members of this structure are referenced by

```
name-of-structure.name-of-member
```

The period (.) is the *member operator*. It is used to reference a member of a particular structure. For example, in

```
struct
    {
    int int_number;
    double doub_number;
    } sample_struct;
```

sample_struct is the name of the structure variable. The two members in sample_struct are sample_struct.int_number and sample_struct.doub_number. They are laid out in memory as shown in Figure 7.1. Each of the members can be used just like a single variable, as in

```
i = sample_struct.int_number + 7;
sample_struct.doub_number = 1.2;
```

Most of the time a structure declaration is broken into two parts. First, *a template name* (or *tag*) is given to a particular organization of members. Then variables are declared as structures of that template. The form to declare the template is

```
struct template-name
    {
    declarations-of-members
    }
```

and the form to declare a variable with this template is

```
struct template-name name-of-structure-variable;
```

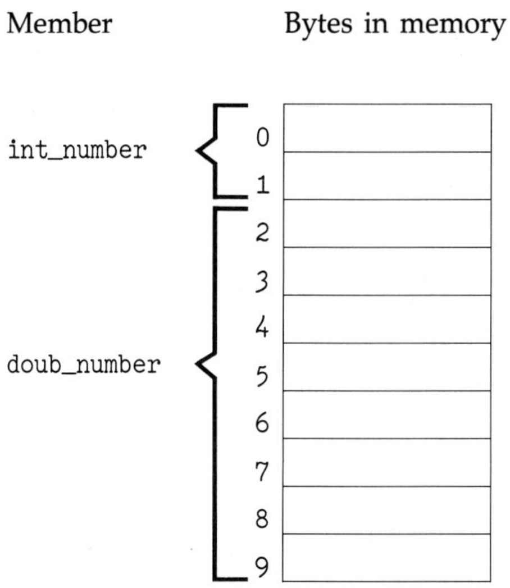

Member                    Bytes in memory

**Figure 7.1 Layout of Sample Structure**

The previous example would be declared as

```
struct sample_template
    {
    int int_number;
    double doub_number;
    } ;
```

```
struct sample_template sample_struct;
```

The template declaration does not cause any storage allocation. It simply defines the layout of the members in the template. Declaring a variable with the template sets aside storage.[1]

The C library includes one tag for a structure that contains the various parts of time. The tag is tm, and it is defined in time.h. Appendix G shows a listing of its members.

A structure as a whole can be passed to a function, returned from a function, and assigned in an assignment. If you declared

```
struct sample_template a_struct, b_struct;
```

you could perform an assignment as

```
a_struct = b_struct;
```

and all the values from b_struct would be assigned to the corresponding variables in a_struct.

You might think the size of sample_template was 10 bytes (2 for the int plus 8 for the double). The compiler may place holes in this structure for purposes of aligning the values on particular locations in memory. The sizeof operator gives the actual size of this structure, if you need it.

You cannot compare two structures as a whole. You can only compare the individual elements. For the example, it is illegal to compute a_struct == b_struct;. To compare the two structures for equality, you can code

```
(a_struct.int_number == b_struct.int_number &&
    a_struct.doub_number == b_struct.doub_number)
```

---

[1] You can declare both the template and a variable using the template in a single statement. However, this is not usually done, because any source file that includes the template is forced to have a variable with that name. For example, the previous example could look like

```
struct sample_template
    {
    int int_number;
    double doub_number;
    } sample_struct;
```

**SAMPLE FUNCTION—date_check**

Grouping the three portions of a date—the month, day, and year—is a natural application for a structure. The date_check function is redone here using a structure as a parameter.

The main routine inputs the values into members of the structure date. The entire structure is passed to date_check, where the values of each member are checked.

**Listing 7.1 date_check with Structure**

```
struct s_date
    {
    int month;                          /* Month of year (1 to 12) */
    int day;                            /* Day of month */
    int year;                           /* Year */
    };

static int days_in_month[2][12] =
    {
    {31, 28, 31, 30, 31, 30, 31, 31, 30, 31, 30, 31},
    {31, 29, 31, 30, 31, 30, 31, 31, 30, 31, 30, 31}
    };

#include <stdio.h>
#define FALSE 0
#define TRUE 1

int date_check(date)
/* Checks a date for validity */
struct s_date date;                     /* Date to check */
                                        /* Returns TRUE if date is good,
                                                FALSE if date is invalid */

    {
    int valid;                          /* Return value */
    int leap;                           /* Flag for leap year */

    /* Assume date is good until proven otherwise */
    valid = TRUE;

    if (date.day <= 0)
        valid = FALSE;
    /* Determine whether leap year */
    if (date.year % 4 == 0)
        leap = 1;
    else
        leap = 0;
```

```
    if ((date.month < 1) | | (date.month > 12))
        valid = FALSE;
    else if (date.day > days_in_month[leap][date.month - 1])
        valid = FALSE;

    return valid;
    }

/****************************  MAIN  ****************************/
int main()
/* Input a date as a structure and check it */
    {
    struct s_date date_in;              /* Date to be checked */
    int result;                         /* Result of check */

    printf("\n This program checks for a valid date");

    /* Input the date */
    printf("\n Enter the month: ");
    scanf("%d", &date_in.month);
    printf("\n Enter the day: ");
    scanf("%d", &date_in.day);
    printf("\n Enter the year");
    scanf("%d", &date_in.year);

    /* Check the date and print the result */
    result = date_check(date_in);
    if (result)
        printf("\n Day is valid");
    else
        printf("\n Day is invalid");

    exit(0);
    }
```

All the values in the structure date_in in the main function are passed to date_check function and placed in the date parameter. This is a call by value, similar to a call by value for simple variables. Affecting the value of date inside of date_check does not affect the value of date_in in main.

The expressions &date_in.month, &date_in.day, and &date_in.year are the addresses of the individual members in date_in. To input values into a structure, enter them into each member that is a simple variable.

## STRUCTURES WITHIN STRUCTURES

Once you have defined a structure template, you can use it inside another structure. For example, if s_date has been defined and you define another template, such as

```
struct s_time
    {
    int hour;
    int minute;
    int second;
    };
```

you can create a template containing both of these structures, such as

```
struct s_date_time
    {
    struct s_date date;
    struct s_time time;
    };
```

If you declared `struct s_date_time instance;`, the members of instance are

| Member | Type |
| --- | --- |
| instance.date | structure of type s_date |
| instance.time | structure of type s_time |
| instance.date.month | int |
| instance.date.day | int |
| instance.date.year | int |
| instance.time.hour | int |
| instance.time.minute | int |
| instance.time.second | int |

Note that if you declare `s_date_time` to be

```
struct s_date_time {
    int month;
    int day;
    int year;
    int hour;
    int minute;
    int second;
    };
```

you cannot use the `date_check` routine in Listing 7.1 or Listing 7.2. Always attempt to build structures from simpler structures. This technique makes creating even larger programs easier.

You should try to create your structures from the lowest level upward. Suppose you created a structure template to contain information about a person:

```
struct person {
    char last_name[SIZE_LAST_NAME];
    char first_name[SIZE_FIRST_NAME];
    char street_address[SIZE_STREET_ADDRESS];
    char city[SIZE_CITY];
    char state[SIZE_STATE];
    char zip[SIZE_ZIP];
    };
```

You then decide to include the work address. You might add more members to the structure, such as

```
char work_street_address[SIZE_WORK_STREET_ADDRESS];
char work_city[SIZE_WORK_CITY];
...
```

If you had started with an address template, such as

```
struct saddress
    {
    char street_address[SIZE_STREET_ADDRESS];
    char city[SIZE_CITY];
    char state[SIZE_STATE];
    char zip[SIZE_ZIP];
    };
```

the person template with the work address included could look like

```
struct sperson
    {
    char last_name[SIZE_LAST_NAME];
    char first_name[SIZE_FIRST_NAME];
    struct saddress home;
    struct saddress work;
    };
```

With this organization, you could have a common routine for printing addresses, sorting addresses, and so forth.

## ARRAYS AND STRUCTURES

You can insert arrays as members of structures. For example,

```
struct s_array
    {
    int a_numbers[100];
    };
struct s_array array_a;
```

has as some of its parts:

| | |
|---|---|
| `array_a` | structure |
| `array_a.a_numbers` | array of `int`s |
| `array_a.a_numbers[3]` | int (4th element in a_numbers) |

If you create another structure of this type, you can assign this structure. This is one way of handling array copying, because the assignment operator does not work with arrays.

```
struct s_array array_b;
array_b = array_a;
```

The second line here copies the entire structure (all of a_numbers).

A common object illustrative of a structure is the playing card. You can define a structure for a card and declare a hand or deck to be an array of these structures, such as

```
#define SIZE_SUIT 9
struct s_card
    {
    int value;                    /* Value of card */
    char suit[SIZE_SUIT];         /* String representing suit */
    };
#define SIZE_HAND 5
struct s_card hand[SIZE_HAND];
```

The variable `hand` has elements in the array that are structures and members of these structures that are arrays, as shown in Figure 7.2. Some of these are

| | |
|---|---|
| `hand` | array of structures of type s_card |
| `hand[1]` | struct of type s_card (one element of hand) |
| `hand[1].value` | int |
| `hand[1].suit` | array of chars |
| `hand[1].suit[0]` | char (first element in array) |

You can write a program in several ways to deal a hand. Listing 7.2 simply gets a random number between 0 and 51, inclusively. It checks whether each number has been dealt before by keeping track of chosen numbers in `card_dealt[]`. If the number has not, the program divides the number by NUMBER_PER_SUIT to get a suit value and uses the remainder to get the card value.

An alternative algorithm is to start with an array filled with all the possible cards and use the random number function to determine which two cards to interchange (shuffle). The problems at the end of the chapter examine this alternative.

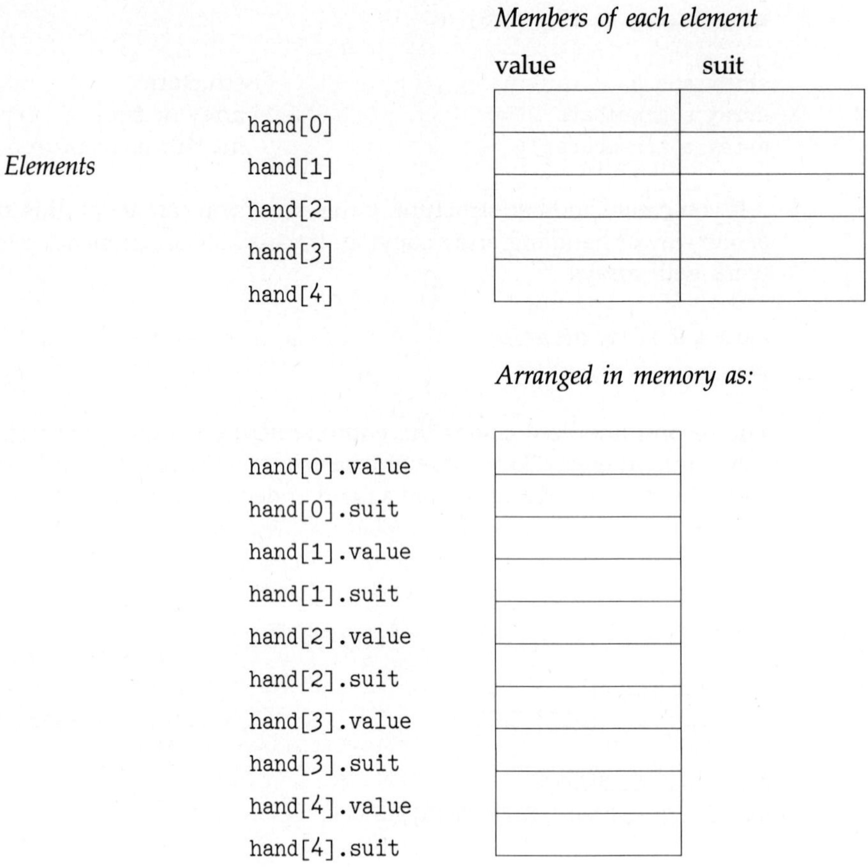

*Members of each element*

| value | suit |
|-------|------|
|       |      |
|       |      |
|       |      |
|       |      |
|       |      |

*Elements*

hand[0]
hand[1]
hand[2]
hand[3]
hand[4]

*Arranged in memory as:*

hand[0].value
hand[0].suit
hand[1].value
hand[1].suit
hand[2].value
hand[2].suit
hand[3].value
hand[3].suit
hand[4].value
hand[4].suit

**Figure 7.2 Layout of Array of Structures**

**Listing 7.2 Deal Hand Program**

```c
#include <stdio.h>
#include <stdlib.h>                     /* For rand function */

#define MAX_SUIT 10
#define NUMBER_SUITS 4
#define NUMBER_PER_SUIT 13
#define NUMBER_CARDS (NUMBER_SUITS*NUMBER_PER_SUIT)
#define TRUE 1
#define FALSE 0

struct s_card
    {
    char suit[MAX_SUIT];                /* Suit */
    int value;                          /* Value (1 to 13) */
    };
```

```
char suits[NUMBER_SUITS][MAX_SUIT] =
{"HEARTS", "SPADES", "CLUBS", "DIAMONDS"};
char card_dealt[NUMBER_CARDS];
                                /* Tracks whether card has been dealt */
int number_dealt;              /* Counts number of cards dealt */

/*************************** NEW-DEAL ****************************/
void new_deal()
/* Starts a new deal */
    {
    int card;                  /* Index for card_dealt */

    for (card = 0; card < NUMBER_CARDS; card++)
        {
        card_dealt[card] = FALSE;
        }

    number_dealt = 0;
    }

/**************************** DEAL HAND ****************************/
int deal_hand(hand, size)
/* Gets a hand of cards */
struct s_card hand[];          /* Array to fill with cards */
int size;                      /* Size of hand */
                               /* Returns number of cards dealt */
    {
    int card;                  /* Card index */
    int dealt_in_hand;         /* Count of cards dealt */

    dealt_in_hand = 0;

    while (dealt_in_hand < size && number_dealt < NUMBER_CARDS)
        {
        card = rand() % NUMBER_CARDS;
        if (card_dealt[card] == FALSE)
            {
            /* Card has not been used */
            card_dealt[card] = TRUE;
            hand[dealt_in_hand].value = card % NUMBER_PER_SUIT + 1;
            strcpy(hand[dealt_in_hand].suit,
                suits[card / NUMBER_PER_SUIT]);
            dealt_in_hand++;
            /* Keep track of total cards dealt */
            number_dealt++;
            }
        }
```

```
      return dealt_in_hand;
      }


/******************************* MAIN *********************************/
#define SIZE_HAND 5

int main()
/* Tests the dealing of a hand */
    {
    struct s_card hand[SIZE_HAND];       /* For the dealt hand */
    int card;                            /* Index into hand */
    int cards_dealt;                     /* Number dealt */
    int hands;                           /* Number of the hands */

    new_deal();

    /* Deal one more hand than the cards will allow */
    for (hands = 0; hands < (NUMBER_CARDS / SIZE_HAND) + 1; hands++)
        {
        cards_dealt = deal_hand(hand, SIZE_HAND);
        printf("\n\n Hand %d : %d Cards dealt", hands, cards_dealt);
        for (card = 0; card < cards_dealt; card++)
            {
            printf("\n Card is %d of %s",
                hand[card].value, hand[card].suit);
            }
        }

    exit(0);
    }
```

A portion of the output from this program looks like

```
Hand 0 : 5 Cards dealt
Card is 1 of HEARTS
Card is 7 of DIAMONDS
Card is 6 of HEARTS
Card is 6 of SPADES
Card is 2 of SPADES
...
Hand 10 : 2 Cards dealt
Card is 2 of HEARTS
Card is 2 of DIAMONDS
```

## PACKAGES OF FUNCTIONS FOR STRUCTURES

You may need to perform different operations on the same type of structure. For example, with the date structure, not only is checking a date necessary but also comparing two dates and learning the day of the week of a particular date are required. Once you have written these functions for one structure, when you reuse the structure in other programs, you can reuse the functions.

Comparing two dates and finding the day of the week of a date may seem like two entirely different operations. However, before you code either one, a little analysis may reduce your coding effort. Say a number is assigned to a date, starting with zero at some point in time. To compare two dates, only their date numbers need be compared, not their individual members. If the difference between two date numbers modulo the number of days in a week is zero, the two dates fall on the same day of the week.

The first function computes a date number. To simplify the example, it assumes the year it is receiving is a number between 1 and 99 that represents years 1901 to 1999. It uses January 1, 1950, as the reference point. If the year is equal to or greater than this year, the date number is positive; if the year is less than this year, the date number is negative.

**Listing 7.3 Date Number Function**

```
struct s_date
    {
    int month;
    int day;
    int year;
    };

#define FIRST_YEAR 50          /* First year for day number calculations */
char days_in_month[2][12] = {
    {31, 28, 31, 30, 31, 30, 31, 31, 30, 31, 30, 31}, /* Nonleap year */
    {31, 29, 31, 30, 31, 30, 31, 31, 30, 31, 30, 31} /* Leap year */
    };
#define INVALID_DATE -32767    /* Date is invalid */


int date_number(date)
/* Computes the number of days since January 1, 1950 */
struct s_date date;             /* Date to determine number */
                                /* Returns date number if date is valid,
                                       INVALID_DATE if date is invalid */

    {
    int leap;                   /* Leap year flag */
    int m;                      /* Month index */
    int year_count;             /* Years from 1950 */
```

```
int day_number;            /* Returned value */
int leap_years;            /* Number of leap years to account for */

if (check_date(date))
    {
    leap = is_leap_year(date.year);
    /* Determine the count */
    year_count = date.year - FIRST_YEAR;
    if (year_count >= 0)
        {
        /* Add number of days in previous years */
        day_number = year_count * 365;

        /* Add the extra leap years */
        leap_years = (year_count + 1) / 4;
        day_number = day_number + leap_years;

        /* Add the number of days in prior months */
        for (m = 0; m < date.month - 1; m++)
            {
            day_number = day_number + days_in_month[leap][m];
            }

        /* Add the day of the month */
        day_number = day_number + date.day - 1;
        }
    else
        {
        /* Number of days in years till FIRST_YEAR */
        day_number = (year_count + 1) * 365;

        /* Add the extra leap years */
        leap_years = (year_count - 1) / 4;
        day_number = day_number + leap_years;

        /* Add the number of days in ending months of current year */
        for (m = 11; m > date.month - 1; m--)
            {
            day_number = day_number - days_in_month[leap][m];
            }
        /* Add the number of days in rest of month */
        day_number = day_number -
            (days_in_month[leap][date.month - 1] - date.day) - 1;
        }
```

```
        }
    else
        day_number = INVALID_DATE;

    return day_number;
    }


/*************************** IS_LEAP_YEAR ***************************/
#define FALSE 0
#define TRUE 1

int is_leap_year(year)
/* Determines whether year is a leap year */
int year;                       /* Year to check */
                                /* Returns TRUE if leap year; FALSE if not
                                        leap year */

    {
    int ret;                    /* Return value */

    if (year % 4)
        ret = FALSE;
    else
        ret = TRUE;

    return ret;
    }
```

Once you find the date number for a date, comparing two dates is easy. Their date numbers are simply compared. You might wonder why the code is not just ret = first_test - second_test. The reason is if first_test is a large positive value and second_test is a large negative, subtraction causes an integer overflow and the result is undefined.

### Listing 7.4 date_compare Function

```
#define INVALID_DATE -32767

int date_compare(first_date, second_date)
/* Compares two dates */
struct s_date first_date;       /* First date to compare */
struct s_date second_date;      /* Second date to compare */
                                /* Returns -1 if first < second */
                                /* 0 if first == second */
                                /* 1 if first > second */
                                /* INVALID_DATE if either date is bad */
    {
    int first_test;             /* Date number of first date */
```

```
    int second_test;          /* date number of second date */
    int ret;                  /* return value */

    first_test = date_number(first_date);
    second_test = date_number(second_date);

    if (first_test != INVALID_DATE && second_test != INVALID_DATE)
        {
        if (first_test < second_test)
            ret = -1;
        else if (first_test == second_test)
            ret = 0;
        else
            ret = 1;
        }
    else
        ret = INVALID_DATE;

    return ret;
    }
```

With the date number, finding the day of the week is easy. The only catch is the sign of the result of the modulo operator (%) for negative numbers is compiler dependent. To ensure the proper day value if day_century was less than zero, the value is negated before the program applies the operator and negated again after the operation.

**Listing 7.5 Day of the Week Function**

```
#define DAYS_IN_WEEK 7        /* Number of days in a week */
#define FIRST_DAY 0           /* Day of week of January 1, 1950 */

int day_of_week(date)
/* Determines the day of the week */
struct s_date date;           /* Date to determine day of week of */
                              /* Returns 0 (SUNDAY) to 6 (SATURDAY)
                                   INVALID_DATE if date is invalid */
    {
    int day_century;          /* Day of century */
    int ret;                  /* Return value */

    day_century = date_number(date);
    if (day_century >= 0)
        ret = day_century % DAYS_IN_WEEK + FIRST_DAY;
    else
        {
        ret = (-day_century) % DAYS_IN_WEEK;
```

```
        ret = (-ret) + FIRST_DAY;
   if (ret < 0)
            ret = ret + DAYS_IN_WEEK;
        }

   return ret;
   }
```

The function next_month in Listing 7.6 demonstrates how to return a structure. This function returns a date that is one month later than the date passed to it. It ensures that the day does not exceed the last day of the month. The function date_out is first set to the input date. All the values in the structure date_in are copied to date_out with this assignment statement. The month is incremented and checked for overflow into the next year. For example, one month after 12/31/90 is 1/31/91. The result is checked to ensure that it is valid. If not, the day is fixed to the last date of the month. For example, one month after 1/31/90 is 2/28/90.

**Listing 7.6 next_month Function**

```
struct s_date {
    int month;
    int day;
    int year;
    };

struct s_date next_month(date_in)
/* Adds one to month and returns the next date */
struct s_date date_in;          /* Date to increment by a month */
   {
   struct s_date date_out;     /* Return value */

   /* Set the return date and increment the month */
   date_out = date_in;
   date_out.month++;
   if (date_out.month > 12)
        {
        date_out.month = 1;
        date_out.year++;
        }

   /* See whether the date is invalid--greater than last day of new month */
   if (!check_date(date_out))
        {
        if (is_leap_year(date_out.year))
            date_out.day = days_in_month[1][date_out.month-1];
        else
            date_out.day = days_in_month[0][date_out.month-1];
        }
```

```
    return date_out;
    }
```

## BIT FIELDS

A structure can contain a member that is a field of bits. These fields access values that are only a part of a memory location, such as a status value in a communication channel. To define a bit field, you define a member of a structure and give its length in bits, such as

```
struct s_bit_example {
    unsigned int one_bit : 1;
    unsigned int five_bit : 5;
    };
struct s_bit_example bit_example;
```

This structure declares that one_bit and five_bit are bit fields. one_bit is one bit long and five_bit is five bits long. Both these members are treated as unsigned ints. This means their high order bit is not treated as a sign bit.[2] The possible values of bit_example.one_bit are 0 and 1.[3] The layout of the bit fields is shown in Figure 7.3. A bit field can be used as if it were a regular integer, as in

```
bit_example.one_bit++
```
Increments by 1. If value was 0, result is 1. If value was 1, result is 0.

```
if (bit_example.five_bit==7)
```
Tests the value of the five bits against the integer value 7

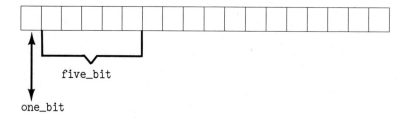

five_bit

one_bit

**Figure 7.3 Layout of Sample Bit Field**

---

[2] You could also declare the fields as int. If the one_bit member were declared as an int, its possible values would be 0 and −1.

[3] Chapter 9 describes signed and unsigned integers.

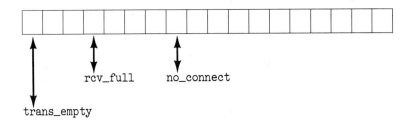

**Figure 7.4 Layout of Sample Bit Field for a Port**

The order in which the bit fields are laid out in memory is dependent on the compiler and the computer system. one_bit may either be the rightmost or leftmost bit in a word. However, it is consistent for a particular compiler/computer combination.

Bit fields have several limitations. They cannot be wider than the number of bits in an int. They are located in integer-wide memory locations starting with the first member. On many compilers, fields cannot overlap integer boundaries. If a member cannot fit into an int, it starts in the next integer location. The address operator (&) cannot be applied to bit fields.

A field of width 0 forces alignment with the next integer. You may also use a field without a name for padding.

A use of bit fields might be in testing the status of a communications port. You might have a port that looks like Figure 7.4.

You could set up a bit field structure looking like

```
struct s_comm_port
    {
    unsigned int trans_empty : 1; /* Transmitter empty */
                             : 2;
    unsigned int rcv_full    : 1; /* Receiver full */
                             : 3;
    unsigned int no_connect  : 1; /* No connection */
    };
struct s_comm_port comm_port;
```

and make references to the fields as

```
if (comm_port.trans_empty==1)
...
if (comm_port.no_connect)
```

## UNIONS

Members of structures do not overlap. Each member has its own memory location. In contrast, union members share the same memory space. The declaration of a union looks like the declaration for a structure.

```
union {
      declarations of members
      } name-of-union-variable;
or

union template-name {
      declarations of members
      };
union template-name name-of-union-variable;
```

A sample union might look like

```
union sample_union_template {
      int int_number;
      double doub_number;
      };
union sample_union_template sample_union;
```

The union is laid out in memory as shown in Figure 7.5. The two members are

```
sample_union.int_number        int
sample_union.doub_number       double
```

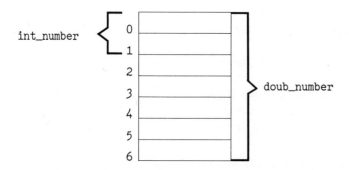

**Figure 7.5 Layout of Sample Union**

The difference between a `struct` and a `union` of this type is when a value is assigned to one member, the value of the other member changes.

```
sample_union.int_number = 5          Assigns 5 to the first two bytes
sample_union.doub_number = 1.0       Assigns 1.0 to the first eight bytes
```

The main uses for unions are either to save space by using the same memory for two purposes or to reference portions of structures whose contents may vary. If you reference a member in a union that is currently being used to store another union member, you may get garbage.

You can initialize a union, but only using the first member of it. For the sample union,

```
union sample_union_template sample_union = 5 ;
```

sets the first two bytes of the union to an integer 5. The size of a union is the size of its largest member.

You can analyze how your computer stores bits in each data type by combining bit fields and unions. For example, if `int`s are 16 bits, you can make up a union of an `int` and a structure of bit fields. When you access a member of the structure, you get the corresponding bit in the `int`.

```
s_bits
    {
    unsigned int bit0: 1;
    unsigned int bit1: 1;
    unsigned int bit2: 1;
    unsigned int bit3: 1;
    unsigned int bit4: 1;
    ...           /* Bits 5 through 14 */
    unsigned int bit15: 1;
    };

union {
    struct s_bits bits;
    int integer;
    } test;

test.integer = 3;
printf("\n The bits in %d are %d%d%d%d%d%d%d%d%d%d%d%d%d%d%d%d",
    test.integer,
    test.bits.bit0,test.bits.bit1,
    ...test.bits.bit15);
```

You can use a union to keep a single array of two different structures. Suppose you want to keep a list of names of companies and persons. For companies, you only want a single name; for persons, two names. You can set up templates as

```
sperson
    {
    char last_name[SIZE_LAST_NAME];
    char first_name[SIZE_FIRST_NAME];
    };

struct scompany;
    {
    char name[SIZE_COMPANY_NAME];
    };
```

Then a master record template could be formed to contain these two structures.

```
union srecord
    {
    struct sperson person;
    struct scompany company;
    };

    struct smaster
    {
    int record_type;
    union srecord record;
    };
struct smaster master[SIZE_MASTER];
```

Each time you reference one of the elements in master, you check the value of record_type to determine which type of record is in that element.

```
if (master[i].record_type == COMPANY)
    printf("\n Company name is %s",master[i].company.name);
    else if (master[i].record_type == PERSON)
    printf("\n Person name is %s %s",
        master[i].person.first_name,
        master[i].person.last_name);
else
    printf("\n Bad record type");
```

## SAMPLE PROGRAM—POKER

This program deals two hands, one to "it" and one to you. It compares the hands using the standard poker rankings. It does not look for straights. You may wish to add the code to do that yourself. The program uses the functions from Listing 7.2 for dealing the hands; from Listing 5.7, yes_no to determine when to stop dealing; and from Listing 6.1 to zero an array. After dealing the hands, the program calls `value_hand` to set a rating for each hand. That routine first checks for a flush, that is, whether all cards are the same suit. It then counts how many cards there are of each value and determines how many pairs, three of a kind, and four of a kind there are.

---

### *Pseudocode for Poker*

Initialize
While not done
    Ask for a bet
    If a bet
        Then deal cards into two hands
        Evaluate the hands
        Compare the evaluations and set the winnings

---

**Listing 7.7  Poker Game**

```c
int main()
    {
    int done = FALSE;                       /* Flag to finish loop */
    int your_cards_dealt;                   /* Number of cards dealt to you */
    int my_cards_dealt;                     /* Number of cards dealt to me */
    int your_hand_value;                    /* Value of your hand */
    int my_hand_value;                      /* Value of my hand */
    struct s_card my_hand[SIZE_HAND];       /* My cards */
    struct s_card your_hand[SIZE_HAND];     /* Your cards */
    double bet;                             /* Your bet */
    double your_pot;                        /* Your current winnings */

    your_pot = 0;
    new_deal();
    while (!done)
        {
        printf("\n Do you want to play?");
        if (yes_no() == YES)
            {
            printf("\n How much do you want to bet?");
            scanf("%lf", &bet);
            if (bet <= 0.0)
                done = TRUE;
            else
                {
```

```
                        my_cards_dealt = deal_hand(my_hand, SIZE_HAND);
                        your_cards_dealt = deal_hand(your_hand, SIZE_HAND);
                        if (my_cards_dealt < SIZE_HAND || your_cards_dealt
                            < SIZE_HAND)
                            {
                            printf("\n End of deck--reshuffling");
                            new_deal();
                            }
                        else
                            {
                            my_hand_value = value_hand(my_hand, SIZE_HAND);
                            your_hand_value = value_hand(your_hand, SIZE_HAND);

                            printf("\n My hand is");
                            print_hand(my_hand, SIZE_HAND);
                            printf("\n Your hand is");
                            print_hand(your_hand, SIZE_HAND);

                            if (my_hand_value > your_hand_value)
                                {
                                your_pot = your_pot - bet;
                                printf("\n You lost. You have %lf", your_pot);
                                }
                            else if (my_hand_value < your_hand_value)
                                {
                                your_pot = your_pot + bet;
                                printf("\n You won! You have %lf", your_pot);
                                }
                            else
                                printf("\n Tie hand");
                            }
                        }                              /* End of if on bet */
                    }                                  /* End of if on yes_no */
            else
                done = TRUE;
            }                                          /* End of while on done */
        exit(0);
        }


/*************************** VALUE_HAND ***************************/
/* Values for each type of hand */
#define FOUR_OF_A_KIND 7
#define FULL_HOUSE 6
#define FLUSH 5
#define THREE_OF_A_KIND 4
#define TWO_PAIRS 3
#define ONE_PAIR 2
```

```
int value_hand(hand, size)
/* This evaluates a hand */
struct s_card hand[];                           /* Hand to evaluate */
int size;                                       /* Number of cards in hand */
    {
    int evaluation = 0;                         /* Result of evaluation */
    char suit[MAX_SUIT];                        /* Holds suit of first card */
    int suit_count;                             /* Number of the same suit */
    int value_count[NUMBER_PER_SUIT + 1];
                                                /* Number of same value */
    int index;                                  /* Index into value_count */
    int number_pairs;                           /* Number of pairs */
    int number_threes;                          /* Number of three of a kind */
    int number_fours;                           /* Number of four of a kind */
    int i;                                      /* Index into hand */

    /* Check for a flush (all cards the same suit) */
    strcpy(suit, hand[0].suit);
    suit_count = 1;
    for (i = 1; i < size; i++)
        {
        if (!strcmp(hand[i].suit, suit))
            suit_count++;
        }
    if (suit_count == size)
        evaluation = FLUSH;

    /* Check for a pair, three, and four */
    zero_array(value_count, NUMBER_PER_SUIT + 1);
    number_pairs = 0;
    number_threes = 0;
    number_fours = 0;

    /* Count how many there are of each value */
    for (i = 0; i < size; i++)
        {
        index = hand[i].value;
        value_count[index] = value_count[index] + 1;
        }

    /* Look at count for each value to see whether a pair, three, or four */
    for (index = 1; index <= NUMBER_PER_SUIT; index++)
        {
        if (value_count[index] == 2)
            number_pairs++;
        else if (value_count[index] == 3)
```

```
                    number_threes++;
            else if (value_count[index] == 4)
                    number_fours++;
        }

    /*Check number of pairs, threes, and fours */
    if (number_fours == 1)
        evaluation = FOUR_OF_A_KIND;
    else if (number_threes && number_pairs)
        evaluation = FULL_HOUSE;
    else if (number_pairs == 2)
        evaluation = TWO_PAIRS;
    else if (number_pairs == 1)
        evaluation = ONE_PAIR;

    return evaluation;
    }

/* PRINT HAND */
int print_hand(hand, size)
/* This prints a hand */
struct s_card hand[];           /* Hand to print */
int size;                       /* Number of cards in hand */
    {
    int card;
    for (card = 0; card < size; card++)
        {
        printf("\n %d of %s", hand[card].value, hand[card].suit);
        }
    return;
    }
```

## SUMMARY

- A structure is a group of variables whose data types need not match.
- Each member of a structure acts as a variable of its type.
- Structures can be passed to functions, returned from functions, and assigned.
- A union is an overlapping set of variables. A change to any one of the variables changes the rest.

## SELF-TEST

1. What is the value of i for each case?

```
struct s_sample {
    int other;
    int array[2];
    };
struct s_sample sample[3] = { {1, {2, 3}}, {4, {5, 6}}, {7, {8, 9}} } ;
```

a. i = sample[0].array[0];

b. i = sample[2].array[1];

c. i = sample[1].other;

d. i = sample[1].array;

2. What is the value of i?

```
union stest {
    int other;
    int another;
    };
union stest test;

test.other = 3;
test.another = test.another + 7;
i = test.other * test.another;
```

---

## ANSWERS

1. a. 2
   b. 9
   c. 4
   d. The compiler will not accept this. You are trying to assign an array to an int.

2. 100. (10 * 10) test.other is set to 3, which sets test.another to 3 as well.

---

## PROBLEMS

1. One way to deal cards is to set up an array of NUMBER_CARDS of type struct s_card. You would fill it in with all possible card values, then shuffle it by randomly switching two cards. Rewrite get_hand to get cards from this array and new_deal to shuffle the cards in this array.
2. Change the poker program to evaluate a straight and a straight flush.

3. Write a game of twenty-one. There is a dealer (the computer) and you, the player.
4. Write a function called `time_check` that checks for a valid time.
5. Write a function to compute the time in seconds from a time in hours, minutes, and seconds.
6. Write a function to add a number of months and years to a date. Use the last day of the month as a limit, for example, January 31, 1990, plus 1 month would be February 28, 1990.
7. Write a function to convert a `time_date` structure to seconds since January 1, 1980. What type should this return?
8. Write a function that determines the difference in seconds between two `time_date` structures. What type should this return?
9. Add a number of seconds to a `time_date` structure.
10. Write a program that uses bit fields to represent binary coded decimal (BCD) values. BCD values are four bits long, each representing a digit from 0 to 9 and the plus and minus signs.
11. Write structures to contain appropriate information for a
    a. driver's license
    b. car registration
    c. ticket for a sporting event, such as football
12. Try printing out the individual bits in an integer. Write a loop that increments the integer value so you can see how the bits change.
13. Write an add-to-date routine that adds or subtracts a number of months and years from a date. For example,

```
struct s_date add_months(date,months,years)
struct s_date date;
int months;
int years;
```

14. Write a general date addition routine, such as

```
struct s_date add_to_date(date,date_to_add)
struct s_date date;
struct s_date date_to_add;
```

This adds the month, days, and years to the date and returns the result.

# Chapter Eight

# Pointers

*Pointers* are variables containing addresses of other variables, much like a mystery game in which each clue points to the location to find the next clue. Pointers enable you to pass parameters by reference, so you can change values in the calling function. They can link complex data structures. You can pass pointers to data, rather than the data itself, which streamlines handling large data items.

After an initial discussion on the concept of pointers, this chapter examines their application to arrays. All processes using arrays can be accomplished with pointers. Pointers are like fire. They are very powerful, but if used improperly, they can be dangerous to a program's execution.

## INTRODUCTION TO POINTERS

The variables discussed in previous chapters contain values meaningful to humans, such as integers and floating point numbers. Variables can also contain values meaningful only in the context of the machine. Values of this type are the addresses of *memory locations*.[1] Variables that contain addresses are called *pointer variables*, because they point at other locations.

### Address Operator, &

Two C operators involve memory locations. The first is the address operator (&). It can only be applied to a variable. Suppose you had declared int i;. Then &i is the address of the memory location where the value of i is stored. For example, suppose i is at location 100 and you had another variable, called p_int. Then these assignments perform the indicated actions.

---

[1] For a review of machine concepts, see Appendix K.

| Assignment | Action |
|---|---|
| i = 6; | sets the value of i to 6. |
| p_int = i; | sets the value of p_int to 6. |
| p_int = &i; | sets the value of p_int to 100. |

### Indirection Operator, *

The other operator is the indirection operator (*). This can only be applied to expressions that have an integer value. The operator assumes the value of the expression is an address. It either retrieves the value at that address or stores a value at that address. For example, suppose the following sequence takes place. The results of executing this sequence in order are shown in Figure 8.1 in the sequence shown for a through f.

| Assignment | Meaning |
|---|---|
| i = 6 | sets the value of i to 6. |
| p_int = &i; | sets the value of p_int to 100 (address of i). |
| j = *p_int; | assigns to j the value at memory address 100 (which is 6). |
| j = p_int; | assigns to j the value of p_int, which is 100. |
| *p_int = 17; | places the value 17 in the memory location to which p_int points (100), so the variable i is set to 17. |
| j = *p_int + 5; | adds the value (17) that is at the memory location that p_int points at (100) to 5 and puts the result (22) into j. |

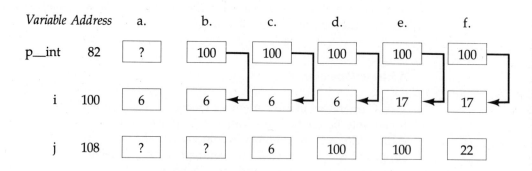

? = value is unknown

**Figure 8.1 Example of Pointers**

---

***Debug Tip***

---

You cannot apply the address operator to a constant or an expression.
&5 and &(x + 3) are both invalid.

---

You declare p_int as a pointer for two reasons. First, the compiler has to know
how many bytes to transfer when a value is stored or retrieved from the address
pointed to. Second, the compiler must know how to use the value being retrieved,
such as an integer or floating point. Thus, a pointer variable must be declared as
pointing to a particular data type. The form is

```
data-type *variable-name;
```

Here *variable-name has the type data-type; variable-name has the type pointer
to data-type. The name can be any valid variable name. One convention is to
always use *p* as the prefix for a pointer name. For the previous example,

```
int *p_int;
```

declares p_int is a pointer variable that points at integers.

When *p_int appears in an expression, the value at the address that p_int points
at is retrieved and treated as an integer. When it appears on the left-hand side
of an assignment, the value assigned is converted to an integer and placed at the
address whose value is in p_int. If it appears in an expression, the value of p_int
is retrieved. If p_int appears on the left-hand side of an assignment, the value
assigned is placed in p_int.

ANSI C makes a sharp distinction between pointers and integers. A pointer variable should only contain a memory address. Integer values are not considered to
be pointer values, so an int variable is not used to contain memory addresses.
Two of the preceding assignments shown would cause the compiler to issue an
error message. These error messages would mean what is shown, although they
might be phrased cryptically by the compiler.

**Assignment**

j = p_int;

p_int = i;

**Error**

assigning the value of a pointer (a memory
address) to an int
assigning an int value to a pointer[2]

---

[2] If for some reason, you really want to assign an int value to a pointer, you can use a cast, as
j = (int) p_int; and p_int = (int *) i. See Chapter 9 for more information on casts.

The address operator and the indirection operator are complementary. This means `& * p_int` and `* & p_int` both have the same value, which is the value of `p_int`. Because registers are not usually memory locations, the address operator cannot be used with register variables.

If the value of a pointer is zero, it is assumed not to point to anything. This is called the null pointer (NULL). By convention, for functions returning pointers, zero is returned as an error value.

One reason pointers are important is that they are the only way to affect the values of variables (other than arrays) passed as parameters. The `swap` function described later in this chapter demonstrates the use of pointers with parameters.

## POINTER TYPES AND INITIALIZATION

Pointers can be declared to point to any data type, such as

```
int *p_f;
double *p_double;
char *p;
```

The values of these pointers are addresses pointing to memory locations containing particular data types. Except in rare instances, you should never assign the value of a pointer to one data type to a pointer to another data type. If you need to, the cast operator should be used. This operator will not change the actual value being assigned.

```
double d = 3.4;
int i;
double *p_double = &d;
int *p_int = &i;
*p_int = *p_double;
```

assigns the double value 3.4 to the integer location pointed at by `p_int`, so `i` is assigned 3.

```
p_int = p_double;
```

should cause a warning or error message.

```
p_int = (int *) p_double
```

casts a pointer to an `int` value and places it in `p_int` so the data types being pointed at agree with their respective pointers.

The syntax for initialization may seem slightly confusing. On the line `double *p_double = &d;`, the initial value of `p_double` is set to the address of `d`. The assignment statement that performs the same action looks like `p_double = &d;`.

In some instances a function may need as a parameter value only an address, rather than an address to a particular type of data. To avoid using the cast operator extensively, you can declare a parameter as a pointer to void. A pointer to void may be converted to and from a pointer to any other type without a cast. For example, with the declarations shown earlier, you could declare

```
void *p_void;               pointer to void type
p_void = p_double;          no cast needed
p_int = p_void              no cast needed
```

When values of pointers are assigned to other pointers, the actual value does not change. What it enables you to do is access the same memory locations as several different data types.

You can assign an absolute memory address to a pointer. For example,

```
char *p_char = (char *) 53;
*p_char = 'A';
```

declares p_char, assigns the value 53 to it, then puts the value of 'A' at the location.[3] The compiler does not check to see whether the absolute address you are assigning is valid. Typically, you only use absolute addresses for computer-dependent features, such as input/output ports or screen memory.

| *Debug Tip* |
| :---: |
| Initialize all pointers. |

## POINTER ARITHMETIC

Because pointers are not integers, you cannot use many of the arithmetic operators on them. C can perform addition and subtraction on pointers. Although these operations look like integer arithmetic, they act somewhat differently. They are based on the size of the object pointed at. You can add or subtract an integer value to a pointer.[4] Suppose ints are two bytes long and the following declarations apply:

---

[3] On a segmented memory system, as the IBM PC, you need to consider that pointers use segment/register pairs. See your compiler manual for details.

[4] You cannot perform pointer arithmetic with pointers to void.

| Declaration | Comment |
|---|---|
| `int i=6;` | i is at address 100 |
| `int *p_int=&i;` | p_int is declared and initialized to 100. |

then

| Expression | Value |
|---|---|
| `p_int` | 100 |
| `p_int + 1` | `100 + 1 * (sizeof int) = 102` |
| `p_int + 2` | `100 + 2 * (sizeof int) = 104` |
| `p_int - 2` | `100 - 2 * (sizeof int) = 96` |

You cannot add two pointers together. However, you can subtract one pointer from another when each points to the same type of object. The difference between two pointers is an integer that represents the difference in the number of objects, not the absolute memory difference. Pointer subtraction is meaningful only if both pointers point to elements in the same array.[5] If you have the following declarations, the expressions would have the values shown. Figure 8.2 diagrams these expressions.

```
int an_array;[6]
int *p_i=&an_array[2];
int *p_j=&an_array[5];
```

| Expression | Value |
|---|---|
| `p_i` | 104 |
| `p_j` | 110 |
| `p_j - p_i` | `3(110 - 104)/sizeof(int)` |

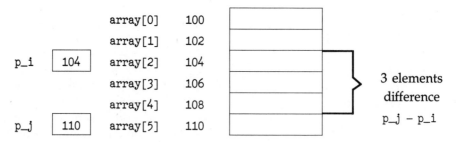

*Address*

Figure 8.2 Example of Pointer Arithmetic

---

[5] On a segmented memory system, such as the IBM PC, pointer subtraction may yield an invalid result if a segment boundary is crossed.

### Table 8.1 Array Subscripting Equivalence to Pointer Arithmetic

| Element | Equivalent | Value | Represents |
|---------|-----------|-------|-----------|
| array | parray | 100 | address of array |
| array[0] | *parray | 501 | value of first element in array |
| array+1 | parray+1 | 102 | address of 2nd element in array |
| array[1] | *(parray+1) | 502 | value of second element in array |

## POINTERS AND ARRAYS

Pointer arithmetic and array subscripting are closely related.[6] An *array subscript* is an offset from the start of an array. The offset is based on the size of the elements in the array. The name of the array represents the address of the first element in the array. As an example, suppose you declare

```
int an_array[6] = {501, 502, 503, 504, 505, 506};
int *p_array = an_array;
```

then, you can reference the elements with either a subscript or a pointer, as shown in Table 8.1. Figure 8.3 shows the layout of the array in memory.

With the preceding declarations, you could zero all the elements in an_array by

```
int i;
for (i = 0; i < 6; i++)
    {
    *p_array = 0;
    p_array++;
    }
```

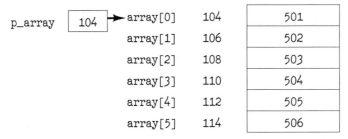

Figure 8.3 Pointers and Arrays

---

[6] The C compiler actually changes all references to arrays to indirect references. array[0] becomes *(array+0), and so forth. Note i[array] is the same as array[i] because of this. The address operator (&) is not required on an array name, so &array is redundant.

---

### *Debug Tip*

Errant pointers—those that have been changed to point to locations outside an array boundary—are a common cause of program problems.

---

Declaring an array sets aside storage for the elements in that array. Declaring
a pointer simply sets aside storage for the value of an address. A pointer can be
used as shown earlier to point to an array whose storage has been allocated.
However, if you instead declare just int *p_array; and execute the code just shown,
you zero out 12 memory locations starting at the address that was initially contained
in p_array;.

One difference between an array name and a pointer variable is that the address
value of the array name is constant. You cannot alter an array name in an expression such as an_array++. That is the equivalent of trying to alter a constant, such
as 5++.

When you use an array as a parameter in calling a function, the address of the
first element is passed. You can use a pointer to receive this address. For example,
Listing 6.1 could be rewritten using pointers, as shown in this listing.

**Listing 8.1 zero_array Function**

```
void zero_array(parray,size)
/* Zero the elements in an array */
int *parray;                    /* Points to array to zero the elements in */
int size;                       /* Number of elements in array */
    {
    int i;                      /* Index for array */

    /* Zero the elements in the array */
    for (i = 0; i < size; i++)
        {
        *parray = 0;
        parray++;
        }

    return;
    }
```

Given the previous declarations, you could call the function with

```
zero_array(an_array, 6);
```

or

```
zero_array(p_array, 6);
```

In either case, the address of the first element is passed to the function. This address becomes the initial value of parray. As the loop continues, it successively points to each element in an_array.

---

## STRINGS AND POINTERS

As discussed with arrays, a string is an array of characters stored as a constant. The name of an array is an address. Likewise, the string constant itself is an address. This address can be assigned to a pointer or passed to a function. For example,

```
char *p_chr="ABCDE";
```

sets up in memory an array of six chars and initializes the value of the pointer p_chr to the address of the array. Figure 8.4 shows the memory layout.

| Expression | Value |
|---|---|
| p_chr | 600 (address of string) |
| *p_chr | 'A' |
| p_chr + 1 | 601 |
| *(p_chr + 1) | 'B' |

In using a string in this way, it is not a good idea to assign a value to it, such as *p_chr = 'Z'. The compiler may not issue a warning. When the program is executed, an error may occur, as you tried to overwrite something that was considered as a constant string of characters. Furthermore, if you use the same string in two places, some compilers use the same memory locations for both appearances. Changing the constant may cause a hidden bug in your program. For example, in

```
char *p_chr_a = "ABCDE";
char *p_chr_b = "ABCDE";
*(p_chr_a) = 'Z';
```

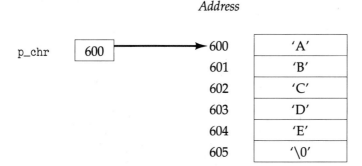

**Figure 8.4 Pointers and Strings**

the string pointed to by p_chr_b will be "ZBCDE", if your compiler does this. You can set up an array that is a string and point to it with a pointer, such as

```
char a_string[] = "ABCDE";
char *p_chr = an_string;
```

This is similar to the previous example, except the string has another way by which it can be referenced: by the name of the array a_string.

## SAMPLE POINTER FUNCTIONS

This section explores some string functions written using pointers. These functions are actually supplied by the compiler.

### The strlen Function

The strlen function computes the length of a string. This function was first introduced in Chapter 6 for arrays. In this version, in_string is incremented until the value it points to is the NUL character ('\0').

**Listing 8.2 strlen Function**

```
int strlen(in_string)
/* Computes the number of characters in a string */
char *in_string;                /* String to count characters in */
                                /* Returns number of characters */
    {
    int count;                  /* Count of characters */

    count = 0;

    /* Keep counting until the null character is reached */
    while (*in_string != '\0')
        {
        count++;
        in_string++;
        }

    return count;
    }
```

You could combine a few operations in the above function and code it as in Listing 8.3.[7]

---

[7] You might see this as for (count=0; *in_string++!='\0'; count++);. Is this more readable?

**Listing 8.3 strlen Function**

```
int strlen(in_string)
/* Computes the number of characters in a string */
char *in_string;                /* String to count characters in */
                                /* Returns number of characters */
    {
    int count;                  /* Count of characters */

    count = 0;

    while (*in_string++ != '\0')
        {
        count++;
        }

    return count;
    }
```

Using pointer arithmetic, you could also code it as the following. start points to the beginning of the string. After the loop terminates, in_string points to the NUL character. The difference between start and in_string is the number of characters in the string.

**Listing 8.4 strlen Function**

```
int strlen(in_string)
/* Computes the number of characters in a string */
char *in_string;                /* String to count characters in */
                                /* Returns number of characters */
    {
    char *start;                /* Points at the start of the string */
    int count;                  /* Count of characters */

    start = in_string;

    while (*in_string != '\0')
        {
        in_string++;
        }
    count = in_string - start;

    return count;
    }
```

---

### *Style Tip*

---

You will commonly see the test for the NUL character as while (*in_string), rather than while (*in_string != '\0'). Either is acceptable, but be consistent.

---

### The strcpy Function

The function strcpy copies a string from one location to another. The last character it copies is the NUL character.

### Listing 8.5 strcpy Function

```
#define FALSE 0
#define TRUE 1

char *strcpy(to, from)
/* Copies one string to another up to and including the NUL character */
char *to;               /* Destination string */
char *from;             /* Source string */
                        /* Returns destination string (to) */
    {
    int done;           /* Flag for when copy is done */
    char *ret;          /* Return value */

    /* Initialize values */
    ret = to;
    done = FALSE;

    /* Copy until and including the NUL character */
    while (!done)
        {
        *to = *from;
        if (*from == '\0')
            done = TRUE;
        else
            {
            to++;
            from++;
            }
        }

    return ret;
    }
```

Because the loop must always execute at least once, you could write it more concisely as shown in Listing 8.6.

**Listing 8.6 strcpy Function**

```
char *strcpy(to, from)
/* Copies one string to another */
char *to;                       /* String to copy to */
char *from;                     /* String to copy from */
                                /* Returns value of destination (to) */

    {
    char *ret = to;             /* Saves the value for the return */

    /* Copy until and including the NUL character */
    do
        {
        *to++ = *from;
        }
        while (*from++);

    return ret;
    }
```

In some programs, the while loop logic just shown might be replaced by either

```
while (*to++ = *from++)
    {
    ;
    }
```

or

```
while (*to++ = *from++);
```

The character at one address is transferred to the other address. If the character is nonzero, the while loop continues. If the character is zero, the loop terminates after the transfer.

If you access an array sequentially, it is generally faster to use a pointer. If you access the elements randomly, using a subscript is appropriate.

**The reverse Function**

This function reverses the characters in a string. The number of characters in the string is added to the starting address in p_start and placed in p_end. This address points to the NUL terminating character, so it is decremented first. The loop need only be repeated for half the length of the string, because two characters are being switched in each iteration.

**Listing 8.7 reverse Function**

```
void reverse(string)
/* Reverse characters in a string */
char *string;                    /* String to reverse */
    {
    char *p_start;               /* Beginning address of string */
    char *p_end;                 /* Ending address of string */
    char temp;                   /* Temporary for the swap */
    int length;                  /* Number of characters in the string */

    p_start = string;
    length = strlen(string);
    p_end = string + length;

    length = length/2;
    while (length--)
        {
        /* Next character from the end */
        p_end--;

        /* Do the swap */
        temp = *p_start;
        *p_start = *p_end;
        *p_end = temp;

        /* Next character from beginning */
        p_start++;
        }

    return;

    }
```

For example,

```
char string[] = "ABCD";
reverse(string);
```

changes the value of string to be "DCBA";.

## ARRAYS OF POINTERS

Pointers are variables, just like any others, so you can create an array of pointers, as in

```
char *strings[10];
```

This is an array of 10 pointers, each of which points to characters or strings of characters. An array of character pointers is typically coded in a routine such as

**Listing 8.8 print_error Function with Pointers**

```
#include <stdio.h>
#define NUMBER_MESSAGES 4

void print_error(error_number)
/* Prints the error message corresponding error for quad_root */
int error_number;            /* Message number to print */
    {
    static char *error_messages[NUMBER_MESSAGES] =
        {
        "No error ",          /* Error number zero is null */
        "Imaginary roots",
        "Coefficient for x**2 is 0",
        "Not an equation",
        };

    if (error_number >= 0 && error_number < NUMBER_MESSAGES)
        printf("\n%s\n", error_messages[error_number]);
    else
        printf("\n UNKNOWN ERROR MESSAGE \n");

    return;
    }
```

The `error_messages` array in this example might be laid out in memory as shown in Figure 8.5.

Using a double dimensioned array, you could have programmed this as shown in Listing 8.9.

**Listing 8.9 print_error Function with Two-Dimensional Array**

```
#include <stdio.h>
#define NUMBER_MESSAGES 4

void print_error(error_number)
/* Prints the error message corresponding error for quad_root */
int error_number;            /* Message number to print */
    {
    static char error_messages[NUMBER_MESSAGES][30]     =
        {
        "No error ",          /* Error number zero is null */
        "Imaginary roots",
        "Coefficient for x**2 is 0",
```

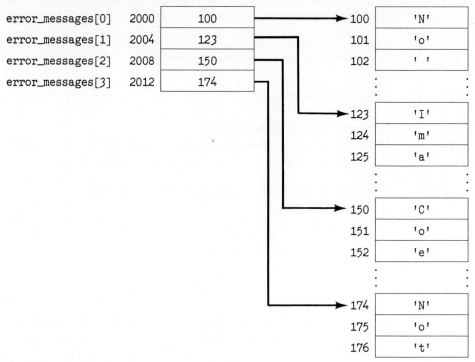

**Figure 8.5 Array of Pointers to Error Messages**

```
        "Not an equation",
        };

if (error_number >= 0 && error_number < NUMBER_MESSAGES)
      printf("\n%s\n", error_messages[error_number]);
else
      printf("\n UNKNOWN ERROR MESSAGE \n");
return;
}
```

This would be laid out in memory as shown in Figure 8.6.

This code avoids having a separate array of pointers as contrasted with the first example. However, if the strings are not all the same length, which is common, you waste space by including unused characters. The array-of-pointer method allows for strings of different lengths.

Note the name of a double dimensioned array, when used with a single subscript, is an address. Because error_messages is actually an array of arrays of chars, error_messages[1] is an array of chars, and thus the address of the second subarray in error_messages.

## CALL BY REFERENCE

The address operator and pointers help functions pass arguments by reference. This enables the called function to change a variable value in the calling function.

As seen in Chapter 4, the arguments to a function are passed by value. To write a function that passes back more than one value, you can use an array as a parameter. An array is passed by reference (address), so any changes to the values of the array are reflected in the calling program.

You may wish to pass back multiple values without using an array. For this the calling function uses the address operators on the names of the parameters.[8] For example, the function scanf, which passes back multiple values, requires the address operator (&) on the names of the variables. The called function uses the indirection operator (*) to show it is receiving an address rather than a value. It must use the indirection operator in all places where the parameter is referenced. For example, if you wanted to swap the values of two variables, you might try to code a function such as in Listing 8.10.

| | | |
|---|---|---|
| error_messages[0] [0] | 2000 | 'N' |
| error_messages[0] [1] | 2001 | 'o' |
| error_messages[0] [2] | 2002 | ' ' |
| error_messages[1] [0] | 2030 | 'I' |
| error_messages[1] [1] | 2031 | 'm' |
| error_messages[1] [2] | 2032 | 'a' |
| error_messages[2] [0] | 2060 | 'C' |
| error_messages[2] [1] | 2061 | 'o' |
| error_messages[2] [2] | 2062 | 'e' |
| error_messages[3] [0] | 2090 | 'N' |
| error_messages[3] [1] | 2091 | 'o' |
| error_messages[3] [2] | 2092 | 't' |

**Figure 8.6 Two-Dimensional Array of Error Messages**

**Listing 8.10 swap Function (Wrong)**

```
void swap(pa_number, pb_number)
/* Attempt to swap two integers */
int pa_number;                    /* One integer to swap */
int pb_number;                    /* Other integer to swap */
    {
    int temp;                     /* Holds temporary value for the swap */

    /* Swap the values */
    temp = pa_number;
    pa_number = pb_number;
    pb_number = temp;

    return;
    }
```

Call the function with the program in Listing 8.11.

**Listing 8.11 swap Program (Wrong)**

```
int main()
/* Tests the swap function */
    {
    int one = 1;                  /* One number to swap */
    int two = 2;                  /* Second number to swap */

    swap(one, two);

    printf("\n One is %d Two is %d", one, two);
    exit(0);
    }
```

Because this is a call by value, the values would not be swapped and One is 1 Two is 2 is printed out. You can code a call by reference as shown here in Listing 8.12.

**Listing 8.12 swap Function (Right)**

```
void swap(pa_number, pb_number)
/* Swaps two integers */
int *pa_number;                   /* Points to one integer to swap */
int *pb_number;                   /* Points to other integer to swap */
    {
    int temp;                     /* Holds temporary value for the swap */
```

---

[8] Note that you cannot pass a constant with a call by reference, because you cannot take the address of a constant.

```
/* Swap the values */
temp = *pa_number;
*pa_number = *pb_number;
*pb_number = temp;

return;
}
```

You then can call the function with the program from Listing 8.13.

**Listing 8.13 swap Program (Right)**

```
int main()
/* Tests the swap function */
    {
    int one = 1;              /* One number to swap */
    int two = 2;              /* Second number to swap */

    swap(&one, &two);

    printf("\n One is %d Two is %d", one, two);
    exit(0);
    }
```

This swaps the values and prints out One is 2 Two is 1. If you call Listing 8.13 with swap(one,two), your program bombs, because swap receives the values of these variables, not their addresses.

---

## SAMPLE FUNCTION—word_break

It is common to break a string into words. There are several means you can employ to do this. The function can find all the words in the string and place pointers to them in an array. Alternatively, it can find the first word in a string. Then it is called again with a pointer that points after this first word. The function word_break operates in the first mode. The function next_word in Listing 12.1 uses the other approach.

The input string is first scanned for nonalphabetic characters. When it finds an alphabetic character, it places the current value of string, which is a pointer to it, in out_array and increments a counter. In the while loop, when the character pointed to by string is no longer alphabetic, the end of the word has been reached. If desired, you could pass back the word size in a separate array. This function places a NUL character into the string to mark the end of the word.

### Listing 8.14 word_break Function

```
#include <ctype.h>

int word_break(out_array, size, string)
/* Returns pointers to words in the input string */
char *out_array[];           /* Pointers will be placed here */
int size;                    /* Maximum number of pointers to return */
char *string;                /* String to break up into words */
                             /* Returns number of pointers up to size
                                    pointers */
                             /* Note that it puts a NUL into string at the
                                    end of each word */
    {
    int count = 0;           /* Count of words found */

    while (*string != '\0')
         {
         /* Take off leading nonletters */
         if (!isalpha(*string))
              string++;
         else
              {
              /* Start of word increment count, set pointer */
              out_array[count] = string;
              count++;
              string++;

              /* Keep going until nonletter */
              while (isalpha(*string))
                   {
                   string++;
                   }

              /* If you want the length of the word, at this point
                   it is equal to string - out_array[count] */

              /* If not at end, set a NUL character after the word */
              if (*string != '\0')
                   {
                   *string = '\0';
                   string++;
                   }
              }
         } /* End of loop on NUL */
    return count;
    }
```

```
/******************************* MAIN ********************************/
#include <stdio.h>
#define MAX_POINTERS 50          /* Maximum number of pointers to find */

int main()
/* Breaks a string into words */
    {
    char *word_pointers[MAX_POINTERS];
                              /* Where to put the pointers */
    int number_pointers;      /* Number of words found */
    int i;                    /* Temporary counter */
    static char string[] = "The rain in Spain stays mainly on the plain";
                              /* String to break into words */

    number_pointers = word_break(word_pointers, MAX_POINTERS, string);

    printf("\n Words are: ");
    for (i = 0; i < number_pointers; i++)
        {
        printf("\n %s", word_pointers[i]);
        }

    exit(0);
    }
```

This produces output in the form

```
Words are:
The
rain
in
Spain
stays
mainly
on
the
plain
```

## POINTER ERRORS

The most frequently made error with pointers is using them before they are assigned a value. A static or external pointer has a default value of 0. Some compilers place a special value in address 0. If you change the value in the location when your program runs, you will get an error indication of Null pointer used.

An automatic pointer variable has a garbage value. There is no telling where it may point. Changing the location to which it points may or may not keep your program running. *Initialize all pointers.*

```
static int *pointer_zero;

func()
    {
    int *pointer_garbage;

    /* This places the value 17 at memory location 0 */
    *pointer_zero=17;

    /* This places the value 29 at some memory location */
    *pointer_garbage=29;
    }
```

## POINTERS AND STRUCTURES

Pointers can point to structure variables, just as they can to any other data type. To declare a pointer to a particular type of structure, you simply use the form

```
struct template-name *name-of-structure-pointer-variable;
```

for example,

```
struct s_date
    {
    int month;
    int day;
    int year;
    };
struct s_date *p_date;
```

declares `p_date` to be a pointer variable to structures with template `s_date`.

If you set `p_date` to point to a structure, such as

```
struct s_date date;
p_date = &date;
```

you can access the member of date with two forms. One uses the indirection operator; the other uses the pointer to structure member operator (->). Table 8.2 summarizes your alternatives.

### Table 8.2 Pointer to Structure Member

| *Member* | *Pointer* | *Alternative* |
|---|---|---|
| date.month | (*p_date).month | p_date->month |
| date.year | (*p_date).year | p_date->year |
| date.day | (*p_date).day | p_date->day |

A function passed a pointer to a structure can alter the values of the structure in the calling function. Listing 8.15, date_correct, is coded to show the parameter being a pointer to a structure, rather than being itself a structure. Compare it to date_correct in Listing 7.1. Note that one of the indices for days_in_month uses an expression involving the integer member of the structure, p_date->month.

### Listing 8.15 Correct Date Function with Pointers

```
#define TRUE 1
#define FALSE 0

struct s_date
    {
    int month;              /* Month of year (1 to 12) */
    int day;                /* Day of month */
    int year;               /* Year */
    } ;

static int days_in_month[2][12] =
    {
    {31, 28, 31, 30, 31, 30, 31, 31, 30, 31, 30, 31},
    {31, 29, 31, 30, 31, 30, 31, 31, 30, 31, 30, 31}
    };

int date_correct(p_date)
/* Checks a date for validity and corrects if */
struct s_date *p_date;          /* Date to check and correct */
                                /* Returns
                                        TRUE if valid
                                        FALSE if not valid */
    {
    int valid;                  /* Return value */
    int leap;                   /* Leap year flag */

    /* Assume date is good until proven otherwise */
    valid = TRUE;

    /* Check for leap year and set the index into days_in_month */
```

```
        if (p_date->year % 4 == 0)
            leap = 1;
        else
            leap = 0;

        /* Check the month */
        if (p_date->month < 0)
            {
            valid = FALSE;
            p_date->month = 1;
            }
        else if (p_date->month > 12)
            {
            valid = FALSE;
            p_date->month = 12;
            }

        /* Check the day for low end */
        if (p_date->day <= 0)
            {
            valid = FALSE;
            p_date->day = 1;
            }
        /* Check the day for high end */
        else if (p_date->day > days_in_month[leap][p_date->month - 1])
            {
            valid = FALSE;
            p_date->day = days_in_month[leap][p_date->month - 1];
            }

        return valid;
        }
```

In this case, the main function in Listing 7.1 would call date_check using

```
result = date_correct(&date);
```

## SAMPLE PROGRAM—COWS AND BULLS

The program in Listing 8.16 plays the game of cows and bulls. It makes up a five-digit number, with no two digits alike. When you guess a number, it reports how many digits are in the right spot (''bulls'') and how many others are in the number, but not in the right place (''cows''). When you have guessed the number (five bulls), the game ends.

The generate function creates a string of digits in mystery and ensures that there are no duplicate digits. It uses the used array to keep track of what digits it has put into the string. Once you have entered five digits, check_guess is called to determine the number of cows and bulls. The individual characters are checked to see if they are digits and that there are no duplicate digits.

The program uses pguess_i and pguess_j to point to the individual elements of guess. If all of the elements are digits, each digit in the mystery string is examined for a match with the guess. pmystery and pguess_i point to the individual elements of mystery and guess. If there is a match, the positions in the string (i and j) are compared to see if the match is a bull or a cow. The function then places the number of cows and bulls at the addresses passed to it and returns an indication if guess contains duplicate digits.

---

### *Pseudocode for Cows and Bulls*

Cows and bulls
    Initialize
    While bulls not equal to length of mystery number
        Get a guess
        Check the guess for validity
        Count the number of cows and bulls

---

**Listing 8.16 Cows and Bulls Game**

```c
#define NUM_DIGITS 5           /* Count of digits in mystery number */
#define TRUE 1
#define FALSE 0

#include <stdio.h>
#include <ctype.h>

int main()
/* Plays the game of cows and bulls */
    {
    char mystery[NUM_DIGITS];   /* Holds the mystery number */
    char guess[NUM_DIGITS + 1]; /* For the current guess plus 1 for NUL */
    int bulls;                  /* Number of digits in right place */
    int cows;                   /* Number of digits guessed in mystery */
    int valid;                  /* Flag whether guess was valid */

    /* Generate digits */
    generate(mystery);
```

```
        bulls = 0;
        while (bulls != NUM_DIGITS)
                {
                printf("\n What is your guess? ");
                scanf("%s", guess);
                valid = check_guess(mystery, guess, &cows, &bulls);
                if (valid)
                        printf("\n You have %d bulls and %d cows ", bulls, cows);
                else
                        printf("\n Invalid guess ");
                }

        exit(0);
        }


/*************************** CHECK_GUESS ****************************/

int check_guess(mystery, guess, pcows, pbulls)
/* Checks a guess and returns number of cows and bulls */
char mystery[];                 /* Mystery number to check against */
char guess[];                   /* Guess to check */
int *pcows;                     /* Where to put the number of cows */
int *pbulls;                    /* Where to put the number of bulls */
                                /* Returns
                                        TRUE if guess is valid
                                        FALSE if guess is not valid
                                */
        {
        int i;                  /* Index for guess and mystery */
        int j;                  /* Index for mystery */
        int valid;              /* Flag for valid or not */
        char *pguess_i;         /* Pointers to guess */
        char *pguess_j;         /* Pointers to guess */
        char *pmystery;

        *pbulls = 0;
        *pcows = 0;
        valid = TRUE;

        /* Check the validity of the guess */
        /* If any two characters are the same, the guess is invalid */
        i = NUM_DIGITS;
        pguess_i = guess;
        while (i--)
                {
                /* Determine whether the current character is a digit */
                if (!isdigit(*pguess_i))
```

```
            valid = FALSE;
        /* Starting at one past current character, see whether any of the
            rest match it */
        pguess_j = pguess_i + 1;
        j = i;
        while (j--)
            {
            if (*pguess_j == *pguess_i)
                /* Duplicate character */
                valid = FALSE;
            pguess_j++;
            }
        pguess_i++;
        }

    if (valid)
        {
        /* Count the number of cows and bulls */
        /* Loop on the guess */
        pguess_i = guess;
        i = NUM_DIGITS;
        while (i--)
            {
            /* Loop on the mystery number */
            pmystery = mystery;
            j = NUM_DIGITS;
            while (j--)
                {
                if (i == j)
                    {
                    /* Point to the same point in sequence */
                    /* If characters match, it is a bull */
                    if (*pmystery == *pguess_i)
                        (*pbulls)++;
                    }
                else
                    {
                    /* If characters match but not at same point in
                        the sequence, it is a cow */
                    if (*pmystery == *pguess_i)
                        (*pcows)++;
                    }
                pmystery++;
                }
            pguess_i++;
            }
```

```
            }
        return valid;
        }


/*****************************  GENERATE  *****************************/

#define DIGITS 10                /* Number of digits */

void generate(number)
/* Generates a mystery number */
char number[];                   /* Where to put the number */
    {
    char used[DIGITS];           /* Which digits have been used */
    int i;                       /* Index into used */
    int num_done;                /* Index into number */
    int value;                   /* Value for a digit */
    char *pused;

    num_done = 0;

    /* Clear the used digit array */
    i = DIGITS;
    pused = used;
    while (i--)
        {
        *pused = FALSE;
        pused++;
        }

    while (num_done < NUM_DIGITS)
        {
        value = rand() % 10;
        /* Make sure value has not already been used */
        if (used[value] == FALSE)
            {
            *number = value + '0';
            used[value] = TRUE;
            num_done++;
            number++;
            }
        }

    return;
    }
```

## SUMMARY

- A pointer is a variable that stores the addresses of other variables. It points to variables of a particular data type.
- Pointer arithmetic is based on the size of the data type pointed at.
- Pointers can efficiently index through arrays.

## SELF-TEST

1. What does this function do?

```
function(a, b)
char *a, *b;
    {
    while (*a++ = *b++);
    }
```

2. List what action each of these calls performs.

```
char array[100];
char *p = array;
```

   a. scanf("%s",p);
   b. scanf("%s",p + 1);
   c. scanf("%s",&p);
   d. scanf("%s",&(p + 1));
   e. scanf("%s",*(p + 1));

3. What is the value of "01234567890"[2]?

4. Given the following declarations, which of the assignment statements (a–f) are valid?

```
int i;
double d;
double dd;
double *p = &dd;
```

   a. i = d;
   b. *p = d;
   c. p = *d;
   d. *p = i;
   e. *p = *&d;
   f. p = &i;

5. Given

```
double d[10];
double *p;
p = &d[3];
p += 4;
```

if d is located at 8000 and doubles are eight bytes, what is the value of p?

---

## ANSWERS

1. It copies the characters from b to a. The while loop terminates after the NUL ('\0') character is assigned.
2. a. Characters input are placed in array starting at array[0].
   b. Characters input are placed in array starting at array[1].
   c. Characters input are placed in p and the locations following it.
   d. Compiler gives an error. You cannot take the address of an expression.
   e. Characters input are placed at a garbage address. The address is the value located at a[1] to a[n], where n is the size of a pointer variable.
3. The value is 2. 01234567890 is the address of a constant character array, so it acts as a pointer to char. So this is equivalent to *(2 + pointer_to_char), or the third element in the string.
4. a. Valid, assigning double to int.
   b. Valid, assigning double to double.
   c. Invalid; d is not a pointer; therefore, indirection operator cannot be applied to it.
   d. Valid, assigning int to a double.
   e. Valid, assigning a double to a double. The expression &d is of type "pointer to double," so *&d is a double.
   f. Invalid; &i is a pointer to int. A cast could be used to make it valid, but this would be of questionable use.
5. 8056. &d[3] is 8000 + 3 * 8, which is 8024. The value of 4 * 8, which is 32, is then added to p.

---

## PROBLEMS

1. A subtle error—which is not a compiler error—occurs if you initialize a variable as

```
*strings[]=
    {
    "Incorrect usage"
    "No terminator"
    };
```

What is it?

2. Write a routine called day_of_week. Have it return a pointer to a character string that is the day ("MONDAY", and so on).

3. All subscripts in C begin at zero. How would you write the code so you could refer to an array that starts at an index value of 200, without having to allow storage for the first 200 elements?

4. Rewrite the hangman program in Chapter 6 to use pointers to chars. Add more words to the list of answers.

5. How would you rewrite the word_break function to avoid writing a NUL character into the string?

6. Write a game of blackjack or twenty-one. The computer can be the dealer. The dealer must stand on 17 or greater. Embellish the program as much as you wish.

7. Write a simplified spelling checker. It should include an array of correctly spelled words. The input should be broken up into words and compared against this list. You can embellish this by any of the following:
   a. Allowing the user to add words to this list.
   b. Outputting an "almost match" word that differs only by a letter from an unfound input word.
   c. Making the checking run as efficiently as possible.

8. Rewrite any program containing arrays that you have written to use pointers instead.

9. Try running this program. It gives the addresses of the subarrays in a two-dimensional array. If your compiler does not support %p, use %lx or %x instead.

```
#define SIZE_J 3
#define SIZE_I 2

main()
    {
    static int array[SIZE_I][SIZE_J]=
        {
        {1,2,3},
        {4,5,6},
        };
    int (*point_at_array)[SIZE_J];
    int i,j;
    int *p;
    p=array;

    /* Print the addresses of the subarrays */
    printf("\n array is %p",array);
    for (i=0;i<SIZE_I;i++)
```

```
    {
    printf("\n array[%d] is %p",i,array[i]);
    printf("\n *(array+%d) is %p",i,*(array+i));
    }
printf("\n Size of array[1][1] is %d",sizeof(array[1][1]));
printf("\n Size of array[1] is %d",sizeof(array[1]));
printf("\n Size of array is %d",sizeof(array));
for (i=0;i<SIZE_I;i++)
    {
    point_at_array[i]=array[i];
    printf("\n point_at_array[%d] is %p", i,point_at_array[i]);
    for (j=0;j<SIZE_J;j++)
        {
        printf("\n point_at_array[%d][%d] is %d",
            i,j,point_at_array[i][j]);
        }
    }
}
```

# Chapter Nine

# Data Types and Operators Revisited

C has many data types. Although you can write most programs with the types described so far—double, int, and char—these additional types permit the efficient storage of data in memory. This chapter covers the conversions among all data types. C has many operators not found in other languages, including bitwise operators, the autoincrement and autodecrement operators, and the compound assignment operators.

## ARITHMETIC DATA TYPES

With the int and double types introduced previously, you have not been concerned with the actual sizes of the data types, but only with the fact that one could only contain integral values and the other floating point numbers. There are many variations of these types, most of which exist to allow efficient use of storage for arrays or to hold numbers whose size exceeds that contained in the regular data types. The possibilities are listed in Table 9.1. For a review of the data representation in a computer, see Appendix K.

Every variable requires a certain amount of memory for its storage. The amount varies from computer to computer, so the sizes given are only representative. The short ints type uses less or the same amount as regular ints; long ints use more than or the same amount as regular ints. The float type uses less space than doubles; long doubles use the same or more space than doubles.[1]

With unsigned integers, the bit normally used as the sign bit is used as another bit for value. Only positive numbers are kept in unsigned ints. All arithmetic is done modulus the largest number plus one, which can be represented in the unsigned int. For example, if 65535 is the largest number that an unsigned int can hold, then for

---

[1] The double data type was formerly known as long float, but this synonym is now obsolete. However, you may see it in older programs and early C literature.

**Table 9.1 Arithmetic Data Types**

| Data Type | Also Can Use | Minimum Range of Values | Typical Size |
|---|---|---|---|
| int | signed int | $-32767^1$ to 32767 | 2 or 4 bytes |
| short int | short<br>signed short<br>signed short int | $-32767^1$ to 32767 | 2 bytes |
| long int | long<br>signed long<br>signed long int | $-2147483647^1$<br>to 2147483647 | 4 bytes |
| float | | 10E−37 to 10E37<br>6 decimal digits | 4 bytes |
| double | | 10E−37 to 10E37<br>10 decimal digits$^2$ | 8 bytes |
| long double | | 10E−37 to 10E37<br>10 decimal digits$^2$ | 8 to 16 bytes |
| unsigned int | unsigned | 0 to 65535 | 2 or 4 bytes |
| unsigned short int | unsigned short | 0 to 65535 | 2 bytes |
| unsigned long int | unsigned long | 0 to 4294967295 | 4 bytes |
| char | | $-127^1$ to $+127$ or 0 to 255 | 1 byte |
| unsigned char | | 0 to 255 | 1 byte |
| signed char | | $-127^1$ to 127 | 1 byte |

[1] The formal description of C specifies −32767, −2147483647, and −127 as the lowest negative numbers that are represented by ints, longs, and signed chars. These are the limits for computers that represent numbers using ones complement. Most computers use twos complement representation that has limits of −32768, −214783648, and −128, respectively.

[2] Although double and long double are shown the same, doubles usually have 10 decimal digits with 1E − 37 to 1E37 in the exponent. long doubles have 16 or more decimal digits of precision and 1E − 300 to 1E300 in range.

```
unsigned int i = 65535;
unsigned int j;
j = i + i;
i++;
```

j is set to 65534 ((65535 + 65535) % 65536), and i is set to 0 (65536 % 65536).

Two ranges apply for a regular char type. This is an ambiguity that has existed in C since its early days. Recall that the char data type is always converted to an integer in an expression. Whether the high order bit of a char is treated as a sign bit depends on the computer. The sign bit is defined for each computer; there is no definitive standard.

The data type char usually stores character values. This does not make a difference with ASCII characters; they only have values between 0 and 127, so the high order bit is never set. To save space, chars might be used to store values varying between 0 and 255 or between $-127$ and $+128$. Using the normal char for this purpose is risky, whereas using either the unsigned char or signed char type always works.

To find out the number of bytes that a data type or variable uses, use the sizeof operator. For example, sizeof(int) gives the size of an integer, whereas sizeof(i) gives the size of the variable i.

## NUMERIC CONSTANTS

Some of these data types have corresponding arithmetic constants. A suffix is applied to the constant of the standard types int or double. These are shown in Table 9.2.

Avoid using l for long, because in print it resembles the number 1 too closely. If an integer constant cannot fit into the size of an int, it implicitly is made a long int. So 324567 would be a long if the machine had a limit of 32767 for ints. If no suffix is applied to a floating point constant, it is of type double.

**Table 9.2 Numeric Constant Suffixes**

| Suffix | Type | Example |
|--------|------|---------|
| U (or u) | unsigned int | 4455U |
| L (or l) | long int | 32456L |
| UL (or LU) | unsigned long int | 32456UL |
| F (or f) | float | 3.2F or 3.2E5F |
| L (or l) | long double | 3.2L or 3.1E5L |

**Table 9.3 Escape Character Sequences**

| Sequence | Meaning | ASCII Value |
|----------|---------|-------------|
| \a | alert (bell) | 7 |
| \b | back-space | 8 |
| \t | tab (horizontal) | 9 |
| \n | new-line | 10 |
| \v | vertical tab | 11 |
| \f | form-feed | 12 |
| \r | carriage-return | 13 |
| \" | quote (in a string) | 34 |
| \' | single quote (as a character constant) | 39 |
| \? | question mark | 63 |
| \\ | backslash (the character itself) | 92 |

## CHARACTER CONSTANTS

To represent nonprintable characters in character constants and strings, C includes a set of escape sequences. Although these sequences appear as more than one character long, they are converted by the compiler into a single character. The new-line character \n has been used extensively in this book in printf functions. It is actually converted into a single new-line character (ASCII value 10) in the program. The escape sequences are shown in Table 9.3.

You can also represent characters by giving their octal or hexadecimal value. These are represented by

*Octal:*

\n or \nn or \nnn

where *n* is a digit from 0 to 7

*Hexadecimal:*

\xn
\xnn
\xnnn

where *n* is a hexadecimal digit (0 to 9 and A to F or a to f).

Octal and hexadecimal notation are covered later in this chapter.

## CONVERSION

If the data type on one side of an operator is not the same as the data type on the other side, one of them is converted to the type of the other before the operation is performed. A char or a short int is converted to an int value before it is used in an expression. Whether there is sign extension on regular chars depends on the system. For all the other types, the value that has a data type lower on this list is converted to the data type that is higher:[2]

```
long double          Highest
double
float
unsigned long int
long int
unsigned int
int                  Lowest
```

For example, given these declarations:

```
char c;
int i;
double d;
float f;
unsigned u;
```

the following expressions cause the conversion shown.

| Expression | Conversion |
|---|---|
| d + i | i converted to double, computation performed in double precision |
| i + c | c converted to int, computation performed as integer |
| f + d | f converted to double, computation performed in double precision |
| d + c | c converted to double, computation performed in double precision |
| u > i | i converted to unsigned int, comparison performed as unsigned int. If i has a negative value, the result is undefined. |

---

[2] Most compilers automatically convert floats to doubles so arithmetic is performed in double precision.

**Table 9.4 Conversion with Assignment Operators**

| Left-Hand Type | Right-Hand Type | Conversion |
|---|---|---|
| double<br>or<br>float | long double | round off or truncate, depending on the compiler |
| float | double | round off or truncate, depending on compiler |
| long<br>or<br>int<br>or<br>char | long double<br>or<br>double<br>or<br>float | truncate fractional part or and if integer cannot fit, result is undefined |
| int | long | high order bits eliminated[1] |
| char | int | high order bits eliminated[1] |

[1]The result is undefined, but most compilers simply eliminate the high order bits.

When a value is being assigned, the value may not fit in the variable to which it is being assigned. In such cases the value assigned is based as listed in Table 9.4.

If you try to assign a value that will not fit, a value is assigned, but you cannot be sure what the result will be. Avoid this situation by using data types big enough to hold all possible values of a variable.

## FORCED CONVERSION

You will occasionally need to force an expression to be of a particular data type. This commonly occurs in passing values to a function, so the types agree. The cast operator forces a conversion. You precede the variable or expression with the data type desired in parentheses, as in

| (data-type) expression | **Action** |
|---|---|
| (int) d + i | d converted to int, computation performed as integer |

| | |
|---|---|
| (double) i + c | i and c converted to double, computation performed in double precision |
| (int) f + (int) d | f and d converted to int, computation performed as integer |
| (unsigned long) d + (unsigned long) c | d and c converted to unsigned long, computation performed as unsigned long integer |

You can use forced conversions with functions, such as the power function in Chapter 4. If you call the function with

```
power( (double) 2 , (int) 3.0 )
```

the arguments are converted to the expected types. If you code power(2,3.0), you may get the wrong answer.[3]

## ENUMERATED VARIABLES

Enumeration (enum) types enable you to use identifiers as values. You specify a list of names as these values. You denote a type of enumerated variable by giving a name for the type and listing the values that a variable of that type can take. You can specify a variable of that type in a manner similar to declaring an ordinary variable.[4]

```
enum enum-type {names-of-values};
enum enum-type enum-variable;
```

Listing 9.1 shows a common example of an enumerated variable, days of the week.

**Listing 9.1 Weekend Function with Enumeration**

```
enum eday {sunday, monday, tuesday, wednesday,
    thursday, friday, saturday};
    /* Declares range of values for variables of enum type eday */

#define TRUE 1
#define FALSE 0
```

---

[3] The exception is if an expanded function prototype is in the source file, as shown in Chapter 10.
[4] You can denote a type and declare a variable in a simple statement by coding

```
enum enum-type {names-of-values} enum-variable;
```

This is seldom used.

```
int weekend(day)
/* Returns true if day is weekend day, false otherwise */
enum eday day;
    {
    int ret;

    if (day == sunday || day == saturday)
        ret=TRUE;
    else
        ret=FALSE;

    return ret;
    }
```

Enumerated variables tend to be self-documenting, because you specify what values a variable can take on. However, an enumerated variable is treated as an integer by the compiler and can take on values not in the list. You can compute expressions as day + 3 or day++, even though these might not make any sense.

Integer values are assigned to identifiers starting with 0. You can specify the integer value of an enum identifier by listing it in the declaration of the enum type:

```
enum eday { sunday=1, monday=4, tuesday=3, wednesday=7};
```

Compare Listing 9.1 with this one that uses #define**s:**

**Listing 9.2 Weekend Function with** #defines

```
#define TRUE 1
#define FALSE 0

#define SUNDAY 0
#define MONDAY 1
#define TUESDAY 2
/* ... and so forth */
#define SATURDAY 6

int weekend(day)
int day;
    {
    int ret;

    if (day == SUNDAY || day == SATURDAY)
        ret = TRUE;
    else
        ret = FALSE;

    return ret;
    }
```

The advantage of enumerated variables over this method is that you are assured your enumerated names will each have a unique value. With the #defines, you could make an error and define two days with the same value. With enumerated variables, this cannot occur.

There is no "next value in set" operation or "is in set" operation, as in other languages that have types similar to enumerated variables. You could create these for each enumerated type, if desired. A next_day function might look like that in Listing 9.3.

**Listing 9.3 next_day Function**

```
enum eday next_day(day)
/* Gives the next day */
enum eday day;
    {

    if (day == saturday)
        /* Wrap around to sunday */

    day = sunday;
    else
        {
        /* Increment the day */
        day++;
        }

    return day;
    }
```

## THE typedef STATEMENT

The typedef statement provides a way of assigning a name to a particular data type. The name is then used as a shorthand way of declaring that particular type. To define a typedef, you make up a declaration for a variable of the type you want to define, replace the variable name with the name you want to use for the data type, and preface the statement with typedef. For example, to use a typedef for

```
float variable;
```

the code would be

```
typedef float FLOAT_NUMBER;
```

You could use this as

```
FLOAT_NUMBER x;
FLOAT_NUMBER y;
```

Using the typedef helps keep your programs portable. If the program was run on a computer that had the minimum limits for float type that were lower than needed by the program, you would simply switch the typedef to read typedef double FLOAT_NUMBER; and recompile. Some compilers use typedef to do such operations as additional type-checking of parameter lists.

   The C language uses several typedefs that are listed in Table 9.5. These names are reserved, so you should not make up typedefs with the same names.

The most common typedef is size_t, which represents units of storage, usually bytes. You can also use the typedefs for structures and arrays. For example,

```
typedef struct s_date DATE;
...
DATE a_date;
```

declares a_date to be a structure with tag-type s_date;. This is useful if the DATE is passed only to functions and the user of the functions does not need to know its internal details. For example, a programmer writing all the routines might define DATE as

```
typedef long DATE;
```

and keep the date value as a count from January 1, A.D. 1. Chapter 16 on packages gives examples of this. The typedef

```
typedef struct s_date DATES[12];
DATES dates;
```

**Table 9.5 Standard typedefs**

| typedef | Defined in | Used for |
|---|---|---|
| clock_t | time.h | time |
| div_t | stdlib.h | div() |
| fpos_t | stdio.h | file position |
| jmp_buf | setjmp.h | setjmp(), longjmp() |
| ldiv_t | stdlib.h | ldiv() |
| prtdiff_t | stddef.h | difference in two pointers |
| sig_atomic_t | signal.h | signals (exceptions) |
| size_t | stddef.h | result of sizeof |
| va_list | stdarg.h | variable parameter list |

declares that DATES is a typedef that defines an array of 12 structures of type s_date. The declaration dates is just as if it had been written

```
struct s_date dates[12];
```

## STORAGE TYPES

The C language uses four types of storage. Three were described previously—the automatic (auto), the static (always allocated), and the external. The other type is a variation on the auto—the register.

On any simple type of automatic variable, you can apply the type register. This is your recommendation to the compiler to use a machine register for this variable. If a register is used, code that contains automatic variables executes faster and is more efficient. Variables for controlling loops are usually prime candidates for register variables. The compiler may choose to accept your recommendation. It may decide on its own which automatic variables to place in registers, or it may not place any variables in registers.

Although you could declare all automatic variables to be register variables, computers limit the number of machine registers—anywhere from 2 to around 16, depending on the computer. If the compiler heeds your recommendations, it only makes the first few variables in a function into registers and ignores the rest. Each function can have its own set of register variables. The function stores the prior values of the registers when it is called.

The storage types discussed so far are those that the compiler allocates. The program itself can request additional memory for data storage or for other purposes. Several functions providing for the allocation and deallocation of storage are described in Chapter 12 on pointers.

Automatic and register simple variables (that is, not arrays) can be initialized with expressions, rather than just constants. For example, you could write the following.

```
function(k)
int k;
    {
    int i = k * 2;
    . . .
```

## TYPE MODIFIERS

ANSI C provides for two type modifiers that can help you write more efficient and bug-free programs. The const modifier (for constant) declares a particular variable is not going to be altered during the program execution. The compiler may place this in a read-only area of memory. An execution error may occur if this location is written, depending on the computer running the program. For example, both

```
const int i = 5;
```

and

```
int const i = 7;
```

declare that i is constant.

The volatile modifier declares the contents of a variable may be altered in ways not readily apparent to the compiler. This prevents the compiler from optimizing code that might appear not to do anything meaningful. It is also useful when you are programming changes in variable values that may be caused by events external to the program, such as input and output or asynchronous interrupts. For example, you might code a routine to simply wait a short amount of time as

```
delay()
    {
    int i;
    for (i=0; i<10;i++)
        {
        ;
        }
    return;
    }
```

The variable i is a local variable that is never referenced in the loop or elsewhere in the function. The compiler may recognize this and compile this as if it read

```
delay()
    {
    return;
    }
```

Using the declaration volatile int i; prevents this optimization.

## SCOPE OF VARIABLES

The sample functions group all their declarations together at the beginning of the function. This is the recommended way of declaring variables. C permits variables to be declared at the beginning of any compound statement. The variables are only recognized from the point of declaration until the close of the compound statement. There are four *scopes* for a variable: block, function, file, and program. A variable declared within a block or function is known only within the block or function. A variable declared external to functions is known within the file in which it appears, from the point of its appearance to the end of the file. A variable declared as an external in one source file and declared as extern in other files has program scope, as Chapter 10 illustrates. For example, given this code, Figure 9.1 shows the scope of each variable i in the following example.

```
function(input)
int input;
    {
    int i                      /* Declaration of 1st i */
    i=input                    /* Value of input to 1st i */
    if (i>5)                   /* Test on 1st i */
        {
        int i                  /* Declaration of 2nd i */
        for (i=0;i<5;i++)      /* For loop using 2nd i */
            {
            int i;             /* Declaration of 3rd i */
            i = 7;             /* Value of 7 into 3rd i */
            }
        }
    return;
    }
```

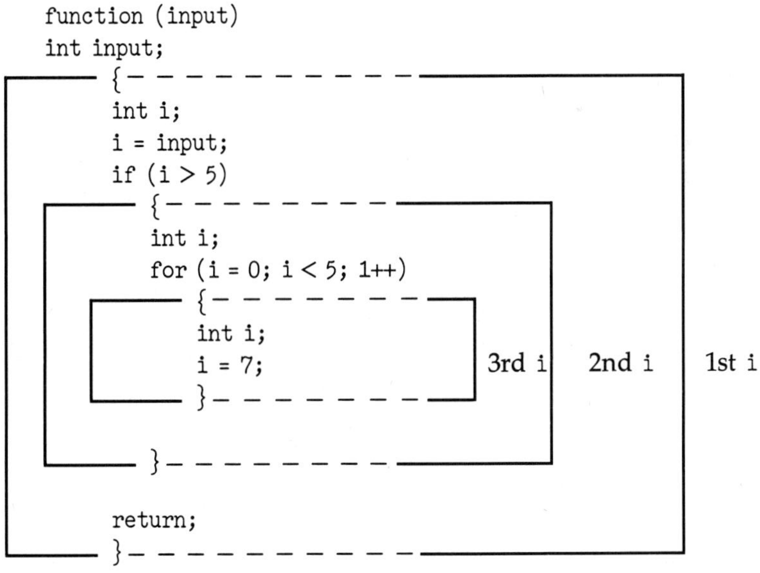

**Figure 9.1 Scope of Variables**

In two places you will find it invalid to redeclare a variable. First, you cannot redeclare a function parameter in the outermost block that begins the function. If you do, you will not be able to access the value passed to the function. This situation triggers a compiler error:

```
int check_char(c)
int c;
    {
    int c;                      /* Redeclaration of parameter */
    ...
    }
```

Second, you cannot redeclare a name in the same block, as in

```
int func()
    {
    int i;
    double i;
    ...
    }
```

## BIT PATTERN CONSTANTS

The constants discussed so far are numeric constants. The actual bit patterns by which these constants are represented in the machine are not usually important to the programmer. In certain programs, you may wish to use a particular bit pattern. This usually occurs if you need to make use of a particular hardware register or if you wish to keep values packed into bits instead of computer words or bytes.

Two common representations for bit patterns are hexadecimal and octal notations. Octal constants begin with the digit 0 and are followed by digits from 0 through 7. Hexadecimal constants begin with the prefix 0X or 0x and are followed by digits 0 through 9 and letters $A-F$ or $a-f$ for the hexadecimal digits 10 to 15. A bit pattern can be represented either way:

| | | |
|---|---|---|
| Octal representation | 0113326 | 1  1   3   3   2   6 |
| Bit pattern | | 1001 0110 1101 0110 |
| Hexadecimal representation | 0x96D6 | 9    6    D    6 |

You can print out integers in hex or octal representation using %x or %o as the format specifier. You can read in integers in hex or octal using %x or %o.

**Listing 9.4 Bit Pattern Program**

```
#include <stdio.h>

int main()
    {
    int a = 123;
    int b = 0x123;
    int c = 0123;
    printf("\n A is hexadecimal %x octal %o decimal %d", a, a, a);
    printf("\n B is hexadecimal %x octal %o decimal %d", b, b, b);
    printf("\n C is hexadecimal %x octal %o decimal %d", c, c, c);
    exit(0);
    }
```

The printout from this program looks like

```
A is hexadecimal 7B octal 173 decimal 123
B is hexadecimal 123 octal 443 decimal 291
C is hexadecimal 53 octal 123 decimal 83
```

# OPERATORS

C has many operators not found in other languages. These include bitwise operators, increment and decrement operators, conditional operators, the comma operator, and assignment and compound assignment operators.

## Bitwise Operators

Bitwise operators treat variables as combinations of bits rather than as numbers. They are useful in accessing the individual bits in memory, such as the screen memory for a graphics display. Bitwise operators can only operate on integral data types, not on floating point numbers. Three bitwise operators act just like the logical operators, but on each bit in an integer. These are the & and, | or, and ˜ one's complement. An additional operator is the exclusive-or (ˆ), also called XOR. The bits are taken one by one and the operations are performed as shown in Table 9.6.

Here is an example of using these operators with the hexadecimal and octal representation of constants. The bit values are shown for comparison.

```
0xF1      &   0x35              yields 0x31 (hexadecimal)
0361      &   0065              yields 061 (octal)
11110001  &   00110101          yields 00110001 (bitwise)
```

**Table 9.6 Bitwise Operators: AND, OR, XOR, and NOT**

| Bit A | Bit B | Result | & (AND) |
|-------|-------|--------|---------|
| 0 | 0 | 0 | |
| 0 | 1 | 0 | |
| 1 | 0 | 0 | |
| 1 | 1 | 1 | |

| Bit A | Bit B | Result | \| (OR) |
|-------|-------|--------|---------|
| 0 | 0 | 0 | |
| 0 | 1 | 1 | |
| 1 | 0 | 1 | |
| 1 | 1 | 1 | |

| Bit A | Bit B | Result | ^ (XOR) |
|-------|-------|--------|---------|
| 0 | 0 | 0 | |
| 0 | 1 | 1 | |
| 1 | 0 | 1 | |
| 1 | 1 | 0 | |

| Bit A | | Result | ~ (ONE'S COMPLEMENT) |
|-------|--|--------|----------------------|
| 0 | | 1 | |
| 1 | | 0 | |

```
0xF1     |  0x35            yields 0xF5 (hexadecimal)
0361     |  0065            yields 0365 (octal)
11110001 |  00110101        yields 11110101 (bitwise)

0xF1     ^  0x35            yields 0xC4 (hexadecimal)
0361     ^  0065            yields 0304 (octal)
11110001 ^  00110101        yields 00000000 11000100 (bitwise)

0xF1                        yields 0xFF0E (hexadecimal)
0361                        yields 0177416 (octal)
11110001                    yields 11111111 00001110[5] (bitwise)
```

There are two shifting operators—the left shift (<<) and the right shift (>>). The left shift moves the bits to the left and sets the rightmost (low order) bit to a zero. The leftmost (high order) bit shifted out is thrown away. For example:

---

[5] 0xFFFFF0FE, 03777777416, and 11111111 11111111 11111111 00001110 if ints are 4 bytes.

| | |
|---|---|
| 0x0F1      << 1 | yields 0x1E2 (hexadecimal) |
| 0361       << 1 | yields 0742 (octal) |
| 11110001   << 1 | yields 111100010 (bit pattern) |
| 0x0F1      << 6 | yields 0x3C40 (hexadecimal) |
| 0361       << 6 | yields 036100 (octal) |
| 11110001   << 6 | yields 11110001000000 (bit pattern) |

The right shift moves bits to the right. The lower order bits shifted out are thrown away. Depending on the compiler and the computer, one of two things occurs with the high order bit of a signed value (the sign bit). It may be set to zero, just like on the left shift. This is termed a *logical shift*. Alternatively, its value may remain what it was. This is termed an *arithmetic shift*. These two differ only if the high order bit is a 1. Unsigned integers do not have a sign bit, so right shifts for them are always logical shifts. Table 9.7 summarizes the concepts of logical and arithmetic right shifts.

You can shift from zero bits to the number of bits in the data type. If you shift more, the result is normally 0. Note the precedence of arithmetic, relational, and equality operators is higher than bitwise operators, so

| | |
|---|---|
| x >> 2 + 3 | shifts it by 5 |
| x & 0x03 == 1 | is equivalent to x & (0x03 == 1) so always 0 |

You could write a program that clears the high order bit of each character in the file. This process would be useful if your word processor used the high order bit for its own purposes and you wanted to transfer the file elsewhere. The input

**Table 9.7 Logical and Arithmetic Shifts**

| *Hexadecimal* | *Logical* | *Arithmetic* |
|---|---|---|
| 0x1E02>>1 | 0x0F01 | 0x0F01 |
| 0xC040>>6 | 0x0301 | 0xFF01[1] |

| *Octal* | *Logical* | *Arithmetic* |
|---|---|---|
| 016402>>1 | 007201 | 007201 |
| 0140100>>6 | 0001401 | 0177401[1] |

| *Bitwise* | *Logical* | *Arithmetic* |
|---|---|---|
| 0001110100000010 >> 1 | 0000111010000001 | 0000111010000001 |
| 1100000001000000 >> 6 | 0000001100000001 | 1111111100000001[1] |

[1] This assumes two-byte `ints`, so that the high order bit is the sign bit. With a four-byte `int`, the high order bits would be zero, so this would be a logical shift.

character returned by getchar is ANDed with a mask having the high order bit
set to 0.

**Listing 9.5 Copy Program**

```
#include <stdio.h>

#define TRUE 1
#define FALSE 0
#define MASK 0x7F              /* Mask to take off high order bit */

int main()                     /* Outputs the input characters with
                                      the high order bit cleared */
    {
    int c;                     /* Input character */
    int eof;                   /* Flag for end-of-file */

    eof = FALSE;

    /* Keep outputting characters until end-of-file is reached */
    while (!eof)
        {
        c = getchar();
        if (c == EOF)
            eof = TRUE;
        else
            putchar(c & MASK);
        }

    exit(0);
    }
```

To convert a file called infile to a file called outfile with the bits cleared, the
executable file named clear would be run with

```
clear < infile > outfile
```

The bitwise operators can be a bit confusing, especially if they are mixed up with
the logical operators. This list shows the differences:

| Expression | Value | |
|---|---|---|
| 1 && 2 | 1 | (Logical AND) |
| 1 & 2 | 0 | (Bitwise AND) |
| 1 \|\| 2 | 1 | (Logical OR) |
| 1 \| 2 | 3 | (Bitwise OR) |

### *Debug Tip*

Watch out for the precedence of the bitwise operators, especially the arithmetic ones. 1 << 2 + 1 is evaluated as 1 << (2 + 1), not (1 << 2) + 1.

## Sample Bit Program

Many times, you want to keep just an indication of whether a particular value is present. You could keep an array of ints or chars containing a 0 or 1 value. However, a more efficient way of doing this is to use the individual bits in the variables. This saves 8 to 16 times the memory. The sample program in Listing 9.6 demonstrates a way to tell quickly what numbers are missing or duplicated in a series. If the numbers had been input to an array, they would need to be sorted before the missing number could be found. The array values would take up much more room than these single bits.

### Listing 9.6 Bit Program

```
#define SIZE_CHAR 8              /* Size of a char in bits */
static unsigned char bit_masks[SIZE_CHAR] = {
0x01, 0x02, 0x04, 0x08,
0x10, 0x20, 0x40, 0x80};


/******************************* SET BIT *******************************/

void set_bit(bit_array, which_bit)
/* Set a bit in an array */
unsigned char bit_array[];      /* Array to set bit in */
int which_bit;                  /* Which bit to set */
    {
    int index;                  /* Which char to use */
    int mask_index;             /* Which bit in char */

    index = which_bit / SIZE_CHAR;
    mask_index = which_bit % SIZE_CHAR;
    bit_array[index] = bit_array[index] | bit_masks[mask_index];
    return;
    }
```

```
/****************************** CLEAR BIT ******************************/

void clear_bit(bit_array, which_bit)
/* Clear a bit in an array */
unsigned char bit_array[];            /* Array to set bit in */
int which_bit;                        /* Which bit to clear */
    {
    int index;                        /* Which char to use *
    /int mask_index;                   /* Which bit in char */

    index = which_bit / SIZE_CHAR;
    mask_index = which_bit % SIZE_CHAR;
    /* Leave the remaining bits by ANDing with the inverse of the bit mask,
        such as ~0X01 is 0XFE */
    bit_array[index] = bit_array[index] & ~bit_masks[mask_index];

    return;
    }


/****************************** TEST BIT ******************************/

int test_bit(bit_array, which_bit)
/* Test a bit in an array */
unsigned char bit_array[];            /* Array to set bit in */
int which_bit;                        /* Which bit to test */
                                      /* Returns bit value (0 or 1) */

    {
    int index;                        /* Which char to use */
    int mask_index;                   /* Which bit in the char */
    int result;                       /* Result of test */

    index = which_bit / SIZE_CHAR;
    mask_index = which_bit % SIZE_CHAR;
    result = bit_masks[mask_index] & bit_array[index];

    return result;
    }


/****************************** MAIN ******************************/

#define MAX_NUMBER 16
#define SIZE_BIT_ARRAY (MAX_NUMBER+7)/8   /* Number of chars needed */
#define TRUE 1
#define FALSE 0
```

```
#include

int main()
/* Determines whether a series number is missing or duplicated */
    {
    char present[SIZE_BIT_ARRAY];   /* Flags to indicate value was present
                                          in input */
    char duplicate[SIZE_BIT_ARRAY];/* Flags to indicate if value was
                                          missing in input */
    int bit;                        /* Index for arrays */
    int number;                     /* Input number */
    int done;                       /* Flag for while loop */

    /* Initialize the arrays */
    for (bit = 0; bit < MAX_NUMBER; bit++)
        {
        clear_bit(present, bit);
        clear_bit(duplicate, bit);
        }

    printf("\n This program checks a series ranging from 0 to %d",
        MAX_NUMBER - 1);
    printf("\n It will see if any numbers are missing or duplicated");
    printf("\n The numbers can be entered in any order");

    /* Get numbers */
    do
        {
        printf("\n Input a number (negative to stop)");
        scanf("%d", &number);
        if (number < 0)
            done = TRUE;
        else if (number < MAX_NUMBER)
            {
            /* If number is already there, it is a duplicate */
            if (test_bit(present, number))
                set_bit(duplicate, number);
            else
                set_bit(present, number);
            }
        else
            printf("\n Number too big to be checked. Maximum is %d",
                MAX_NUMBER - 1);
        }
        while (!done);
```

```
/* See what numbers were missing or duplicated */
for (bit = 0; bit < MAX_NUMBER; bit++)
    {
    if (!test_bit(present, bit))
        printf("\n Number %d was missing", bit);
    else if (test_bit(duplicate, bit))
        printf("\n Number %d was duplicated", bit);
    }

exit(0);
}
```

### Increment and Decrement Operators

The increment and decrement operators have been shown earlier as sole operators in an expression. If you use these operators in complex expressions, you have
to consider when the increment or decrement actually takes place.

The postfix increment (++) uses the value of the variable in the expression and
then increments it. The prefix operator increments the value of the variable first,
then uses it in the expression. Using arrays as an example, say an array was zeroed
with

```
int i;
int an_array[SIZE];
i = 0;
while (i < SIZE)
    {
    an_array[i] = 0;
    i++;
    }
```

This could be written as

```
int i;
int an_array[SIZE];
i = 0;
while (i < SIZE);
    {
    an_array[i++] = 0;
    }
```

The value of i is used as the index to an_array; then i is incremented. However,
if the array is written as

```
int i;
int an_array[SIZE];
i = 0;
while (i < SIZE)
    {
    an_array[++i] = 0;
    }
```

the value of i would be incremented before it was used. an_array[0] would never be set to 0 and an_array[SIZE], which is beyond the end of the an_array, would be set to 0.

If you use an incremented variable in an expression more than once, be careful about side effects. *Side effects* are changes in variables resulting from the evaluation of an expression. Suppose you wanted to set each element in the an_array to the value of its index. You could do so with

```
int i;
int an_array[SIZE];
i = 0;
while (i<SIZE)
    {
    an_array[i] = i;
    i++;
    }
```

If you did it the following way you might run into problems:

```
int i;
int an_array[SIZE];
i = 0;
while (i < SIZE)
    {
    an_array[i] = i++;
    }
```

The question is when the variable i is incremented. Three possibilities could occur:

1. Its value could be used as the index for an_array. Then its value would be put into that element of an_array. Finally, i would be incremented.
2. Its value could be retrieved to evaluate the right-hand side of the assignment. The value would then be used as the index for the an_array and the assignment made. Then i would be incremented. Either of these two orders would produce the correct result.
3. Its value could be retrieved for the right-hand side, then i would be incremented. The variable's new value would then be used as the index of an_array. This would produce an incorrect result. an_array [0] would not be set, an_array [1] would be set to 0, and an_array[SIZE] would be set to SIZE-1.

As you can see, you should not use the increment and decrement operators on a variable that appears more than once in an expression. The ANSI standard simply states the variable values will have been changed by the time the entire statement is executed.[6] The assignment above may work correctly with one compiler and not with another.

Although the warning has been described for the increment operator, the same caution applies to the decrement operator. The prefix and postfix decrement operator works the same way as the increment operator, except it decrements the variable.

Use parentheses to group expressions with increment and decrement operators in them. Even though i+++j makes sense to the compiler, (i++)+j is clearer to the human reader.

## Conditional Operator

The conditional operator can be used in normal coding, but its main use is creating macros, as Chapter 11 explains. The operator has the syntax

```
condition ? true-expression : false-expression
```

If the condition is true, then the value of the conditional expression is *true-expression*. Otherwise, it is the value of *false-expression*. For example,

```
x > 7 ? 5 : 3
```

has the value of 5 if x is greater than 7; it has the value of 3 if x is less. Using the conditional, the if statement

```
if (x > 7)
    j = 5;
else
    j = 3;
```

could be written as

```
j = (x > 7 ? 5 : 3);
```

Nested if statements are much easier to read than nested conditional operators, so limit your use of this conditional operator

---

[6]There are intermediate points in an expression for which the variable values will be known. These are called sequence points. They are listed in Appendix E.

## Comma Operator

The comma operator evaluates two expressions where the syntax allows only one. The value of the comma operator is the value of the right-hand expression. The format for the expression is

*left-expression, right-expression*

One place where the comma operator commonly appears is in a for loop, where more than one variable is being iterated. For example, this function reverses the characters in a string. The index i starts at the beginning of the array, and index j starts at the end of the array. The two values are switched, and each index sets another element closer to the middle. When the indexes meet or cross, all elements have been swapped.

**Listing 9.7 Reverse a String**

```
int reverse_string(string)
/* Reverses the characters in a string */
char string[];                 /* String to reverse */
    {
    int length;                /* Length of the string */
    int i;                     /* Index from start */
    int j;                     /* Index from end */
    int temp;                  /* For swapping */

    length = strlen(string);
    for (i = 0, j = length - 1; i < j; i++, j--)
        {
        temp = string[i];
        string[i] = string[j];
        string[j] = temp;
        }

    return;
    }

int main()
/* Demonstrates reverse_string function */
    {
    static char string[] = "ABCDE";

    printf("\n String is %s", string);
    reverse_string(string);
    printf("\n Reversed string is %s", string);
```

```
    exit(0);
    }
```

The output looks like

```
String is ABCDE
Reversed string is EDCBA
```

The comma operator sometimes gets in the way. With other languages, you reference an element of a double dimensioned array using commas, as in `array[i,j]`. In C, this would not reference the element in the ith row, jth column of the array, but would refer to the `array[j]`, the entire jth row. Another place the comma operator is sometimes used is to show that a particular sequence of operations should not be separated. You might show swapping two values, as in

```
temp = a, a = b, b = temp;
```

The comma operator is always evaluated from left to right, so these three expressions will be computed in the order shown.

### Assignment Operator

The assignment operator in C is unlike that of other languages. It is performed by an assignment operator, rather than an assignment statement. Like other C operators, the result of an assignment operator is a value. This value is that which is assigned. An expression with an assignment operator can be used in a larger expression, such as

```
a_number = 7 * (b_number = 3);
```

b_number is set to 3 here. The value assigned (3), is multiplied by 7 and the result (21) is assigned to a_number.

You may imagine that overuse of this feature could rapidly lead to unmanageable expressions. There are two places in which this feature is normally applied. First, it can be used to set several variables to a particular value, as in

```
a_number = b_number = c_number = 0;
```

Second, it is often seen in the condition of a `while` loop, such as

```
while ((c = getchar()) ! = EOF)
    {
    ...
    }
```

This assigns the value that getchar returned to c and then tests the value against EOF. If it is EOF, the loop is not executed. The parentheses are necessary, because the assignment operator has lower precedence than the nonequality operator. Otherwise, this line would be interpreted as c = (getchar() != EOF). c would be assigned a value of 1 (TRUE) each time until getchar returned EOF.

## Compound Assignment Operators

The assignment operator initially introduced is similar to the assignment statement in other languages. C has an additional set of assignment operators that allow a more concise way of expressing certain computations. What they do is to use the left-hand variable twice, when it only appears once. A regular assignment that is expressed as

```
left-variable = left-variable operation expression
```

can be expressed as

```
left-variable operation = expression
```

The most common one is the add and assign. A typical assignment may look like

```
result = result + 2;
```

With the compound assignment, this can be abbreviated to[7]

```
result += 2;
```

This does not result in any change in execution speed. However, for assignments to array elements, a slight increase in speed might be noted because the index is only computed once. For example, changing

```
var_array[i + j] = var_array[i + j] + 3;
```

to

```
var_array[i + j] += 3;
```

may result in slightly faster execution speed.[8] If the index involved a complex computation, using a compound assignment like this would give a more readable program.

---

[7]Some older compilers may accept = operation as a synonym for the compound assignment. This may cause a few error messages in certain situations.
[8]Optimizing compilers (ones that eliminate unneeded instructions) may eliminate the redundant index computation.

If you had wanted to include an autoincrement operation in the first expression, as in

```
var_array[i] = var_array[i++] + 3;
```

to add 3 to an array element and then increment the index, you could not be sure whether this would execute properly, because the order of evaluation is undefined. However,

```
var_array[i++] += 3;
```

will execute properly, because there is only one reference to i.

This same compound assignment works with the *, /, %, +, -, <<, >>, &, ^, and | operators.

## ORDER OF EVALUATION

The order of evaluation of an expression in C is determined by the compiler. This normally does not alter the value of the expression, unless you have written one with side effects. Side effects are those operations that change the value of a variable while yielding a value that is used in the expression, such as was shown with the increment and decrement operators. The other operators that have side effects are the assignment and compound assignment. Calls to functions that change values of external variables also are subject to side effects. An example of side effects with the increment and decrement operators has been shown. Another example is with the assignment operator. If you coded

```
a = 3;
c = (a = 4) + a;
```

this could be evaluated as either of the following orders:

```
a = 4                       a assigned value of 4
c = 4 + a                   c assigned value of 8 (sum of 4 + 4)
```

or

```
c = (a = 4) + 3             value of 3 retrieved from a
c = 4 + 3                   4 assigned to a, sum put in c
```

There are four operators for which the order of evaluation is guaranteed to be left to right. These are the logical AND (&&), logical OR (| |), the comma operator, and the conditional operator. These operators are listed in Table 9.8. This order enables you to specify a typical test as

```
while ((c=getchar()) != EOF) && (c!='\n') )
```

and to be assured the second part of the logical AND is performed after the character value is assigned in the first part.

## PRECEDENCE AND ASSOCIATIVITY

*Precedence* ranking determines that operators are interpreted first. *Associativity* determines how operators of equal precedence may be interpreted. Table 9.8 lists the operators in order of precedence, from highest to lowest. Operators with equal precedence are grouped together. For example, based on the precedence chart,

```
a_number + b_number * c_number
```

is interpreted as

```
a_number + (b_number * c_number)
```

Based on associativity, given in the table,

```
a_number + b_number + c_number
```

is interpreted as

```
(a_number + b_number) + c_number
```

Notice that the order of a few operators can be tricky. For example, a & 0xF == 0x7 is interpreted as a & (0xF == 0x7).

| *Debug Tip* |
|---|
| Use parentheses in expressions other than those involving the arithmetic operators. |

## SUMMARY

- Variations on integer and floating point data types contain smaller or larger numbers than can fit in the standard sizes.
- Unsigned integers contain only positive integer values.

**Table 9.8 Precedence and Associativity**

| Operator | Meaning | Associativity | Order of Evaluation |
|---|---|---|---|
| () | function call | left to right | |
| [] | array element | | |
| -> | pointer to structure member | | |
| . | member of structure | | |
| ! | logical negation | right to left | |
| ~ | ones complement | | |
| ++ | increment | | |
| -- | decrement | | |
| - | unary minus | | |
| + | unary plus | | |
| (type) | cast | | |
| * | indirection (pointer) | | |
| & | address | | |
| sizeof | size of object | | |
| * | multiplication | left to right | |
| / | division | | |
| % | modulus | | |
| + | addition | left to right | |
| - | subtraction | | |
| << | left shift | left to right | |
| >> | right shift | | |
| < | less than | left to right | |
| <= | less than or equal to | | |
| > | greater than | | |
| >= | greater than or equal to | | |
| == | equality | left to right | |
| != | inequality | | |
| & | bitwise AND | left to right | |
| ^ | bitwise XOR | left to right | |
| \| | bitwise OR | left to right | |
| && | logical AND | left to right | left to right |
| \|\| | logical OR | left to right | left to right |
| ? : | conditional | right to left | left to right |
| = | assignment | right to left | |
| op= | shorthand assignment | | |
| , | comma | left to right | left to right |

- The `register` storage type is a variation of the automatic type that may produce more efficient code.
- Storage type modifiers, `const` and `volatile`, describe the way in which variables may be used.
- Enumerated types provide a set of values that a variable can be assigned.
- Bitwise operators treat integers as collections of bits.
- The increment and decrement operators add one to or subtract one from a variable.
- Precedence and associativity determine how an expression is interpreted.

## SELF-TEST

1. What is the value of `l` in the following?

```
long l;
double d = 50.3;
int i = 10001;
l = i * d;
```

2. What is the value of this expression if `int i = 5`?

```
i-- == 5 && ++i == 5
```

3. What is the decimal value of `027 & 0X12`?

## ANSWERS

1. `503050` is the value; `i` is converted to a double, then the result of fractional part of `i * d` is thrown away.
2. `1` is the value; `i-- == 5` is evaluated first. It is true. `i` then has a value 4, because the logical AND operator is guaranteed to be evaluated left to right.

```
++i == 5
```

is true, because `i` is incremented before the comparison.
3. `18` is the decimal value. In binary, `10111 & 10010 = 10010` or 18 decimal.

## PROBLEMS

1. Make up a `clear_all_bits` routine.
2. Make up a `count_how_many_set_bits` routine.

3. Change the routines so they pack a set of bits (say two or four bits, instead of just one bit). The routine would be called with something like

```
pack_bits(bit_array, value_index, value, number_of_bits)
char bit_array[];          /* Bit array to pack */
int value_index;           /* Index where to pack the value */
int value;                 /* Value to pack */
int number_of_bits;        /* Size of bits in each value to pack */
```

4. If the size of characters was 8, the two statements in Listing 9.6 could read

```
index = which_bit >> 3;
mask_index = which_bit & 0x7;
```

and the program might run somewhat faster. Why?

5. A popular book entitled *Numerical Recipes* contains a routine for creating a random sequence of bits looking like

```
#define BIT18 ((long)1<<18)
#define BIT5  ((long)1<<5)
#define BIT2  ((long)1<<2)
#define BIT1  ((long)1<<1)
#define BIT0  ((long)1<<0)

random_bit()
    {
    int shift_bit;
    static long seed;
    shift_bit=(seed&BIT18)^(seed&BIT5)^(seed&BIT2)
        ^(seed&BIT1)^(seed&BIT0);
    seed <<= 1;
    if (shift_bit)
        seed |= 0x1;
    return shift_bit;
    }
```

Test this to see whether the bits are random.

6. *Numerical Recipes* also has a random number generator that looks like

```
static unsigned long jran;
srand(seed)
long seed;
    {
    jran=seed;
    }
```

```
#define IM 233280
#define IA 9301
#define IC 49297
rand()
    {
    rand = jran*IA+IC%IM;
    return rand;
    }
```

Test this to see how random it is.

7. Write a circular bit shift function (both left and right). This might have a function header such as

```
int circle_shift(a,n)
int a;                      /* Value to shift */
int n;                      /* How much to shift */
                            /* If n is negative shift right */
                            /* If n is positive shift left */
```

8. Write a program that converts a binary file to hexadecimal characters (for data transmission). Write a program that does the reverse.

9. Write a function that computes the log to the base 2 of an int value. It should return the highest value such that $2^{log2(x)}$ is less than or equal to x. It might start something like

```
int log2(x)
int x;
```

(Hint: Try shifting the value.)

10. Write a program to determine how your machine treats right shifts of negative numbers.

11. Write a program to determine how truncation of negative floats to ints is done on your machine.

12. Write a program to see if char is signed or unsigned on your machine.

13. Given

```
char x = 126;
char y = 126;
printf("%d",(x+y));
printf("%c %d",x,x);
```

What prints on your machine?

14. If i is 7, what does this code do?

    ```
    a[i]=i++
    ```

    If i is 7, what does this code do?

    ```
    funct(a[i],i++)
    ```

15. What is the value of i in each of these cases?

    ```
    i = 1.6 + 1.5
    i = (int) 1.6 + (int) 1.5
    ```

16. Suppose i had a value of 5. Then the expression

    ```
    j = (i++) + (--i);
    ```

    has 3 possible values: 10, 9, and 8. Explain how each of these is possible.

17. Try register variables in a program, such as making i a register in the following function. Does it make any difference with your compiler?

    ```
    delay(count)
    int time;
        {
        volatile i;
        for (i=0;i<count;i++)
            {
            ;
            }
        return;
        }
    ```

18. Write a routine to compute day_of_week. Have it return an enumeration type.

19. One way to encrypt a file is to exclusive OR each character with a key character. To decrypt the file, you simply exclusive OR with the same key characters. For example, if the key were a single character long, then

    "ABC" is the unencoded string
    \x41\x42\x43 is the hexadecimal representation for the string
    "z" is the key
    \x7A is the hexadecimal representation for the key
    \x3B\x38\x39 is the hexadecimal for the encrypted string
    ";89" is the encrypted string

    Write a program that encrypts a file. Use a key that has several characters in it.

20. In this chapter, `test_bit`, `set_bit`, and `clear_bit` do not check to see what the size of the `bit_array` is. Should they? Rewrite the routines to provide for a check. What should they return if the size is exceeded?

# Chapter Ten

# Control Flow and Functions Revisited

You can write any function with the control constructs introduced so far—the `if` and the `while`. Additional constructs can help make your code more readable (or less readable). They include the `switch` and the `goto`.

Until this point, all functions have been assumed to be in one source file. The process of linking source code from multiple files is described here, as well as how to make your own library of functions.

## THE for STATEMENT REVISITED

The `for` loop has been introduced before. In C, unlike most other languages, the expressions in the control of the `for` statement do not have to increment or decrement a variable. They do not even have to have any variable in common with each other. Statements in the body of the `for` loop may alter any variable in the control portion. For example,

```
for (k=0; i < m; j++)
    {
    m--;
    }
```

is a perfectly valid, though meaningless, `for` loop. Using the comma operator, you could code this loop as

```
for (k = 0; i < m; j++, m--);
```

though this makes it a bit more unreadable. One or more of the expressions in the `for` statement can be eliminated as long as the semicolon is there to mark its place. A loop that adds the numbers 1 through 5 could be written as

```
sum = 0.0;
i = 5;
for (; i >= 1; i--)
    {
    sum = sum + i;
    }
```

or

```
sum = 0.0;
i = 5;
for (; i >= 1;)
    {
    sum = sum + i;
    i--;
    }
```

The example just shown is the equivalent of while (i>=1). A for statement like for(;;) is the equivalent of while (1). Both are infinite loops. A break statement is needed to escape an infinite loop.

When a for loop is used just for counting instead of indexing an array, a decrementing variable can be used. When the variable reaches 0, the loop ends. So in place of the beginning of the loop,

```
for (i = 0; i < n; i++)
```

you could use

```
for (i = n; i--;)
```

or

```
i = n;
while (i--)
```

---

### Style Tip

The for loop should be the primary way to control loops using a counter that is incremented or decremented.

## THE goto STATEMENT

The goto alters the normal execution flow of a C routine. You use goto to set the next statement to be executed by naming that statement. A statement that a goto can branch to has a name, called a *label*. The form for a goto is

```
goto label-name;
```

A label is created by appending a colon to a name, as in

```
label-name: statement
```

The goto statement is extensively used in languages that do not have the numerous control structures that C has. Suppose C did not have an if-else structure. You would have to write

```
if (i < 5)
     j = 7;
else
     j = 3;
```

as:

```
    if (i < 5)
        {
        j = 7;
        goto next;
        }
     j = 3;
next:;
```

The goto statement is probably the most controversial control statement ever invented. The statement exists in most languages, but irresponsible use of it has created program disasters. However, in a few situations, responsible use of the goto may make good sense.

These cautions are necessary, nevertheless.

1. Never use the goto to branch to a label coming before it in the source code. This is a hidden way of creating a loop and C has sufficient loop structures.
2. Never have more than one or two (at the most) labels in a function to branch to.

Labels have the scope of the entire function, so you cannot repeat a label within a function. The compiler will goto a label within a compound statement (such as the middle of a for loop). However, what will happen when the program executes is undefined.

The basic rationale for a goto is to escape from a sequence of code because some condition occurred that made it impossible to continue. If you were testing a three-dimensional array to see which element is zero, one way would be

```
for (i = 0; i < I_SIZE; i++)
    {
    for (j = 0; j < J_SIZE; j++)
        {
        for (k = 0; k < K_SIZE; k++)
            {
            if (array_3d[i][j][k] == 0)
                /* Found the zero element */
                goto end;
            }
        }
    }
end:
```

Using the goto might be clearer than using a flag, as in

```
done=FALSE;
for (i = 0; i < I_SIZE && !done; i++)
    {
    for (j = 0; j < J_SIZE && !done; j++)
        {
        for (k = 0; k < K_SIZE && !done; k++)
            {
            if (array_3d[i][j][k] == 0)
                /* Found the zero element */
                done=TRUE;
            }
        }
    }
...
```

---

### *Style Tip*

Justify why you need a goto every time you code one.

---

---

## SWITCH STATEMENT

Many times you may want to test a variable or an expression against several values. You could use nested if-else to do this, as in

```
if (x == 3)
      y = 7;
else if (x == 5)
      y = 9;
else if (x == 9)
      y = 8;
else
      y = 12;
```

The switch statement provides a clear structure for doing these multiple tests. Its form is[1]

```
switch (integral-test-expression)
      {
case integer-value-1:
      statements
case integer-value-2:
      statements

            . . .
default:
      statements
      }
```

The integral-test-expression is evaluated, and the next statement to be executed is the one following the case label having a value that matches this expression. If there is no matching case label, the next statement to be executed is the one following the default label. If no case value matches and there is no default, the next statement is the one following the switch.

The switch statement acts like a controlled goto. It selects a label to branch to for a particular value. You might try to write the nested if logic just shown as

---

[1] The exact form is actually

```
switch (expression)
      statement
```

However, without case labels in a compound statement, the switch is pretty but useless.

```
switch (x)
    {
case 3:
    y = 7;
case 5:
    y = 9;
case 9:
    y = 8;
default;
    y = 12;
    }
```

If x had a value of 3, the first statement to be executed would be y = 7;. The next statement would be y = 9;, followed by y = 8 and y = 12;. The following summarizes what statements will be executed. Figure 10.1 shows this graphically. However, this does not follow the same logic as the if statements.

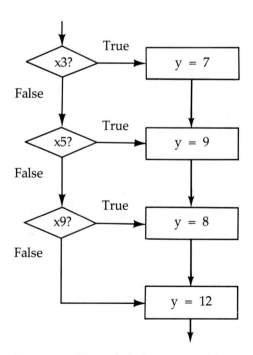

**Figure 10.1 The switch Statement Without Breaks**

| Value of x | Statements Executed |
|---|---|
| 3 | y = 7; |
|  | y = 9; |
|  | y = 8; |
|  | y = 12; |
| 5 | y = 9; |
|  | y = 8; |
|  | y = 12; |
| 9 | y = 8; |
|  | y = 12; |
| anything else | y = 12; |

The break control terminates the execution of statements within the switch body and continues execution with the first statement following the switch. The case statements would be written as

```
switch (x)
    {
case 3:
    y = 7;
    break;
case 5:
    y = 9;
    break;
case 9:
    y = 8;
    break;
default:
    y = 12;
    }
```

If x had the value of 3, the statement y = 7; would be executed, then execution would continue with the statement after the switch. Figure 10.2 shows the flow of this switch construct. The statements would be executed as follows:

| Value of x | Statement Executed |
|---|---|
| 3 | y = 7; |
| 5 | y = 9; |
| 9 | y = 8; |
| anything else | y = 12; |

Use a break with every case label or group of case labels in every switch. Any inconsistency should be thoroughly documented with comments explaining why you want the execution to flow through the next case label.

Listing 10.1 is the familiar date_check function using the switch. The code tests the value of the month against each case label. If the value does not match one of those values, execution is switched to the default label.

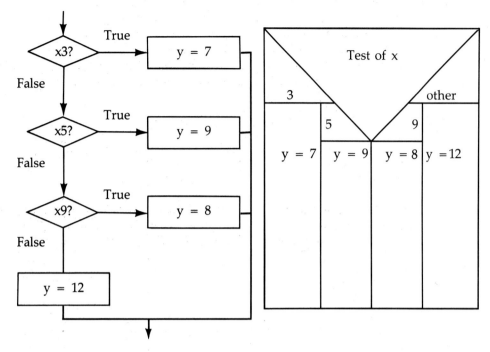

**Figure 10.2 The switch Statement With Breaks**

**Listing 10.1 date_check with switch**

```
#define TRUE 1
#define FALSE 0
/* Months of the year */
#define JAN 1
#define FEB 2
#define MAR 3
#define APR 4
#define MAY 5
#define JUN 6
#define JUL 7
#define AUG 8
#define SEP 9
#define OCT 10
#define NOV 11
#define DEC 12

int date_check(month, day, year)
/* Checks a date for validity */
int month;                        /* Month to check */
int day;                          /* Day to check */
int year;                         /* Year to check */
```

```
                               /* Returns
                                   TRUE if valid date
                                   FALSE if invalid date */
{
int valid;                 /* Return value */

/* Assume date is good until proven otherwise */
valid = TRUE;

if (day <= 0)
    valid = FALSE;
else
    {
    switch (month)
        {
    case FEB:
        if (year % 4 == 0)
            {
            /* Month is February in a leap year */
            if (day > 29)
                valid = FALSE;
            }
        else if (day > 28)
                valid = FALSE;
        break;
    case JAN:
    case MAR:
    case MAY:
    case JUL:
    case AUG:
    case OCT:
    case DEC:
        /* All have 31 days */
        if (day > 31)
            valid = FALSE;
        break;
    case APR:
    case JUN:
    case SEP:
    case NOV:
        /* All have 30 days */
        if (day > 30)
            valid = FALSE;
        break;
    default:
        /* Month is invalid */
        valid = FALSE;
```

```
    break;
        }                          /* End of switch */
    }                              /* End of else */

return valid;
}
```

<table>
<tr><td align="center">*Debug Tip*</td></tr>
<tr><td>Always have a <code>default</code> label in a <code>switch</code> statement. It may catch values that you never thought could occur.</td></tr>
</table>

## THE break STATEMENT

The break is used both for terminating a series of statements in a switch and for ending a loop. The break only terminates one level. For example,

```
for (i = 0; i < n; i++)
    {
    switch (j)
        {
    case 0:
        ...
        break;
    case 1:
        ...
        }
    }
```

With this example the break statement only ends the execution of the statements in the switch.

## THE continue STATEMENT

With the continue statement you can skip the remainder of a loop and go to the test condition. If your code resembled

```
while (test-expression)
    {
    /* Beginning of loop */
```

```
        if (test)
            {
            /* Rest of loop */
            }
        }
```

you could replace it with a continue, as in

```
while (test expression)
    {
    /* Beginning of loop */
    if (!test)
        continue;
    /* Rest of loop */
    }
```

The continue statement works with while, do-while, and for loops. With the for loop, it goes to the third expression instead of the test, so

```
for (expression1;expression2;expression3)
    {
    /* Beginning of loop */
    continue;
    /* Rest of loop */
    }
```

acts like

```
expression1;
while (expression2)
    {
    /* Beginning of loop */
    goto endloop;
    /* Rest of loop */
endloop:
    expression3;
    }
```

You can write most functions without using the continue. However, if you have deeply nested if statements in a loop, sometimes a single continue makes the program more readable. This example of a continue counts the number of positive values in the array and sums them.

```
#define SIZE 5
int i;
int array[SIZE];
int sum = 0;
```

```
for (i = 0; i < SIZE; i++)
    {
    if (array[i] <= 0)
        continue;
    count++;
    sum += array[i];
    }
```

The loop could be replaced by

```
for (i = 0; i < SIZE; i++)
    {
    if (array[i] > 0)
        {
        count++;
        sum += array[i];
        }
    }
```

## FUNCTIONS—LINKING MULTIPLE SOURCE FILES

So far, all the functions in the programs (other than the library functions) have been written in a *single* source file. Usually, a program consists of functions compiled in separate source files. Each source file is compiled separately and then linked together with the linker. Table 10.1 shows how to compile and link multiple source files, called file1.c and file2.c. Figure 10.3 diagrams how multiple files are linked together.

For functions called by several programs you could compile the source files and then combine the object files into a library. This library of object files can be accessed by the linker. Figure 10.4 shows how multiple files are combined into a library. The commands for the librarian vary, so check your operating system's manual.

## EXTERNAL NAMES

When a function is defined in a source file, the compiler automatically makes the name global. When another file calling the function is linked to the file in which the function is defined, it will find that name. The name is "globally" known among all files linked into a program. External variables work differently. As seen in Chapter 4, an external variable is any variable declared outside of a function. The variable is accessible to any function following it in the source file. A function in another source file may wish to access that variable. To do so, the function must tell the

**Table 10.1 Compiling and Linking Two Source Files**

| *MS/DOS* | *UNIX* | *VAX/VMS* |
|---|---|---|
| cc file1 | cc file1.c file2.c | cc file1 + file2 |
| cc file2 | (linker called | |
| | implicitly) | link file1 |
| link file1+file2;;; | | |

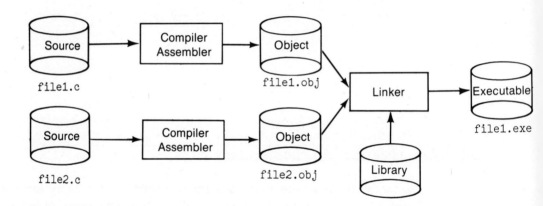

**Figure 10.3 Linking Multiple Source Files**

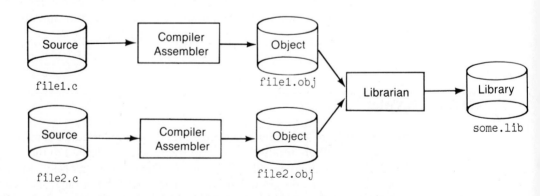

**Figure 10.4 Diagram of Making a Library**

compiler that the definition of the variable will be found when the file is linked. The keyword extern starts the declaration of these references. For example,

Source file one:

```
int number;
```
Defines an external variable known by functions in this source file

Source file two:

```
extern int number;
```
Declares number is an external variable defined in another source file.

For example, Listing 4.8 contained three functions—start_average, add_to_average, and compute_average. If these were in separate source files, you could not use a plain external for count and sum. In one file, you would write

```
double sum;
int count;
```

and in the other two, you would code

```
extern double sum;
extern int count;
```

The definition of the variables (without the extern) sets aside storage for the variables. The declarations referencing the variables, using the extern keyword, do not set aside storage. You can have a definition and multiple extern references to the same variable in the same source file. You can only define the variable once.[2]
  If you declared the following in a single source file,

```
int i;
extern double i;
```

then the compiler would report an error. If you declared

Source file one:

```
int i;
```

Source file two:

---

[2]The ANSI standard requires there to be only one definition of an external variable in all source files linked together. However, the standard permits multiple definitions of an external variable of int number; form in a single source file. One is taken as the definition, the remainder as if they had the keyword extern.

```
extern double i;
```

the compiler would not report an error. However, the program would probably not run correctly. This is a reason for using the `lint` program, discussed in Chapter 4; `lint` would report the mismatch in the data types.

You cannot declare a function and an external variable as having the same name. This code causes a compile error:

```
int f;
int f() {;}
```

---

## errno—GLOBAL ERROR VARIABLE

The `errno` global variable is part of the standard C library. If an error occurs in a library function, `errno` may be set to indicate information on the error. The standard headers include a declaration such as

```
extern int errno;
```

With some compilers, you can test `errno` to see why a file could not be written (for example, when a disk unit is off- line). Unfortunately, the meanings of `errno` values are not standardized.

---

## STATIC EXTERNAL VARIABLES

The keyword `static` may precede an external variable definition. A `static` external variable is known only within the source file in which it is defined. Even if another source file tries to declare the same variable as an external, the source file cannot access the variable.

**Source file one:**

```
static int number;
```
Defines an external variable known only by functions in this source file.

**Source file two:**

```
extern int number;
```
Declares `number` is an external variable defined elsewhere. This is not matched by the `static` external variable in source file one.

Practically all external variables should be classed as `static` externals. The main use for externals is to allow related functions access to the same variables. Because related functions should be kept in the same source file, static externals can be used. Functions for general use should not pass values using external variables, but rather through the parameter list.

Table 10.2 summarizes the scope of all the types of variable declarations.

## STATIC FUNCTIONS

When the compiler comes across the definition of a function, it creates an external definition for the name, similar to an external variable definition. If another source file is linked in to your program with a function of the same name, you will get a "Multiple definition" error from the linker.

Although functions cannot be nested in C, many times a function is called only by routines in the same source file. You may make the function unknown to all other source files by prefixing its name with the word static. Although the

**Table 10.2 Scope of Variable Names**

| Keyword | Use Relative to Function Definition | Referenced | Initialization | Storage Class |
|---|---|---|---|---|
| static | Outside | Only in source file | constant expression default 0 | external |
|  | Inside | Only in function[1] | constant expression default 0 | static |
| extern | Outside | In source file | Not initializable[2] | external |
|  | Inside | Only in function | Not initializable[2] | external |
| auto | Outside | Invalid | | |
|  | Inside | Only in function | Any expression | auto |
| register | Outside | Invalid | | |
|  | Inside | Only in function | Any expression | register |
| none | Outside | In source file and in other source files that use extern | constant expression default 0 | external |
|  | Inside | Only in function | Any expression | auto |

[1]Where the use is given as "Only in function," this also means that if it were defined inside a block, it could be referenced only in that block and not in the entire function.

[2]ANSI permits the initialization of a variable with the extern keyword, but it is not considered good programming practice.

function is not "static," the keyword is used in the same manner as making an external variable static. Even if a function in another source file has the same name, the linker does not give a "Multiple definition" error.

**Source file one:**

```
static func()
    {
    ...
    }
```

This code defines a function known only by functions in this source file.

**Source file two:**

```
static func()
    {
    ...
    }
```

The second sample code defines a function known only by functions in this source file.

---

## EXPANDED FUNCTION PROTOTYPES

Suppose power (the function introduced in Chapter 4) was in a separate source file and was called from the main program with

```
power(root)
```

or

```
power(exp,root)
```

or

```
power()
```

The C compiler would not report an error in processing the file, but the program would either not give the correct answer or would hang up the computer ("bomb"). C does no inherent checking on the number of parameters and their data types in the function call if the function's definition is in another source file.

The ANSI standard provides an extension to the function prototype for performing this checking. The types of parameters are inserted in the parentheses of the prototype. The form is

```
data-type function-name(parameter-types);
```

Instead of declaring the function as double power();, it would be declared as

```
double power(double, int);
```

Alternatively, the parameter names can be included as

```
double power(double base, int exp);
```

If this prototype appeared in the source file in which a call to power was made using one of the three examples above, the compiler would report an error.[3]

If this prototype is in a source file, the parameters will be automatically converted if they can be. For example, if you called power with

```
answer = power( 2 , 5.0 );
```

```
answer = power( 2 , 5 );
```

```
answer = power( 2.0 , 5.0 );
```

the first parameter would be converted to a double and the second parameter would be converted to an int.

The compiler needs to distinguish between a prototype that simply declares the return type and an expanded prototype for a function with no parameters. So the syntax for an expanded function prototype for a function with no parameters is

```
data-type function-name(void);
```

New style function prototypes are not in the code in this book, because many current compilers do not support them and give an error if such prototypes are present.[4]

To match the expanded function prototype, ANSI C provides an alternative function header. The form of a function can be written as

```
data-type function-name(declaration-of-parameters)
    {
    declarations-of-local-variables
```

[3]The names of the parameters are simply for convenience in making a prototype. They do not declare any actual variables.

[4]A variable parameter list is denoted with ellipses (...), as function (int number,...);. You should usually avoid creating functions having variable parameter lists. The prototypes for printf and scanf, which are standard functions with variable parameters, are in your compiler's stdio.h file.

```
      statements
      }
```

Using this alternate form, the power function would begin as follows:

```
double power(double base,int exp)
    {
    ...
    }
```

The corresponding function headers are not prevalent in this book, so comparison of these functions with those in other books will be easier.

Expanded function prototypes can be very useful in ensuring that you call each function with the proper types. If you use them, you need to have some discipline. In every source file in which a function is called, the corresponding prototype should appear. The easiest way to do this is to create one or more #include files with the prototypes in them. Appendix J has an example of this.

With a function call using the regular header, parameters that are chars are converted to ints and those that are floats are converted to doubles. Functions written with this new style header have one basic difference. If the function has parameters of type char or a float, and a prototype for the function appears in the source file calling it, then the values may be passed as char or float, instead of being converted to int and double. If you write a function with this type of header, be sure to include a prototype for it in every source file that calls it, or you may run into problems. For example, if you defined power as

```
float power(base, exp)
float base;
int exp;
```

and there was a prototype in the source file that called power, such as

```
float power(float base, int exp);
```

when the function is called with

```
float f = 5.5;
int i = 2;
float r;
r = power(f, i);
```

the value of f might not be converted to a double, but could be passed as a float value.

The keyword void can be used as the return type of a function that does not return a value. The compiler will ensure that the result of a call to a function of void type is not used in an expression. For example,

```
void func(int, int);
```

declares that func does not return a value, and the compiler signals an error if you coded a = func(1, 1);.

If a parameter is a pointer, it may be declared to point to a const type.[5] The compiler will verify that the function does not modify the values being pointed to. For example, the strcmp library function, which compares two strings, has a header and expanded prototype that looks like

```
int strcmp(char const *string1, char const *string2);
```

When strcmp is compiled, if it alters the strings pointed to, the compiler reports an error. In addition, when a function that uses strcmp is compiled with this prototype, the compiler may take advantage of the knowledge that the two strings will not be changed by the called function.

| *Debug Tip* |
| --- |
| With either type of function header, be sure to avoid making calls to functions with parameters that have side effects, as in func(i,i++). |

## THE lint PROGRAM

If you do not use expanded function prototypes to check for return type and parameter agreement, you can use the lint program discussed in Chapter 4. You specify the source files that lint is to check. It treats the list as if they had all been put in one file and reports any mismatches.

You normally specify two or more files to lint by typing

```
lint fileone filetwo
```

Each lint program varies slightly in how multiple files are specified, so you should check your computer manual. The lint program is also valuable in ensuring that your function prototypes agree with the definition of the function. If you make a modification in the parameters of a function, you need to be sure to change the corresponding prototype, or you will have a false sense of security that the program should work.

[5]If the parameter is not a pointer (or equivalently, an array), the function cannot modify it in the calling routine, so const is unnecessary.

The `lint` program will even pick up definition-reference mismatches. For example, if you had in separate source files

**Source file one**                    **Source file two**

`int d;`                                `extern double d;`

then your program would not work right. The `lint` program would notify you of the error.

---

## MORE ALGORITHMS

Many functions perform a mathematical algorithm, such as computing the root of a quadratic equation or applying formulas as the ones in the lunar lander program. Some merely automate an algorithm that was formerly done by hand. For example, in math calculations frequently you will need to find the root of an equation. One way of doing this is to use the Newton-Raphson Approximation.

This method states you can find the root of an equation by guessing what the root is and using the guess to find a better guess. Suppose the equation to be solved is represented by f(x) and the derivative of the equation is represented by fprime(x). You make a guess, symbolized by $x_0$. Then the next guess (symbolized by $x_1$) is

$$x_1 = x_0 - f(x_0) \; / \; fprime(x_0)$$

In general, for the iteration i + 1, the guess is

$$x_{i+1} = x_i - f(x_i) \; / \; fprime(x_i)$$

When the difference between $x_{i+1}$ and $x_i$ is small, you assume you have found the root. Solving for the square root of a number with the equation

$$square = root^2$$

gives

$$f(root) = root^2 - square = 0$$
$$fprime(root) = 2 * root$$

Substituting these in the formula yields

$$root_{i+1} = root_i - (root_i^2 - square) \; / \; (2 * root_i)$$

which can be subsequently reduced to

$$root_{i+1} = (root_i + square \; / \; root_i) \; / \; 2$$

and finally, to

$$\text{root}_{i+1} = .5 * (\text{root}_i + \text{square} / \text{root}_i)$$

This is restated in C in the square_root function in Listing 10.2 with $\text{root}_i$ as root_old and $\text{root}_{i+1}$ as root_new. An initial guess for root_old is 1.0. A value for root_new is computed using the value of root_old. When the difference between root_new and root_old is less than a small number (ALMOST_ZERO), the loop ends. If difference was tested for exact equality to 0.0, the loop might never end, due to the representation of floating point numbers.

**Listing 10.2 Square Root Program**

```
#include <stdio.h>
#define ALMOST_ZERO .000001        /* Error allowed for the root */


double square_root(square)
/* Computes the square root of a number */
double square;                     /* Number to take the square root of */


    {
    double root_old;               /* Original guess */
    double root_new;               /* New guess */
    double difference;             /* Difference between the two */

    /* Start the old guess somewhere */
    root_old = 1.0;
    difference = 1.0;

    /* If number is greater than 0.0, find the square root */
    if (square > 0.0)
        {
        /* Keep going until the difference is close to zero */
        while ((difference > ALMOST_ZERO)
            || (difference < -ALMOST_ZERO))
            {
            root_new = .5 * (root_old + (square / root_old));
            difference = root_new - root_old;

            printf("\n Difference %lf root_old %lf root_new %lf",
                    difference, root_old, root_new);

            root_old = root_new;


            }
        }
    else root_new = 0.0;
```

```
        return root_new;
        }

int main()
/* Demonstrates square root */
        {
        double square = 16.;        /* To find root of */
        double root;                /* Answer */

        root = square_root(square);
        printf ("\n Square root of %lf is %lf", square, root);

        exit(0);
        }
```

As the program searches for the root, the output looks like

```
Difference 7.500000 root_old 1.000000 root_new 8.500000
Difference -3.308824 root_old 8.500000 root_new 5.191176
Difference -1.054512 root_old 5.191176 root_new 4.136665
Difference -0.134407 root_old 4.136665 root_new 4.002258
Difference -0.002257 root_old 4.002258 root_new 4.000001
Difference -0.000000 root_old 4.000001 root_new 4.000000
Square root of 16.000000 is 4.000000
```

## CALL BY REFERENCE

Many functions return both a result and an error indicator. A good way to code this is to return the error indicator as the value of the function and pass the result back through the parameter list.

The root solver for a quadratic function must be able to pass back three values. The first is an error indication. Errors include A_COEF_ZERO if the value of a is zero, ROOT_IMAGINARY if the root is imaginary, and NOT_EQUATION if the value of b is zero. The other two are the two possible roots. To do this the quad_root function could look like that in Listing 10.3.

**Listing 10.3 Root of a Quadratic**

```
#define A_COEF_ZERO 2
#define ROOT_IMAGINARY 1
#define NOT_EQUATION 3
#define ROOT_OKAY 0
#define ALMOST_ZERO .0000001       /* Tolerance for zero test */

#include <math.h>                   /* For the square root prototype */
```

```
int quad_root(a, b, c, proot1, proot2)
/* Determines both positive roots for quadratic */
double a;                       /* x**coefficient */
double b;                       /* x**1 coefficient */
double c;                       /* x**0 coefficient */
double *proot1;                 /* Where to put first root */
double *proot2;                 /* Where to put second root */
                                /* Returns
                                        ROOT_OKAY is all okay
                                        ROOT_IMAGINARY if root is imaginary
                                        A_COEF_ZERO if value of x**2
                                            coefficient is 0
                                        NOT_EQUATION if value of a and b are 0
                                */
    {
    int ret_value;             /* Return indicator */
    double temp;               /* To hold temporary value */

    /* Determine if a is close to zero */
    if ((a < ALMOST_ZERO) && (a > -ALMOST_ZERO))
        {
        /* Linear equation--try to answer anyway */
        ret_value = A_COEF_ZERO;

        if ((b < ALMOST_ZERO) && (b > -ALMOST_ZERO))
            {
            /* Not an equation at all */
            ret_value = NOT_EQUATION;
            *proot1 = 0;
        }
        else
            /* Linear equation */
            *proot1 = -c / b;
            }
    else
        {
        temp = b * b - 4 * a * c;
        if (temp < 0.0)
        ret_value = ROOT_IMAGINARY;
        else
            {
            temp = sqrt(temp);
            *proot1 = (-b + temp) / (2 * a);
            *proot2 = (-b - temp) / (2 * a);
            ret_value = ROOT_OKAY;
            }
        }
```

```
        return ret_value;
        }


/****************************** MAIN ********************************/

#include <stdio.h>

int main()
/* Demonstrate quad_root */
    {
    double a = 1.;            /* x**2 coefficient */
    double b = 5.;            /* x**1 coefficient */
    double c = 4.;            /* x**0 coefficient */
    double root1;             /* To hold first root */
    double root2;             /* To hold second root */
    int result;              /* To hold result */

    result = quad_root(a, b, c, &root1, &root2);
    if (result == ROOT_OKAY)
        printf("\n Roots of %lfx**2 + %lfx + %lf are %lf, and %lf",
            a, b, c, root1, root2);
    else
        printf("\n Error, number is %d", result);

    exit(0);
    }
```

The output of the program would look like

```
Roots of 1.000000x**2 + 5.000000x + 4.000000 are -1.000000 and -4.000000
```

## STACKS IN PARAMETER PASSING

Many compilers use the stack mechanism of the processor hardware to pass parameters. A *stack* is a block of memory addressed by a special purpose register called the *stack pointer*. This memory is allocated when the program initially starts up. When a function is called, the value of each parameter is placed in the stack at the address specified by the stack pointer. Each time a value is transferred, the stack pointer is decremented by the size of the type of value. This transfer is called "pushing" onto the stack.

When the function returns, each value is "popped" off the stack by transferring it to a temporary register. For each transfer, the stack pointer is incremented. Popping all the values is the equivalent to increasing the stack pointer by the total size of all the parameters.

Many processors use the same stack to allocate the automatic variables for a function and to store the return address. Calling a function typically occurs in three steps. The values of the parameters are pushed onto the stack. The order in which they are pushed is compiler dependent. The function is called with a machine instruction termed "jump to subroutine." This instruction stores the return address on the stack. When the function is entered, the current value of the stack pointer is copied into a register called the *frame pointer*. Then the stack pointer is incremented by the number of bytes necessary for the automatic variables in the function.

When the `return` statement is encountered, the stack pointer is set back to the value of the frame pointer. Then a "return from subroutine" machine instruction is executed. This pops the return address off the stack and jumps to that address. The calling function then either pops the parameter values off the stack or simply sets the stack pointer to the value it had before the parameters were passed.

Figure 10.5 demonstrates how the parameters are passed when the function `power` is called from another function, `func`.

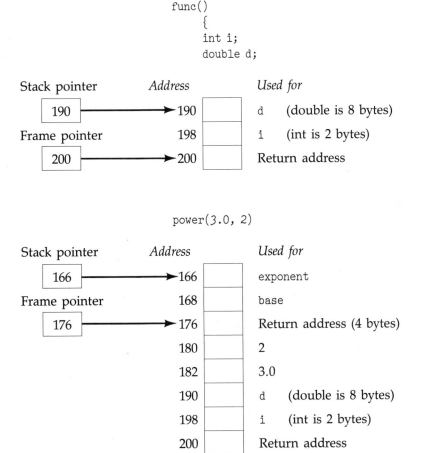

**Figure 10.5 Stack in Parameter Passing**

## RECURSION

Functions in C can call not only other functions but also themselves. These can be part of *mutual recursion,* in which one function calls another function that calls the first, and so forth. A recursive function uses itself as a function that is called. There are several instances in which recursion is useful. Some algorithms, especially those that deal with analyzing languages, are naturally recursive. Most of the time, an algorithm that is recursive can be made iterative (such as by using a loop) and vice versa.

Listing 10.4 is a simple example of a recursive routine. The out_function is called four times—once by main and three times by itself. If in_times is greater than zero, the function will call itself.

**Listing 10.4 Recursive Function**

```
#include <stdio.h>

int main()
/* Demonstrate a recursive function */
    {
    recur_function(3);
    }

void recur_function(in_times)
/* A recursive demonstration function */
int in_times;                    /* Number of times to go through function */
    {
    static int out_times = 0;

    printf("\n Coming into recur_function in_times %d", in_times);

    /* Call it again, if not at zero */
    if (--in_times > 0)
         recur_function(in_times);

    out_times++;
    printf("\n Going out of recur_function out_times %d", out_times);

    return;
    }
```

The output of this program will look like

```
Coming into recur_function in_times 3
Coming into recur_function in_times 2
Coming into recur_function in_times 1
Going out of recur_function out_times 1
Going out of recur_function out_times 2
Going out of recur_function out_times 3
```

If out_times were not static, that is, if it were automatic, a new location would be allocated for it every time out_function was entered. The last three lines would all read Going out of recur_function out_times 1. Something has to stop the recursion. This is usually a parameter decremented to 0, a string terminator (NUL), or an end of file.

Figure 10.6 demonstrates how the stack works with recursion. Each time the function is called, another location is allocated on the stack for the local variable in_times. Static variables as out_times are not allocated on the stack. The diagram shows the state of the stack after the call from main and the first call to itself.

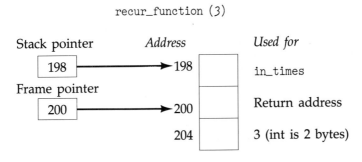

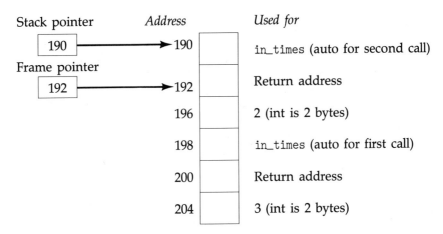

**Figure 10.6 Stack in Recursive Function Call**

## SAMPLE RECURSIVE FUNCTIONS

### Factorial

The factorial has a recursive algorithm. The recursive definition of a factorial is

```
factorial(0) = 1
factorial(i) = factorial(i-1) * i
```

You could implement this in an iterative manner, as has been shown before (in Listing 4.4). Listing 10.5 gives the new implementation.

**Listing 10.5 factorial Function Without Recursion**

```
int factorial(number)
/* Computes factorial of a number */
int number;                      /* Number to compute factorial for */
                                 /* Returns factorial of number */

    {
    int result;                  /* Return value */

    result = 1;

    if (number > 0)
        {
        result = number;
        while (--number)
            {
            result *= number;
            }
        }

    return result;
    }
```

You could implement it as a recursive function, as in the following function.

**Listing 10.6 factorial Function with Recursion**

```
int factorial(number)
/* Computes factorial of a number */
int number;                      /* Number to compute factorial for */
                                 /* Returns factorial of number */
```

```
{
int result;                    /* Return value */

if (number <= 0)
    result = 1;
else
    result = number * factorial(number - 1);

return result;
}
```

If you coded the function as in Listing 10.6, each time the function was called, room for another automatic variable would be allocated. So it is better to code it as Listing 10.7.

**Listing 10.7 factorial Function with Recursion**

```
int factorial(number)
/* Computes factorial of a number */
int number;                    /* Number to compute factorial for */
                               /* Returns factorial of number */
    {
    if (number <= 0)
        return 1;
    else
        return number * factorial(number - 1);
    }
```

### The power Function Revisited

The power function described in Chapter 4 could be coded in a recursive manner. The function in Listing 10.8 calls itself until the exponent value goes to zero. If the exponent was initially negative, it will invert base, negate exponent, and call itself.

**Listing 10.8 power Function with Recursion**

```
double power(base, exponent)
/* Computes the result of a base raised to an integer power */
double base;                   /* value to be raised to a power */
int exponent;                  /* power to which to raise base */
    {
    if (exponent == 0)
        return 1;
    else if (exponent > 0)
        return power(base, --exponent) * base;
    else
        return power(1 / base, -exponent);
    }
```

## SAMPLE PROGRAM—ACEY-DEUCEY

This program plays acey-deucey. This is a card game that deals two cards. You bet whether the third card will fall between the values of the two cards. If it matches the cards or falls outside the range, you lose. As long as the pot is positive and the bet is not negative, you keep playing. Two cards are dealt by card. swap is called to switch the order if the second card is less than the first. After players get a third card, the results are printed out and the pot either increases or decreases by bet.

**Listing 10.9 Acey_deucey Game**

```c
#include <stdio.h>
#include <stdlib.h>

#define TRUE 1
#define FALSE 0
#define MAX_CARD 13            /* Maximum value for a card */
#define START_POT 100          /* Starting pot of money */

/* Expanded prototypes for the functions in this program */
void main(void);
int card(void);
void swap(int *, int *);
int in_bet(int);
void print_card(int);

void main(void)
/* Plays acey-deucey */
    {
    int bet;                   /* Current bet */
    int pot;                   /* Current pot */
    int card_one;              /* First card value */
    int card_two;              /* Second card value */
    int card_three;            /* Third card value */

    /* Initialize bets */
    pot = START_POT;
    bet = 0;

    /* Until pot is 0 or bet is negative, keep dealing two cards */
    while ((pot > 0) && (bet >= 0))
        {
        card_one = card();
        card_two = card();
```

```
                    /* Put them in numerical order */
                    if (card_two < card_one)
                         swap(&card_one, &card_two);

                    /* Print the cards */
                    printf("\n\n Your two cards are ");
                    print_card(card_one);
                    printf(" and ");
                    print_card(card_two);

                    bet = in_bet(pot);
                    if (bet > 0)
                         {
                         /* Get a third card; check it against the first two */
                         card_three = card();

                         printf("\n Your card is ");
                         print_card(card_three);

                         if ((card_three > card_one) && (card_three
                             < card_two))
                             {
                             pot += bet;
                             printf("\n You won. You now have %d", pot);
                             }
                         else
                             {
                             pot -= bet;
                             printf("\n You lost. You now have %d", pot);
                             }
                         }
                    }                   /* End of loop on pot and bet */

        printf("\n Thanks for playing");
        exit(0);
        }

/*************************** CARD ***************************/

int card(void)
/* Returns a card value from 1 to MAX_CARD */
        {
        int ret;                 /* Return value */

        ret = rand() % MAX_CARD + 1;
```

```
        return ret;
        }


/*************************  SWAP  *************************/

void swap(pone, ptwo)
/* Swaps two integer values */
int *pone;                    /* First value to swap */
int *ptwo;                    /* Second value to swap */
        {
        int temp;             /* Used to hold temporary value */

        temp = *pone;
        *pone = *ptwo;
        *ptwo = temp;

        return;
        }


/*************************  IN_BET  *************************/

int in_bet(pot)
/* Returns a bet that is less than or equal to pot */
int pot;
        {
        int done;             /* Flag when bet is okay */
        int bet;              /* Value of bet returned */

        done = FALSE;

        while (!done)
            {
            printf("\n What is your bet (negative bet to end)?");
            scanf("%d", &bet);
            if (bet > pot)
                printf("\n You don't have that much!!");
            else
                done = TRUE;
            }

        return bet;
        }


/*********************  PRINT_CARD  *********************/

void print_card(card)
/* Prints the alphabetic value of a card */
```

```
int card;                          /* Value of card to print */
    {
    switch(card)
        {
    case 1:
        printf("ACE");
        break;
    case 11:
        printf("JACK");
        break;
    case 12:
        printf("QUEEN");
        break;
    case 13:
        printf("KING");
        break;
        default:
        printf("%d",card);
        }
    return;
    }
```

## SUMMARY

- A `for` statement can do more than use a variable as a counter.
- The `switch` statement handles tests for multiple values of an expression. It should be used with `break`s.
- The `goto` and `continue` should be used only to make potentially messy code cleaner.
- The types of parameters in a function definition need to agree with those in the call. Expanded function prototypes or the `lint` program will help you check that they do.
- Regular external variables may be accessed from other source files using the `extern` keyword.
- Static externals are known only in the source file in which they are declared.
- Functions are known through the entire program that is linked together, unless they are declared static.

## SELF-TEST

1. What does the following code do to the values in a and b?

```
int a[2], b[2];
swap(a, b);
```

2. How many times will this loop be executed?

```
for (k=1;--k;)
    {
    j++;
    }
```

3. If these two functions are in separate source files, what is the value of i after function_one is executed?

```
int k = 7;
function_one()
    {
    int i;
    i = function_two() * 3;
    i += k;
    }
...
extern int k;
function_two()
    {
    return k++;
    }
```

4. What is the value of j if this code is executed four separate times starting with i equal to 1, 2, 3, and 4?

```
j = 5;
switch(i)
    {
case 1:
case 2:
    j++;
    break;
case 3:
    j++;
default:
    j--;
    }
```

5. What prints when this code is executed?

Source file one:

```
main()
    {
    printf("\n %d", func_a());
    printf("\n %d", func_b());
    }
```

Source file two:

```
static int i = 5;
func_a()
    {
    i++;
    return i;
    }
```

Source file three:

```
int i;
func_b()
    {
    i--;
    return i;
    }
```

6. What is wrong with this code?

```
    int i;
    i = 3;
start:
    if (i > 7)
        goto done;
    a[i] = 9;
    i++;
    goto start;
done: ;
```

7. What occurs in a call by reference?

## ANSWERS

1. The values of a[0] and b[0] are swapped. An array name is the address of the first element in the array.

2. None. k is set to 1. Then the value of k is decremented to 0 by the prefix decrement operator. The result of 0 is tested. Because it has the value of false, the loop exits immediately.

3. 29. function_two will return a 7. 7 * 3 is 21. But k has been changed to 8, so i is set to 21 + 8 is 29.

4. For the respective values of i and j, these are the results:

```
i  j
1  6
2  6  Same code is executed for these two cases.
3  5  Both j++ and j-- are executed, because there is no break statement
4  4  The default is selected, because the value does not match a case.
```

5. 6 and -1. The i in source file two is not the same i as in source file three, because it is static. The i in source file three is initialized to zero by default.

6. The code uses the goto to create a loop. This is bad programming practice. The for statement does the same operation in a much cleaner manner.

```
for (i = 3; i <= 7; i++)
    {
    a[i] = 9;
    }
```

7. The addresses of the parameters, rather than the values of the parameters, are passed.

---

## PROBLEMS

1. Write a program that accepts a string of characters and outputs the string in reverse order. Assume that the string will end with either a blank space or a carriage return. The program should also count the number of characters inputted and print and identify the original and the reversed string. The function that does the actual string reversal should be a recursive function.

2. The Fibonacci numbers are a sequence of numbers that are defined in the following manner:

$$\text{Fib}(n) = 0, \qquad\qquad\qquad\quad n = 0$$
$$\text{Fib}(n) = 1, \qquad\qquad\qquad\quad n = 1$$
$$\text{Fib}(n) = \text{Fib}(n-1) + \text{Fib}(n-2) \quad n > 1$$

The first 12 Fibonacci numbers are 0, 1, 1, 2, 3, 5, 8, 13, 21, 34, 55, 89.

Write two functions that calculate the first 30 Fibonacci numbers. The first function should not use a recursive algorithm. The second function should use a recursive algorithm.

3. Write program that calculates the sum of n, n − 1, n − 2, ..., 1 . The number n is a positive integer. Use a recursive function to compute the sum.

4. Write a recursive program that outputs a * on the terminal for each character in a string.

5. A table for withholding taxes is given by

| Dependents | Tax |
|---|---|
| 0 | 25% |
| 1 | 22% |
| 2 | 19% |
| 3 | 16% |
| 4 | 13% |
| 5 or more | 10% |

Create a function that computes the withholding tax for a given income.

6. An efficiency you could add to the square root function (Listing 10.2) would be to make a better initial guess than 1.0. How would you do this?

7. If the cards were not swapped in Listing 10.9, how many comparisons would it take to make sure that card_three was in between the values of the two cards?

8. Write a program that helps a bank loan officer decide whether a loan candidate should be given a loan. The basic rules and inputs to be used in the program are

| | |
|---|---|
| Age rule | The loan candidate must be over 18 years but under 65 years old. |
| Employment rule | The loan candidate must be employed and monthly take-home pay (after expenses and taxes) must be 5 times the monthly loan payments. |
| Credit History rule | The candidate must have a good credit history. If there is no history, the loan officer must get three positive references or a cosigner. |
| Loan Type rule | The loan must be to purchase a car, home, or boat. No other kinds of loans are to be made. |

The monthly payments are calculated by this simple rule:

Monthly payment $=$ loan amount $(1 + rate)^{years} / (12 * years)$

rate for cars   $= .12$
rate for homes $= .11$
rate for boats  $= .14$

An example of a four-year, $10,000 car loan's monthly payments is

$10000 * (1.1)^4 / (4 * 12)$

Here the monthly payment = $305.02.

# Chapter Eleven

# The Preprocessor

The preprocessor helps you to keep your C programs readable and maintainable. You can also use it to customize the language to fit your own programming style. The preprocessor performs some textual conversions on your source file before it is actually compiled. The commands to the preprocessor are called *directives*. You are already familiar with the #define directive. It and #include are examined in detail; then the remainder of the directives are described.

## THE #define DIRECTIVE

The #define is coded in almost every example in this book. It has a few other properties that should be mentioned. So far the only use of the #define has been to textually substitute a number. The syntax for the directive looks like

```
#define define-label text-of-define
```

All preprocessor directives end at the new-line (or carriage return). If the text for a #define must run onto the next line, the line continuation sequence ('\' followed by a carriage return), is placed at the end of the line. The replacement text can be anything, such as

```
#define FUNCTION /* */
#define FILE_NAME "ABCDE"
#define extra_long_external_name short_name
```

You could use #defines as these to document your code or use long external names with compilers that only support the six characters of significance. If you coded something similar to

```
int extra_long_external_name;
FUNCTION func()
```

```
        {
        char *p = FILE_NAME;
        int a = extra_long_external_name;
        }
```

it would actually be compiled as

```
int short_name;
/* */ func()
        {
        char *p = "ABCDE";
        int a = short_name;
        }
```

You can also use defined values in a definition, as in

```
#define X 10
#define Y X + 5
```

If you use an expression like this one in a definition, when the text is substituted in an expression such as

```
a = Y * 2;
```

you will get

```
a = 10 + 5 * 2;
```

You should enclose all expressions in #defines in parentheses, such as

```
#define Y (X + 5)
```

so the previous expression would yield

```
a = (10 + 5) * 2;
```

In C, expressions composed of just numeric constants are evaluated at compile time, not execution time. Using a set of #defines, each of which refers to the previous one, will not slow the execution time of the program, only the compilation time.

You cannot define a #define in terms of itself. For example, the following is invalid:

```
#define X X + 1
```

There is no substitution of a name within a string literal. For example,

```
#define CHARACTER A
printf("Character is CHARACTER")
```

is preprocessed to

```
printf("Character is CHARACTER");
```

Instead, you should use implicit string concatenation, such as

```
#define CHARACTER "A"
printf("Character is " CHARACTER);
```

to get the result of

```
printf("Character is A");
```

   The #define directive's names are known from the point of their appearance in the source file to the end. If you try to reference a name before it is defined, you get an error.
   ANSI C reserves some #define names for common uses. These are shown in Table 11.1. You may find some of them useful. There are many other names defined by ANSI C, which are listed in Appendix G. For example, you might write

```
printf("\n This program was compiled on %s at %s",
     __DATE__, __TIME__);
printf("\n Program logic error at line %d File %s",
     __LINE__, __FILE__);
```

   The # in all preprocessor directives can start anywhere on the line. You can insert space between the # and the name of the directive itself. Any of the spacing formats shown in the following list is acceptable, but the first form is usually preferred for lines outside functions and the third for lines inside functions. Usually you place all #defines outside functions and at the beginning of the source file so they are easy to spot.

```
#define TOKEN 1
#      define TOKEN 1
     #define TOKEN 1
```

**Table 11.1 Predefined Macro Names**

| *Macro Name* | *Meaning* |
|---|---|
| __LINE__ | line number of current source line (integer) |
| __FILE__ | file name of source file (string) |
| __DATE__ | translation date of source file (string) |
| __TIME__ | time of translation (string) |
| __STDC__ | the version number of the C standard (the integer value 1) |

### #define with Tokens

You can pass actual tokens to a #define. The code looks similar to that for passing parameters to a function. The text passed is substituted in the #define wherever the matching parameters appear. This type of #define is sometimes called a *macro*, although the term is often applied to simple #defines. The form for a macro is

```
#define define-label(tokens...) text-of-define
```

The left parenthesis that starts the token list in the #define must be adjacent to the name. Otherwise, the preprocessor assumes it to be the replacement text for a simple #define. A sample macro is:

```
#define absolute_value(x) ((x) >= 0 ? (x) : -(x))
```

When the macro is used as

```
if (absolute_value(y + 3))
```

it is interpreted as

```
if ((y + 3) >= 0 ? (y + 3) : -(y + 3))
```

Multiple tokens can be passed to a macro. These are separated by commas, such as

```
#define greater(x, y) ((x) > (y) ? (x) : (y))
```

You could call this macro with

```
d = greater(a, b);
```

which would give

```
d = ((a) > (b) ? (a) : (b));
```

By usual C conventions, uppercase is used for names for #defines with no tokens. Lowercase is used for macro names. This makes them look more like function calls.

As with simple #defines, omitting the parentheses in macro definitions causes errors. You should always enclose expressions in parentheses. Notice if you had left off the parentheses in the definition of the macro, you would get the incorrect expression:

```
if (y+3 > 0 ? y+3 : -y+3)
```

Sometimes a macro can create an erroneous program, if you use expressions with tokens that have side effects. For example, if your definition is

```
#define SQUARE(x) ((x) * (x))
```

and you code

```
a = SQUARE(y++);
```

you get

```
a = ((y++) * (y++));
```

which will more than likely not give you the right value, as you saw in Chapter 9 for the increment operator.

You can use macros to add a few features to the C language. Some other languages have a do-until loop structure. With this the loop is repeated until a particular condition is true. The loop is always executed at least once. You could create a do-until by defining

```
#define until(x) while (!(x))
```

and using it as:

```
do
    {
    ...
    } until(x)
```

With a macro, you can make operations that look like functions expand "in-line." The instructions are then duplicated each place the macro is used, rather than being coded once and called. For example, you can write a macro that clears an array to zero, as in

```
#define clear_array(array,size)   \
    {                              \
    int i;                         \
    for (i = 0; i < size; i++)     \
        {                          \
        array[i] = 0;              \
        }                          \
    }
```

This macro uses the potential for declaring variables at the beginning of any compound statement that will be known only within the compound statement. When you use this macro, as in

```
#define SIZE_DEMO 10;
int demo_array[SIZE_DEMO];
...
```

```
clear_array(demo_array, SIZE_DEMO);
```

it is preprocessed to execute as if you had written the last line as

```
{
int i;
for (i = 0; i < 10 ; i++)
    {
    demo_array[i] = 0;
    }
}
```

There is a trade-off between using a macro and a function call. A macro expands to in-line code, so that it avoids the overhead of calling a function. However, each time a macro is used, it requires more memory for the additional code. Calling a function requires more time to pass the parameters, but the code for the function is stored only in one place.[1]

A #define cannot be recursive; that is, it cannot use itself in its definition. However, it can be called with itself. For example, with the definition

```
#define ADDONE(X) ((X) + 1)
```

the line

```
ADDONE(ADDONE(2))
```

expands to

```
((((2) + 1)) + 1)
```

A macro can call other macros. If a #define name is formed when the macro is expanded, the replacement is made for those macros. For example, if you had the following two macros:

```
#define old_func new_func
#define new_func() (x)
```

old_func() yields new_func(), which yields (x).

---

[1]For a very short macro, the additional code may be less than the code required to pass the parameters to a function.

---
***Style Tip***

---

If your linker does not support long function names, you can still use them if you include a macro that redefines the name. For example,

```
#define compute_average(a,b) comp1(a,b)
```

changes all references to compute_average to comp1.

---

### The #undef Directive

If a name has been #defined, you can "undefine" it using the #undef command. This removes the definition from the preprocessor. One reason to #undef a name is you want to redefine it. You may have a second #define of the same name, without an #undef, but only if the text value of the macro is the same as the previous definition. So to change the definition, you must #undef it. For example,

```
#define EOF -1
#define EOF -1            Redefinition is okay, value is the same.
```

```
#define EOF -1
#undef EOF
#define EOF -3            Redefinition is okay because of #undef.
```

---

## THE #include DIRECTIVE

There are many pieces of source code that you might want to use in more than one source file. Declarations of function prototypes and #defines are common elements. Instead of using your word processor to simply duplicate the source code, you can use the #include directive.

The #include directive specifies a source file for the compiler to read in. The compiler continues as if the text were in the source file being compiled. For example,

| **Source File** test.c | **Source File** test.h |
|---|---|
| `#include "test.h"` | `#define PI 3.14159` |
| `...` | |
| `a=PI;` | |

A source file that is included can contain #include directives. The compiler reads the named source file at that point and then returns to the original included file. At least five levels of nesting of include files can occur.

Three forms exist for naming the source file to be included. They are

| | |
|---|---|
| `"filename"` | file searched in current directory |
| `<filename>` | file searched in system directory |
| `DEFINE-NAME` | name given by #define DEFINE-NAME |

On most operating systems, the user operates in what is called a *current directory*. This usually contains only files that he or she has created. The system directory contains files that are readable by all users. A `filename` in quotes is searched only in this current directory. A `filename` in brackets (< >) is looked for in the system directory. The value of the `DEFINE-NAME` is used as the filename. It must be surrounded by either quotes or brackets (< >). If an include file cannot be found, the compiler reports an error.

The C compiler uses include files that are listed in Table 11.2. These are the names you enter to use the corresponding functions. The names are reserved words—do not name your own #include files with any of these names.

## CONDITIONAL COMPILATION

Not all statements in a source file are compiled into executable code. Comments, for example, are ignored by the compiler. You may have some statements you wish to execute only for debugging your program. Once you have finished the debugging phase, you no longer want the statements to be executed, but you might like

**Table 11.2 Standard Header Files**

| File | Usage |
|---|---|
| assert.h | program diagnostics |
| ctype.h | character typing functions |
| error.h | error values |
| float.h | ranges of floating point values |
| limits.h | limits of integer values |
| locale.h | setting the locale of a program |
| math.h | mathematical functions |
| setjmp.h | doing long jumps back through code |
| signal.h | setting functions to handle signals (exceptions) |
| stdarg.h | variable parameter lists |
| stddef.h | standard definitions |
| stdio.h | input and output |
| stdlib.h | miscellaneous functions |
| string.h | string functions |
| time.h | time functions |

them to remain in the source file. In other languages, you can "comment out" executable code, such as

```
/*
    printf("\n Value of x is %d",x);
*/
```

Although you could do this in C, if you have comments in the code you are trying to eliminate, you will have problems, because comments do not nest. The conditional compilation directives solve this problem, as well as make for more maintainable code. The #if set of directives is similar to if statements. If the test result is true, the code following is compiled. If it is not true, the code is ignored by the compiler. The #endif directive marks the end of the statements compiled if the test is true. The most common #if directive is #ifdef. This tests if a particular name has been defined with a #define. For example,

```
#ifdef DEBUG
    printf("\n Value of x is %d",x);
#endif
```

If a #define DEBUG had appeared before this code, the printf call will be compiled. Otherwise, it would be ignored, as if it were a comment. With most compilers you can also define a name on the command line when the compiler is invoked. For example,

```
cc -DDEBUG test.c
```

defines DEBUG, as if a #define DEBUG had appeared in the source.

---

### Debug Tip

Use #ifdef DEBUG to keep all your debugging statements in the function. If you ever make changes to the function and you have problems, your debug output will only be a -DDEBUG away.

---

There are a few other types of #if directives. The #ifndef tests to see whether the expression's name has been defined. The #if tests an expression to see if it is nonzero. The expression must be something that can be evaluated at compilation time.

You can use the #else directive to compile code if the #ifdef is false. If the condition is true, then the code up to the #else is compiled. Otherwise, the code between the #else and the #endif is compiled. A typical use is to determine the smallest type of variable to use for storing values. The file limits.h includes #defines for the largest possible values for each integer type.

```
#define MY_MAX_NUMBER      60000
#include <limits.h>
#if MY_MAX_NUMBER < INT_MAX
int size;
#else
long size;
#endif
```

You can nest conditional compilations using the #elif directive. Logically this acts like an else if of the regular language.

```
#define MY_MAX_NUMBER      60000
#if MY_MAX_NUMBER < SHRT_MAX
short size;
#elif MY_MAX_NUMBER < INT_MAX
int size;
#else
long size;
#endif
```

You can also test in an #if to see whether a name has been #defined. The expression defined(*name*) returns a true or false value, depending on whether *name* has been #defined. You can use this value in an expression, such as

| | |
|---|---|
| `#if defined(NAME)` | same as #ifdef NAME. |
| `#if defined(NAME_A)&&defined(NAME_B)` | The code is compiled only if both NAME_A and NAME_B are defined. |

Avoid nesting conditional compilation directives. It becomes confusing to determine what really has been compiled for a particular set of #defines.

## QUOTING AND TOKEN CONCATENATION

A couple of operators are available only in preprocessor directives. These are the quote operator and the tokenizing operator.

The quote operator (#) takes a set of characters and inserts quotes around them. If you had

```
#define STRING(string) #string
```

then

```
STRING(abc)
```

would compile as if you had written

```
"abc"
```

The example on #defines could be written using the quote operator, as

```
#define CHARACTER #A
printf("Character is " CHARACTER);
```

The quote operator enables you to create a debug macro, as in

```
#define debug(x) printf("\n Value of " #x " is %d",x);
...
debug(variable_name);
```

This is interpreted by the preprocessor in stages. First, the value variable_name is substituted for x, so the code is

```
printf("\n Value of " #variable_name " is %d",variable_name);
```

Then the quote operator gives

```
printf("\n Value of " "variable_name" " is %d",variable_name);
```

Then the string constants are concatenated by the compiler to yield

```
printf("\n Value of variable_name is %d",variable_name);
```

The token concatenator (##) takes two sets of characters and concatenates them. It operates on unquoted strings. For example,

```
#define VAR_NUMBER(number) var##number
int VAR_NUMBER(3)
```

is compiled as if it were int var3.

Table 11.3 gives a few more examples of quoting and tokenizing.

These operators can be combined with macros to form complex definitions. This one is given as a sample.

```
#define VARIABLE(X) abc ## X
#define ANOTHER(Y) # VARIABLE(Y)
```

**Table 11.3 Effects of Quoting and Tokenizing**

| Expression | After Preprocessing | After Compiling |
|---|---|---|
| "x" "y" | "x" "y" | "xy" |
| x ## y | xy | xy |
| # x | "x" | "x" |
| # x "y" | "x" "y" | "xy" |

The interpretation of the expansion of

ANOTHER(1)

yields successively

| Expression | Comment |
| --- | --- |
| ANOTHER (1) | original |
| # VARIABLE(1) | after substitution |
| # abc##1 | after substitution |
| # abc1 | after token concatenation |
| "abc1" | after quote operator |

## OTHER DIRECTIVES

Other preprocessor directives are seldom used by the typical programmer. They are included here for completeness. The #line directive forces the compiler line counter to be set to a new value. This is used in computer-generated C programs.

The #error directive forces the compiler to issue an error message. One use is in conditional compilation, to act as a flag if an odd case comes up, similar to using an error message in the default of a switch.

The #pragma directive is a compiler-specific directive for commanding it to do actions not handled in standard C. The null directive (#) is permitted but has no effect.

## CRAPS GAME

This program makes extensive use of #defines. In the game of craps, the player rolls two dice. If the first roll is 2, 3, or 12, the player loses. If it is 7 or 11, he or she wins. Otherwise, the value becomes the "point" the player must match. He or she keeps rolling until the point occurs again (a winner) or the dice count totals 7 (crap out).

This program continues play until either the pot is zero or the bet is not positive. It uses the in_bet function from the Acey-deucey Program, Listing 10.9. The roll_dice function returns the value of a throw. The value is compared in the switch statement to the possible outcomes. If a win is undetermined, the while loop is repeated until the throw is either the value of point or CRAP_OUT. The out_win function outputs the current amount after each throw.

If DEBUG had been #defined when this program was compiled, then the printf calls would be included in the executable code. If RAND_MACRO was #defined, the rand macro would be defined. This macro generates a known sequence of numbers and is useful in testing the program.

**Listing 11.1 Craps Game**

```c
#include <stdio.h>
#define TRUE 1
#define FALSE 0
#define UNDETERMINED -1
#define START_POT 100              /* Starting value for pot */
#define MAX_DIE 6                  /* Maximum value for a die */

/* Values for the various throws */
#define BOX_CARS 12
#define SNAKE_EYES 2
#define THREE_EYES 3
#define CRAP_OUT 7
#define WINNER1 7
#define WINNER2 11

/* Determine whether to use macro or function for rand() */
#ifdef RAND_MACRO
int random;
#define rand() (random++)
#else
#include <stdlib.h>                /* For rand */
#endif

int main()
/* Plays craps */
    {
    int pot;                       /* Current pot */
    int bet;                       /* Current bet */
    int throw;                     /* Value for current throw */
    int point;                     /* Point to be made */
    int win;                       /* Flag whether a win */

    /* Initialize */
    printf("\n Welcome to craps");
    pot = START_POT;

    while (pot > 0)
        {
        /* Get a bet */
        bet = in_bet(pot);
        if (bet <= 0)
            break;

        /* First throw */
        throw = roll_dice();
        switch (throw)
            {
```

```
        case SNAKE_EYES:
        case THREE_EYES:
        case BOX_CARS:        /* All are losers */
            win = FALSE;
            break;
        case WINNER1:
        case WINNER2:         /* Both are winners */
            win = TRUE;
            break;
        default:              /* Must make a point */
            win = UNDETERMINED;
            point = throw;
            break;
            }
        pot = out_win(win, bet, pot);

        /* Have a point to make */
        while (win == UNDETERMINED)
            {
            throw = roll_dice();
            if (throw == CRAP_OUT)
                win = FALSE;
            else if (throw == point)
                win = TRUE;
            pot = out_win(win, bet, pot);
            }
        }      /* End of loop on pot */

    printf("\n You leave the game with %d", pot);
    exit(0);
    }

/****************************** OUT_WIN ******************************/
int out_win(win, bet, pot)
/* Determines the new pot based on the result */
int win;                      /* Current win flag */
int bet;                      /* Current bet */
int pot;                      /* Current pot */

    {
#ifdef DEBUG
    printf("\n OUTWIN receiving win %d bet %d pot %d",
        win, bet, pot);
#endif

    switch (win)
        {
    case TRUE:
```

```
              printf("\n You won");
              pot += bet;
              printf("\n Your pot is %d", pot);
              break;
       case FALSE:
              printf("\n You lost");
              pot -= bet;
              printf("\n Your pot is now %d", pot);
              break;
       case UNDETERMINED:
              printf("\n Keep rolling");
              break;
              }

#ifdef DEBUG
       printf("\n OUTWIN returning %d", pot);
#endif

       return pot;
       }


/****************************** ROLL_DICE ******************************/

int roll_dice()
/* Rolls dice and prints their value */
       {
       int die_one;        /* Count for die one */
       int die_two;        /* Count for die two */
       int total;          /* Total for two dice */

       die_one = rand() % MAX_DIE + 1;
       die_two = rand() % MAX_DIE + 1;
       total = die_one + die_two;
       printf("\n Your throw is %d and %d", die_one, die_two);

#ifdef DEBUG
       printf("\n ROLL_DICE returning %d", total);
#endif

       return total;
       }
```

## SUMMARY

- The #define directive specifies text to be inserted in the program.
- A macro permits the user to specify the values of tokens that are replaced in #define text.
- The #include directive specifies a source file to insert into the code before compilation.
- Conditional compilation directives allow the same source file to be compiled in various ways, depending on #define values and other testable values.

## SELF-TEST

1. What is the value of i in the following?

```
#define SOMETHING 1 + 2
#define SOMETHING_ELSE 3
int i;
i = SOMETHING * SOMETHING_ELSE;
```

2. What is the value of j?

```
#if INT_MAX< CHAR_MAX
    j = 7;
#else
    j = 5;
#endif
```

3. Given

```
#define a 7
#define A a + 1
#define B(x) x + 3
c = B(A);
```

what value will be assigned to c?

## ANSWERS

1. 7. When the substitutions are made, the statement looks like i = 1 + 2 * 3;.
2. 5. The size of an int is never less than the size of a char, so the statement j = 5; is compiled.

3. 11. The interpretation is

```
c = B(A);
c = A + 3;
c = a + 1 + 3;
c = 7 + 1 + 3;
```

## PROBLEMS

1. Set up a list of #defines for constants you might use for a geometry program.
2. Put some conditional #ifdef DEBUG directives in one of the functions you have written.
3. Look at stdio.h and see whether your compiler implements getchar and putchar as macros. If so, write a short program that calls either of these without having a #include <stdio.h> and see what happens.
4. Look at the ctype.h file for your compiler to see whether isdigit and the other character functions are defined as macros.
5. Revise Listing 3.3 using the concepts presented in this chapter. Keep in mind that the program must be easy to read, especially by novice programmers.
6. Revise a prior program you have written using the concepts presented in this chapter. Keep in mind that the program must be easy to read, especially by novice programmers.
7. The names of operating system functions vary from machine to machine and from compiler to compiler. Explain how you might write a program that accounts for these variations. Show how your program could be written so that one version could be compiled on different systems and by different compilers without any changes.

# Chapter Twelve

# Pointers Revisited

Pointers can be used in many ways. They can point to memory locations that are allocated by the operating system. As part of structures, they can help form linked lists, which make it easy to add an item between two previously stored items. Function pointers can be used to pass addresses of functions to other functions.

## POINTERS TO POINTERS

Pointers can point not only to simple data types, but also to other pointers. Suppose you had this code, as annotated:

```
int x = 6;                  x has address 602
int *p_int = &x;            p_int has address 610
int **p_p_int = &p_int;     p_p_int has address 620[1]
```

These values are diagramed in Figure 12.1. If you suppose pointers are four bytes long and ints are two bytes, then the following expressions yield the values shown.

| Expression | Value | |
|---|---|---|
| x | 6 | (Integer) |
| p_int | 602 | (Pointer to integer) |
| *p_int | 6 | (Integer) |
| p_p_int | 610 | (Pointer to pointer to integer) |
| *p_p_int | 602 | (Pointer to integer) |

---

[1] Note that you would declare and assign this as

```
int **p_p_int;
p_p_int = &p_int;
```

*Variable Address*

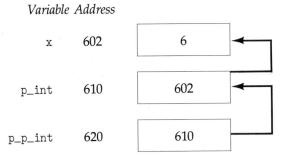

**Figure 12.1 Pointer to Pointer**

| | | |
|---|---|---|
| **p_p_int | 6 | (Integer) |
| p_p_int + 1 | 614 | (Pointer to pointer to integer) |
| *p_p_int + 1 | 606 | (Pointer to integer) |
| **p_p_int + 1 | 7 | (Integer) |

Listing 8.14 broke up a string into words using an array of pointers. The function called next_word in Listing 12.1 operates in another manner. It returns two values—a pointer to the word and the length of the word. The string is parsed in the same manner as in word_break. However, a pointer to the start of the word is placed in the location pointed to by pword. pword is a pointer to a variable that is a pointer to char. Each time next_word is called, the value of string should be incremented by the size of the word plus one for the NUL character.

**Listing 12.1 Next Word**

```
#include <ctype.h>

int next_word(string, pword)
/* Returns pointer to start of a word in string */
char *string;                   /* String to look for word in */
char **pword;                   /* Pointer to start of word is put in the
                                   variable whose address is passed */
                                /* Returns
                                      length of word
                                      - length of word if last word
                                      0 if at end and no word
                                */
                                /* Note that it puts a NUL into string at the
                                   end of each word */
{
int count;                      /* Count of characters in word */

count = 0;

/* Take off leading nonletters */
while (!isalpha(*string))
```

```
        {
        string++;
        }
/* Put the start of word into the pointer whose address was passed,
    then loop until at end of word */
*pword = string;
while (isalpha(*string))
        {
        string++;
        count++;
        }

/* See if at end */
if (*string == '\0')
        count = -count;
/* Put on a terminating null */
if (count > 0)
        *string = '\0';

return count;
}
```

/*******************************  MAIN  *******************************/

```
#include <stdio.h>

int main()
/* Breaks a string into words */
    {
    static char string[] =
        "The rain in Spain stays mainly on the plain";
                                /* String to break into words */
    char *pword;                /* Pointer to word */
    char *pstring;              /* Points to string to break up */
    int count;                  /* Size of word */

    pstring = string;
    do
        {
        count = next_word(pstring, &pword);
        if (count > 0)
            {
            printf("\n Word length is %d word is %s ",
                count, pword);
            /* Step over word and NUL */
            pstring = pstring + count + 1;
```

```
            }
        if (count < 0)
            {
            /* Last word */
            printf("\n Word length is %d word is %s ",
                    -count, pword);
            printf("\n Last word");
            }
        }
    while (count > 0);

    exit(0);
    }
```

The output for this listing looks like

```
Word length is 3 word is The
Word length is 4 word is rain
Word length is 2 word is in
Word length is 5 word is Spain
Word length is 5 word is stays
Word length is 6 word is mainly
Word length is 2 word is on
Word length is 3 word is the
Word length is 5 word is plain
Last word
```

How you choose to write the function depends on the ultimate use of the function. The word_break is limited, because only MAX_POINTER words can be found. However, word_break is more efficient than calling next_word many times and is less dependent on the user incrementing the starting position each time. Note that both of these routines write NUL characters into the passed string, so you should not pass a string that is in read-only memory.

## THE argc AND argv ARGUMENTS

Two arguments are passed to the function called main when the program begins. They represent what was typed on the command line to the operating system when the program was executed. These arguments are conventionally named argc and argv. The argc argument is the count of how many words (strings of characters separated by spaces) the program contains. The argv argument is an array of pointers to these words. These function just as if word_break was called from the command line. The first element in argv usually points to the name of the program. If you use these, your main function may look like

```
#define FALSE 0
#define TRUE 1
static int debug;              /* Debug flag */

main(argc,argv)
int argc;
char *argv[];
    {

    debug=FALSE;
    if (argc>1)
        {
        /* Test to see if debug should be set */
        if (toupper(*argv[1])=='D')
            debug=TRUE;
        ...
```

The characters in the strings may be converted to lowercase, depending on your operating system, so if you are testing for a specific character, you ought to use toupper, as shown.

By convention, options on the command line are passed by preceding them with a hyphen. Filenames are passed with no hyphen. So the main function code might look like

```
if (argc > 1)
    {
    for (i=1; i < argc; i++)
        {
        if (*argv[i] == '-')
            /* check for option */
            {
            if (toupper(argv[i][1]) == 'D')
                debug=TRUE;
            ...
```

For example, if you executed this program as

```
test -R -D
```

then the values of argc and argv[2] would be

---

[2] Some systems cannot set the value of the argv[0] (shown in the second line of the list here) and will set it to point to a NULL string ("").

| Expression | Value |
|------------|-------|
| argc | 3 |
| argv[0] | "test" |
| argv[1] | "-R" |
| argv[2] | "-D" |

Chapter 13 contains a file copying program that uses the argc and argv arguments.

## POINTERS AND ALLOCATED MEMORY

The storage types described so far (automatic, external, static) are all provided by the compiler. Either storage is allocated only while you are using a function (automatic) or during the entire program execution (external and static). There is a compromise between these two positions. This is memory that can remain allocated after a function is exited, but that may not be needed during the full program execution. Such a process is called *allocated storage*. It is allocated from the heap, as shown in Figure 12.2.

The C library provides several routines that allocate storage. The most common is malloc. This returns a pointer to the first byte of a block of memory. It requires the stdlib.h file. Its calling sequence is

```
void *malloc(size)
/* Allocates a block of memory */
size_t size;                    /* Number of bytes to allocate */
```

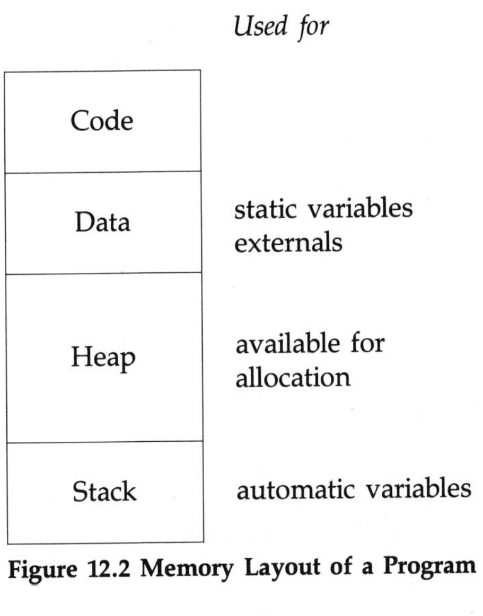

*Used for*

| | |
|---|---|
| Code | |
| Data | static variables<br>externals |
| Heap | available for<br>allocation |
| Stack | automatic variables |

**Figure 12.2 Memory Layout of a Program**

```
/* Returns pointer to block, if available */
/* NULL if not available */
```

The `void` data type declaration means that this function returns a pointer value that can be assigned to any type of pointer, such as a pointer to `int`s or a pointer to `char`. The data type `size_t` is a `typedef` that is the equivalent of an integer. The corresponding routine to deallocate memory is `free`. It is passed an address that must have been returned by an allocation function as `malloc`. If the address is anything else, the program will not behave correctly. The calling sequence for the declaration is

```
void free(pointer)
/* Frees a block of memory */
void *pointer;               /* Pointer to block to free */
```

One common use for `malloc` is getting storage for arrays, whose size may vary each time the program runs. Another use is for self-referential structures, which are covered later in this chapter. If you call it as

```
size_t size;
int *an_array;
an_array=malloc(size * sizeof(int));
```

then you could reference the storage as `an_array[0]` to `an_array[size-1]`, just as if you had declared `an_array` to be a regular array.

---

### Style Tip

Static or external arrays are fixed in size. The size of allocated arrays can be determined at execution time. They can decrease the memory requirements of your program.

---

## MAKING ALLOCATION EFFICIENT

There is a good deal of overhead associated with allocating and freeing memory. This overhead is both in time and space. The memory allocator keeps its own linked list of allocated and unallocated portions of memory. This requires room each time an allocation occurs. There is an alternative method of allocating memory to make it more efficient and safe.

The allocation routines work regardless of the size of elements. For general applications, an allocation routine should have all these capabilities. However, specific applications may require more efficiency or control over the allocation process. For example, suppose the function was in a real time system. Suddenly the program runs out of memory. The operator is faced with an error stating

```
OUT OF MEMORY
```

and some error explanation as

```
Increase main memory
```

It might be better to set some expected maximum plus an overflow factor (called a "fudge factor" in engineering applications). When the stack gets close to the expected maximum, the message could appear as

```
STACK SPACE FOR XXXX PROCESS IS APPROACHING DESIGN LIMITATION
```

and an error explanation might be

```
Contact application programmer so space can be increased.
```

As the stack comes closer to the maximum, the message could be made stronger.

In addition, writing your own allocation routines enables you to use indices rather than addresses for pointers to structures. This may save space (such as 2 bytes for an int versus 4 bytes for a pointer), but its prime use is in debugging. It is far easier to check whether an index is out of bounds than it is to see whether an address points at an incorrect memory location.

The following functions form a package for efficiently allocating storage. The init_element routine calls the operating system to get all the required memory at one time. The allocated array is a map of which elements in the memory have been allocated by alloc_element. That function checks the map to see whether there is a zero bit by calling first_bit_not_set. If there is, init_element returns the address of the corresponding location in memory. The dealloc_element routine simply checks to see which location corresponds to the address that is to be deallocated. If the address is bad (that is, it was not an allocated address), dealloc_element returns BAD_ADDRESS. The functions call the bit functions from Listing 9.6.

**Listing 12.2 Memory Allocation Functions**

```c
#include <stdlib.h>

#define MAX_ELEMENTS 100

static char allocated[(MAX_ELEMENTS + 7) / 8];
                                /* Bit array for allocation */
```

```
static int size;                          /* Size of allocation */
static void *memory_pointer;              /* Points at allocated memory */
int current_allocated = 0;                /* Number allocated */
int max_allocated;                        /* Maximum to allocate */

#define BAD_ADDRESS 1                     /* Trying to free unallocated ad-
                                             dress */
#define OKAY 0
```

/***************************** INIT_ELEMENT *****************************/

```
int init_element(size_element, number_element)
/* Initialize the memory allocation system */
int size_element;                         /* Size of an element */
int number_element;                       /* How many elements to allocate */
                                          /* Return
                                                  number_element or
                                                  0 if no room
                                          */
    {
    int ret;                /* Return value */
    int i;                  /* Index into allocation buffer */

    /* Get the memory */
    memory_pointer = calloc(size_element, number_element);
    if (memory_pointer == NULL)
        ret = 0;
    else
        {
        size = size_element;
        ret = number_element;
        max_allocated = number_element;
        current_allocated = 0;
        /* Clear the allocation buffer */
        for (i = 0; i < size / 8; i++)
            {
            allocated[i] = 0;
            }
        }
        return ret;
    }
```

/***************************** ALLOC_ELEMENT *****************************/

```
void *alloc_element(p_remaining)
/* Allocates an element */
int *p_remaining;                           /* Where to put count remaining */
                                            /* Returns pointer to element */
```

```
        {
        int result;              /* Result of find */
        void *address;           /* Address to return */

        if (current_allocated < max_allocated)
             {
             result = first_bit_not_set(allocated, sizeof (allocated));
             if (result >= 0)
                  {
                  set_bit(allocated, result);
                  address = memory_pointer + (result * size);
                  current_allocated++;
                  }
             }
        else
             address = NULL;

        *p_remaining = max_allocated - current_allocated;

        return address;
        }

/**************************** DEALLOC_ELEMENT ****************************/

int dealloc_element(address)
void *address;                   /* Address to deallocate */
                                 /* Returns
                                        OKAY if deallocation worked
                                        BAD_ADDRESS if address was bad
                                 */
        {
        int element;             /* Which element in array */
        int ret;                 /* Return value */

        element = (address - memory_pointer) / size;
        if (element >= 0 && element < max_allocated)
             {
             clear_bit(allocated, element);
             current_allocated--;
             ret = OKAY;
             }
        else
             ret = BAD_ADDRESS;

        return ret;
        }
```

```
/************************ ADDITIONAL BIT FUNCTIONS *********************/

#define SIZE_CHAR 8

int first_bit_not_set(bit_array,size_array)
/* Finds first bit not set in an array */
unsigned char bit_array[];          /* Array to set bit in */
int size_array;                     /* Size of array in chars */
                                    /* Returns
                                         index of bit
                                         -1 if not found
                                    */
    {
    int index;                      /* Which char to use */
    int mask_index;                 /* Which bit in the char */
    int result;                     /* Index of bit */

    result=-1;

    for (index=0;index<size_array;index++)
        {
        /* See whether the char is all bits set */
        if (bit_array[index]!=0XFF)
            {
            /* If not, find out which bit is not set */
            for (mask_index=0;mask_index<SIZE_CHAR;mask_index++)
                {
                if (bit_masks[mask_index] & bit_array[index]==0)
                    {
                    result=index*SIZE_CHAR + mask_index;
                    break;
                    }
                }
            break;
            }
        }

    return result;
    }
```

## SELF-REFERENTIAL STRUCTURES—LINKED LIST

Self–referential structures contain one or more members that point to other structures of the same type. This enables you to link structures in chains, in either a simple list or in complex trees. Simple lists are covered here. The binary tree is explained later in this chapter.

A linked list is a chain of structures. Each structure in the list points to another structure. The last structure in the list contains an indication that it is last by pointing to an invalid place (the null pointer). Each structure in the list also holds the value of a data item. You can use a linked list in place of an array. An array is declared to contain a given number of data elements. The advantage of a linked list is that the number of data items it can hold is limited only by the size of memory.

You can construct a linked list to store data in an organized manner. This program uses links to store words. Each link will contain a string representing a word. The link will point to the next word in the list, if any. The words will be kept in alphabetical order (ASCII sort order).

This is a one-way linked list, because each link only contains a pointer to the next link. You could make this a two-way link by having each link have pointers to the next and previous links. The problem set will examine this possibility.

Each value is kept in a structure of type s_link. The link stores both the value and a pointer to the next link. When an item is added to the list, memory for a link is obtained from malloc. The pointer in the link is set to point to the next link, and the pointer in the previous link is set to point to the new link.

The link functions are divided into several portions. The make_link function gets memory for a link and initializes it. It is called by add_list every time a new link is required. That function searches all the links current in the list to see where to put a word. If the word is already on the list, it does not add it. The end of the list is found when the pointer to the next link is NULL.

The root variable points to the start of the list. A word to be added can come before the first link or after it. If the word comes before, root is set to point to the new link. Otherwise, the new link's pointer is set to the pointer in the link it follows, and the pointer is set to point to the new link. The search_list function determines whether a word is on the list.

**Listing 12.3 Linked List Functions**

```c
#include <stdio.h>
#include <stdlib.h>              /* For malloc */

#define FOREVER 1
#define TRUE 1
#define FALSE 0

#define SIZE_WORD 15            /* Size of word in a link */
struct s_link                   /* Structure for a link */
    {
    struct s_link *next;        /* Points to next link */
    char word[SIZE_WORD + 1];  /* Word value for this link with NUL */
    };

static struct s_link *root;     /* Points to the first link on the list */
```

```
/*************************** MAKE_LINK **********************************/

struct s_link *make_link(new_word)
/* Create a new link */
char new_word[];                        /* Word to put in the link */
                                        /* Returns pointer to the new link */
    {
    struct s_link *pointer;        /* Pointer for new link */

    /* Get memory for the link */
    pointer = (struct s_link *) malloc(sizeof(struct s_link));

    if (pointer != NULL)
        {
        /* Move the word into it */
        strncpy(pointer->word, new_word, SIZE_WORD);
        /* Put a NUL on it */
        pointer->word[SIZE_WORD] = '\0';
        pointer->next = NULL;
        }

    return pointer;
    }

/***************************** ADD_LIST ********************************/

int add_list(new_word)
/* Add a word to the list */
char new_word[];                        /* Word to add */
                                        /* Returns
                                           NULL if not added
                                           address of new link if added
                                        */
    {
    int compare;                   /* Result of comparison */
    struct s_link *new_pointer;    /* Pointer for new link */
    struct s_link *pointer;        /* Pointer to each link */
    struct s_link *previous_pointer; /* Pointer to previous link */
    int to_add;                    /* Whether to add or not */
    int ret;                       /* Return */

    if (root == NULL)
        {
        /* First word, set up the root */
        root = make_link(new_word);
        new_pointer = root;
        }
```

```
else
    {
    /* Start at the root */
    pointer = root;
    previous_pointer = NULL;

    while (FOREVER)
        {
        compare = strncmp(new_word, pointer->word, SIZE_WORD);
        if (compare == 0)
            {
            /* Already in list */
            to_add = FALSE;
            break;
            }
        else if (compare < 0)
            {
            /* Past where it should be in the list */
            /* Insert it in the list after previous link */
            pointer = previous_pointer;
            to_add = TRUE;
            break;
            }
        else
            {
            /* Keep going in the list */
            if (pointer->next == NULL)
                {
                /* At end, put it here */
                to_add = TRUE;
                break;
                }
            else
                {
                /* Not at end, keep going */
                previous_pointer = pointer;
                pointer = pointer->next;
                }
            }
        }                    /* End of the while loop */

    if (to_add)
        {
        new_pointer = make_link(new_word);
        /* If okay, then put it in the list */
        if (new_pointer != NULL)
            {
```

```
                              if (pointer != NULL)
                                  {
                                  /* Not at beginning of list */
                                  new_pointer->next = pointer->next;
                                  pointer->next = new_pointer;
                                  }
                              else
                                  {
                                  /* Comes before the first link on the list */
                                  new_pointer->next = root;
                                  root = new_pointer;
                                  }
                              }
                      }
              }           /* End of if (root != NULL) */

      if (new_pointer == NULL)
          ret = FALSE;
      else
          ret = TRUE;

      return ret;
      }

/*************************** SEARCH_LIST ****************************/

int search_list(match_word)
/* Searches list for a word */
char match_word[];              /* Word to match */
                                /* Returns
                                     TRUE if found
                                     FALSE if not found
                                */
      {
      int found;                /* Result of search */
      int compare;              /* Result of comparison */
      struct s_link *pointer;   /* Pointer to links */

      found = FALSE;
      pointer = root;
      while (pointer != NULL)
          {
          compare = strncmp(match_word, pointer->word, SIZE_WORD);
          if (compare == 0)
              {
              /* Found it */
              found = TRUE;
```

```
                break;
                }
        else if (compare < 0)
                {
                /* Passed it by */
                found = FALSE;
                break;
                }
        else
                {
                if (pointer->next == NULL)
                    {
                    /* End of list */
                    found = FALSE;
                    break;
                    }
                else
                    /* Go to next item on list */
                    pointer = pointer->next;
                }
        }

    return found;
    }

/*************************** PRINT_LIST ****************************/

void print_list()
/* Prints the list */
    {
    struct s_link *pointer;          /* Pointer to links */

    for (pointer = root; (pointer != NULL); pointer = pointer->next)
        {
        printf("\n Word is %s", pointer->word);
        }

    return;
    }

/*************************** MAIN ****************************/

#define NWORDS (sizeof(words)/sizeof(char *))

int main()
/* Test routine for the list functions */
```

```
        {
        static char *words[] = {"RUN", "WALK", "CRAWL", "GO", "RUN"};
                                        /* Last one is a duplicate */
        int result;                     /* Results from functions */
        int i;                          /* Index for words */

        /* Add the words */
        for (i = 0; i < NWORDS; i++)
            {
            result = add_list(words[i]);
            printf("\n Adding to list %s result is %d", words[i], result);
            print_list();
            }

        /* Look for some words */
        for (i = 0; i < NWORDS; i++)
            {
            result = search_list(words[i]);
            printf("\n Searching for %s Result is %d", words[i], result);
            }

        printf("\n Print of list is");
        print_list();

        exit(0);
        }
```

Figure 12.3 shows how the created list appears. The printout from this program
looks like this:

```
Adding to list RUN result is 1
Word is RUN
Adding to list WALK result is 1
Word is RUN
```

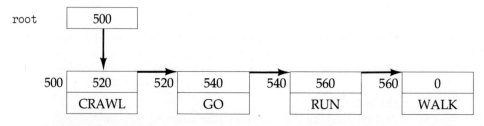

**Figure 12.3 Linked List**

```
Word is WALK
Adding to list CRAWL result is 1
Word is CRAWL
Word is RUN
Word is WALK
Adding to list GO result is 1
Word is CRAWL
Word is GO
Word is RUN
Word is WALK
Adding to list RUN result is 0
Word is CRAWL
Word is GO
Word is RUN
Word is WALK
Searching for RUN Result is 1
Searching for WALK Result is 1
Searching for CRAWL Result is 1
Searching for GO Result is 1
Searching for RUN Result is 1
Print of list is
Word is CRAWL
Word is GO
Word is RUN
Word is WALK
```

You may note that it is very easy to insert a value in a linked list. Only two pointers need to be changed. If you try to insert a value into the middle of an array, all subsequent values have to be moved one element down. The same comparison applies to deletion of a value. However, without using an index, you need to search the entire list for an item link by link, even if it is kept in order. With an array that is kept in order, you could use a binary search.

## BINARY TREE

Another way to have data easily searchable is to keep it in a binary tree. A *tree* is a type of linked list. Each node in a tree has two links to other nodes. The links are to nodes that contain key values that come before and after the key value of the node. These are called the *left and right pointers.* A *binary tree* has only right and left pointers. Figure 12.4 diagrams how a binary tree appears. A *nonbinary tree* can have more than two pointers. This possibility is left for advanced books.[3]

---

[3] See Knuth, *Sorting and Searching,* and Wirth, *Algorithms and Data Structures.* These books are listed in the bibliography.

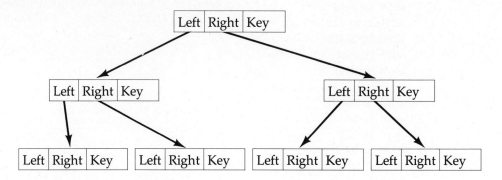

**Figure 12.4 Diagram of Binary Tree**

If nodes are added to a tree in a sorted order, the tree will degenerate into a single linked list. There are several methods for keeping a tree balanced so this does not happen. These techniques are covered in the reference books.

The structure template s_node is used for each node in the tree. Each time a new node is needed, memory is allocated and initialized by make_node. The add_tree function searches the tree for the proper spot to place a new value. If the value is already in the tree, the word is not added. search_tree searches for a particular value. To simplify the initialization, the first node is created by tree_start.

Both add_tree and search_tree are implemented as recursive routines. If the value of the current node does not match the word to be added or matched, either the right or left link is chosen. If the pointer to that link is NULL, this is the place to add either the word or to indicate that the word is not in the tree. If the pointer is not NULL, the functions call themselves to check that node.

**Listing 12.4 Binary Tree**

```
#define TRUE 1
#define FALSE 0

#define SIZE_WORD 20

#include <stdio.h>
#include <stdlib.h>

struct s_node                           /* This is a node */
    {
    struct s_node *left;                /* Left pointer */
    struct s_node *right;               /* Right pointer */
    char word[SIZE_WORD + 1];           /* Value for the node with NULL */
    };
```

```
/***************************** MAKE_NODE *****************************/

struct s_node *make_node(new_word)
/* Makes a new node */
char new_word[];                        /* Word to put into new node */
                                        /* Returns
                                                pointer to new node
                                                NULL if no room
                                        */
    {
    struct s_node *pointer;             /* Pointer to return */

    pointer = (struct s_node *) malloc(sizeof(struct s_node));
    if (pointer != (struct s_node *) NULL)
        {
        strncpy(pointer->word, new_word, SIZE_WORD);
        pointer->word[SIZE_WORD] = '\0';
        pointer->left = (struct s_node *) NULL;
        pointer->right = (struct s_node *) NULL;
        }

    return pointer;
    }

/***************************** ADD_TREE *****************************/

int add_tree(pointer, new_word)
/* Add a node to the tree */
struct s_node *pointer;                 /* Pointer to current node */
char new_word[SIZE_WORD];               /* Word to add */
                                        /* Returns
                                                TRUE if added
                                                FALSE if not added
                                        */
    {
    int added;                          /* Flag if added */
    int compare;                        /* Comparison result */

    compare = strncmp(new_word, pointer->word, SIZE_WORD);
    if (compare == 0)
        /* Already in tree */
        added = FALSE;
    else if (compare < 0)
        {
        /* Go to left branch */
        if (pointer->left == (struct s_node *) NULL)
            {
```

```
                          pointer->left = make_node(new_word);
                          added = TRUE;
                          }
                 else
                      added = add_tree(pointer->left, new_word);
                 }
         else
             {
             /* Go to right branch */
             if (pointer->right == (struct s_node *) NULL)
                      {
                      pointer->right = make_node(new_word);
                      added = TRUE;
                      }
             else
                      added = add_tree(pointer->right, new_word);
             }
         return added;
         }
```

```
/****************************** TREE_START ******************************/
```

```
struct s_node *tree_start(new_word)
/* Starts the tree */
char new_word[SIZE_WORD];          /* Word to put into first node */
     {
     return make_node(new_word);
     }
```

```
/****************************** SEARCH_TREE ******************************/
```

```
int search_tree(pointer, match_word)
/* Searches a tree for a match */
struct s_node *pointer;            /* Pointer to current node */
char match_word[SIZE_WORD];        /* Word to search for */
                                   /* Returns
                                           TRUE if found
                                           FALSE if not found
                                   */
     {
     int found;                    /* Found flag */
     int compare;                  /* Result of comparison */

     compare = strncmp(match_word, pointer->word, SIZE_WORD);
     if (compare == 0)
         found = TRUE;
     else if (compare < 0)
         {
```

```
        /* Go to left branch */
        if (pointer->left == (struct s_node *) NULL)
            found = FALSE;
        else
            found = search_tree(pointer->left, match_word);
        }
    else
        {
        /* Go to right branch */
        if (pointer->right == (struct s_node *) NULL)
            found = FALSE;
        else
            found = search_tree(pointer->right, match_word);
        }

    return found;
    }

/****************************** MAIN ********************************/

static char *words[] = {"RUN", "SPOT", "RUN", "JANE", "DICK"};
                                        /* Test array of words */

#define NWORDS (sizeof(words)/sizeof(char *))  /* Size of test array */

int main()
/* Test program for the tree */
    {
    struct s_node *root;            /* Pointer to root node */
    int ret;                        /* Return value from
                                            functions */
    int i;                          /* Index for words */
    void print_node();              /* Function declaration */
    void print_word();              /* Function declaration */
    void in_order();                /* Function declaration */

    /* Add the first word */
    root = tree_start(words[0]);

    /* Add the remaining words */
    for (i = 1; i < NWORDS; i++)
        {
        ret = add_tree(root, words[i]);
        printf("\n Adding %s return is %d", words[i], ret);
        }

    /* Search for a word */
```

```
        ret = search_tree(root, words[3]);
        printf("\n Searching for %s return is %d", words[3], ret);

        /* Try searching for one that is not there */
        ret = search_tree(root, "NONE");
        printf("\n Search for NONE return is %d", ret);

        /* Print the tree */
        printf("\n Print of tree in order is");
        in_order(root, print_word);

        /* Print the tree */
        printf("\n Print of nodes in tree in order is");
        in_order(root, print_node);

        exit(0);
        }

/****************************** IN_ORDER ******************************/

void in_order(pointer, function)
/* Performs a function on a tree in order */
struct s_node *pointer;      /* Points to the current node */
int (*function)();           /* Points to function for each node */
    {
    if (pointer != (struct s_node *) NULL)
        {
        in_order(pointer->left, function);
        (*function)(pointer);
        in_order(pointer->right, function);
        }
    return;
    }

/****************************** PRINT_WORD ******************************/

void print_word(pointer)
/* Prints the word in a node */
struct s_node *pointer;      /* Points to which node to print */
    {
    printf("\n Node is %s", pointer->word);
    return;
    }

/****************************** PRINT_NODE ******************************/

void print_node(pointer)
/* Prints the values of a node */
```

```
struct s_node *pointer;      /* Points to which node to print */
    {
    printf("\n Word %-10.10s Node %8p, left is %8p, right is %8p",
        pointer->word, pointer, pointer->left, pointer->right);
    }
```

The finished tree appears in Figure 12.5. The printout from this program looks like

```
Adding SPOT return is 1
Adding RUN return is 0
Adding JANE return is 1
Adding DICK return is 1
Searching for JANE return is 1
Search for NONE return is 0
Print of tree in order is
Node is DICK
Node is JANE
Node is RUN
Node is SPOT
Print of nodes in tree in order is
Word DICK    Node 5d5f000c,    left is        0,    right is        0
Word JANE    Node 5d560010,    left is 5d5f000c,    right is        0
Word RUN     Node 5d07000c,    left is 5d560010,    right is 5d0f0004
Word SPOT    Node 5d0f0004,    left is        0,    right is        0
```

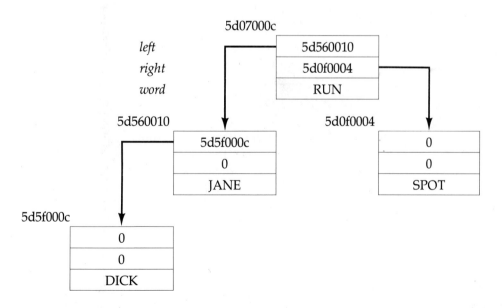

**Figure 12.5 Binary Tree for the Example**

## POINTERS TO FUNCTIONS

The pointers described so far point to data objects. C provides pointers to functions, as well. You declare a pointer as a function returning a particular type by coding a statement in the form

```
data-type (*pointer-name)();
```

If a function prototype or a call to the function has appeared, you can set the value of the pointer.

```
int int_function();              prototype
int (*p_function)()=int_function;   declaring and initializing pointer to
                                     function.
```

The name of a function is its address, so &int_function is not required. Because function parentheses () have higher precedence than the pointer operator *, if you code

```
int *p_function();
```

this declares p_function as a function returning a pointer to an int. Once you have declared and assigned a value to p_function, you can use it as

```
(*p_function)(5);
```

which calls the int_function() and passes it the value of 5 as a parameter.[4]

## PASSING FUNCTIONS AS PARAMETERS

You can pass a pointer to a function to a routine, but not the function itself. A common use for this is to pass the comparison function to a sort routine. For example, the qsort function in the library is called with

```
qsort(array,size,size_of_element,compare)
char array[];            /* Array to be sorted */
```

---

[4] With ANSI C you can specify this call to the function as either the above or as p_function(5); because p_function has been declared as a pointer to a function, it can interpret this as a call to the function pointed to.

```
int size;               /* Number of elements in array */
int size_of_element;    /* Size of an element */
int (*compare)();       /* Comparison function */
```

The compare function is passed two pointers to values to compare. For example, if you wanted an ascending sort, you would use a function like

```
int ascending(pvalue_a, pvalue_b)
/* Compares two integer values */
int *pvalue_a;          /* Pointer to first value */
int *pvalue_b;          /* Pointer to second value */
    {
    int ret;

    if (*pvalue_a < *pvalue_b)
        ret = -1;
    else if (*pvalue_a > *pvalue_b)
        ret = 1;
    else
        ret = 0;

    return ret;
    }
```

To sort an array, you would call qsort as

```
#define SIZE_ARRAY 5
int array[SIZE_ARRAY];
...
qsort(array, SIZE_ARRAY, sizeof(int), ascending);
```

You could create a routine to find the root of an equation by Newton-Raphson's approximation. This algorithm was described in Chapter 10. The function solve_for_zero is passed the addresses of two functions. One should return the value of f(x). The other should return the value of fprime(x), the derivative. The address of a variable is passed as the third parameter. The initial guess should be placed in this variable when the function is called. The solution will be placed in it when the function returns. It is possible there is no solution, so a limit (MAX_ITERATIONS) is placed on the number of times the function will loop. The function whose address was passed (function) is called, passed the value at pguess, and new_value is set to the returned value. If it is close to zero, then the solution has been found. Otherwise, another value for the *pguess is computed, using new_value and the address of the other function (function_deriv). For all, solve_for_zero returns either OKAY if it was able to find a solution or BAD_VALUE if unable to do so.

### Listing 12.5 Newton-Raphson

```
#include <stdio.h>
#define ERROR_VALUE .0000001     /* How close to the zero */
#define MAX_ITERATIONS 50        /* When to stop if not close */
#define BAD_VALUE -1             /* Unable to find solution */
#define OKAY 0                   /* Found solution */

#define TRUE 1
#define FALSE 0

/***************************** SOLVE FOR ZERO ****************************/

int solve_for_zero(function, function_deriv, pguess)
/* Solve for root of a function */
double (*function)();          /* Pointer to routine that returns value of
                                   function */
double (*function_deriv)();    /* Pointer to routine that returns derivative
                                   */
double *pguess;                /* Points to initial pguess of root */
                               /* Root is placed in *pguess, if found */
                               /* Returns
                                   OKAY if root found
                                   BAD_VALUE if
                                   MAX_ITERATIONS exceeded*/
    {
    int counter;          /* How many iterations */
    double new_value;     /* Keeps the new value of the function */
    int done;             /* Flag for finishing loop */
    int ret;              /* Return value */

    /* Initialize */
    done = FALSE;
    counter = 0;
    ret = OKAY;

    while (!done)
        {
        /* Call the function whose address was passed to get a value */
        new_value = (*function)(*pguess);

        /* This print statement is to show what is going on */
        printf("\n Values for pguess %lf new_value %lf",
            *pguess, new_value);

        if ((new_value < ERROR_VALUE) && (new_value > -ERROR_VALUE))
            done = TRUE;
        else
            {
```

```
                    /* Call the function whose address was passed to get the
                        derivative*/
                    *pguess = *pguess - new_value / (*function_deriv)(*pguess);

                    /* This print statement is to show what is going on */
                    printf("\n Iteration %d derivative %lf",
                        counter, (*function_deriv)(*pguess));

                    counter++;
                    if (counter > MAX_ITERATIONS)
                        {
                        ret = BAD_VALUE;
                        done = TRUE;
                        }
                    }
                }

        return ret;
        }

/******************************* FUNC *******************************/

double func(x)
/* Function to solve for */
double x;                               /* Value for x */
        {
        double result;                  /* Value to return */

        result = x * x - 16.;

        return result;
        }

/***************************** FUNC_DERIV *****************************/

double func_deriv(x)
/* Derivative of function to solve for */
double x;                               /* Value for x */
        {
        double result;                  /* Value to return */

        result = 2 * x;

        return result;
        }
```

```
/********************************* MAIN *********************************/

int main()
/* Demonstrates the solve for zero function */
    {
    double answer;              /* Where the answer is */
    int ret;                    /* Return value */

    answer = 1.0;

    ret = solve_for_zero(func, func_deriv, &answer);

    printf("\n Answer is %lf return was %d", answer, ret);

    exit(0);
    }
```

The output for this program looks like

```
Values for pguess 1.000000 new_value -15.000000
Iteration 0 derivative 17.000000
Values for pguess 8.500000 new_value 56.250000
Iteration 1 derivative 10.382353
Values for pguess 5.191176 new_value 10.948313
Iteration 2 derivative 8.273329
Values for pguess 4.136665 new_value 1.111995
Iteration 3 derivative 8.004515
Values for pguess 4.002258 new_value 0.018065
Iteration 4 derivative 8.000001
Values for pguess 4.000001 new_value 0.000005
Iteration 5 derivative 8.000000
Values for pguess 4.000000 new_value 0.000000
Answer is 4.000000 return was 0
```

Expanded function prototypes enable you to specify the parameter and return types for pointers to functions. The solve_for_zero function would have a prototype like

```
int solve_for_zero(double (*function)(double),
    double (*function_deriv)(double), double *pguess);
```

You can have an array of pointers to functions, but not an array of functions themselves. An array of pointers to functions would be declared as

```
#define S_ARRAY 5
double (*p_function_array[S_ARRAY])();
```

If you assigned

```
p_function_array[3]=func;
```

then

```
value=(*p_function[3])(3.2);
```

would call func and pass it the value 3.2. An array of pointers to functions is sometimes useful in interfacing device drivers to an operating system and in multiway branching.

## DOUBLE DIMENSIONED ARRAYS AND POINTERS

Double dimensioned arrays, which were discussed in Chapter 6, have an implicit pointer to pointer, as in

```
int array[5][3];
```
address 500

```
array[4]
*(array + 4)
```
where 4 is times sizeof(int [3])
address value of 524.

```
array[4][2]
*(*(array+4)+2)
```
where the 2 is sizeof (int)
value of int at address 528.

Using an array of pointers can speed up access to individual elements in a double dimensioned array. If you had a terminal screen image such as

```
#define NUM_ROWS 25
#define NUM_COLUMNS 80
char screen[NUM_ROWS][NUM_COLUMNS];
```

you could put a character into this array by something like

```
screen[row][col] = 'A';
```

A faster way of doing this is to create a second array and store the addresses of each row of the first array in it. This would be accomplished by

```
char *pscreen[NUM_ROWS];
for (i = 0; i < NUM_ROWS; i++)
    {
    pscreen[i] = screen[i];
    }
```

Using this second array, you can put a character into an element of screen coding:

```
*(pscreen[row]+col) = 'A';
```

Because array indexing is equivalent to pointer references, this could alternatively be written as

```
pscreen[row][col] = 'A';
```

Although the results of this precomputation take up memory, your program will run faster, because it will not have to perform these computations each time.

## MULTIPLE DIMENSIONS HANDLED AS ONE

You can use a multidimensional array as a parameter to a called function. The called function needs to know the size of all the dimensions except the first one to access each element properly. If you dealt with an entire multidimensional array as a whole, such as summing all the elements, you could treat it as a single dimensioned array. However, at times you may want to treat it as a two-dimensional object, say for summing each row.

If the number of elements in each row is constant, such as NUM_COLUMNS, you can write a summing function using a function header as shown in Chapter 6. Listing 12.6 shows such a function.

**Listing 12.6 sum_rows Function**

```
void sum_rows(sum_of_rows, array, number_rows)
int sum_of_rows[];                  /* Sum for the rows */
int array[][NUM_COLUMNS];           /* Array to sum */
int number_rows;                    /* Number of rows in array */
    {
    int row;                        /* Counter for rows */
    int col;                        /* Counter for columns */

    /* Add the elements in each row */
    for (row = 0; row < number_rows; row++)
        {
        /* Clear the sum */
        sum_of_rows[row] = 0.0;
        /* Add the elements in each row */
        for (col = 0; col < NUM_COLUMNS; col++)
            {
            sum_of_rows[row] += array[row][col];
            }
        }
```

```
    return;
    }
```

If you have these declarations:

```
#define NUM_ROWS 3

int my_array[NUM_ROWS][NUM_COLUMNS] =
    {
    {1,2},
    {3,4},
    {5,6}
    };

int sum_of_rows[NUM_ROWS];
```

then you can call this function with

```
sum_rows(sum_of_rows, my_array, NUM_ROWS);
```

If the size of each row is not constant, you will have to compute the actual offset from the beginning of the array. To do this, the macro elnum in the Listing 12.7 determines the equivalent index into a single dimension array for an element of a two-dimensional array.

**Listing 12.7 sum__rows Function**

```
#define elnum(row, col) (row * number_cols + col)
        /* At what index is an element in the array */

void sum_rows(sum_of_rows, array, number_rows, number_cols)
/* Computes the sum of each row in a two-dimensional array */
int sum_of_rows[];          /* Sums for the rows */
int array[];                /* Array to sum */
int number_rows;            /* Rows in array */
int number_cols;            /* Columns in array */

    {
    int row;                /* Counter for rows */
    int col;                /* Counter for columns */

    for (row = 0; row < number_rows; row++)
        {
        /* Clear the sum */
        sum_of_rows[row] = 0.0;
        /* Add the elements in each row */
        for (col = 0; col < number_cols; col++)
```

```
            {
            sum_of_rows[row] += array[elnum(row, col)];
            }
        }

    return;
    }
```

This `sum_rows` function is more general than the previous one. If you have the declarations previously shown, you call this function with[5]

```
sum_rows(sum_of_rows, my_array, NUM_ROWS, NUM_COLS);
```

Alternatively, you can use the following function that sums up all the elements in a single dimensioned array.

**Listing 12.8 sum_entire_array Function**

```
int sum_entire_array(array, number_elements)
/* Computes sum of all elements in an array */
int array[];                    /* Array to sum */
int number_elements;            /* Number of rows in array */
    {
    int element;                /* Counter for element */
    int sum;                    /* Sum */

    sum = 0;
    for (element = 0; element < number_elements; element++)
        {
        sum += array[element];
        }

    return sum;
    }
```

You could sum up each row in `my_array` by calling it with the individual sub-arrays in a loop, as in

```
for (i = 0; i < NUM_COLS; i++)
    {
    sum_of_rows[i] = sum_entire_array(my_array[i], NUM_COLS)
    }
```

---

[5] To use this with expanded function prototypes (see Chapter 10), you need to have a cast on the second parameter, as in

```
sum_rows(sum_of_rows, (int []) my_array, NUMBER_ROWS, NUMBER_COLS);
```

# COMPLEX DECLARATIONS WITH POINTERS

With the indirection declarator, you can create complex declarations of variables. In order to create or interpret these declarations, simply use the precedence rules. When in doubt, you can always overparenthesize your declarations.

| Declaration | Meaning |
|---|---|
| `int a;` | a is an integer |
| `int *p;` | p is a pointer; it points at integers |
| `int *p[3];` | p is an array (brackets have higher precedence than *); it is an array of 3 pointers; the pointers point at integers |
| `int (*p)[3];` | p is a pointer (* has higher precedence inside parentheses); it points to arrays three long; they are arrays of integers |
| `int p();` | p is a function; the function returns an integer |
| `int *p();` | p is a function (parentheses have precedence over *); it returns a pointer; the pointer points to integers |
| `int (*p)();` | p is a pointer (* has higher precedence due to the parentheses); it points to a function; the function returns an integer |
| `int *(*p)();` | p is a pointer; it points to a function; the function returns a pointer; the pointer points to integers |
| `int (*p[3])();` | p is an array; it is an array of three pointers; they point to functions; the functions return integers |

You should remember pointers can point to objects that are not just simple data types, as the declaration `int (*p)[3]` shows. If you had an array

```
static int an_array[7][3];
p = (int (*)[3]) an_array[2];
```

you could reference the elements of the an_array as summarized in Table 12.1.

The odd-looking cast simply converts the address given by an_array[2], a pointer to integers, to a pointer to a three-element array of integers.

The const data type modifier can promote confusion about what is actually constant when the modifier is combined with a pointer. Suppose you have[6]

```
int const *pointer_to_constant;
int * const constant_pointer;
```

then if you code the references to these variables as shown next, some of them cause compiler errors.

**Reference**                          **Result**

```
pointer_to_constant++;                 okay
(*pointer_to_constant)++;              error trying to modify const int
constant_pointer++;                    error trying to modify const pointer
(*constant_pointer)++;                 okay
```

The ANSI standard library uses const char * in function descriptions to show the values in the parameter string will not be modified.

---

## SAMPLE PROGRAM—TIC-TAC-TOE

This program keeps track of a game of tic-tac-toe between two players. Instead of fixing the number of boxes on a side to three, the number is entered on the command line when the program is executed. You might want to alter the pro-

**Table 12.1 Using a Pointer to Reference an Array**

| Reference | Equivalent | Type |
|---|---|---|
| p[0] | an_array[2] | pointer to int, &an_array[2][0] |
| p[-1] | an_array[1] | pointer to int, &an_array[1][0] |
| p[0][0] | an_array[2][0] | int |
| p[-1][0] | an_array[1][0] | int |

[6] This is the same as

const int *pointer_to_constant;

gram so that instead of asking player two for an input, the program decides where to move.

The playing board is a one-dimensional array. The functions act as if it is a two-dimensional array.

The `init_board` function clears the array `board`, which acts as the playing board. The `print_the_board` function prints the board. The `play_tic_tac_toe` function keeps track of the player's turns, calling `get_input` for each player's input. Finally, `check_for_win` tests the current board to see whether the current player has won.

---

**Pseudocode for Tic-Tac-Toe**

```
Initialize
Set current player to 1
  While not done
    Print the board
    Get input from current player
      Check for a win
      If win
        Then set done
      Else
        Switch to other player
```

---

**Listing 12.9 Tic-Tac-Toe Game**

```
#define SIDE_MAX 25        /* Maximum boxes on a side */
#define SIDE_MIN 3         /* Minimum boxes on a side */
#define TRUE 1
#define FALSE 0
#define PLAYER _1 1
#define PLAYER _2 2
#include <stdlib.h>        /* For malloc() */
#include <stdio.h>


/*************************** MAIN ****************************/

int main(argc, argv)
/* Plays tic-tac-toe */
/* This program is executed with the following progname size-of-side
 */
```

```
int argc;                              /* Count of arguments */
char *argv[];                          /* Pointers to arguments */
    {
    int side = 0;                      /* How many sides */
    char *board;                       /* Pointer to array to be allocated
                                          */


    /* Be sure there is at least one argument */
    if (argc < 2)
        printf("\n Usage is progname size-of-size");
    else
        {
        /* Scan the size of the side */
        sscanf(argv[1], "%d", &side);
        if (side > SIDE_MAX)
            {
            printf("\n Side too big %d reducing to %d", side, SIDE_MAX);
            side = SIDE_MAX;
            }
        else if (side < SIDE_MIN)
            {
            printf("\n Side too small %d expanding to %d", side,
                SIDE_MIN);
            side = SIDE_MIN;
            }

        /* Get memory for the board */
        board = malloc(side * side);
        if (board == NULL)
            printf("\n Not enough memory");
        else
            {
            printf("\n Playing the game");
            init_board(board, side);
            play_tic_tac_toe(board, side);
            }
        }
    exit(0);
    }


/*********************     INIT_BOARD     *********************/

int init_board(board, side)
/* Initialize the board to all zeros */
```

```
char *board;            /* Playing board */
int side;               /* Size of a side */
    {
    int i;
    i = side * side;
    while (i--)
        {
        *board++ = 0;
        }
    return;
    }


/***************************** PLAY_TIC_TAC_TOE **********************/

int play_tic_tac_toe(board, side)
/* Plays one game of tic-tac-toe */
char *board;            /* Playing board */
int side;               /* Size of one side */
    {
    int done = FALSE;
    int player;
    int count;
    player = 1;

    while (!done)
        {
        printf("\n Here is the current board");
        print_the_board(board, side);
        /* Get the input */
        if (player == PLAYER_1)
            {
            printf("\n What is your move, player one (*)? ");
            get_input(board, side, player);
            if (check_for_win(board, side, player))
                {
                printf("\n Congrats Player one--You won");
                print_the_board(board, side);
                done = TRUE;
                }
            player = PLAYER_2;
            if (++count == side * side)
                {
                printf("\n No more room--END OF GAME");
                done = TRUE;
                }
            }
```

```
                    else
                        {
                        printf("\n What is your move, player two (X)? ");
                        get_input(board, side, player);
                        if (check_for_win(board, side, player))
                            {
                            printf("\n Congrats Player two--You won");
                            print_the_board(board, side);
                            done = TRUE;
                            }
                        player = PLAYER_1;
                        }
                if (++count == side * side)
                    {
                    printf("\n No more room--END OF GAME");
                    done = TRUE;
                    }
                }
        return;
        }


/***************************** PRINT_THE_BOARD *****************************/

int print_the_board(board, side)
/* Prints the board */
char *board;              /* Playing board */
int side;                 /* Size of one side */
    {
    int row;
    int col;
    int i;

    /* Just print each side */
    i = 0;
    for (row = 0; row < side; row++)
        {
        printf("\n");
        for (col = 0; col < side; col++)
            {
            if (*board == PLAYER_1)
                printf(" * ");
            else if (*board == PLAYER_2)
                printf(" X ");
            else
                printf("%2d ", i);
            board++;
```

```
                        i++;
                        }
                }
        return;
        }


/****************************** GET_INPUT ******************************/

int get_input(board, side, player)
/* Gets input from a player */
char *board;            /* Playing board */
int side;               /* Size of one side */
int player;             /* Which player */
        {
        int move;
        int done;


        /* Get the input */
        done = FALSE;
        while (!done)
                {
                scanf("%d", &move);
                if (move < 0 || move >= side * side)
                        printf("\n Invalid move %d move again", move);
                else
                        if (board[move] != 0)
                                printf("\n Box %d filled move again", move);
                        else
                                {
                                board[move] = player;
                                done = TRUE;
                                }
                }
        return;
        }


/***************************** CHECK_FOR_WIN **************************/

#define board_el(row, col) (*(board + row * side + col))

int check_for_win(board, side, player)
/* Checks for a win */
char *board;            /* Playing board */
int side;               /* Size of one side */
int player;             /* Which player */
        {
```

```
int count;
int win;
int row;
int col;
win = FALSE;

/* Check the rows */
for (row = 0; row < side; row++)
    {
    count = 0;
    for (col = 0; col < side; col++)
        {
        if (board_el(row, col) == player)
            count++;
        }
    if (count == side)
        win = TRUE;
    }

/* Check the columns */
for (col = 0; col < side; col++)
    {
    count = 0;
    for (row = 0; row < side; row++)
        {
        if (board_el(row, col) == player)
            count++;
        }
    if (count == side)
        win = TRUE;
    }

/* Check the two diagonals */
count = 0;
for (row = 0; row < side; row++)
    {
    if (board_el(row, row) == player)
        count++;
    if (count == side)
        win = TRUE;
    }

count = 0;
for (row = 0; row < side; row++)
    {
    if (board_el(row, (side-1)-row) == player)
```

```
            count++;
        if (count == side)
            win = TRUE;
        }

    return win;
    }
```

## SUMMARY

- Pointers can point to pointers, as well as simple data types.
- Pointers are used to store the addresses of allocated memory.
- A linked list stores data items so it is easy to insert and delete items.
- The binary tree can be an index for data items.

## SELF-TEST

1. Given the following declarations, which of the assignment statements are valid?

```
int i;
double d;
double dd;
double *p = &dd;
double **p = &p;
```

   a. *p = d;
   b. d = **p;
   c. p = *pp;
   d. **p = *d;
   e. **p = i;
   f. p = pp;
   g. **p = *&d;
   h. p = &i;

2. What are major uses of pointers?

3. If the values added to a binary tree are added in sorted order, what happens?

# ANSWERS

1. Five assignment statements are valid and three are invalid.
   a. Valid; assigns double to double.
   b. Valid; assigns double to double.
   c. Valid; assigns pointer to double to a pointer to double.
   d. Invalid; d is not a pointer; therefore, the indirection operator cannot be applied to it.
   e. Valid; assigns int to a double.
   f. Invalid; cannot assign "pointer to pointer to double" to a type "pointer to double." A cast could be used to make it valid as: p = (double *) pp;.
   g. Valid; assigns a double to a double. The expression &d is of type "pointer to double," so *&d is a double.
   h. Invalid; &i is a pointer to int. A cast could be used to make it valid, but this would be of questionable use.
2. Following are the major uses of pointers:
   a. They are chain links in linked lists and nodes in trees.
   b. They point to data items, so the actual data item does not need to be moved.
3. The binary tree degenerates to a simple linked list.

# PROBLEMS

1. The arguments in the command line follow a convention that a hyphen precedes an option. Write a routine that interprets command line options. It could look something like

```
arg_interpret(argc,argv,options_set,options_list,number_options)
    int argc;                /* Number of command line arguments */
    char *argv[];            /* Pointer to arguments */
    int options_set[];       /* TRUE if option set */
                             /* FALSE if option not set */
    char options_list[];     /* Character values for options */
    int number_options;      /* Size of option_set and options_list */
                             /* Returns
                                  BAD_OPTION if option was bad
                                  OKAY if options are okay
                                  NON_OPTION if there was a
                                  nonoption*/
```

It might be called as

```
#define SIZE_OPTIONS 3
int option_value[SIZE_OPTIONS];
char options[SIZE_OPTIONS]={'D','Q','M'}

ret=arg_interpret(argc,argv,option_value,options,SIZE_OPTIONS);
```

2. Given these values:

```
int x = 6;                  x has address 602
int *p_int = &x;            p_int has address 610
int **p_p_int = &p_int;     p_p_int has address 620
int y = 7;                  y has address 604
int *p_y = &y;              p_y has address 614
```

and that the sizeof (int) is 2, sizeof (int * ) is 4, and the sizeof(int **) is 4, what are the values of

```
p_int + 1
*p_int + 1
*p_p_int + 1
**p_p_int + 1

*(p_int + 1)
*(p_int + 1)
**(p_p_int + 1)
*(*p_p_int + 1)
*++*p_p_int + 1
```

3. You could have defined argv as char **argv. Is this clearer than *argv[]? Why would one be preferred over the other?

4. Preorder traversal starts at the root, then visits the left subtree, then the right subtree. In postorder traversal, the left subtree is visited first, then the right subtree, and then the root. Write routines to do these two operations.

5. Write a routine to delete a node from a binary tree. (Hint: One way is to find the next element in order in the tree, then move it up.)

6. Write an iterative form of add_node or search_node. Why would an iterative form be better or worse?

7. Write a delete_list function that deletes a word from a linked list.

8. Write a function to count how many words there are on a linked list.

9. Write a function that merges two linked lists.

10. A double-linked list has a structure like

```
struct s_double
    {
    struct s_double *p_next;        /* Points to next */
```

```
struct s_double *p_previous;    /* Points to previous */
int data;                       /* Data here */
}
```

Write a function that adds a link to a double-linked list.

11. Write the add_list and search_list routines in a recursive manner.

12. When arrays are used to hold values, there are times when only a few elements in the array have nonzero values. Sometimes the amount of memory required for the array is larger than what is available. For such cases you can use a sparse array technique. This one uses sets of linked lists. A link looks like

```
struct s_element
    {
    double data;                        /* Data value */
    struct s_element *next_in_row;      /* Next in row */
    struct s_element *next_in_col;      /* Next in column */
    int row;                            /* Row */
    int col;                            /* Column */
    };
```

There are pointers to the first elements in each row and column, such as

```
struct s_element *first_in_row[MAX_ROWS];
struct s_element *first_in_col[MAX_COLS];
```

Write a routine to sum the values in a given row or given column.

13. The add_list routine placed a word in the list in the proper order. It might be quicker simply to place it at the beginning of the list and then sort the list after all words have been added. Write a routine to sort a linked list.

14. At some point you might want to delete a link in a list. Write a routine to delete a link in the list of Listing 14.5.

15. With strings, it can be inefficient to use an array in the link to store the string, as it has to be big enough to hold the maximum possible string. Rewrite Listing 12.3 to use a pointer to a char in the link, rather than an array. Allocate memory in make_link to hold the word and then store the address in the link.

16. Typically, a binary tree does not hold the actual values of the data items, but pointers to those values. Each node has a pointer to the value, rather than the actual value. Alter the binary tree functions to use pointers to values, rather than the values themselves.

17. Write a program that compresses the data elements of a large sparse array into a compact file. Add to this program a function that permits rapid addition and multiplication of two similar sized sparse arrays.

18. Rewrite the `word_break` function to call the `next_word` function.
19. Write an allocation function that follows Listing 12.2, which checks to see if an address is valid.

# File Input and Output

The input and output functions presented so far handle only one input file and one output file. Many programs require access to multiple files simultaneously. The functions presented in this chapter enable you to access more than the standard input and output files.

## INPUT/OUTPUT FUNCTIONS

The C library provides four basic ways to perform I/O. The first is character-oriented, with `getchar` and `putchar`. The second is with formatting, as `scanf` and `printf`. The third is block-oriented, which reads or writes several characters at a time. The functions that do this, `fread` and `fwrite`, will be discussed shortly. The fourth is block oriented using a terminator, which reads or writes some number of characters, depending on a terminating character. These are `gets` and `puts`, which read or write a string of characters until a terminating character (new-line or NUL-character).

## FILE INPUT AND OUTPUT

So far the only files described are standard input and output—typically the screen and the keyboard. These files can be redirected on the command line to input and output to different devices, such as disk files. You may need to access more than just one file for input and one file for output. The C library has functions that perform input and output to any device supported by the operating system.

Because C began with an association with UNIX, its approach to files is that they are streams of bytes. The routines input and output bytes and strings to different devices. Unlike the standard files, these devices must be explicitly opened. Although the term *file I/O* is used, which typically is the term for a disk file, these routines work with any device supported as a file by the operating system, such as a printer or a modem.

You first must make an explicit connection to a file by calling fopen(). The form is

```
FILE *fopen(file_name,file_mode)
/* Opens a file for reading or writing */
char *file_name;          /* Name of file to open */
char *file_mode;          /* Mode to open it in */
```

The fopen function returns a pointer to a library-defined structure called FILE. It is declared in <stdio.h>. If fopen is unable to open the file, it returns the value NULL. This pointer value, referred to as a *file pointer*, is passed to the other file functions to indicate which file you want to operate on. You can open a file for reading, writing, or appending (adding to the end of the file). The corresponding values of file_mode are r, w, and a. Opening a disk file for writing (w) erases any data currently in the file. You can open a file for both reading and writing by adding + to the string, such as r+, w+, and a+.

Two types of disk files are supported: text files and binary files.[1] The first is the text file. The end of the text file is usually marked with an end-of-file character (in ASCII, the value 26). When the file is read, the read routine reports the end of file when this character is read. New-line characters written to this file may be expanded to a carriage-return (ASCII value 13) and a new-line character (ASCII value 10). When the file is read back in text mode, these two characters are combined into a single line-feed.

A binary file has no end-of-file character representation. The operating system keeps a count of how many bytes are in a file. When this number of bytes has been read, the read routine reports the end of file. There is no special treatment for any characters. You may read more characters than are actually in the file, because the operating system count includes padding characters that fill out a physical disk sector.

A binary file may be read as a text file, and vice versa. You simply indicate in file_mode which way you want it opened. The default is text. To indicate binary, a b is added to the string, as rb, wb, and ab. Usually, though, you read the file in the same mode as you created it. The possible modes are shown in Table 13.1.

When you are done with a file, a recommended way to close it is with fclose. This ensures that characters written to the file but not yet physically placed in the file will be stored there. If you do not call fclose, the exit function will close any open files.

```
int fclose(file_pointer)
FILE *file_pointer;       /* Pointer to file to close */
```

---

[1] Under UNIX, there is little distinction between these two types of files.

**Table 13.1 Modes for fopen**

| Text Streams | Binary Streams | Meaning |
|---|---|---|
| "r" | "rb" | open stream for reading |
| "w" | "wb" | create stream for writing |
| "a" | "ab" | open stream or create stream for appending (writes appended to end of file) |
| "r+" | "r+b" or "rb+" | open stream for updating |
| "w+" | "w+b" or "wb+" | create stream for updating |
| "a+" | "a+b" or "ab+" | open stream or create stream for updating (writes appended to end of file) |

Once a file has been opened, you can read or write to it. The operation of the following functions is diagramed in Figure 13.1. The fgetc function reads one character at a time.

```
int fgetc(file_pointer)
FILE *file_pointer;              /* Pointer to file to read from */
```

The fgetc function returns either a character or the value EOF. EOF is usually #defined as −1, so an integer should be used for the return value, as in[2]

```
int c;
...
c=fgetc(file);
if (c==EOF)
     ...
```

The corresponding function to output a character is

```
fputc(character,file_pointer)
int
int character;
FILE *file_pointer;
```

If for some reason fputc is unable to output the character (perhaps the disk is full or you have closed the file), fputc returns EOF as its value.

You can write to a file using formats like printf with the fprintf function. This is called by

```
int fprintf(file_pointer,format,values...)
FILE *file_pointer;            /* Pointer to file to write to */
char *format;                  /* Format string */
values ...                     /* Values to output */
```

---

[2] If you defined c as a char and chars were unsigned on a particular machine, c would never equal −1 (EOF).

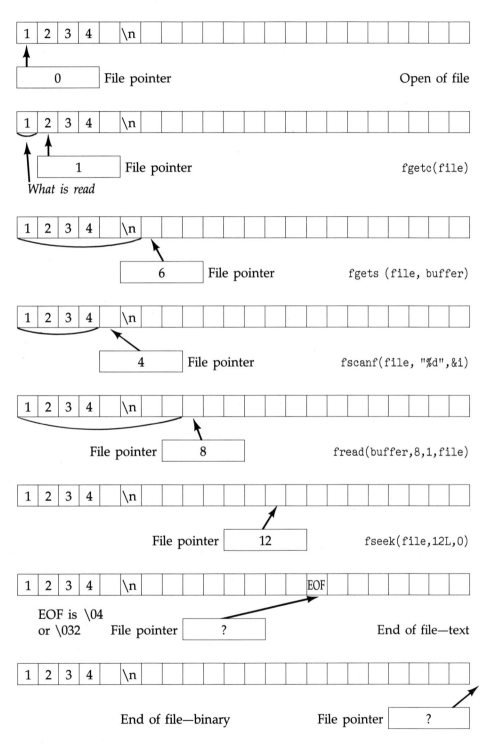

**Figure 13.1 File Input/Output**

The fprintf function works exactly like printf, except it prints to a file. If you specify stdout as the file_pointer, output goes to the terminal screen. Both fprintf and printf return a value that is the number of characters written. If the output fails, the return value is EOF. In most programs, the return value of printf is not used, because output to the terminal hardly ever fails. However, with disk files or other devices, the output could fail (the disk could be full or the disk drive off-line). You should always check the return value from fprintf.

The corresponding input function is fscanf. This is coded like

```
int fscanf(file_pointer,format,addresses...)
FILE *file_pointer;        /* Pointer to file to read from */
char *format;              /* Format string */
addresses...               /* Where to put input values */
```

---

### Debug Note

It is easy to leave out the file pointer in the parameter list for fscanf and fprintf, such as in

```
fprintf("The value is %d",i);
```

This would print to a file whose file pointer was the address of the string. The result of the function when executed is indeterminate.

---

You can read or write a number of bytes with fread and fwrite. An address is passed as the location to read to or write from. The calling sequences are shown here. A program using them is given later in the chapter.

```
size_t fread(array, size_of_element, size_of_array, file_pointer)
char *array;              /* Where to put the bytes read */
size_t size_of_element;  /* How big each element is in array */
size_t size_of_array;    /* Number of elements in array */
FILE *file_pointer;      /* Pointer to file to read from */
```

and

```
size_t fwrite(array,size_of_element,size_of_array,file_pointer)
char *array;              /* Where to read the bytes from */
size_t size_of_element;  /* How big each element is in array */
size_t size_of_array;    /* Number of elements in array */
FILE *file_pointer;      /* Pointer to file to write to */
```

The fseek function enables you to set the position in the file so the next character will be read from or written to that position. The ftell function returns the current position in the file that you can pass to fseek to go back to a particular position in the file.

```
int fseek(file_pointer, offset, mode)
FILE *file_pointer;          /* Pointer to file */
long int offset;             /* Where to position the file */
int mode;                    /* How to use the offset
                                   SEEK_SET from beginning
                                   SEEK_CUR from current position
                                   SEEK_END from end of file */


long ftell(file_pointer)
FILE *file_pointer;          /* Pointer to file */
```

These functions are demonstrated in Listing 13.4.

You can read or write a line to a file using fgets and fputs. fgets returns a pointer to the buffer read or written, if the operation was successful. If it was not, it returns the NULL pointer. fput returns EOF, if unsuccessful.

```
char *fgets(buffer, size, file_pointer)
char *buffer;                /* Where to put the bytes read */
int size;                    /* Maximum number of characters  to  read */
FILE *file_pointer;          /* Pointer to file to read from */

int fputs(buffer, file_pointer)
char *buffer;                /* Where to read the bytes from */
FILE *file_pointer;          /* Pointer to file to write to */
```

Three file pointers point to files already opened when your main program starts execution: stdin, stdout, and stderr. They are the standard input, standard output, and standard error files. The standard error file is usually sent to the terminal screen. Any of the functions introduced will work with these files by simply using one of these values as the file pointer. For example, fprintf(stdout,"Hi"); prints to the standard output. The getchar function is usually implemented as a macro #define getchar() fgetc(stdin).

---

| *Debug Tip* |
| --- |
| Use the stderr file for error messages, especially if the program output may be redirected. If you use standard output, your error messages may get lost. |

## SAMPLE PROGRAM—COPYFILE

This program copies one file to another. The copy program in Chapter 5 copied from stdin to stdout. If you want to copy from one file to another, you executed it as

```
copy < in_file > out_file
```

The following copyfile program operates in a similar manner. However, it is executed by specifying the input and output files on the command line, as in

```
copy in_file out_file
```

It opens both files in binary mode. Then copyfile gets a character from the input file and writes that to the output file. The loop ends when the end-of-file is returned. Note it checks every return value from the file functions. The values passed to the exit function can be checked by the operating system. These may need to change, if your operating system requires other values for success or failure of a program.

**Listing 13.1 copyfile Program**

```c
/* copyfile program */
/* Copies one file to another */
/* Command line: copyfile in-file out-file */
#include <stdio.h>

/* Exit returns */
#define BAD_CALL 10
#define BAD_INPUT_FILE 11
#define BAD_OUTPUT_FILE 12
#define GOOD_COPY 0
#define BAD_WRITE 1

/* Values for fopen */
#define READ_BINARY "rb"
#define WRITE_BINARY "wb"

#define TRUE 1
#define FALSE 0

int main(argc, argv)
/* Copies one file to another */
int argc;                /* Argument count */
char *argv[];            /* Pointers to arguments */
                         /* Returned values are
                              0 GOOD_COPY
```

```
                            10 BAD_CALL (not enough arguments)
                            11 BAD_INPUT_FILE (unable to open input)
                            12 BAD_OUTPUT_FILE (unable to open output)
                            1 BAD_WRITE (to output file) */
{
int result;              /* Return value */
int character;           /* Current character */
int done;                /* Flag when done with input */
FILE *file_in;           /* Input file */
FILE *file_out;          /* Output file */

if (argc < 3)
    {
    fprintf(stderr, "You should specify two files");
    result = BAD_CALL;
    }
else
    {
    file_in = fopen(argv[1], READ_BINARY);
    if (file_in == NULL)
        {
        fprintf(stderr, "\n Cannot open input file %s", argv[1]);
        result = BAD_INPUT_FILE;
        }
    else
        {
        file_out = fopen(argv[2], WRITE_BINARY);
        if (file_out == NULL)
            {
            fprintf(stderr, "\n Cannot open output file %s",
            argv[2]);
            result = BAD_OUTPUT_FILE;
            }
        else
            {
            done = FALSE;
            while (!done)
                {
                character = fgetc(file_in);
                if (character == EOF)
                    {
                    done = TRUE;
                    result = GOOD_COPY;
                    }
                else
```

```
                              {
                                if (fputc(character, file_out) == EOF)
                                  {
                                    result = BAD_WRITE;
                                    done = TRUE;
                                  }
                              }
                        } /* End of while on done */
                    } /* End of else on fopen-write */
                } /* End of else on fopen-read */
            } /* End of else on argc */

        exit(result);
        }
```

---

## SAMPLE PROGRAM—FILE COMPRESSION

To save space on a disk or to save time in transmitting a file, you can compress the information in the file. There are several methods for file compression; the method presented here compresses the file by shortening strings of duplicate characters. These strings are usually a series of spaces.

In this compression technique, when three or more of the consecutive characters are the same, they are replaced by a special sequence of characters composed of a special character (COMPRESS_CHAR) followed by a count and the duplicated character. To keep the operation of the compression visible, an OFFSET has been added to the count. You could set it to 0.

If COMPRESS_CHAR is in the file, a sequence is created for it. Its value should be a character not appearing in a file or one appearing rarely. Otherwise, the technique will increase rather than decrease the size of the file.

The program reads the input file and keeps track of the last character read. If the current character is equal to the last character, repetition_count is increment. Otherwise, the previous character is output. When repetition_count reaches a maximum, the compression sequence is output to avoid having wraparound on the count. With & as the compression character and the offset as 0, a sample compression looks like this:

*Input file:*

```
abcddddddddefg        abcdef
aaaaaaaaaaa
```

*Output file:*

```
abc&7defg&: abcdef
&;a
```

**Listing 13.2 File Compression Program**

```
/* Compression program */
/* Compresses character string on input file and places it in output file */
/* Command line: compress in-file out-file */
#include <stdio.h>

#define MINIMUM_COMPRESS 3      /* Minimum number of characters to compress */
#define COMPRESS_CHAR '&'       /* Compression character */
#define OFFSET '0'              /* Offset to use for repetition count */
#define MAXIMUM_COMPRESS 126-OFFSET
                                /* Maximum number of characters to compress */
#define NO_CHAR -2              /* No previous character */
static FILE *in_file;           /* Input file */
static FILE *out_file;          /* Output file */

int main(argc, argv)
int argc;
char *argv[];
    {
    int old_character;      /* Previous character */
    int repetition_count;   /* Repetition counter */
    int character;          /* Input character */

    old_character = NO_CHAR;
    repetition_count = 0;

    if (argc >= 3)
        {
        in_file = fopen(argv[1], "r");
        out_file = fopen(argv[2], "w");

        if ((in_file != NULL) && (out_file != NULL))
            {
            /* Loop until the end of file */
            while ((character = fgetc(in_file)) != EOF)
                {
                /* If current character matches previous one, just
                   increment counter */
                    if (character == old_character)
                        {
                        repetition_count++;
                        /* Output the compression sequence if at
                            maximum */
                        if (repetition_count ==
                            MAXIMUM_COMPRESS)
```

```
                                    {
                                    out_char(old_character, repetition_count);
                                    old_character = NO_CHAR;
                                    repetition_count = 0;
                                    }
                                }
                        else
                                {
                                /* Output the previous character */
                                out_char(old_character, repetition_count);
                                repetition_count = 1;
                                old_character = character;
                                }
                        }
                    /* Output the last character */
                    out_char(old_character, repetition_count);
                    fclose(in_file);
                    fclose(out_file);
                    }
            else
                    printf("File open error ");
            }
    else
            printf("\n You need to specify two files");
    exit(0);
    }


/****************************** OUT_CHAR ******************************/

void out_char(character, repetition_count)
/* Outputs a character, based on repetition_count */
int character;              /* Character to output */
int repetition_count;       /* How many of character to output */
    {
    int count;             /* Counter */
    int ret;               /* Return value from fgetc */

    if ((repetition_count < MINIMUM_COMPRESS)
            && (character != COMPRESS_CHAR))
            {
            /* Less than minimum to compress and not the compression character */
            for (count = 0; count < repetition_count; count++)
                    {
                    ret = fputc(character, out_file);
                    if (ret == EOF)
                            printf("\n Output error");
                    }
```

```
        }
        else
            {
            /* Output the compression string */
            ret = fputc(COMPRESS_CHAR, out_file);
            if (ret == EOF)
                printf("\n Output error");
            ret = fputc(repetition_count + OFFSET, out_file);
            if (ret == EOF)
                printf("\n Output error");
            ret = fputc(character, out_file);
            if (ret == EOF)
                printf("\n Output error");
            }
        return;
        }
```

The corresponding program shown in Listing 13.3 decompresses the file. When it reads a character equal to the COMPRESS_CHAR, it gets the next two characters and outputs the duplicated character repetition_count times.

### Listing 13.3 File Decompression Program

```
/* Decompression program */
/* Decompresses character string on input file and puts it on output file */
/* Command line: decomp in-file out-file */
#include <stdio.h>

#define COMPRESS_CHAR '&'       /* Compression character */
#define OFFSET '0'              /* Offset to use for repetition count */
#define C_INIT 0                /* Initial condition */
#define C_COMPRESS 1            /* Compression character found */
#define C_COUNT 2               /* Compression count found */

static FILE *in_file;           /* Input file */
static FILE *out_file;          /* Output file */

int main(argc, argv)
int argc;
char *argv[];
    {
    int repetition_count;       /* Repetition counter */
    int character;              /* Input character */
    int next;                   /* Next case in switch to use */
    int count;                  /* Counter */
    int ret;                    /* Return value */
```

```
    next = C_INIT;

if (argc >= 3)
    {
    in_file = fopen(argv[1], "r");
    out_file = fopen(argv[2], "w");

    if ((in_file != NULL) && (out_file != NULL))
        {
        while ((character = fgetc(in_file)) != EOF)
            {
            switch (next)
                {
            case C_INIT:
                /* See whether character is compression character */
                if (character == COMPRESS_CHAR)
                    next = C_COMPRESS;
                else
                    {
                    ret = fputc(character, out_file);
                    if (ret == EOF)
                        printf("\n Output error");
                    }
                break;
            case C_COMPRESS:
                /* Set the repetition count */
                repetition_count = character - OFFSET;
                next = C_COUNT;
                break;
            case C_COUNT:
                /* This is the character to repeat */
                for (count = 0; count < repetition_count;
                    count++)
                    {
                    ret = fputc(character, out_file);
                    if (ret == EOF)
                        printf("\n Output error");
                    }
                next = C_INIT;
                break;
                }
            } /* End of while on character == EOF */
        fclose(in_file);
        fclose(out_file);
        }
    else
        printf("File open error ");
```

```
            }
        else
            printf("\n You need two filenames");
        exit(0);
        }
```

## VIEW PROGRAM

The next program displays the contents of a text file. It displays a screen of lines in the file. You can then go forward or backward through the file by either a line at a time or a page at a time.

Listing 13.4 uses linepoint, an array of long integers, to store the position in a file at the start of each line. Space for the array is allocated by a call to calloc. It calls line_break to determine where the ends of the lines are. This calls ftell to get the current position in the file, and fgets to get one line of the file. After it has finished reading the file, the program calls the display routine.

The display routine uses the values linepoint to position the file before each fgets call. Going forward or backward is simply a matter of altering start_line, the initial index into linepoint.

---

### Pseudocode for File Viewing Program

View
    Initialize
    Determine line breaks
    While not done
        Display one page of file
        Get a command
        If movement
            Go backwards or forwards in the file
        If exit
            Set done true

---

**Listing 13.4 File Viewing Program**

```
/* View program */
/* View a text file on the screen */
/* Command line:
   view file
*/
#include <stdio.h>
#include <stdlib.h>
```

```
#define TRUE 1
#define FALSE 0

#define LINESIZE 2000        /* Maximum number of lines */
#define BUFFER_LENGTH 300     /* Maximum length of line */

int main(argc, argv)
/* Views a file on the terminal screen */
int argc;
char *argv[];
    {
    char *cret;              /* Return value from fgets */
    int number_lines;        /* Number of lines */
    FILE *file;              /* File pointer to file to read */
    long *linepoint;         /* Points to where start of each line in file
                                    is */
    char filename[30];       /* Filename */

    /* If there is a filename */
    if (argc > 1)
        {
        /* Open the file */
        strcpy(filename, argv[1]);
        file = fopen(argv[1], "r");
        if (file == NULL)
            printf("\n File not found");
        else
            {
            /* If file is open, then read it */

            /* Get space for the array of line pointers */
            linepoint = (long *) calloc((unsigned) LINESIZE, sizeof(long));
            if (linepoint == NULL)
                {
                printf("\n Insufficient memory for viewing");
                printf("\n Press Enter key to continue");
                getchar();
                goto end;
                }
            number_lines = line_break(linepoint, file);
            if (number_lines >= LINESIZE)
                printf("\n Unable to show entire file");

            display_file(linepoint, file, number_lines, filename);
            }
        }
    free(linepoint);
```

```
end:
    exit(0);
    }


/***************************** LINE_BREAK *****************************/

int line_break(linepoint, file)
/* Determines where line breaks are in a file */
long linepoint[];          /* Where to put the pointers */
FILE *file;
    {
    int number_lines;    /* Number of lines */
    char *cret;          /* Return value */
    unsigned char buffer[BUFFER_LENGTH];
                         /* Buffer to use for reading file */

    number_lines = 0;
    while (number_lines < LINESIZE)
        {
        linepoint[number_lines] = ftell(file);
        cret = fgets(buffer, BUFFER_LENGTH, file);
        if (cret == NULL)
            {
            clearerr(file);
            break;
            }
        number_lines++;
        }

    return number_lines;
    }


/***************************** DISPLAY_FILE *****************************/

#define PAGE_LENGTH 23      /* Number of lines to display for a page */
#define LINE_LENGTH 78      /* Number of characters to display on a line */

/* Characters for control of display */
#define PAGE_UP 'P'
#define PAGE_DOWN 'N'
#define ESCAPE 'E'
#define CURSOR_UP 'U'
#define CURSOR_DOWN 'D'

/* Ending line for each page */
static char lineend[] =
    "E-exit P-prev page N-next page D-down line\U-up line (CR)";
```

```
int display_file(linepoint, file, number_lines, filename)
/* Display a screen full of lines from a file with controls */
int number_lines;       /* Maximum lines to display */
long linepoint[];       /* Pointers to beginning of lines */
FILE *file;             /* File to read from */
char filename[];        /* Filename */
    {
    unsigned char *pc;  /* Pointer to wind way through buffer */
    int c;              /* Input command */
    int start_line;     /* Line to start with */
    int i;              /* Counter for number of characters output */
    int line;           /* Counter for number of lines output */
    int command;        /* Flag set true if input is a command */
    char *cret;         /* Return from fgets */
    int ret;            /* General return value */
    unsigned char buffer[BUFFER_LENGTH];
                        /* Buffer to use for reading file */

    /* Initialize */
    start_line = 0;

    while (TRUE)
        {
        /* Position the file to the starting line */
        ret = fseek(file, linepoint[start_line], 0);
        printf("\n File :%s: First line is %d of %d", filename,
            start_line, number_lines);
        printf("First byte position %ld \n", linepoint[start_line]);

        for (line = 0; line < PAGE_LENGTH; line++)
            {
            /* Display each line */
            cret = fgets(buffer, LINE_LENGTH, file);
            if (cret == NULL)
                {
                printf("\n Error in reading file");
                goto end;
                }
            pc = buffer;
            for (i = 0; i < LINE_LENGTH; i++)
                {
                if (*pc == 0)
                    break;
                if (*pc < ' ')
                    *pc = ' ';
                putchar(*pc++);
                }
```

```
            putchar('\n');
        }
/* Print prompt and get a command */
printf("%s", lineend);
do
        {
        command = TRUE;
        c = getchar();
        c = toupper(c);
        switch (c)
            {
        case PAGE_UP:
            start_line -= PAGE_LENGTH;
            break;
        case PAGE_DOWN:
            start_line += PAGE_LENGTH;
            break;
        case CURSOR_UP:
            start_line--;
            break;
        case CURSOR_DOWN:
            start_line++;
            break;
        case ESCAPE:
            goto end;
            break;
        default:
            command = FALSE;
            }
        }
        while (!command);

/* See whether beyond limits */
if (start_line < 0)
    start_line = 0;
if (start_line >= (number_lines - PAGE_LENGTH))
    start_line = number_lines - PAGE_LENGTH;
}
end:
    return;
    }
```

---

## STRING FORMATTING

Two functions perform the same operations as printf and scanf but use strings, rather than files. Their calling sequences are

```
int sprintf(buffer, format, values...)
char *buffer;                    /* Array of characters to write to */
char *format;                    /* Format string */
values ...                       /* Values to output */
```

and

```
int sscanf(buffer,format,addresses...)
char *buffer;                    /* Array of characters to read from */
char *format;                    /* Format string */
addresses...                     /* Where to put input values */
```

The introductory chapters noted problems with scanf. You might want to input an integer with scanf. If you or your program's users type characters other than digits, scanf stops. You then have to "clear the buffer" using getchar to eliminate these characters. Instead, you can write

```
int int_num;
char input_buffer[SIZE_INPUT];

get_line(input_buffer,SIZE_INPUT]);
sscanf(input_buffer, "%d", &int_num);
```

This gets a line of input from the user and then converts it to an int. The get_line function was defined in Chapter 5. Because get_line inputs all characters to the end of a line, any nondigits are read into input_buffer, and the next get_line starts with a clean buffer. If you want to be able to input characters other than a number, change the call to scanf to a call to a function such as get_number:

```
get_number(input_buffer,SIZE_INPUT);
switch(toupper(input_buffer[0]))
     {
case 'E':
     /* Exit from program */
     exit(0);
     break;
case 'S':
     /* Special function */
     func_special();
     break;
default:
     /* Input a number */
     sscanf(input_buffer, "%d", &int_num);
     break;
     }
```

All the formatting features of sprintf and sscanf are described in Appendix G.

## SAMPLE PROGRAM—GRADES

GRADES is a typical data entry program. It can keep track of any type of structure by changing the structure definition and altering the user input and output to request and display additional data items.

In keeping track of grades, the program uses structures of type s_student to contain the name of a student and the grade. The structures are written and read from a data file, using fread and fwrite. The first few bytes of the data file store the number of structures (also called *records*) that have been written to the file.

The functions contain several printf calls so you can trace what is going on. The init_file function opens the data file. main_menu gets a selection from the user. Based on the selection, the program calls end_file to close the data file and exits, or it performs an operation. It calls add_name_ to ask for a name to add, find_name to find a name and get a new grade, or print_name to print all the names and grades. Notice that return values from the input/output functions are checked to verify that the operation has been performed. The error is passed back to the main routine. A simple message is output if an error occurs. However, you can program a more elaborate error recovery process.

There is no index of names in the file. In order to find a name, the program searches through all the records in the file. This could take some time with many records. Using an index of names, which could be searched quickly with a binary search, would dramatically decrease the time.

---

### *Pseudocode for Grade Program*

```
Grades
        Initialize—open files
        While not done
                Get command
                If command is Exit
                        set done
                Else if command is Add
                        Input name and grade
                Else if command is Find
                        Input name
                        Get matching record
                        Input and update grade
                Else if command is Print
                        Start at beginning of file
                        Print all records
                Else
                        Bad command
        Terminate—close files
```

**Listing 13.5 Grade Program**

```c
#include <stdio.h>
#define OKAY 1              /* Value for good return */
#define NOT_OKAY 0          /* Value for bad return */
#define FALSE 0
#define TRUE 1


/* Structure of the student record */
#define SIZE_NAME 20            /* Size of name */

struct s_student
    {
    char name[SIZE_NAME + 1];
        /* Name of student with space for NUL char */
    int grade;              /* Grade */
    };

#define RECORD_SIZE sizeof(struct s_student) /* Size of a record */

#define ADD_NAME 1          /* Menu value for adding a name */
#define FIND_NAME 2         /* Menu value for finding a name */
#define PRINT_NAME 3        /* Menu value for printing names */
#define END_PROGRAM 4       /* Menu value for ending program */


/******************************* MAIN *******************************/

int main()
/* This program keeps track of student's grades */
    {
    int ret;                /* Return values */
    int main_select;        /* Main menu option */

    /* Open the data file */
    ret = init_file();
    if (ret == OKAY)
        {
        do
            {
            main_select = main_menu();
            switch (main_select)
                {
            case ADD_NAME:
                ret = add_name();
                break;
            case FIND_NAME:
                ret = find_name();
```

```
                        break;
                case PRINT_NAME:
                        ret = print_name();
                        break;
                }
        if (ret != OKAY)
                printf("\n File error ");
        }
    while (main_select != END_PROGRAM);

    ret = end_file();
    if (ret != OKAY)
            printf("\n Error in closing data file");
    }
else
    printf("\n File error in opening data file");

exit(0);
}


/****************************** MAIN_MENU *******************************/


int main_menu()
/* This displays the choices for the main menu */
        /* Returns one of the choices
                ADD_NAME        Menu value for adding a name
                FIND_NAME       Menu value for finding a name
                PRINT_NAME      Menu value for printing names
                END_PROGRAM     Menu value for ending program
        */
{
int chr;                /* For input character */
int done;               /* Flag for while loop */
int ret;                /* Return value */

printf("\n\n What would you like to do ?");
printf("\n Add a name");
printf("\n Print the names");
printf("\n Find a name");
printf("\n End the program");
printf("\n\n Type the first letter of your choice");
printf("\n followed by CR : ");

done = FALSE;
while (!done)
        {
```

```
            chr = getchar();
            switch (toupper(chr))
                {
            case 'A':
                /* Add a name */
                ret = ADD_NAME;
                done = TRUE;
                break;
            case 'P':
                /* Print names */
                ret = PRINT_NAME;
                done = TRUE;
                break;
            case 'F':
                /* Find a name */
                ret = FIND_NAME;
                done = TRUE;
                break;
            case 'E':
                /* End the program */
                ret = END_PROGRAM;
                done = TRUE;
                break;
            default:
                /* Ignore all other characters */
                break;
                }
            }

    /* Get the last new-line character */
    chr = getchar();
    return ret;
    }


/************************ EXTERNAL VARIABLES *************************/

/* These are used by the add, find, and print routines */

static int current_record;      /* Current record in the file */
static int last_record;         /* Last record in the file */
                                /* The first record contains this number */
                                /* Data records start with the second record
                                 */
static FILE *data_file;         /* Pointer to data file */
#define FILENAME "student.dat"  /* Name of data file */

static FILE *print_file;        /* File pointer for print file */
#define PRINT_FILE "PRINTER"    /* Printer file */
```

```
/****************************** INIT_FILE ******************************/

int init_file()
/* Opens the data file */
    {
    int ret;                        /* Return value */
    int count;                      /* Count of bytes read */
    char buffer[RECORD_SIZE];       /* Buffer for read */

    data_file = fopen(FILENAME, "r+");
    if (data_file == NULL)
        {
        /* Open a new file */
        data_file = fopen(FILENAME, "w+");
        if (data_file == NULL)
            ret = NOT_OKAY;
        else
            {
            /* Write record count on new file */
            sprintf(buffer, "%d", last_record);
            count = fwrite(buffer, RECORD_SIZE, 1, data_file);
            if (count != 1)
                ret = NOT_OKAY;
            else
                ret = OKAY;
            }
        }
    else
        {
        /* Read record count from file */
        count = fread(buffer, RECORD_SIZE, 1, data_file);
        if (count != 1)
            ret = NOT_OKAY;
        else
            {
            ret = OKAY;
            sscanf(buffer, "%d", &last_record);
            }
        }
    if (ret == OKAY)
        printf("\n File contains %d students", last_record);

    return ret;
    }

/****************************** END_FILE ******************************/

int end_file()
```

```
/* Ends the data file */
    {
    int ret;                           /* Return value */
    int count;                         /* Count of bytes read */
    char buffer[RECORD_SIZE];          /* Buffer for read */
    int ret_seek;                      /* Return from seek */

    /* Write the record count on the first record */
    sprintf(buffer, "%d", last_record);

    ret_seek = fseek(data_file, (long) 0, SEEK_SET);
    if (ret_seek != 0)
        ret = NOT_OKAY;
    else
        {
        count = fwrite(buffer, RECORD_SIZE, 1, data_file);
        if (count != 1)
            ret = NOT_OKAY;
        else
            {
            ret = OKAY;
            printf("\n File now contains %d students", last_record);
            }
        }
    fclose(data_file);
    return ret;
    }

/***************************** ADD_NAME ******************************/

#define SIZE_BUFFER 3                  /* Buffer size for grade */

int add_name()
/* Add a name to the file */
    {
    int ret;                           /* Return value */
    int count;                         /* Write count */
    char buffer[SIZE_BUFFER + 1];      /* Buffer for integer input */
    struct s_student student;          /* Buffer for record */
    int ret_seek;                      /* Return from seek */

    /* Input the name */
    printf("\n Adding a name");
    printf("\n Name: ");
    get_line(student.name, SIZE_NAME);
    printf("\n Grade: ");
    get_line(buffer, SIZE_BUFFER);
    sscanf(buffer, "%d", &student.grade);
```

```
    /* Record the name and grade */
    last_record++;
        current_record = last_record;
    ret = OKAY;

    ret_seek = fseek(data_file, (long) last_record * RECORD_SIZE,
    SEEK_SET);
    if (ret_seek != 0)
        ret = NOT_OKAY;
    else
        {
        count = fwrite(&student, RECORD_SIZE, 1, data_file);
        if (count != 1)
            ret = NOT_OKAY;
        else
            printf("\n Students on file %d", last_record);
        }

    return ret;
    }

/****************************** FIND_NAME ******************************/

int find_name()
/* Find a name in the file */
    {
    int ret;                    /* Return value */
    int count;                  /* Read/write count */
    struct s_student match;     /* Buffer for matching values */
    struct s_student student;   /* Buffer for record */
    char buffer[SIZE_BUFFER + 1]; /* Buffer for grade */
    int found;                  /* Flag for found */
    int ret_seek;               /* Return from seek */

    found = FALSE;
    ret = OKAY;
    /* Input the name to find */
    printf("\n Find a name");
    printf("\n Name: ");
    get_line(match.name, SIZE_NAME);

    /* Rewind file and look for matching name in the file */
    ret_seek = fseek(data_file, (long) RECORD_SIZE, SEEK_SET);
    if (ret_seek != 0)
        ret = NOT_OKAY;
    else
```

```
            {
            for (current_record = 1; current_record <= last_record;
            current_record++)
                {
                count = fread(&student, RECORD_SIZE, 1, data_file);
                if (count != 1)
                    ret = NOT_OKAY;
                else
                    {
                    if (strncmp(match.name, student.name, SIZE_NAME) == 0)
                        {
                        printf("\n Student was found");
                        printf("\n Grade was %d", student.grade);
                        printf("\n New grade: ");
                        get_line(buffer, SIZE_BUFFER);

                        /* If buffer is blank, grade will not be changed */
                        sscanf(buffer, "%d", &student.grade);

                        /* Rewrite the record */
                        ret_seek = fseek(data_file,
                        (long) current_record * RECORD_SIZE, SEEK_SET);
                        if (ret_seek != 0)
                            ret = NOT_OKAY;
                        else
                            {
                            count = fwrite(&student, RECORD_SIZE, 1,
                                data_file);
                            if (count != 1)
                                {
                                ret = NOT_OKAY;
                                }
                            else
                                found = TRUE;
                            break;
                            }
                        } /* End of else on strncmp */
                    } /* End of else on count */
                } /* End of for */
            } /* End of else on ret_seek 0 */

    if (!found)
        printf("\n Student not found");

    return;
    }
```

```
/***************************** PRINT_NAMES ****************************/

int print_name()
/* Print all the names in the file */
     {
     int ret;                        /* Return value */
     int count;                      /* Read count */
     struct s_student student;       /* Buffer for record */
     int ret_seek;                   /* Return from seek */

     printf("\n Printing the names on %s", PRINT_FILE);

     ret = OKAY;
     print_file = fopen(PRINT_FILE, "w");
     if (print_file == NULL)
          {
          printf("\n Unable to open printer");
          ret = NOT_OKAY;
          }
     else
          {
          /* Rewind the file and print the records */
          ret_seek = fseek(data_file, (long) RECORD_SIZE, SEEK_SET;
          if (ret_seek != 0)
               ret = NOT_OKAY;
          else
               {
               for (current_record = 1; current_record <= last_record;
                    current_record++)
                    {
                    count = fread(&student, RECORD_SIZE, 1, data_file);
                    if (count != 1)
                         ret = NOT_OKAY;
                    else
                         {
                         fprintf(print_file,
                              "\n Student %30.30s Grade %5d",
                              student.name, student.grade);
                         }
                    }
               }
          fclose(print_file);
          }

     return ret;
     }
```

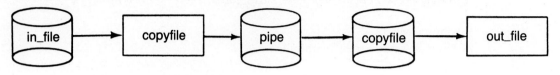

**Figure 13.2 Pipes and Filters**

## FILES AND PIPES

There are a few more operations you can do on the command line on UNIX and
MS-DOS systems. To append to a file (add information at the end of an existing
file), you can use >>. If you run the copy program in Chapter 5 as

```
copyfile < in_file >> out_file
```

the contents of in_file are added at the end of "out_file."
   The pipeline operator (|) takes the standard output of one program and uses
it as the standard input of another program. This is shown in Figure 13.2, for
example.

```
copyfile < in_file | copyfile > out_file
```

pipes the standard input (from in_file) to a pipe. The second copy program reads
the standard input from the pipe and copies it to out_file.

## SUMMARY

- The C library has functions for opening, closing, reading, writing, and appending to files.
- All files are treated as strings of characters.
- Types of files include disk files, printer files, modem files, or ones from other
  devices.

## SELF-TEST

1. If you execute this code, what is the value of c?

```
char c = 'A';
f = fopen("FILE","w");
fputs("a",f);
fclose(f);
f = fopen("FILE","w+");
c = fgets(f);
```

2. What could happen if the stdio.h file was not included in this code?

```
int file;
file = fopen("SOMEFILE","w");
fputc('a',file);
```

## ANSWERS

1. The value is EOF. The file was opened the second time for writing, so the contents of the file were erased. Just after the fclose, the file had one character in it—the letter *a*.
2. The value returned from fopen is a pointer. If the value cannot fit into an integer, it is truncated. When fputc is called, it is passed an invalid file pointer. The result is indeterminate—your program may hang, bomb, or yield garbage.

## PROBLEMS

1. Rewrite the copying program using one of the following:

| | |
|---|---|
| fgets() / fputs() | Till a new line |
| fscanf("%s") / fprintf("%s") | Till a space |
| fread() / fwrite() | For a certain number of characters |

Copy a large file twice, first using the copy program in Listing 13.1 and then using the program you just rewrote. Which code is the faster?

2. Here is the copy program rewritten to use gotos. Is this acceptable, better, or worse than the one in the text?

```
main(argc,argv)
int argc;
char argv[];
    {
    int result;
    int character;
    int char_out;
    FILE *file_in = NULL;
    FILE *file_out = NULL;

    if (argc! = 3)
        {
        fprintf(stderr,"You should specify two files");
        result=BAD_CALL;
        goto end;
        }
```

```
            file_in=fopen(argv[1],READ_BINARY);
            if (file_in==NULL)
                  {
                  fprintf("\n Cannot open input file %s",argv[2]);
                  result=BAD_INPUT_FILE;
                  goto end;
                  }
            file_out=fopen(argv[2],WRITE_BINARY);
            if (file_out==NULL)
                  {
                  fprintf(stderr,"\n Cannot open output file %s" argv[1]);
                  result=BAD_OUTPUT_FILE;
                  goto end;
                  }
        while (FOREVER)
                  {
                  character=fgetc(file_in);
                  if (character==EOF)
                        {
                        result=GOOD_COPY;
                        goto end;
                        }
                  if (fputc(file_out,character)==EOF)
                        {
                        result=BAD_WRITE;
                        goto end;
                        }
                  }
    end:
        fclose(file_in);
        fclose(file_out);

        exit (result);
        }
```

3. Write a program to compare two files character by character. The program should print the differences between the two files.

4. Write a program to compare two files line by line. Why would you prefer this program to the one in Problem 3?

5. Write a program that concatenates two or more files into a third file.

6. Write a program that prints a file in a nicely formatted output. It should have a header on each page that has the file name and page number. Allow a margin at the top and bottom of the page. If the file ends in the middle of a page, print extra blank lines so the next printout does not start in the middle of the page.

7. Write a program that produces a dump of a file. The dump is a listing in hex-adecimal format of the contents of each byte in the file (Hint: Use %02x as the format specifier and use unsigned chars). Alternatively, print the file in octal format.

8. Write a function to convert a date in a structure s_date (see Listing 7.1) to a string in the form of month day, 19year.

9. Convert a date to several formats:

| | |
|---|---|
| string with MM/DD/YY | 12/31/90 |
| string with DD/MM/YY | 31/12/90 |
| MON D,Y | DEC 12, 90 |

10. On many systems, there is a program called MORE that displays a screen full of lines of a file until a character is typed. Create a program that does this. You can enhance it by permitting backup to a previous screen.

11. Write a function that takes a double value and outputs it as a string with commas inserted at the thousand, million, and billion marks. For example,

    1023334445.5   should be output as   1,023,334,445.5.

12. Write a program that sorts lines (strings ending with a new-line) in a file.

13. Add commands to the view program to go to the beginning and the end of the file.

14. In the view program, if a line is longer than the screen width, it is truncated. Add commands such as cursor left and right that begin the display of each line with a character to the left or right a given number of the current first character. You may want to add a screen buffer, so you do not have to keep reading the file when you go right or left.

15. Alter Listing 13.2 to provide a more elaborate error recovery process if an error occurs. Integrity of the data file is important. You may wish to flush the file after every write.

# Chapter Fourteen

# Program Style

Style is a matter of how you write your C code. Brief tips on style have been placed throughout this book. This chapter reviews those tips and suggests a few more. It can become your style manual for writing C applications. The most important aspect of style is to pick a convention and stick with it. Then anybody reading your code can easily determine what you are doing. C enables you to create unintelligible expressions and unreadable code. If you discipline yourself to a certain style of writing, programs will be both more readable and maintainable. Common errors are reviewed in this chapter so you will have one place to turn to for suggestions on how to find a bug.

Style is a matter of visual appearance, appropriate code style, and clarity. Using white space and following indentation guidelines makes the code easy to read. Using a consistent style, with few gotos or multiple returns makes it easy to trace the flow. Names and comments should be long enough to be understandable, but short enough so they will be read.

## WHITE SPACE USAGE

Use blank space to break up programs. It graphically helps in understanding the program. Use comments to explain the code, not repeat it. You might set up white space standards; these are recommended as a start:

1. Binary operators (such as + and *) shall be surrounded by spaces.
2. Unary operators (such as ++ and --) shall have no space.
3. Do not use a space between the function name and the ().
4. Use one statement per line.
5. Skip a line after the last declaration in each function.

When in doubt, tend toward the overuse of parentheses and braces. Use more parentheses than precedence requires to break up an expression into simpler expressions. Use braces around even a single statement that forms the body of a while or for loop. Debugging statements can then be placed in the body of the loop without additional effort.

## INDENTATION AND BRACES

There are several styles for the placement of braces and the amount of indentation. Four choices are shown in Table 14.1. It is a good idea to comment the closing brace of a loop if the body is longer than 10 or 15 lines.

**Table 14.1 Indentation Styles**

| Alignment Style | Sample |
| --- | --- |
| Style of Kernighan and Ritchie | ```while (i<0) {```<br>```    i++;```<br>```}``` |
| Braces aligned with the loop body | ```while (i<0)```<br>```    {```<br>```    i++;```<br>```    }``` |
| Braces aligned with the control statement | ```while (i<0)```<br>```{```<br>```    i++;```<br>```}``` |
| A combination of styles | ```while (i<0) {```<br>```    i++;```<br>```    }``` |

## CODE STYLE

You can write C in several different styles. Many of the examples in this book perform the same function. They have been written in different styles to show the variety of ways of addressing the same problem. Because C is such a versatile language, there are many ways of attacking the same problem. For example, the following represents a standard way of choosing two alternatives:

```
if (a == 10)
    b = 5;
else
    b = 0;
```

You can make use of some of the C operators that do not exist in other languages, such as

```
b = a == 10 ? 5 : 0;
```

You can also use the freedom C gives you in expressions such as

```
b = (a == 10) * 5;
```

Most programmers probably prefer the first form. On a different tack, you might prefer using a C idiom, which appears often in routines. Suppose you want to read a file until the end of file. It is often done as

```
while ((c = getchar() != EOF)
    {
    /* Rest of loop */
    }
```

But it could be written as

```
#define FOREVER 1
...
while (FOREVER)
    {
    c = getchar();
    if (c == EOF)
        break;
    /* Rest of loop */
    }
```

or in a more structured manner as

```
#define FALSE 0
#define TRUE 1
...
done = FALSE;
while (!done)
    {
    c = getchar();
    if (c == EOF)
        done = TRUE;
    else
        {
        /* Rest of loop */
        }
    }
```

The first form may be preferable, because it shows immediately what the loop termination condition is.

If you had to test for multiple variables, you might write the testing code as

```
while ((c = getchar()) != EOF && c != END_CHAR1 && c != END_CHAR2)
    {
    /* Rest of loop */
    }
```

or as

```
while (FOREVER)
    {
    c = getchar();
    switch(c)
        {
    case EOF:
    case END_CHAR1:
    case END_CHAR2:
        goto end;
    default:
        /* Rest of loop */
        }
    }
end:;
```

or in a more structured manner as

```
done=FALSE;
while (!done)
    {
    c=getchar();
    switch(c)
        {
    case EOF:
    case END_CHAR1:
    case END_CHAR2:
        done=TRUE;
        break;
    default:
        /* Rest of loop */
        }
    }
```

If you want to trace the value of c being returned by getchar, or to add additional characters as terminators, the latter two forms are much easier to modify.

Two types of operators in C not found in other languages can make your code somewhat more readable. The increment and decrement operators and the compound assignment operators help reduce the amount of your source code.

| **Use** | **For** |
|---|---|
| a++; | a = a + 1; |
| a += 5; | a = a + 5; |

Do not use the comma operator and place an entire loop in the header:

```
int array[SIZE];
for (i = 0; i < SIZE; array[i] = 0, i++);
```

Though this may save you keystrokes, it makes it harder to follow the flow of the program.

Use logical consistency as your criterion for adopting a particular style of programming. For a short loop with a single test, the C idiom can be coded. For a longer loop, in which there might be another test for breaking the loop, the structured method is preferable.

## USE OF goto STATEMENTS

Try to avoid the use of gotos. If you must use them, limit them to one or two labels per function, at the bottom of a loop or for error recovery. Start the labels at the first character of the line.

One well-planned goto can simplify a program. For example, if you needed to see which element of a triple dimensioned array provided some value, you could write the code as

```
for (i = 0; i < n; i++)
    {
    for (j = 0; j < n; j++)
        {
        for (k = 0; k < n; k++)
            {
            if (array[i][j][k] == VALUE) goto end;
            /* Rest of loop */
            }
        }
    }
end:;
```

Otherwise, you would need to introduce another flag and the code would look like

```
done=FALSE;
for (i = 0; i < n && !done; i++)
```

```
    {
for (j = 0; j < n && !done; j++)
    {
    for (k = 0; k < n && !done; k++)
        {
        if (array[i][j][k] == VALUE)
            done=TRUE;
        else
            {
            /* Rest of loop */
            }
        }
    }
}
```

## USE OF MULTIPLE return AND exit STATEMENTS

If a function returns a value, use a variable for the value instead of an expression. Do not use multiple return statements in a function. By following these rules, you will spend much less time debugging your programs. For example, you could write an absolute value function as:

```
int absolute(number)
/* Computes the absolute value of a number */
int number;                    /* Number to return absolute value for */
    {
    if (number < 0)
        return -number;
    else
        return number;
    }
```

or as

```
int absolute(number)
/* Computes the absolute value of a number */
int number;                    /* Number to return absolute value for */
    {
    int ret;

    if (number < 0)
        ret = -number;
    else
        ret = number;

    return ret;
    }
```

Although this is a simple function, suppose it was not working. To debug your function you would have to change the first function to look like

```
int absolute(number)
/* Computes the absolute value of a number */
int number;                          /* Number to return absolute value for */
    {
    if (number < 0)
        {
        printf("\n Result is %d", -number);
        return -number;
        }
    else
        {
        printf("\n Result is %d", number);
        return number;
        }
    }
```

The latter could simply look like

```
int absolute(number)
/* Computes the absolute value of a number */
int number;                          /* Number to return absolute value for */
    {
    int ret;

    if (number < 0)
        ret = -number;
    else
        ret = number;

    printf("\n Result is %d", ret);
    return ret;
    }
```

It is simple to debug a function that has a single return, as shown later in the section on debugging. If you find it necessary to have multiple returns, the lesser evil may be to use gotos to a return statement at the end of the function.

You should have only one call to the exit function in your program. If you need to exit from several locations, devise your own exit routine to call exit. With this routine you can trace where you might be exiting from, as well as returning an exit value.

## EXTERNAL VARIABLES

External variables may be either global (program-wide) or static (declared only within a source file). Try to avoid using global variables. If you must use them, declare them as externs in a header file. Place all corresponding definitions in a single file that also includes this header file. This will allow the compiler to check that you have not redeclared a variable to be a different data type.

Global variables should preferably be used only for reference. Functions should never change their value, otherwise programs can be difficult to debug.

You should refrain from creating packages that require the user to set global variables. There is a simple way of avoiding this necessity. For example, suppose you have the global variable mode_setting. This variable needs to be set and tested throughout the program. You could simply create source files as

*Source file:* setting.h

```
extern int mode_setting;
```

*Source file:* setting.c

```
int mode_setting;              /* Declares global variable */
```

*User's source file:*

```
#include "setting.h"
...
if (mode_setting == 0) ...
```

However, a better way to implement this is to code two functions to access the variable and have the user call these functions instead. This would look like

*Source file:* setting.h

```
void set_mode();
int get_mode();
```

*Source file:* setting.c

```
static int mode_setting;

void set_mode(value)
int value;
    {
    mode_setting = value;
    return;
    }
```

```
get_mode()
    {
    return mode_setting;
    }
```

and the user's code would look like:

```
#include "setting.h"

if (get_mode() == 0) ...
```

This method has several advantages. First, if you want to track the changes to mode_setting, one print statement in set_mode() is sufficient. Second, if you slip and code if (get_mode()=0), the compiler will signal an error. This is not the case if the error is if (mode_setting=0).... Third, many debuggers do not have a "watch" feature that interrupts execution when a variable's value changes. You have to step through the code carefully to find when mode_setting changes. With these functions, you simply break on each call to set_mode.

After the program is thoroughly debugged, you may want to create a slightly faster version. To avoid the overhead of calling functions, you can change the files to

*Source file:* setting.h

```
extern int mode_setting;
#define set_mode(x) mode_setting=(x)
#define get_mode() (mode_setting)
```

*Source file:* setting.c

```
int mode_setting;                /* Declares global variable */
```

## VARIABLE NAMES

Use meaningful variable names. Do not abbreviate names unless they are overly long. If you need to abbreviate, use meaningful abbreviations. You should adopt a consistent method for naming variables. A typical table of style conventions appears in Table 14.2. You could make exceptions to the rules, but deviations should be carefully commented.

Do not reuse variable names every time an opening brace appears, even though C permits this practice. If you see number = 0; in one portion of the code, without a careful reading of the intervening lines you might assume this value for a latter reference to number. For example, (number == 0) in another section might be true. If number had been redeclared for the block in which this appeared, then this assumption might be wrong.

Within packages of functions (source file of related functions), any functions or external variables used only within the package should be declared static. This prevents conflict of local names between source files.

### Table 14.2 Naming Standards

| *Element* | *Style* |
| --- | --- |
| Function names | All lowercase. |
| Variable names | All lowercase. |
| External variable names | Start with a unique letter sequence (such as g_). |
| #defines | All uppercase if simple define. |
| | All lowercase if with tokens (as a function). |
| Structure and union tag-types | Start with a unique letter sequence (such as s_ or u_). |
| Pointer names | Start with a unique letter, such as p. |

Do not use names beginning with underscores, because they may conflict with names reserved by the compiler.

---

## #defines

As a rule of thumb, all constants should appear in #defines. Only 0 (and maybe 1) should appear in the body of a function. All arrays should be sized with either a #define or implicitly as

```
#define SIZE_ARRAY 30
...
int array[SIZE_ARRAY];
```

or

```
#define SIZE_ARRAY sizeof(array)/sizeof(int)
...
int array[] = {1, 2, 3, 4};
```

Any for loops would use SIZE_ARRAY as the size for the end test, such as for (i = 0; i < SIZE_ARRAY; i++).
    You should #define filenames, such as

```
#define FILENAME "B:NAME.FIL"
#define WRITE "w"

file = fopen(FILENAME,WRITE);
```

This makes it easy to switch filenames without looking through a program for fopen calls.
    Strings that are format specifications for printf and scanf need not follow this convention. However, it is a good idea to use #define for error messages, because they become easier to spot. For example, the following error message stands out:

```
#define ERROR_NO_FILE "No file has been found"
...
printf(ERROR_NO_FILE);
```

Other than TRUE and FALSE, which are usually defined as 1 and 0, never make an assumption about the value of a `#define`. Always test explicitly against a value, as if (c == END), rather than assuming END has a value of 0, as with if (!c).

---

## HEADER FILES

You should use header files for definitions of system-wide information. C compilers use header files to contain machine-dependent information, such as the I/O stream information. Header files can create "information hiding," as the set_mode example demonstrated.

A `#define` should never be repeated in two separate files if it refers to the same thing. For example, if you decide to use `#define PI 3.14159` in several different source files, keep it in a common header file. The declaration of all `extern` variables should be kept in a header file. The corresponding definitions of these `extern` variables should be kept in one source file.

A `#define` in a header file can create in-line code expansion for what would appear to be a function call. For example, many compilers have a header file for `isdigit(chr)` and other similar routines that simply turn the call into an index into a character array.[1] This translation is transparent to the user.

Similarly, you can create a `#define` file that renames functions. This is particularly useful if a compiler supports function names longer than the linker allows. For example,

```
#define StrToInt(string) atoi(string)
```

Another novel use of `#defines` is by Mike Cogan of Modern Systems Consulting, who created a header file having macros for many of the common C keywords. Listing 14.1 shows some of these `#defines`. Cogan included `#defines` for FUNCTION and CALL so he can quickly find the beginning of each function and the places where it is called.

**Listing 14.1 Cogan's Naming Header**

```
#define AND &&
#define OR ||
#define NOT !
```

---

[1] For example, into `ctype[(chr) + 1]&0x4`, where bit 2 in each element of `ctype` is a 1 if the corresponding character is a digit.

```
#define LT <
#define GT >
#define EQ ==
#define NE !=
#define GE >=
#define LE <=

#define AND_D &
#define OR_D |

#define FUNCTION /**/
#define CALL /**/

#define BEGIN {
#define END }
#define IF if
#define THEN {
#define ELSEIF } else if
#define ELSE } else {
#define ENDIF }
#define FOR for
#define ENDFOR }
#define CASE break; case
```

Using these #defines, you can write a piece of C code like

```
if ((x == 4) | | ( y <= 3))
     j = 7;
else
     {
     b = a & MASK;
     }
```

to look like

```
IF ( (x EQ 4) OR ( y LE 3))
     THEN J = 7;
ELSE
     b = a AND_D MASK;
ENDIF
```

## CODE DOCUMENTATION

There are a variety of guidelines for documenting your program. One tends to write more functions in C than in other languages, so it is important each function be documented sufficiently to be readable and understandable.

Establish guidelines for documenting code. An example of guidelines is shown in Table 14.3. Consistently using a standard form helps people reading your programs to know where to find necessary information. It also helps with the later creation of an automatic documentation program to extract the comments.

Keep related functions in the same source file. Having #define FUNCTION /* */ and using it at the start of each function helps each stand out. Each source file or package of functions and each function should have documentation following the guidelines in Table 14.3.

Sample documentation looks like

```
/* BINARY TREE PACKAGE */
/* Provides a way to create and print a binary tree */
/* Functions are
     int search_tree(pointer, match_word)
     int add_tree(pointer, new_word)
     void in_order(root, print_node);
     struct s_node *tree_start(new_word)
*/
/* Header file is "bintree.h" */

/* 8/29/86 First release Dan T. */
/* 9/30/86 Fixed bug add_tree Ken P.*/
...
int add_tree(pointer, new_word)
/* Add a node to the tree */
struct s_node *pointer;        /* Pointer to current node */
```

**Table 14.3 Package Documentation**

| Documentation Element | Items Included |
|---|---|
| Package header | Title of package<br>Summary of what is in it |
| Various system dependent information | Revision number<br>Status of revision (fully tested, user tested, and so on) |
| Update information for the entire file after the initial release | Date of change<br>Explanation and reason for change |
| Function header | One line explaining purpose of function<br>Explanation of each argument of function<br>Explanation of return values<br>Comments on errors that might occur<br>General comments (including algorithm) |

```
char new_word[SIZE_WORD];        /* Word to add */
                                 /* Returns
                                       TRUE if added
                                       FALSE if not added
                                 */
```

If you comment your code well, documentation like that just shown can be produced directly from the code. You could write a sample program that reads the file and outputs the appropriate comments.

If you must write tricky code, use the star system for documentation to highlight your comment blocks. Here's an example of the star system.

```
/**********************************************************************/
/*                                                                  */
/*                          WARNING                                 */
/*    Do not change the following lines unless you fully understand */
/*    this program.                                                 */
/*                                                                  */
/*    Because I needed to meet real-time requirements, I had to do it */
/*    this way. Sorry. D. Turney                                    */
/*                                                                  */
/**********************************************************************/
```

Documenting code is important, both for yourself and other programmers. Days or months after you have written a program, you may need to go back and modify it. If you keep notes in the form of comments that appear directly in the code with the program modules, you will have an easier time remembering why you created the module in a particular way.

If your programs and functions are going to be called by other users, it is especially important to comment well. Otherwise, you may find yourself spending a great deal of time explaining the use of your code.

## AIDS TO MAINTENANCE

Suppose you are faced with the task of altering code that is not documented or has been written in a sloppy manner. There are several programs you can use to help you create some semblance of order. Most systems have a "pretty print" program that indents and inserts spaces in code according to a standard pattern, as shown in Table 14.1.

The lint program, which has been described in Chapters 4 and 9, can also analyze source code for other purposes. It can report on variables that are not used in functions and portions of code that are unreachable. There are cross-reference programs on many systems that document which functions call particular functions and which functions access global variables.

## OPTIMAL FUNCTION SIZE

Functions can be big or small. Some guidelines suggest a function be kept to a page or two (about 60 to 120 lines long). This simplifies both reading and understanding functions. There may be reasons for needing to write a longer function. Try to make sure the execution of a long function takes place in small blocks, each of which is less than a page in length. On the whole, keep functions simple.

Breaking a program into manageable functions makes the debugging job easier. It is quicker to recompile a small function after you fix an error than a function 30 pages long. When you find yourself using your text editor to copy lines of source code for reuse in another function, it is time to consider making those lines a function.

There is another simple rule of thumb you can use. If you start indenting more than three or four levels, a function becomes difficult to follow. Though a function may be shorter than the maximum length of two pages, when it breaks this rule, it is time to subdivide it.

You should use functions (or macro equivalents) for small repeatable segments of code. Even if the segment is only a single line long, a function might be in order. Functions that have several nested `if` or `while` loops appear much easier to read if some of the inner loops are placed in a separate function.

You can also create functions with names closer to their purpose. For example, you could use

```
#define zero_buffer(buffer,size_buffer) setmem(buffer,size_buffer,0);
#define clear_buffer(buffer,size_buffer) setmem(buffer,size_buffer,' ');
```

Maintain a common order of parameters between functions. With the C library functions, output parameters usually come first, input parameters second. For example, the string copy function has the order `strcpy(out_string, in_string)` instead of `strcpy(in_string, out_string)`. Whichever method you choose, use it consistently. Unfortunately, some of the library functions are not consistent (for example, `fputc` and `fprintf` have the file pointer in different places).

Use the `void` type for function returns if the function does not return a value. This helps prevent a garbage return value from being used in an expression.

## HOW TO HANDLE ERRORS IN FUNCTIONS

Each function should check its arguments for validity. It should also attempt to check any intermediate results for validity. If it detects an error, there are several options for what the function can do. These are

1. Return the error value from the function—if there are unique values that do not normally apply. You can use values as NULL for pointers or negative numbers for array indices.

2. Call a separate error routine (or as in the C library, a global variable, such as errno) after every use of the function to check for errors.

3. Have the function abort the program due to an error. This is usually permissible if an error was due to an internal logic error. However, in most cases you would want to return to the user.

4. Print an error message on stderr. Because stderr is usually defaulted to the terminal, this might mean your program displays a message in the midst of normal output. Avoid using printf function to output in a procedure, other than error messages that are really not supposed to occur. stderr can be directed elsewhere using freopen().

5. For routines in large programs, have the routine output an error message to a log file. This is a file produced as the program is running, and it can be checked at the end of the run for error messages. If stderr is redirected to this file, this option is the same as option 4.

6. Combine some of the techniques in items 1 through 5.

If you use a log file, make your messages meaningful but short, so you can use a word processor to search through the file quickly for a particular error message.

You can implement the last three methods in a way that allows you to change the output easily. For example, if you coded

```
#define ERROR(MESSAGE) printf("\n" MESSAGE)

#define ERR_FILE "Bad value for routine xxx"
    . . .
if (value > MAX_VALUE)
    ERROR(ERR_FILE);
else
    . . .
```

you could simply change ERROR(MESSAGE) to

```
#define ERROR(MESSAGE) fprintf(error_file,"\n" MESSAGE);
```

or

```
#define ERROR(MESSAGE) fprintf(stderr,"\n" MESSAGE);
```

In the former, the error messages would then go to the file opened as error_file. With the latter they would go to wherever stderr was directed.

---

## DEBUGGING

Debugging is the art of determining why a program does not work properly. Even the best of designs can fail to be coded properly. The key to debugging is knowing what is failing and precisely when it fails. Otherwise, debugging resembles trying to fix a car when the owner simply says, "it doesn't run right."

Plan and code your programs so they are easy to test and debug. Develop your testing procedure *before* you code, not afterwards.

### Types of Program Failures

Failures come in many flavors. First is the program that always runs, but produces wrong answers. Second is the program that runs, but hangs up (refuses to respond to more input) at certain spots. Third is the program that does either of the first two, but in a seemingly unpredictable manner. ("If I type this, then that, and next I press that key, this error occurs, but not all the time and then....")

Information is essential in debugging. The more internal values of variables you can obtain, within reason, the easier it will be to try to determine the outcome.

### Debugging Techniques

You can debug your code in several ways. Debug statements can be either conditionally compiled into the code or the code can test some flag to see if debug should be output. The former is more efficient for routines that may be executed many times, such as library routines. The latter is good for programs themselves.

For example, a function called often might look like

```
check_date(month,day,year)
    {
#ifdef DEBUG
    printf("\n In check_date.");
    printf("Input is month %d day %d year %d", month,day,year);
#endif
    ...
#ifdef DEBUG
    printf("\n Check_date return is %d",result);
#endif
    return result;
    }
```

Alternatively, you could set up code like this:

```
#include <stdio.h>

FILE *debug_file;            /* Debug file pointer */
int debug;                   /* Debug flag */
main(argc,argv)
int argc;                    /* Argument count */
char *argv[];                /* Pointers to arguments */
    {
    if (argc > 1)
```

```
        {
        debug = TRUE;
        debug_file = fopen(argv[1], "w");
        if (debug_file == NULL)
                {
                printf("\n Unable to open debug file");
                exit(1);
                }
        }
    ...
    if (debug)
        fprintf(debugfile, "\n Value of x is %d", x);
    }
```

Supposing this program is called test, if you started it up as

```
test run1
```

the debug output goes to a file called run1. The output slows down the execution
of the program. However, the user is otherwise unaware of its existence. You simply
would use a text editor to search for the various values in the debug output file.
    You might have several levels of debug, for example,

```
#define DEBUG1 (debug & 0x01)
#define DEBUG2 (debug & 0x02)
#define DEBUG3 (debug & 0x04)
```

```
...
```

```
#include <stdio.h>

FILE *debug_file;              /* Debug file pointer */
int debug;                     /* Debug flag */

main(argc,argv)
int argc;                      /* Argument count */
char *argv[];                  /* Pointers to arguments */

    {
    if (argc > 2)
        {
        sscanf(argv[2], "%x", &debug);
        debug_file=fopen(argv[1],"w");
        if (debug_file == NULL)
                {
                printf("\n Unable to open debug file");
                exit(1);
```

```
                }
             }
             ...
         if (DEBUG1)
             fprintf(debugfile,"\n Value of x is %d",x);
```

Then, executing it with

```
test run1 2
```

only outputs statements that tested DEBUG2. Depending on the size of the final program, the additional work to break debug statements into levels might be worthwhile.

Another use of the conditional directive is to be able to include the test program for a routine with the routine itself. That way, if the routine is changed, the source can be recompiled with the same test as before. For example,

```
#ifdef DEBUGMAIN
main()
/* Test driver for check_date */
    {
    int result;
    /* Test for bad month */
    result=check_date(0,1,40);
    printf("\n For bad month (0) result is %d",result);
    result=check_date(13,1,40);
    printf("\n For bad month (13) result is %d",result);
    ...
    }
#endif
```

## ERRORS

There are several forms of errors:

1. Compiler errors—those the compiler tells you about because it cannot understand what you have coded
2. Compiler warnings—those the compiler warns you about because it can determine there may be an error in your program
3. Run-time errors—errors reported when you try to run your program, such as a divide by 0
4. Writing errors—errors in thinking that what you wrote is what you meant
5. Design errors—those that result because your design is wrong

The only good thing about making errors is that if you remember them, you should not make them a second time. Each type of error is covered in the remainder of this section, and guidelines for avoiding errors should help you minimize their occurrence.

### Compiler Errors

*Compiler errors* are ones occurring during the compilation process. They may be reported a line later or so than the line on which they actually occurred. Some common errors are

1. Missing braces around a compound statement, as in

```
if (x==5)
      y=3;
      z=7;
else
      x=2;
      y=9;
```

2. Redefining a function return:

```
double function();
...
int function()
    {
    ...
    }
```

3. Putting a semicolon after a function name that is being defined.

```
function();
    {
    ...
    }
```

### Compiler Warnings

*Compiler warnings* are potential errors that indicate you are trying to force something in the code that may not be proper. These include

1. Forgetting to define a function parameter
2. Omitting a function declaration return type
3. Passing incorrect parameters

These warnings are reported by the compiler, if there are expanded function prototypes in the source file. The `lint` program also reports these errors.

### Run-Time Errors

There are very few run-time error messages with programs written in C. The most frequent run-time error is trying to divide a number by 0. Your system may also report addressing exceptions (accessing the 0 location, writing into read-only memory, and so on) and floating point exceptions (such as overflow).

### Writing Errors

*Writing errors* are mistakes in your use of the language. You will get no warnings from the compiler. The code is compiled, but it does not execute the way you assumed it would. Types of writing errors include

1. Global errors, such as

   ```
   int i;     in one source file
   double i;  in another source file²
   ```

2. Array initialization, such as

   ```
   char string[5]="abcde"
   ```

   which means that there is no room for a terminating NUL.

3. Going beyond an array's boundaries. Always check for the size of an array.
4. Error in usage, such as

   ```
   root = b + discriminant/2*a
   ```

   or

   ```
   root = (b+discriminant)/2*a
   ```

   for

   ```
   root = (b+discriminant)/(2*a)
   ```

5. Floating point errors: 1./3. − .33333333 may not produce 0.0. Check all floating points against some tolerance.
6. Redefining a library function, especially if your function does something different than the library function.

---

² Some linkers may catch this error.

7. Operator confusion, such as

   && versus &
   == for =

8. Operator misuse—usually of operators with side-effects, such as

   a = a++;

9. Function parameter and return data type mismatch. This can be avoided by including expanded function prototypes or by using the `lint` program.
10. Using variables, especially pointers, before they are initialized.
11. Leaving off the address operator (&) on parameters passed to `scanf`.
12. Not checking for pointers equal to NULL.
13. Ignoring the order of the prefix and postfix increment and decrement operators: `*(p++)` is not the same as `*(++p)`.
14. Using `'A'` for `"A"`, and vice versa.
15. Returning the address of an automatic variable from a function. The memory location for an automatic is only reserved while the function is executing.
16. Clobbering constants, such as a function that alters a parameter passed by reference. Use the `const` modifier for parameters that should not be altered.
17. Not being aware of precedence with bit operators. For example, a >> 5 + 3 is processed as a >> (5 + 3).
18. Type coercion (silent truncation), such as

    ```
    int i;           /* Assuming two byte ints */
    int j = 256;
    i = 257 * j;
    ```

## Design Errors

*Design errors* are logic errors in the program. The most common are

1. Errors in loops. Your code either loops one too many times or one too few times.
2. Error in termination. The last object to be processed is ignored because you terminated a function prematurely.
3. Not testing all possible conditions. You have several tests of a variable against a value, but they do not test all possible values.

## Preventing Errors

There are many ways of preventing common errors, or at least determining what errors there are. These include

1. Checking all return values from functions. Don't write simply

```
fwrite(buffer,count,1,file);
```

rather, use

```
if (fwrite(buffer,count,1,file)!=count)
    {
    printf("\n Error in file writing ");
    exit(0);
    }
```

2. Testing for floating point values close to zero with a tolerance.

```
#define TOLERANCE .0000001
int test_zero(value)
/* Checks to see if floating number is close enough to equal zero */
double value;                /* Value to check */
    {
    return ( (value>-TOLERANCE) && (value<TOLERANCE) );
    }
```

3. Using a default case in every switch.

```
switch(value)
    {
case ONE:
    ...
default:
    printf("\n In routine SOMENAME, value was %d in switch",value);
    error_check(NOT_FATAL);
    ret = ERROR:
    goto end;
    }
```

4. Using a common error reporting routine as[3]

---

[3] Suppose you specify the routine in the following code with

```
enum error_level = {non_fatal,fatal};
error_check(severity)
enum error_level severity;
    ...
```

and you use a function prototype within the source file. You should get a compilation error or warning
if you call the routine with any value other than non_fatal and fatal. Thus, the default in the switch
would not have been required.

```
error_check(severity)
/* Checks for the severity of an error */
int severity;
    {
    switch(severity)
        {
    case NOT_FATAL:
        printf("\n Please notify program office");
        printf("\n Program will continue after you press Enter");
        while (getchar() != '\n')
            {
            ;
            }
        break;
    case FATAL:
        printf("\n Please notify program office immediately");
        printf("\n A programming error has occurred");
        printf("\n Program is exiting");
        exit(1);
    default:
        printf("\n Please notify program office immediately");
        printf("\n An error has occurred in the error handler");
        }
    return;
    }
```

You should check all values input to your program or functions. This eliminates a common source of program malfunctions.

Validate the input as close to the source as possible. Ideally, it should be when the user types it in. There are several checks for input. First there are checks such as dates (with the check_date function) and times that can only use certain values. Second are ones that can be checked for definite ranges (employee salary must be positive and less than the president's). Third are those that can only be checked for reasonableness. (Did you really want 10000 boxes of paper clips?)

Some input can be cross-checked. For example, given hours worked per day, you can see if the total number of hours per week is a reasonable number.

If the input data is invalid, you should display a helpful message. Just writing "Input data is invalid" does not help a user very much. "Value should be between 10 and 100" is much more meaningful.

Each function should check its input as much as practical. Pointer values are difficult to check as anything but NULL could be a valid value. It is easy to check the index of an array against 0 to some maximum value. You should check for division by zero before all divisions.

# TESTING

## Types of Tests

Commercial firms have a standard policy of at least several testing levels for programs. The first is the *unit test.* At this level, each programmer on the project tests to make sure his or her functions are working according to specification. The next level is called the *system test* or *system integration.* At this level, the modules are linked together in the final form and the program tested for completeness. The next level is the *alpha test,* which is usually performed by in-house nonprogrammers. They make sure all features of the program work and the program does not bomb out.

After the program passes the alpha test, it is released in *beta test* to selected outside firms. These firms try the program in real-life situations. These operations usually uncover bugs, as the users try combinations of features not covered by the alpha testers. After a period of beta testing, the program is ready for production.

Checking each function involves several different tests. You can write a driver program to provide various input to the module. Some of the programs in this book act as drivers. The parameters passed to each function should test all possible paths (for example, each branch on `if` statements and each `case` on switches).

## What to Test

You should test for input values that fall on the boundary of permissible values. These usually include zero, one, and some maximum. You should also try a null case (such as sorting an array with all zero values) and illegal cases (such as passing a negative number as a size).

If you decide not to test all these values (and even if you do), you should include the appropriate `#ifdef DEBUG` statements in the functions, so you can check the values when the functions are called in programs.

# DEBUGGERS

*Debuggers* are programs that trace the execution of your code a statement at a time. *Assembly language debuggers* use the machine code that has been compiled and assembled as the source for tracing. To use debuggers you need an understanding of how your processor works and how the compiler and assembler use the various features of the computer. Normally you use debuggers only to debug any assembly language routines you have written.

*Source language debuggers* trace statements on the C level source code. You can stop the execution of your program, print out the values of variables, and alter variable values. Several interpreters available currently not only act as source language debuggers, but also have a built-in editor, compiler, and linker, so if you make a change in the source, the function will be quickly recompiled and relinked.

Debuggers are useful in checking out small sets of routines or small programs. Using them in combination with some means of debug output (either conditional compilation or test of a debug flag) is an excellent way of checking out larger programs.

Do not use debuggers and interpreters as crutches. You should write your programs so they are easily debuggable. Interpreters should help you save time in recompiling code that might need a small change. Relying on a debugger's features as the primary means for developing code may lead to sloppy code.

Many of the example programs include what you might term "useless." The value is only used in one place and therefore does not really need to be assigned to a variable. These variables were created with the debugging process in mind. It is easier to have a `printf` output a single variable than to print out the expression being computed.

## SUMMARY

- Write your code for visual appearance and clarity.
- Use appropriate code style.
- Plan your programs so they are testable.
- Use #defines everywhere.
- Do not write tricky code. It will trick you.
- Comment sufficiently, but not excessively.
- Plan your testing before writing the code. Write code that is easy to test.

## SELF-TEST

1. What are some types of errors?
2. What is the best way to debug?
3. What is wrong with the following code?

```
if (a > d) {
     k = 3;
     }
while (f < 7)
{
     f++;
}
if (a == b) { i = 1; j = 2;}
```

## ANSWERS

1. Compilation errors, logic errors, design errors, execution errors, and misuse of the language.
2. Plan for debugging in advance. Structure your programs so tracing their execution is easy.
3. It does not follow a consistent style for indents and placement of braces.

## PROBLEMS

1. Look at the first few programs you wrote in C. How would you improve their appearance? Did you document what you were doing?
2. Give a sample of your programs to some programming friends. Ask them if they can tell what the program is supposed to do.
3. Look at the examples in the first part of this book. Which style for the if (a==b) example do you like? How about the c=getchar()? And the multiple test on C? Explain your reasons.
4. If you use many of the #defines in Table 14.3, your code will not look like C. Is this good or bad? Why?
5. Does your code meet the white space guidelines? Which indentation guideline does it meet? Write a program that takes a source file that does not meet these guidelines and produces one that does.
6. Are your functions consistent in the order of parameters? How consistent are your names for variables and parameters?
7. Someone coded a tax table as

```
if (income<=5000.)
     tax_rate=0.0;
else if (income<=7000.)
     tax_rate=.14
else
     ...
```

How could this be better structured?

8. Following the guidelines presented in this chapter, modify Listings 2.3, 3.3, 4.4, and 9.1.
9. Revise your earlier assignments to conform to this chapter's guidelines. Exchange several revised programs with fellow classmates for comments.
10. Redo problem 8 from Chapter 13 using the guidelines in this chapter.

11. Investigate the creation and use of standard library functions using your compiler. Comment how you might design and use library functions to write large application programs.

12. Select sample programs from the literature such as *Dr. Dobb's Journal* and *Computer Language*. Comment on how closely these programs follow the guidelines presented in this chapter. How might you make these programs conform?

# Chapter Fifteen

# Design, Coding, and Approaching Problems

Designing a program is a developed skill. The more you design and code, the better you become at it. Program design systems include top-down, bottom-up, data flow, control flow, and graphical design. You should always design a program before coding it. Though the design takes time, in the end the total time spent designing and coding will be less than launching into coding blind and spending time repairing your programs.

## PROGRAM SPECIFICATION PHASE

The first step in designing a program is specifying what it is supposed to do. This is actually the hardest part of application development. Fully specifying every input and output of a program is much of the design effort. Incomplete specifications from program users are common, leaving you to your imagination about what to do.

It is tough to write a program that does exactly what it is supposed to do, if it cannot be clearly stated. Depending on the type of program, a user's manual could be written first, instead of a complete specification. Your users will know what they are getting and the design is essentially specified by the manual.

Sometimes it is easy to make a prototype of a proposed program. Commercially available prototyping programs show the users what will be happening, if they cannot visualize it from a specification or user's manual.

It is possible to design a program without complete specifications. As you program more and more, you will get a feeling for what specifications are essential and what can be left till later. For example, with typical programs, exact report layouts can usually be put off till late in the design process.

## DESIGN PHASE

Once the specifications for a program are set, there are several approaches to the design. As your programming experience increases, the proper time to apply each approach will become more readily apparent.

### Top-Down and Bottom-Up Design

Two common approaches are top-down and bottom-up design. The top-down approach concentrates on the overall picture. It looks at the forest and breaks it into trees. The bottom-up approach starts with the smallest details and builds them into a program. It starts with trees and creates a forest. Each approach has its applications and advocates.

Top-down design starts with a general outline of a program. Then it breaks each entry in the outline into its constituents. The process continues until an entry becomes a process about the size of a function. For example, most programs can start with an outline that looks like:

Initialize
Process
Terminate

or

Input
Process
Output

Each of these large tasks is broken down into smaller tasks as the details of each task increase and take their final forms. For example, you might start with:

| | |
|---|---|
| Initialize | Display title screen |
| | Open files |
| | |
| Process | Pick one of: |
| | Add word |
| | Delete word |
| | Edit word |
| | Print words |
| | |
| Terminate | Clear screen |
| | Close files |

The bottom-up approach works in reverse. Small, simple solutions to problems are designed. These are combined into larger tasks that solve larger problems. These larger solutions are usually for problems that are general, rather than specific, to a program. These might look more like

Do a little thing
Do another little thing
Do still another little thing

which would get combined as

Do a combination of things

For example, you might start by writing functions that do the following:

Position a cursor
Set an attribute (highlight or normal)
Write a character

These could be called by a routine that writes a field (a string of characters at a position with a certain attribute) onto the terminal screen. It would be this field routine you call in your program. You might create higher level routines that output entire screens (arrays of fields).

Often the most practical method is a combination of these two methods. The bottom-up approach produces common tools that can be called by several programs. The top-down approach divides a program into tasks. The act of division may be affected by the tools you use. The combined approach will be demonstrated in Chapter 16.

If you designed a program purely from the top down, you might find yourself using similar, but different, code in separate parts of the program. If you approached it purely from the bottom up, you might write a disjointed program.

One way to solve a problem is to break the problem down into smaller problems, for which you already have solutions. In learning to program, you started with simple problems and worked your way up into bigger ones. In designing a program, you use these solutions as the potential answers to portions of bigger problems.

You can use smaller solutions several ways. First, you can *pipe* them: The output of one solution becomes the input of the next. This is often performed with UNIX and MS-DOS commands that perform input/output redirection. Second, you can call a solution from a larger one, as in normal function calling. Third, you can put two solutions together, as with creating packages. Fourth, you can make minor modifications to a solution. For example, you could change a function to use long integers rather than regular sized ones. The more you construct a repertoire of solutions for problems, the easier it will be to break problems down. For example, if you develop solutions like a generalized sorting routine, your design breakdown stops at that level. Make sure each solution does its task well. You might have multiple solutions, each of which makes trade-offs in speed or space.

Don't reinvent the wheel—use what somebody wrote before, if it works well. Use the compiler-supplied library for its functions. You can buy commercial packages with solutions to particular problems, such as math and statistical libraries.

### Control Flow and Data Flow Design

There is another dichotomy in a way of approaching the design. This is control flow versus data flow. The former concentrates on how the execution of a program occurs, whereas the latter describes how the data is passed from one portion of a program to another.

Once again, both design strategies have their applications. Control flow is useful for examining small portions of a program, about the size of a routine or so. Data flow is useful for looking at the big picture of a program, seeing how the portions relate to one another. Control flow tends to be detailed; data flow general. The structure chart attempts to combine some features of both.

Control flow can be expressed in at least three ways. The most common are the conventional flowchart (ANSI X3.25 symbols), the Nassi-Schneiderman (N-S) chart, and pseudocode. The conventional chart and the N-S chart use symbols that have been introduced in the text. The N-S diagrams are structure-oriented. *Structured code* is based on the concept that control has three forms—sequential, looping, and conditional. If you produce a chart using just the N-S symbols, the code you produce using it will be structured.

Pseudocode is simply a word description of what the process is doing. It can look much like the actual code itself. Indentation of loops and blocks helps to depict the structure graphically.

The power function of Chapter 4 could be expressed in each of these ways as shown in Figures 15.1, 15.2, and 15.3.

The conventional flowchart and the N-S charts can be produced mechanically from actual code using one of several commercial programs. This can help to make a graphic representation of what an unfamiliar routine is doing. The state diagram, which is introduced later on, is another way of showing control flow for complex algorithms.

Data flow shows how the information flows through the program modules. A data flowchart has five basic features: sources of data, destinations for data, data streams, data stores, and processes.

A source of data is anything that produces data, such as someone typing on a keyboard. The destination of data is something that simply uses data, such as a report. A data store is like a file—permanent or temporary—that saves data. A data stream is a flow of data from one process to another, from a source or data store to a process, or from a process to a destination or data store. A process uses a data stream from sources or data stores and produces a data stream to destinations or data stores.

The actual symbols to employ for each of the features is up to you. Abstract symbols can be used, so you do not automatically assume a particular device as a source, destination, or store. Some symbols are shown in Figure 15.4. These are from an IBM flowchart template.

Note that the lines in a data flowchart indicate which data is being passed to a process, not the actual flow of execution in a process. A program that does a spelling check might look like Figure 15.5.

The input from the data source (a keyboard or a file) is broken into words by the first process. The list of words is passed to the second process, which sorts

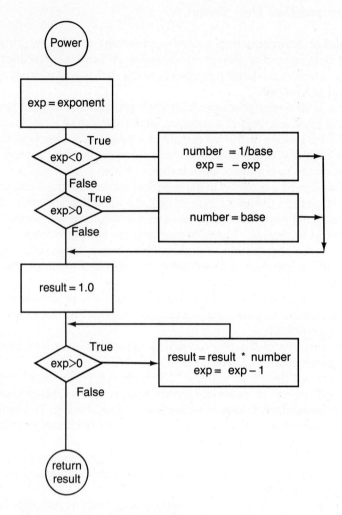

**Figure 15.1 Flowchart Example**

them. The sorted list is passed to a third process, one that removes duplicates. The next process looks up each unique word in a dictionary and passes only the unmatched words to the destination (a printed report or a file).

**Structure Chart**

An alternative method, which attempts to combine some of the features of both the data flow method and the control flow, is the structure chart. With this type of chart, the lines represent control flow and separate arrows depict the data flow. This is useful to show the basic organization of modules within a program. It cannot show looping or conditional execution. The chart for the power program in Chapter 4 would look like Figure 15.6.

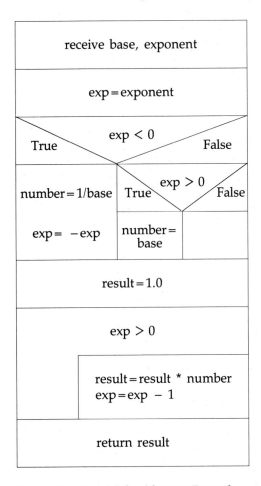

**Figure 15.2 Nassi-Schneiderman Example**

```
power: computes base raised to an exponent

input base, exponent

if exponent is negative
     invert the base
     negate the exponent
set result to 1
while exponent is positive
     set result to result times base
     subtract one from exponent

output result
```

**Figure 15.3 Pseudocode Example**

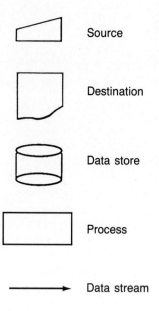

Source

Destination

Data store

Process

Data stream

**Figure 15.4 Data Flow Symbols**

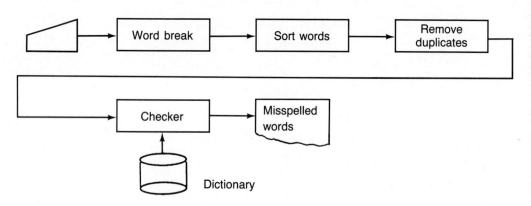

**Figure 15.5 Data Flow Example**

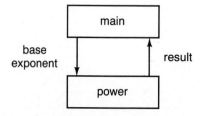

**Figure 15.6 Structure Chart Example**

## CONVERTING THE DESIGN INTO CODE

The essential idea in creating a program design is that the code should be able to be easily derived from it. Regardless of which type of design aid you adopt, you should structure your program or modules to match it. Otherwise, maintenance of the program becomes more complex.

You should strive to be able to say each thing once. If you include in your design a list of data item names, then you can describe these once. All descriptions of the processes and data should use these data item names. It helps keep the code consistent.

In creating designs you may make assumptions about the actual language in which it will be coded. However, you should not make assumptions about the *form* in which it will be coded. For example, if you recognize that you will need a stack, you should not specify whether the stack will be an array or a linked list. That is a detailed decision that you can make at coding time.

Before starting to code, you, any other programmers, and a sampling of users should "walk through" the design. You start with the beginning of the program and trace through the operations to be performed for the various sorts of input. This helps to ensure that the design meets the specifications.

A large portion of the effort in a software project is in the testing stage. Write your code so it is easy to test. Sample testing methods were given in Chapter 14. Using general routines previously written and tested will decrease the number of functions you must test.

## GOALS IN DESIGN

Your goals in designing programs are multiple. A working program is the first goal. Once you are able to write working programs, your emphasis should be on writing good programs. Two primary goals stand out:[1]

1. Clarity over speed.
2. Simplicity.

A few subgoals that go along with these goals are

1. Make it readable before you make it work.
   The Style section in Chapter 14 gave points on this.
2. Make it work before you make it fast.
   The Debugging section in Chapter 14 covered this.

---

[1] These are adapted from P. J. Plauger's design column in *Computer Language* magazine.

3. Make it general after you make it work once.
   Chapter 16 covers this.

4. Design robust code—do not let it bomb on bad input.
   Let it gracefully degrade, if possible.
   Have it report errors, not just abort.
   The Error section in Chapter 14 described this.

## MODULAR CODE AND INTERFACES

Regardless of the design approach chosen, you should write modular code. This means each function or package of functions acts like a plug-in circuit card. You should be able to pull a set of functions out, rewrite them, and put them back in a program without concern for what is going on in the rest of the program.

The most important aspect of writing modular code is to define the interface precisely. The values passed to and from a function or a program need to be exactly defined. The actual method by which a module performs a particular operation is insignificant, but the operation that is to be performed needs to be detailed.

Tight specifications of interfaces make it easy to break up a large programming project into pieces that can be easily integrated later.

Modular code also implies that each function or set of functions will have no side-effects outside of the function. This means that it should not affect any global variables. You should attempt to have functions input all values and output all values through the parameter list.

## ITERATIVE PROCESS

One important aspect in designing and coding programs is that they are iterative processes. The functions in this book were not all written in a single pass from start to finish. They were first written. Then problems developed or an insight into a better method occurred, and they were revised. You may follow all the rules—use top-down design, break down the major actions into modules—only to have problems develop in such a way that the best solution is to start over.

The more experience you have designing and programming, the fewer iterations you will go through on a particular design. You should be able to foresee potential problems and develop methods for meeting these problems in advance. Breaking up a problem into pieces will become easier as you program more.

## APPROACHES TO SOME DESIGN PROBLEMS

Several problems occur commonly in handling program design. State-based systems enable you to code some difficult problems easily. Storing variable length data can be handled in several ways. Other approaches can be found in the "Programming Pearls" column by John Bentley in the *Communications of the ACM.* Other occasional articles in that magazine explain solutions to particular problems.

## State-Based Systems

Many problems do not fit neatly into conventional design aids. State-based design is an alternative. State processing is a way of describing a program as where one is now and what one can possibly want to do next. The beginning of a typical program might be represented in pseudocode as

```
(1)   Input a_thing
(2)   If a_thing is A
            then Input another_thing
                  If another_thing is A1 then
(3)                     do something3
                  else if another_thing is A2 then
(4)                     do something4
(5)   Else if a_thing is B
            then Input still_another_thing
                  If still_another_thing is B1 then
(6)                     do something6
```

The corresponding state program would look something like:

```
State 1:  Input a_thing
          If a_thing=A then goto state 2
          If a_thing=B then goto state 5
State 2:  Input another_thing
          If another_thing=A1 then goto state 3
          If another_thing=A2 then goto state 4
State 3:  Do something3
State 4:  Do something4
State 5:  Input still_another_thing
          If still_another_thing=B1 then goto state 6
State 6:  Do something6
```

This "state way" of thinking is shown in Table 15.1 and diagramed in Figure 15.7.

**Table 15.1**

| State Number | Action | Result | goto State |
|---|---|---|---|
| 1 | Input | A | 2 |
|  |  | B | 5 |
| 2 | Input | A1 | 3 |
|  |  | A2 | 4 |
| 3 | Something3 |  | . . . |
| 4 | Something4 |  | . . . |
| 5 | Input | B1 | 6 |
| 6 | something6 |  | . . . |

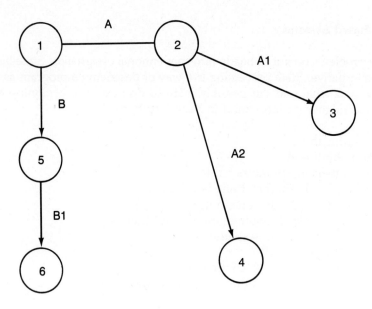

**Figure 15.7 State-Based Example**

Notice that the table clearly shows that for certain states and certain inputs, the next state is undefined. For example, for state 1, if the result is C, then the next state is undefined. You have to look for all the matching else-ifs in the normal code to determine this.

A "state processor" could implement these actions by something beginning like

```
Switch (Action(state))
     Case Input:
          Get an input
          Switch (Input)
               case Input1:
                    newstate=state(Input1)
               case Input2:
                    newstate=state(Input2)
               ...
     Case Something3:
          Do something 3
          Newstate=state
     Case Something4
          Do something 4
          Newstate=state
```

An example of a state-based routine might clarify this. Take a minute to figure out how to solve this problem: Given a string, determine if the characters in the string represent a valid decimal number. The rules for a valid number are

1. It may start with spaces.
2. There may be no spaces within the number.
3. There may be an optional sign (+ or -).
4. There is a series of digit characters optionally followed by a decimal point and another string of digits.
5. There may be trailing spaces.
6. It may be the null string.

A typical C routine to solve this problem might look like this:

**Listing 15.1 check_float Function—Standard**

```
#include <ctype.h>              /* For isdigit() */
#define YES 1
#define NO 0

int check_float(string, length)
/* Checks whether the string is a valid decimal number */
char *string;                   /* String to check */
int length;                     /* Maximum number of characters to check */
                                /* If NUL is not reached */
                                /* Returns
                                     YES if good
                                     NO if no good
                                */
{
int number_chars;              /* Number of characters to check */
int ret;                       /* Return value */

/* Get the real length */
number_chars = strlen(string);
if (number_chars < length)
    length = number_chars;

/* Take off leading spaces */
while ((length > 0) && (*string == ' '))
    {
    string++;
    length--;
    }

/* Check for a + or - */
if (length > 0 && (*string == '+' || *string == '-'))
    {
    string++;
    length--;
    }

/* Check digit part */
```

```
while ((length > 0) && (isdigit(*string)))
    {
    string++;
    length--;
    }

/* If characters still left, look for period and decimal part */
if (length > 0)
    {
    if (*string == '.')
        {
        string++;
        length--;
        while (length > 0)
            {
            /* Check remainder of characters */
            if (!isdigit(*string))
                break;
            else
                {
                string++;
                length--;
                }
            }
        }
    }

/* Check for trailing spaces */
while (length > 0)
    {
    if (*string != ' ')
        break;
    string++;
    length--;
    }

/* If length is nonzero, invalid characters were in string */
if (length != 0)
    ret = NO;
else
    ret = YES;

return ret;
}
```

There are a few alterations you can make in this code to take advantage of some of the C expressions (such as eliminating the test against 0). However the basic flow would remain unchanged. You could use a state-based design in coding this routine, using the state description in Table 15.2.

**Table 15.2 State Table—Version One**

| State | Meaning | Character input | Increment | New state |
|-------|---------|-----------------|-----------|-----------|
| INIT | Initial spaces | space | yes | INIT |
| | | anything else | no | SIGN |
| SIGN | Optional sign | + or − | yes | DIGIT |
| | | anything else | no | DIGIT |
| DIGIT | Whole part | digit | yes | DIGIT |
| | | anything else | no | PERIOD |
| PERIOD | Optional point | . | yes | DECIMAL |
| | | anything else | no | END |
| DECIMAL | Fraction part | digit | yes | DIGIT |
| | | anything else | yes | END |
| END | Trailing spaces | space | yes | END |
| | | anything else | yes | Terminate |

**Listing 15.2 check_float Function—State-Based**

```
#include <ctype.h>              /* For isdigit() */
#include <stdio.h>

#define S_INIT 0
#define S_SIGN 1
#define S_DIGIT 2
#define S_PERIOD 3
#define S_DECIMAL 4
#define S_END 5

#define YES 1
#define NO 0

int check_float(string, length)
/* Checks whether the string is a valid decimal number */
char *string;                   /* String to check */
int length;                     /* Maximum number of characters to check */
                                /* If NUL is not reached */
                                /* Returns
                                      YES if good
                                      NO if no good
                                */
    {
    int state;                  /* Current state */
    int number_chars;           /* Number of characters to check */
```

```
int ret;               /* Return value */
char chr;              /* Current character */
int step_char;         /* How many characters to step */

/* Get the real length */
number_chars = strlen(string);
if (number_chars < length)
    length = number_chars;

/* Now check all the characters */
ret = YES;
state = S_INIT;
step_char = NO;

while ((length > 0) && (ret == YES))
    {

    chr = *string;
    printf("\n State %d chr %c length %d", state, chr, length);
    switch (state)
        {
    case S_INIT:
        /* Get rid of leading spaces */
        if (chr == ' ')
            step_char = YES;
        else
            state = S_SIGN;
        break;
    case S_SIGN:
        /* Check on a + or - */
        if (chr == '+' || chr == '-')
            step_char = YES;
        state = S_DIGIT;
        break;
    case S_DIGIT:
        /* Get the digits in front of the decimal */
        if (isdigit(chr))
            step_char = YES;
        else
            state = S_PERIOD;
        break;
    case S_PERIOD:
        /* check for a period */
        if (chr == '.')
            {
            step_char = YES;
            state = S_DECIMAL;
            }
```

```
              else
                  state = S_END;
              break;
         case S_DECIMAL:
              /* Get the digits to right of the decimal */
              if (isdigit(chr))
                  step_char = YES;
              else
                  state = S_END;
              break;
         case S_END:
              /* Check for trailing blanks */
              if (chr != ' ')
                  ret = NO;
              else
                  step_char = YES;
              break;
         default:
              printf("\n CHECK_FLT Logic error state %d", state);
              }   /* End switch */

         /* Go to next character, if step_char is YES */
         if (step_char == YES)
              {
              string++;
              length--;
              }
         step_char = NO;
         }   /* End while */

    return ret;
    }
```

For the string "1.2" this printout shows the trace of the states:

```
State 0 chr    length 7
State 0 chr    length 6
State 0 chr 1 length 5
State 1 chr 1 length 5
State 2 chr 1 length 5
State 2 chr . length 4
State 3 chr . length 4
State 4 chr 2 length 3
State 4 chr   length 2
State 5 chr   length 2
State 5 chr   length 1
```

Notice no elaborate if-then-else statements appear in this function. At each state, only particular types of characters are accepted. If they do not appear, then either an error is signaled (that is, ret=) or the next state is attempted.

The preceding state function is not the most compact code. A reduction might look like Listing 15.3. See Table 15.3 for the second version of the state table.

**Table 15.3 State Table Example—Version Two**

| State | Meaning | New State If | | | |
|---|---|---|---|---|---|
| | | *Space* | *Digit* | *Period* | *Sign* |
| INIT | initial spaces | INIT | DIGIT | DECIMAL | DIGIT |
| DIGIT | whole part | END | DIGIT | DECIMAL | ERROR |
| DECIMAL | fraction part | END | DECIMAL | ERROR | ERROR |
| END | terminating | END | ERROR | ERROR | ERROR |
| ERROR | error occurred | | | | |

**Listing 15.3 check_float Function—State-Based (Compact Version)**

```
#include <ctype.h>                          /* For isdigit() */
#include <stdio.h>

#define S_INIT 0
#define S_DIGIT 1
#define S_DECIMAL 2
#define S_END 3
#define S_ERROR 6

#define C_SPACE 0
#define C_DIGIT 1
#define C_PERIOD 2
#define C_SIGN 3

static int change_state[][4] =
    {
    {S_INIT, S_DIGIT, S_DECIMAL, S_DIGIT},    /* S_INIT */
    {S_END, S_DIGIT, S_DECIMAL, S_ERROR},     /* S_DIGIT */
    {S_END, S_DECIMAL, S_ERROR, S_ERROR},     /* S_DECIMAL */
    {S_END, S_ERROR, S_ERROR, S_ERROR},       /* S_END */
    };

    /* newst[][0] new state if space */
    /* newst[][1] new state if digit */
    /* newst[][2] new state if period */
    /* newst[][3] new state if + or - */
```

```
#define YES_ 1
#define NO 0

int check_float(string, length)
/* Checks whether the string is a valid decimal number */
char *string;                   /* String to check */
int length;                     /* Maximum number of characters to check */
                                /* If NUL is not reached */
                                /* Returns
                                        YES_ if good
                                        NO if no good
                                */

        {
        int state;              /* Current state */
        int number_chars;       /* How many characters in the string */
        int ret;                /* Return value */
        char chr;               /* Current character */
        int chr_case;           /* Type of character */
        int new_state;          /* Next state to go to */

        /* Get the real length */
        number_chars = strlen(string);
        if (number_chars < length)
            length = number_chars;

        /* Now check all the characters */
        ret = YES_;
        state = S_INIT;
        while (length--)
            {
            chr = *string++;
            /* Determine the type of character */
            if (chr == ' ')
                chr_case = C_SPACE;
            else if (isdigit(chr))
                chr_case = C_DIGIT;
            else if (chr == '.')
                chr_case = C_PERIOD;
            else if (chr == '+' || chr == '-')
                chr_case = C_SIGN;
            else
                {
                /* Bad character, terminate now */
                ret = NO;
                break;
                }
            new_state = change_state[state][chr_case];
```

```
                    printf("\n State %d new state %d chr_case %d", state,
                        new_state,chr_case);

            if (new_state == S_ERROR)
                {
                ret = NO;
                break;
                }
            state = new_state;
            }
        return ret;
        }
```

For the same string, "1.2", the state transitions look like

```
State 0 new state 0 chr_case 0
State 0 new state 0 chr_case 0
State 0 new state 1 chr_case 1
State 1 new state 2 chr_case 2
State 2 new state 2 chr_case 1
State 2 new state 3 chr_case 0
State 3 new state 3 chr_case 0
```

The primary difference between state based code and conventional code is that a number (the "state") designates where you are in a process. In the conventional code, when you find the decimal point, you are a little over halfway down through the code. From that point, you continue to the end. In the state based system, when you find the decimal, state has the value S_DECIMAL, and you go around through the same loop again.

## Data Input and Storage

You can handle data that has a variable number of elements in two ways. Either the number of elements can be explicitly kept in a separate variable or a unique terminating value can be the last element. The former is the method C uses for arrays passed to bsearch. The latter convention is used for strings in C. If a value exists (such as '\0') that does not represent a valid value then the latter approach can be employed.

In inputting a series of values for different variables, you can use one of three approaches. The first uses the order in which the variables appear. A terminator appears at the end of each value. This is similar to the parameter list of functions or some commands (for example, copy a_file b_file assumes the first file is the source file).

The second approach is to give the name of the variable (or a keyword for it) and the value. This is usually used on the command line (such as -DDEBUG=7). The third method uses a fixed length field for each variable. This was used mostly

**Table 15.4 Input Forms**

| Approach | Input | Explanation |
|---|---|---|
| Order | namevalue,agevalue | where , is the terminator |
| Keyword | Name=namevalue,Age=agevalue | in either order |
| Length | Character position | |

```
          0         1
          123456787901234567
          namevalue      agevalue
```

name starts in character position 1
age starts in character position 15

with punched card input and is commonly used for data storage (records usually have fixed length fields).

For example, if you wanted to input a name and an age, you could input it in any of the ways in Table 15.4.

In a different area, but one with similar concerns, suppose you needed to store pixels (individual bits on a picture). Each pixel can be on (value 1) or off (value 0).

You could store these using a straight bit map, as in this sample:

**Bit number**

```
0         1         2         3
0123456789012345678901234567890
0001100000001000000000000010000
```

This makes it easy to turn on or off a particular bit. However, the bit consumes the same space regardless of the number of on bits.

You can keep track of which bits are on by simply having a list (or array) of bit positions, for example,

```
3 4 12 26
```

This takes up less space if only a few bits are on. If most bits are on, you could keep track of the off bits. In this form, it would take more time to turn on or off a particular bit, because these values should be kept in order.

As another alternative, you could store the sizes of blocks of bits that are off and on.

```
off on off on off on off
3   2  7   1  13  1  5
```

Depending on the way the pattern of bits is set, this alternative may take up much less room. This is usually a good way to store fixed maps. It is easy to shorten or expand the length of a block, thus shrinking or expanding the map. However, it takes more time to determine whether a bit is on or off.

You can use a combination of these latter two methods. Here the starting position of a block of on bits and the count of bits in the block are stored.

```
Position Count Position Count Position Count
   3       2     12      1     26      1
```

This has the advantages and disadvantages of the two approaches. The bit map approach is the most general. However, the others have advantages in storage space and particular uses. The technique you choose depends on what the program may be doing. These are examples of trade-offs you will have to make in designing programs.

### Multiple Return Values

There are three ways in which a function can return multiple values to a calling program. They all have to do with the concept of call by reference. The first is to use a string of variables, each of which is a call by reference. The second is to use an array as a parameter, which works if the variables are the same data type. The third is to pass a pointer to a structure, which will work for different data types.

### Interacting with the User

You should help the user of your program use it. Some guidelines for you to follow are

1. Always prompt for input. Do not make the user guess what is expected.
2. Have error messages give meaningful reasons explaining why the input is wrong.
3. Always try to have an escape mode to get a user out of performing some task accidentally.
4. Let users signify an end to input instead of making users supply a count of how many input items there are.
5. If an item value is bad and you cannot ask the user for correction, try one of the following. In any case, put out a message telling what you have done.
   a. Make a reasonable assumption item.
   b. Discard the item.
   c. Discard the minimum amount of information that the item relates to (itself, a structure, a file, and so on).
6. Always have programs die gracefully if they cannot continue. Put out error messages—both meaningful to the user and meaningful to you.
7. Try to make your program run even if the user does not select any options.

## PROGRAM APPLICATIONS

As you design programs, consider the application and lifetime of the program. You may write quick prototype programs that explore some aspect of a problem. These do not need to be as meticulously designed as the final program. Programs run infrequently need not be as efficient as those run often.

The area of application and the way in which the program runs may affect your design decisions. There are several facets of applications and a program may be classified within each facet.

### Timing

The following modes handle program timing in unique ways.

- Batch mode: Programs that are run unattended. They can usually be run at any time without difference in their results.
- Interactive mode: Programs that interact in some way with the user. These may be data entry programs that produce a file of data read by other programs or they may be standalone programs in themselves. Most personal computer programs are of this type. Although they must respond within a reasonable amount of time to user input, much of the time is spent simply waiting for the user to type.
- Timesharing mode: Programs that must respond to a variety of inputs, within some amount of time. These are interactive programs that operate on a shared processor.
- Real-time mode: Programs that must respond within a certain time to external events. A program controlling the firing of the spark plug in an electronic ignition system is a good example.

### Usage

Two basic categories of programs—other than operating environments—are developed.

- Application programs: Programs that perform some function that is not part of the programming effort. (An inventory system and an accounting package are examples.) Applications are usually the types of programs you write.
- System programs: Programs for writing programs. They include the C compiler, `lint`, and so on. They also include such tools as the UNIX programs `make` and `yacc`.

### Order of Execution

Two basic categories apply to the order of program execution.

- Dependent mode: Here, results may be determined by the order in which the operations are applied. For a banking program, suppose an overdrawn situation is tested after each check and deposit. If checks are subtracted first, then deposits added, an overdrawn situation may occur for an account even if deposits cover the checks.

- Independent mode: For this situation, results are not dependent on the order in which actions occur. For a banking application, suppose an overdrawn situation were only tested for at the end of a series of deposits and checks. Then the order in which the checks and deposits were applied has no effect.

## EFFICIENCY

Efficiency should be a consideration as you write a program, but not the overriding consideration. Several elements contribute to efficiency. One is how much time it takes the user to learn how to use the program. Another is how much time it takes for someone maintaining the program to understand how it works. Third is the algorithmic efficiency. Doing it one way may make a significant difference in time than doing it another way. Finally, there is efficiency in coding—how well you use processor time and memory space.

Normally the algorithmic efficiency and coding efficiency should be the least concern for the programmer, if a program runs in a reasonable amount of time and works. Usually only in real-time applications, or on small computers with limited memory or with programs run frequently, do the latter factors become significant. Choosing the proper algorithm usually has far more impact on a program's execution than any particular coding techniques. However, C does provide the means for you to code particular operations efficiently.

Languages are basically designed either to enable the application developer to be efficient, or to enable the developer to be abstract. On the one end is assembly language. It makes little use of abstractions, although some macro processors help programmers to be clever. On the other end are languages such as Prolog or LISP, which separate the abstractions from the actual way that the data is manipulated. Pascal is an example of a language that separates character data from integer variables. This makes it a superb language for teaching, because the compiler can check for programmer errors in mixing the two. However, if you want to be very efficient, Pascal may be the wrong choice.

A prime example of these differences is the ability of languages to address the screen memory of various computers. The IBM-PC enables you to directly address its memory (see portability example). Pascal does not allow this. Prolog and LISP, in their standard form, do not have the capability of addressing the screen. C enables you to directly address the memory with a pointer.

## SPEEDING UP THE PROGRAM

Never design a program for speed to the exclusion of all other considerations. If speed is a necessity, the program design may be tilted toward that goal, but it should not be the primary effort. Except in a few specialized areas, such as putting a game into 8K of ROM, program trickery should be only a last resort. Good overall design, such as choice of a sorting algorithm, has a far greater effect on execution time than saving a few instructions in an initialization routine.

A typical rule of thumb is that 80 percent of the code only accounts for 20 percent of the execution time. Thus to speed up a program, looking at the 20 percent of the code executed 80 percent of the time is an efficiency-producing exercise.

A *run-time profiler*, which is offered by several vendors, can help determine the bottlenecks in a program. A good modular design should allow you to concentrate your efforts on just a few modules.

Here are a few routines shown previously, but this time they have been written for maximum speed, rather than readability. You should compare these against their prior versions in Listings 7.1 and 5.6.

**Listing 15.4 date_check Function**

```
static char month_days[2][13] =
    {
    {0, 31, 28, 31, 30, 31, 30, 31, 31, 30, 31, 30, 31},
    {0, 31, 29, 31, 30, 31, 30, 31, 31, 30, 31, 30, 31},
    };

struct sdate
    {
    int month;
    int day;
    int year;
    };

int date_check(pdate)
/* Checks validity of date */
struct sdate *pdate;            /* Points to date structure to check */
                                /* Returns 1 if valid
                                          0 if not-valid */

    {
    return (pdate->month > 0 && pdate->month <= 12 ? ((pdate->day > 0)
        && (pdate->day <= month_days[!(pdate->year % 4)][pdate->month]))
        : 0);
    }
```

**Listing 15.5 toupper Function**

```
int toupper(chr)
int chr;
    {
    return ((chr >= 'a') && (chr <= 'z') ?
        chr - ('a' - 'A') : chr);
    }
```

Avoid using assembly language. It makes code less portable and maintainable. If you must use assembly language routines, try to make them general, such as inport and outport for hardware input and output or callsys with register structures for operating system calls. Put all assembly language programs together in a single file with full documentation of why they had to be written in assembler.

## ALGORITHMIC EFFICIENCY

Picking an algorithm can make more of a difference than coding practices. The power function introduced in Chapter 4 was inefficient. If you raised a value to the 14th power, there would be 13 multiplication operations. You might realize there is a faster way to get the same value. You can break the multiplications into steps:

$$x^2 = x * x$$
$$x^4 = x^2 * x^2$$
$$x^8 = x^4 * x^4$$
$$x^{14} = x^8 * x^4 * x^2$$

By calculating $x^2$, then $x^4$, and so forth, you can solve $x^{16}$ with only 4 multiplication operations. If you use the modulus operator, you can determine whether you need a particular power. You could take the power function and modify it to look like Listing 15.6.

**Listing 15.6 power Function Made Efficient**

```
double power(base, exponent)
/* Computes a power of base raised to a number */
double base;                /* Number to raise to a power */
int exponent;               /* Power to raise base to */
    {
    double power_of_two;    /* Current value of base raised to power of two */
    double result;          /* Result */
    int use_this_power;     /* Flag whether to use this power */

    /* If a negative power, then invert the base */
    if (exponent < 0)
        {
        base = 1 / base;
        exponent = -exponent;
        }

    result = 1.0;
    power_of_two = base;
    while (exponent > 0)
        {
        use_this_power = exponent % 2;
        exponent /= 2;
        if (use_this_power)
                result = result * power_of_two;
```

```
            power_of_two *= power_of_two;
            }

        return result;
        }
```

The function determines whether a particular factor (power_of_two) is needed by taking the exponent modulo 2. If it is, then the function multiplies result by the factor.[2]

---

## EFFICIENCY OF CODE

You can make code efficient simply by avoiding some common inefficiencies. An optimizing compiler may actually help you by performing some of these suggestions, but you should be aware of them. The following advice is true in general. For each given rule, there may be exceptions. Some compilers can optimize certain code segments more efficiently than alternative segments expressing the same logic.

1. Avoid unnecessary computation of subexpressions.
2. Reduce repetitive subscript calculations.
3. Remove constant expressions from loops, such as:

```
for (k=0;k<n;k++)
    {
    array[k]=i * j + 1;
    }
```

4. Use int instead of float variables if you only need discrete values.
5. Use the op= assignment operator.
6. Use expanded function prototypes and designate parameters as chars or floats. The compiler may avoid converting them to ints and doubles and thus save time.
7. If accessing elements sequentially in an array, use a pointer and increment it instead of using an index.

```
n = size;
pointer = array;
while (n--)
```

---

[2] You could also look at the bits in the integer power to determine whether a particular power of x is needed. For example, 14 has the bit value 000000000001110.

```
        {
        *pointer++ = x;
        }
```

is faster than

```
for (i = 0; i < size; i++)
        {
        array[i] = x;
        }
```

8. Similarly, if computing a set of values, use addition over multiplying. For example, if elements in an array were being set to some multiple of a number, then

```
x = number;
pointer = array;
while (n--)
        {
        *pointer++ = x;
        x += number;
        }
```

is faster than

```
n = size;
pointer = array + n;
while (n--)
        {
        *(--pointer) = number * n;
        }
```

9. Make a trade-off of data space versus speed. Look up results in tables, rather than computing them every time. For example, you might store the square roots for certain numbers in a table, as in

```
double square_root(x)
double x;
        {
        static double table [][2] =
                {
                /* Number, square root */
                {1., 1.},
                {2., 1.414.},
                {3., 1.7},
                /* Any more common ones */
                };
        /* Look up x in the table (using binary search routine) */
        /* If found, return corresponding value */
```

```
/* Else compute it using sqrt */
...
}
```

10. Use the smallest size data type for a variable that holds the range required. This is especially true for arrays.

11. Put code in-line versus calling a function. For example, calling an absolute value function is slower than simply computing it as:

```
(a > 0 ? a : -a )
```

which could be coded using a #define. For longer expressions, in-line code will require more memory, but it will still be faster than calling a function. Using a macro for an expression computation (one called many times) enables you to easily switch from in-line to function or vice versa.

12. Use register variables.

13. Pass pointers to objects, not the objects themselves. When an object is passed, all of the storage that it uses is copied onto the stack. For large objects this could take a good deal of time. When a pointer to that object is passed, only the address is copied onto the stack.

   Do not worry about removing expressions composed entirely of constants from a loop. The compiler computes expressions involving just constants at compile time. For example, if you have

```
#define I 5
#define J 17
#define L 32
      for (k=0;k<n;k++)
      {
      array[k]= I * J + L;
      }
```

the expression I * J + L is computed at compile time, and removing it from the loop does not make any difference.

## SUMMARY

- Top-down design, breaking a program into pieces, and bottom-up design, creating large solutions from small ones, complement each other.
- Data flow shows an overall view of how variables are passed.
- Control flow gives a detailed view of how they are operated upon.
- State-based design can simplify complex design problems.
- Algorithmic selection is more important than tricky coding in writing efficient programs.

## SELF-TEST

1. What are some approaches to design?
2. What is the first goal in programming?
3. Why is a program specification so important?
4. What is one important aspect of interacting with users?

## ANSWERS

1. Top-down, bottom-up, control flow, data flow, pseudocode, N-S charts, and flowcharts.
2. Make a working, readable program.
3. You cannot design a program until you know what it is supposed to do.
4. Let users know what is going on. Use meaningful prompts and error messages.

## PROBLEMS

1. For a life-insurance company, the mortality rates for various ages are given by a table:

   | Age at Issue | Rate per Thousand |
   |:---:|:---:|
   | 0 | 3.4 |
   | 1 | 1.3 |
   | 2 | 1.31 |
   | . . . | . . . |
   | 99 | 93.4 |
   | 100 | 99.7 |

   This was stored as an array of doubles. How might it be changed to save space?
2. Is the efficient version of the date_check function understandable? Why should you code it this way?
3. Time the power function in this chapter and the earlier version in Listing 4.2. How much of an improvement is there? Code it by testing the bits in the exponent. How much of an increase in speed is there? Is it worth the extra effort?
4. The memcpy function in the standard library may not copy properly if the memory locations being copied to overlap the memory being copied from. The memmove function will work properly in any instance. How much do you think you would save using the memcpy function? What do you think you might lose using it? Which one would you use?

5. A change to `check_flt` would be to allow an exponent (such as E33 or E+33) on a number. Change each function in this chapter to do this. You should first state whether blanks will be allowed before and after the E.

6. Following the guidelines presented in this chapter, modify Listings 2.3, 3.3, 4.4, and 9.1.

7. Revise your earlier assignments to conform to this chapter's guidelines. Exchange several revised programs with fellow classmates for comments.

8. Write and demonstrate the use of a function that accepts criteria for numeric data input. The function should be able to set upper and lower limits of acceptable data. The function should provide consistent error messages and looping for data.

9. Write and demonstrate the use of a function that accepts name input. The function should be able to check the name against a table of acceptable names. The function should provide consistent error messages and looping for correct data.

10. Write and demonstrate the use of a function that accepts date and time input. The function should be able to check the date and time against acceptable formats and limits. The date input should be *month/day/year* format and the time should be in *hour.min.sec*. The function should provide consistent error messages and looping for correct data.

11. Write and demonstrate a simple menu selection function. The idea is to enable the user to select an item from a menu displayed on the screen. The function should echo back the selection and permit alteration of the names and number of the selections.

12. Put into a library the functions created in the earlier exercises and write or modify an earlier assignment to make use of the library functions.

# Packages of Functions

Creating reusable functions decreases the amount of code you have to write to implement a design. *Packages* are groups of functions that perform related operations. Creating and using packages eliminates repetitive coding and debugging of the same problems over and over. Good software engineering uses many packages.

## MODULAR PROGRAMMING

As you saw several times earlier in the book, modular programming is the art of designing a routine or program to perform one task well. A *modular system* is a modular set of programs. A modular program contains a modular set of functions. Whether a particular sequence of operations is performed by a series of programs or by a single program with a series of functions is relatively unimportant. The trade-off between the two is mostly a memory space versus speed consideration. A series of programs requires less code space but takes more time to develop.

There are several natural areas in programming for creating modules. They include I/O packages, data access packages, and mathematical operation packages. The first step in designing a package is to determine whether what you require has already been written by other programmers in your organization or by commercial developers. There is no sense in reinventing the wheel, if the wheel works for your application. Packages are commercially available to perform graphics, communications, and statistics.

## PACKAGE ORGANIZATION

Most packages consist of two parts: the library of functions the user can call and the header file, which the user includes in the program. A typical package is a collection of mathematical routines, such as the one provided by the C compiler.

Function prototypes and definitions of error returns are provided in the math.h header file. The functions themselves are in the C library.

The date_check function, Listing 8.1, could be part of a package of date manipulation routines. You might have other functions to handle dates, as shown in this function description:

```
int date_check(date)
/* Checks the validity of a date */
struct s_date date;            /* Date to check */

struct s_date subtract_dates(first_date,second_date)
/* Returns the number of days between two dates */
struct s_date first_date;      /* First date */
struct s_date second_date;     /* Second date */
     /* If first_date is greater than second_date, result is negative */

long day_number(date)
/* Returns the number of days from Jan. 1, 1800 */
struct s_date date;            /* Date for which to compute number */
```

You would also have a header file, say date.h, containing the following:[1]

```
struct s_date
    {
    int month;                 /* Month of date (1 to 12) */
    int day;                   /* Day of date (1 to 31) */
    int year;                  /* Year of date (1800 or greater) */
    };
#define TRUE 1                 /* Return for valid dates (date_check) */
#define FALSE 0                /* Return for invalid dates (date_check) */

int date_check();
struct s_date subtract_dates();
long day_number();
```

If you keep all the functions in a single source file, say date.c, you simply compile the file and produce date.o (or date.obj). If not, you compile each file and produce object files that could be gathered together by the librarian program (discussed in Chapter 10).

---

[1] You could use expanded function prototypes:

```
int date_check(struct s_date date);
struct s_date subtract_dates(struct s_date first_date, struct s_date second_date);
long day_number(struct s_date date);
```

and the compiler will type check the parameters.

Finally, you should publish a manual on the functions you collect. If you comment each function with the guidelines shown in Chapter 15, you can simply extract the head of each function as a quick form of documentation. A general outline of the purposes of the functions and a note saying "date.h" is the header file and date.o or date.lib contains the routines would round out the necessary information.

Design these functions to be as robust as possible. All possible errors should be reported back to the user. The user in this case is the programmer calling your functions, not the person running the program.

## ABSTRACTIONS AND OBJECTS

An abstraction is a way of thinking about something conceptually, without getting into its details. On one level, you have already been using abstractions. The preprocessor #defines create abstract values you can use without knowing the exact replacement value. An object is a type of abstraction. If you consider a date as an object, you can call the preceding routines to manipulate dates without worrying about the details of how they do it.

Using structures to represent objects is a first step in abstraction. The user of the date routines presented in the first part of the chapter needs to know the actual names of the members in the structure. To keep it more abstract, you could write a routine to create a structure with the appropriate values. You can first define the object as a structure with

```
typedef struct
    {
    int month;
    int day;
    int year;
    } DATE;
```

and then create a routine that returned an object of this type:

```
DATE create_date(month,day,year)
/* Creates a DATE object */
int month;                      /* Month (1 to 12) */
int day;                        /* Date (1 to 31) */
int year;                       /* Year (1800 to 2399) */
    {
    DATE ret;
    ret.month = month;
    ret.day = day;
    ret.year = year;
    return ret;
    }
```

Although the date routines in the package do not change in the execution, you probably want to change their header so they look like they operate on objects, such as

```
int date_check(date)
/* Checks the validity of a date */
DATE date;                      /* Date to check */
```

The test of whether you have made your objects truly abstract is whether you can change the order of members or member names or data types without users having to make any change in their programs. This usually means you have to supply some way of getting at the individual members of your library, if necessary. With less abstraction, the user could have found the value of the month in a date simply by accessing date.month. If you changed the member month to mon, that code would not work. So you might need to create auxiliary functions, such as

```
int date_month(date)
/* Returns the month of the date */
DATE date;
    {
    return date.month;
    }
```

If the user simply creates objects with an initialization statement, such as

```
DATE date = {1, 3, 93};
```

and you decide to change the way months are stored in the routines (say, from 1 to 12 to 0 to 11), the user must change every initialization statement. With the create_date function, the only change would be in one line, to

```
ret.month = month - 1;
```

Just as with structures depicted in Chapter 7, you can create higher-order objects from objects previously defined. For example, once DATE has been defined, you could create such objects as

```
typedef struct
    {
    int hour;
    int minute;
    int second;
    } TIME;

typedef struct
    {
```

```
        DATE date;
        TIME time;
        } DATE_TIME;
```

---

## ACCESSING A VIRTUAL ARRAY

Depending on the computer, there is a limit on the size of an array that you can create, due to the memory limitations. You may need larger arrays. One alternative is to call a set of functions to access the array. For example, you might have an array such as

```
#define MAX_ARRAY 10000
int an_array[MAX_ARRAY];
```

that is referenced with

```
an_array[5]=32;
j=an_array[7];
```

Suppose the requirements of the program change so you need an array 10 million bytes long. There is not enough memory in the computer, although there is sufficient disk space to store this number of elements. You could create two functions to access an_array:

```
int get_value_an_array(index)
```

and

```
int put_value_an_array(index,value)
```

Throughout the program you reference an_array using these functions. Now an_array does not even have to be in memory. It can reside on a disk file. If it fits in memory, these routines might look like Listing 16.1.[2]

### Listing 16.1 Virtual Array Functions

```
#define NO_GOOD -32767
#define GOOD 1

#define MAX_ARRAY 100
static int an_array[MAX_ARRAY];
```

---

[2] The value returned by get_value_an_array for an error must be unique. If it is impossible to do this, the value must be returned through a pointer, or by other means described in Chapter 15.

```
/*********************** GET_VALUE_AN_ARRAY ************************/

int get_value_an_array(index)
/* Get a value from an array */
int index;                      /* Index to retrieve value from */
                                /* Returns value of element in array NO_GOOD
                                   if index was bad */


    {
    int ret;                    /* Return value */
    if ((index >= 0) && (index < MAX_ARRAY))
        ret = an_array[index];
    else
        ret = NO_GOOD;

    return ret;
    }


/*********************** PUT_VALUE_AN_ARRAY ************************/

int put_value_an_array(index, value)
/* Place a value in an array */
int index;                      /* Where to put value */
int value;                      /* Value to put into array */
                                /* Returns
                                        GOOD if index was good
                                        NO_GOOD if index was not good
                                */
    {
    int ret;                    /* Return value */
    if ((index >= 0) && (index < MAX_ARRAY))
        {
        an_array[index] = value;
        ret = GOOD;
        }
    else
        ret = NO_GOOD;

    return ret;
    }
```

If the array will not fit in memory, the following functions could be substituted.
No references to these functions need change in the functions that call them. Only
an initial call to init_value_an_array and a terminating call to end_value_an_array
need to be included in the program.

### Listing 16.2 Virtual Array Functions

```c
#include <stdio.h>

#define ARRAY_FILE "array.dat"    /* Name for array file */
static FILE *array_file = NULL;   /* File pointer */
static int init = 0;              /* Initialization flag */
static int array_size;            /* Size of array */

#define GOOD 1
#define NO_GOOD -32767            /* Error return */


/*********************** INIT_VALUE_AN_ARRAY ***********************/

int init_value_an_array(size)
/* Initializes array */
int size;                         /* Size to initialize array to */
                                  /* Returns
                                        GOOD if able to initialize
                                        NO_GOOD if not able */
    {
    int ret;                      /* Return value */
    int zero = 0;                 /* For writing to file */

    array_file = fopen(ARRAY_FILE, "w+");
    if (array_file == NULL)
        ret = NO_GOOD;
    else
        {
        ret = GOOD;
        /* Initialize the array to zeros */
        array_size = size;
        while (size--)
            {
            fwrite(&zero, sizeof(int), 1, array_file);
            }
        }

    return ret;
    }
```

```
/*********************** END_VALUE_AN_ARRAY ***********************/


int end_value_an_array()
/* Ends array */
                                /* Returns
                                        GOOD if able to close array file
                                        NO_GOOD if error occurred
                                */
    {
    int ret;
    if (fclose(array_file) == 0)
        ret = GOOD;
    else
    ret = NO_GOOD;
    return ret;
    }


/************************* GET_VALUE_AN_ARRAY **************************/


int get_value_an_array(index)
/* Get a value from an_array */
int index;                      /* Index into array */
                                /* Returns
                                        value of element or
                                        NO_GOOD if index was bad or file error
                                */

    {
    int value;                  /* Value to return */
    int read_count;             /* Count from the read */

    if ( (index < array_size) && (index >= 0) )
        {
        fseek(array_file, (long) index * sizeof(int), SEEK_SET);
        read_count = fread(&value, sizeof(int), 1, array_file);
        if (read_count != 1)
            value = NO_GOOD;
        }
    else
        value = NO_GOOD;
    return value;
    }
```

```
/************************ PUT_VALUE_AN_ARRAY *************************/

int put_value_an_array(index, value)
/* Place a value in an_array */
int index;                        /* Index in array */
int value;                        /* Value to put into array */
                                  /* Returns
                                        GOOD if index was good
                                        NO_GOOD if index was bad or file error
                                  */
    {
    int ret;                      /* Return value */
    int read_count;               /* Count from the read */

    if ( (index < array_size) && (index >= 0) )
        {
        fseek(array_file, (long) index * sizeof(int), SEEK_SET);
        read_count = fwrite(&value, sizeof(int), 1, array_file);
        if (read_count != 1)
            ret = NO_GOOD;
        else
            ret = GOOD;
        }
    else
        ret = NO_GOOD;

    return ret;
    }
```

## .COMPLEX NUMBER PACKAGE

Complex numbers are composed of a real and an imaginary part. They have many applications in engineering and science. There are no operators in C that handle complex numbers, so you need to devise functions to perform arithmetic operations on complex numbers. Using a structure is an excellent way of representing a complex number. These routines have structures for parameters and return the result as a structure. Using this structure you can nest calls to these routines, as shown in the main program. The structure would look like

```
typedef struct
    {
    double real;
    double imag;
    } COMPLEX;
```

The routines could look like Listing 16.3.

**Listing 16.3 Complex Number Functions**

```c
#include "complex.h"
#include <stdio.h>


/***************************** INIT_COMPLEX *****************************/

COMPLEX init_complex(real,imaginary)
/* Initializes a complex number object */
double real;                    /* Real portion */
double imaginary;               /* Complex portion */
    {
    COMPLEX ret;                /* Returned value */

    ret.real = real;
    ret.imag = imaginary;
    return ret;
    }


/*************************** ADD_COMPLEX ****************************/

COMPLEX add_complex(operand1,operand2)
/* Adds two complex numbers */
COMPLEX operand1;               /* One number to add */
COMPLEX operand2;               /* Second number to add */
    {
    COMPLEX result;

    result.real = operand1.real + operand2.real;
    result.imag = operand1.imag + operand2.imag;

    return result;
    }


/**************************** MUL_COMPLEX ****************************/

COMPLEX mul_complex(operand1,operand2)
/* Multiplies two complex numbers */
COMPLEX operand1;               /* First number to multiply */
COMPLEX operand2;               /* Second number to multiply */
    {
    COMPLEX result;
```

```
        result.real = operand1.real * operand2.real
            - operand1.imag * operand2.imag;
        result.imag = operand1.imag * operand2.real
            + operand1.real * operand2.imag;

        return result;
        }



/*************************** INPUT_COMPLEX ***************************/

COMPLEX input_complex()
/* Inputs a complex number */
        {
        COMPLEX result;

        printf("\n Real part is: ");
        scanf("%lf",&result.real);
        printf("\n Imaginary part is: ");
        scanf("%lf",&result.imag);

        return result;
        }



/*********************** OUTPUT_COMPLEX ***********************/

void output_complex(operand)
/* Outputs a complex number */
COMPLEX operand;
        {
        printf("\n Real part is %lf Imaginary part is %lf", operand.real,
        operand.imag);

        return;
        }
```

The header file, "complex.h", would look like Listing 16.4.

**Listing 16.4 Header File complex.h**

```
typedef struct
        {
        double real;
        double imag;
        } COMPLEX;
```

```
COMPLEX init_complex(double,double);
COMPLEX add_complex(COMPLEX,COMPLEX);
COMPLEX mul_complex(COMPLEX,COMPLEX);
COMPLEX input_complex(void);
void output_complex(COMPLEX);
```

As an example, these functions could be called with a program like Listing 16.5.

**Listing 16.5 Complex Number Example**

```
#include <stdio.h>
#include "complex.h"

main()
/* This program is an example of complex operations */
    {
    COMPLEX number1;
    COMPLEX number2;
    COMPLEX result;
    COMPLEX constant;

    constant = init_complex(2.0,1.0);

    /* Get the numbers */
    printf("\n Input first number (a) ");
    number1=input_complex();
    printf("\n Input second number (b) ");
    number2=input_complex();

    /* Compute and print (number1+number2)*constant */
    result=mul_complex(add_complex(number1,number2),constant);
    printf("\n Result of ((a+b)*(2.+1.i) is ");
    output_complex(result);

    exit(0);
    }
```

This is the printout for the program, with the user's responses in this font.

```
Input first number (a)
Real part is: 1.
Imaginary part is: 2.
Input second number (b)
Real part is: 4.
Imaginary part is: 3.
Result of ((a+b)*(2.+1.i) is
Real part is 5.000000 Imaginary part is 15.000000
```

## TERMINAL I/O PACKAGE

The C I/O functions treat all devices as a string of bytes. Terminals are treated as teletypes. There are no standard C routines that recognize the full screens available on most terminals. A screen package is a useful tool. It is developed here from the bottom up and made as portable as possible.

UNIX has a package called curses that provides many of these screen functions. Those functions were incorporated into this package. Alternatively, the corresponding curses functions can be written for MS-DOS. The complexity involved with duplicating all the curses operations is beyond the scope of this book.

The basic operations in writing to the screen are to position the cursor, to set the attributes (including elements like the highlight or inverse video), and to write the character. Commands to most video terminals are a sequence of ASCII characters. For example,

```
ESC [ 1 3 ; 1 5 H
```

tells the terminal to position the cursor at row 13, column 15. This sequence varies from terminal to terminal, but most terminals understand a common set of sequences that are ANSI standard. These functions output the ANSI sequences. A common header for both these lower-level routines and the upper-level routines—to be shown later—is that in Listing 16.6.

**Listing 16.6 Header File terminal.h**

```
/* For set_attribute */

#define NORMAL 0               /* Normal output */
#define HIGHLIGHT 1            /* Highlighted output */

/* For field routines */

struct sfield
    {
    int line;                  /* Which line */
    int column;                /* Which column */
    int width;                 /* How wide */
    char *string;              /* Points to string to input or output */
    };

/* Returns from field_in */

#define END_UP_CURSOR 1
#define END_DOWN_CURSOR 2
#define END_CARRIAGE_RETURN 3
```

```
#define END_ESCAPE 4
#define END_ACCEPT 5

/* Internals */

#define MAX_COLUMN 80
#define MAX_LINE 24
#define ESCAPE '\033'                      /* Escape character */

#define C_UP_CURSOR '\025'                 /* Control-U */
#define C_DOWN_CURSOR '\002'               /* Control-B */
#define C_RIGHT_CURSOR '\022'              /* Control-R */
#define C_LEFT_CURSOR '\014'               /* Control-L */
#define C_CARRIAGE_RETURN '\015'           /* CR */
#define C_ESCAPE '\033'                    /* ESC */
#define C_ACCEPT '\001'                    /* (Control-A) */

#define TRUE 1
#define FALSE 0
```

The functions for positioning the cursor, clearing the screen, and setting the attributes for subsequent output look like the following:

| | |
|---|---|
| cursor(line, column) | Positions the cursor to line and column for output |
| in_cursor(line, column) | Positions the cursor to line and column for input |
| clear_screen() | Clears the screen |
| set_attribute(attribute) | Sets the attribute for output character |
| init_terminal() | Initializes the terminal package |
| end_terminal() | Ends the terminal package |
| charin() | Retrieves a character from the keyboard |
| charout(c) | Outputs the character c to the screen |

**Listing 16.7 Basic Screen Operations**

```
#include <stdio.h>
#include <terminal.h>

/****************************** CURSOR ******************************/

void cursor(line, column)
/* Position the cursor for output */
int line;                          /* Line */
int column;                        /* Column */
```

```
       {
       charout(ESCAPE);
       charout('[');

       /* Check the line and column */
       /* This is optional and might be removed in a production system */
       if (line < 1)
           line = 1;
       else if (line > MAX_LINE)
           line = MAX_LINE;
       if (column < 1)
           column = 1;
       else if (column > MAX_COLUMN)
           column = MAX_COLUMN;

       /* Convert line to ASCII characters */
       charout(line / 10 + '0');
       charout(line % 10 + '0');
       charout(';');

       /* Convert column to ASCII characters */
       charout(column / 10 + '0');
       charout(column % 10 + '0');
       charout('H');

       return;
       }


/****************************** IN_CURSOR ******************************/

void in_cursor(line, column)
/* Position the cursor for input */
int line;                       /* Line */
int column;                     /* Column */
    {
    /* This is the same as the output, so simply call that routine */

    cursor(line, column);

    return;
    }
```

```
/**************************** CLEAR_SCREEN ****************************/

void clear_screen()
/* Clears the screen of all characters */
    {
    charout(ESCAPE);
    charout('[');
    charout('2');
    charout('J');

    return;
    }

/**************************** SET_ATTRIBUTE ****************************/

void set_attribute(attribute)
/* Set attributes for subsequent output */
int attribute;                  /* What attribute to set */
                                /* These are
                                    NORMAL normal output
                                    HIGHLIGHT highlighted output
                                */
    {

    charout(ESCAPE);
    charout('[');

    switch (attribute)
        {
    case NORMAL:
        charout('0');
        break;
    case HIGHLIGHT:
        charout('7');
        break;
    default:
        charout('0');
        break;
        }

    charout('m');

    return;
    }
```

The character input and output routines can either be general or specific to the computer. The general routines look like Listing 16.8.

**Listing 16.8 Character In and Out**

```
#include <stdio.h>

void init_terminal()
/* Initializes the terminal I/O system */
    {
    /* Unbuffer the input */
    setbuf(stdin, NULL);
    return;
    }

void end_terminal()
/* Ends the terminal system */
    {
    /* Nothing here, but may be needed on some systems */
    return;
    }

int charin()
/* Inputs a character in unbuffered mode */
/* Returns the character that is input */
    {
    return getchar();
    }

void charout(c)
/* Outputs a character */
int c;
    {
    putchar(c);
    return;
    }
```

Functions specific to the IBM-PC look like the following. The bdos function is a common routine supplied with compilers for the IBM-PC. Its calling sequence varies, but the one shown is common.

**Listing 16.9 IBM-PC Terminal Routines**

```
#define READ_KEYBOARD 0x08     /* DOS call to read keyboard */
#define DISPLAY_CHAR 0x02      /* DOS call to display character */
#define CHAR_MASK 0xFF

void init_terminal()
/* Initializes the terminal I/O system */
    {
    return;
    }
```

```
void end_terminal()
/* Ends the terminal system */
    {
    return;
    }

int charin()
/* Inputs a character in unbuffered mode */
/* Returns the character that is input */
    {
    int ret;
    ret = bdos(READ_KEYBOARD, 0) & CHAR_MASK;
    return ret;
    }

void charout(c)
/* Outputs a character */
int c;
    {
    int ret;
    ret = bdos(DISPLAY_CHAR, c);
    return;
    }
```

The curses package on UNIX and VAX/VMS already provides terminal command codes for many of the common terminals. It can determine your terminal type, then output the appropriate command sequences. The curses system is also written to minimize the number of characters needing to be sent to the terminal. It is arranged so the characters are not sent until you tell it to send them. It has many other features, such as windowing, which are described in the UNIX manual. Using the curses package, the routines could be written as shown in Listing 16.10.

**Listing 16.10 UNIX Terminal Routines**

```
#include <stdio.h>
#include <curses.h>
#include <terminal.h>


/******************************* CURSOR *****************************/

void cursor(line, column)
/* Position the cursor for the next output */
int line;                        /* Line */
int column;                      /* Column */
    {
    if (line < 1)
        line = 1;
```

```
        else if (line > MAX_LINE)
            line = MAX_LINE;
    if (column < 1)
        column = 1;
    else if (column > MAX_COLUMN)
        column = MAX_COLUMN;

    /* Decrement by 1, because 0,0 is upper left */
    move(--line, --column);

    return;
    }


/****************************** IN_CURSOR ******************************/

void in_cursor(line, column)
/* Position the cursor for input */
int line;                       /* Line */
int column;                     /* Column */
    {
    cursor(line, column);
    refresh();

    return;
    }


/**************************** CLEAR_SCREEN ****************************/

void clear_screen()
/* Clears the screen of all characters */
    {

    erase();

    return;
    }


/*************************** SET_ATTRIBUTE ***************************/

void set_attribute(attribute)
/* Set attributes for subsequent output */
int attribute;                      /* What attribute to set */
                                    /* Possible are
                                            NORMAL for normal output
                                            HIGHLIGHT for highlighted output
                                    */
```

```
        {
        switch (attribute)
            {
        case NORMAL:
            standend();
            break;
        case HIGHLIGHT:
            standout();
            break;
        default:
            break;
            }

        return;
        }
```

```
/*************************** END_TERMINAL ***************************/
```

```
void end_terminal()
/* Ends the terminal system */
        {
        endwin();
        return;
        }
```

```
/*********************** INIT_TERMINAL ***********************/
```

```
void init_terminal()
/* Initializes the terminal I/O system */
        {
        initscr();
        raw();
        nonl();
        noecho();
        return;
        }
```

```
/************************** CHARIN **************************/
```

```
int charin()
/* Inputs a character in unbuffered mode */
/* Returns the character that is input */
        {
        return getch();
        }
```

```
/******************************* CHAROUT ********************************/

void charout(c)
/* Outputs a character */
int c;                          /* Character to output */
    {
    addch(c);
    refresh();
    return;
    }
```

Once lower-level functions are defined, you can create higher-level functions to call them. With these functions, it should not matter which of the alternative lower functions are really executed. The interface to them has been well defined.

The basic operations for a full screen are to input and output strings of characters at a particular location on the screen called *field*. When inputting to a field, you may wish to cursor across the field to fix an input error or go to another field. A common set of commands for a field might look like

| Key | Operation |
| --- | --- |
| Cursor left | Go one character to left, if possible |
| Cursor right | Go one character to right, if possible |
| Escape | Exit the input operation and do something else |
| Cursor up | End of input, go to previous field |
| Cursor down | End of input, go to next field |
| Carriage return | End of input, go to next field |
| Accept key | End of input, done with all fields |

The field_out and field_in functions output or input fields. The screen_out function outputs a number of fields. The screen_in function inputs the number of fields and handles which field to go to next.

### Listing 16.11 Field Functions

```
/* Higher level constructs for input/output */

#include "terminal.h"


/***************************** STRING_OUT *****************************/

void string_out(string, length)
/* Outputs a field */
char *string;                   /* String to output */
int length;                     /* Maximum length to output */
    {

    while ((*string != '\0') && (length--))
```

```
        {
        charout(*string++);
        }

    return;
    }

/*************************  FIELD_OUT  **************************/

void field_out(pfield)
/* Outputs a field */
struct sfield *pfield;          /* Field to output */
    {

    cursor(pfield->line, pfield->column);
    string_out(pfield->string, pfield->width);

    return;
    }

/****************************** FIELD_IN ******************************/

int field_in(pfield)
/* Inputs a field */
struct sfield *pfield;          /* Field to output */
                                /* Return based on ending character
                                        END_UP_CURSOR
                                        END_DOWN_CURSOR
                                        END_CARRIAGE_RETURN
                                        END_ESCAPE
                                        END_ACCEPT
                                */
    {
    char *pc;                   /* Pointer for string output */
    int length;                 /* Length of field */
    int current_pos;            /* Current position from start */
    int done;                   /* Flag when finished */
    int chr;                    /* Input character */
    int ret;                    /* Return value */

    set_attribute(HIGHLIGHT);
    /* Output the current field */
    field_out(pfield);

    done = FALSE;
    length = pfield->width;
    pc = pfield->string;
    current_pos = 0;
```

```
while (!done)
    {
    in_cursor(pfield->line, pfield->column + current_pos);
    chr = charin();
    switch (chr)
        {
    case C_UP_CURSOR:
        ret = END_UP_CURSOR;
        done = TRUE;
        break;
    case C_DOWN_CURSOR:
        ret = END_DOWN_CURSOR;
        done = TRUE;
        break;
    case C_CARRIAGE_RETURN:
        ret = END_CARRIAGE_RETURN;
        done = TRUE;
        break;
    case C_ESCAPE:
        ret = END_ESCAPE;
        done = TRUE;
        break;
    case C_ACCEPT:
        ret = END_ACCEPT;
        done = TRUE;
        break;
    case C_LEFT_CURSOR:     /* Decrement position */
        current_pos--;
        if (current_pos < 0)
            current_pos++;
        break;
    case C_RIGHT_CURSOR:    /* Increment position */
        current_pos++;
        if (current_pos > length)
            current_pos--;
        break;
    default:
        /* Only accept if not at end of field */
        if (current_pos < length)
            {
            /* Only accept noncontrol characters */
            if (chr >= ' ')
                {
                *(pc + current_pos) = chr;
                charout(chr);
                current_pos++;
                }
```

```
                  }
            }                            /* End of switch */
      }                                  /* End of while on !done */

      /* Write fields out as normal */

      set_attribute(NORMAL);
      /* Output the current field */
      field_out(pfield);

      return ret;
      }
```

```
/****************************** SCREEN_OUT ******************************/

void screen_out(screen, size)
/* Outputs a set of fields */
struct sfield *screen;                   /* Points to array of fields */
int size;                                /* Number of fields */
      {
      while (size--)
            {
            field_out(screen++);
            }
      return;
      }
```

```
/*************************** SCREEN_IN ***************************/

int screen_in(screen, size)
/* Inputs a set of fields */
struct sfield *screen;                   /* Points to array of fields */
int size;                                /* Number of fields */
                                         /* Return based on ending character
                                               END_ESCAPE
                                               END_ACCEPT
                                         */
      {
      int number;                        /* Counter for fields */
      struct sfield *field;              /* Pointer to current field */
      int current_field;                 /* Index of current field */
      int done;                          /* Flag when done with screen */
      int ret;                           /* Return value */

      /* First output them */
      number = size;
      field = screen;
      while (number--)
```

```
                    {
                    field_out(field++);
                    }
            current_field = 0;
            done = FALSE;
            while (!done)
                    {
                    /* Input each field */
                    field = screen + current_field;
                    ret = field_in(field);
                    switch (ret)
                            {
                    case END_UP_CURSOR:
                            current_field--;
                            if (current_field < 0)
                                    current_field = size - 1;
                            break;
                    case END_DOWN_CURSOR:
                    case END_CARRIAGE_RETURN:
                            current_field++;
                            if (current_field >= size)
                                    current_field = 0;
                            break;
                    case END_ESCAPE:
                    case END_ACCEPT:
                            done = TRUE;
                            break;
                    default:
                            printf("\n field_in return error %d", ret);
                            }
                    }

            return ret;
            }
```

The field_out routine does not set the attribute for the characters to be output. A separate call to set_attribute is required. If many fields contain different attributes (such as colors), it is more efficient to change the field structure to include an attribute value and have field_out call set_attribute, as in

**Listing 16.12 field_out Alternative**

```
struct sfield
        {
        int line;                       /* Which line */
        int column;                     /* Which column */
        int width;                      /* How wide */
        char *string;                   /* Points to characters to input/output */
```

```
        int attribute;              /* Attribute to use for output */
        } ;
void field_out(pfield)
/* Outputs a field */
struct sfield *pfield;/* Field to output */
        {

        set_attribute(pfield->attribute);
        cursor(pfield->line, pfield->column);
        string_out(pfield->string, pfield->width);

        return;
        }
```

Another common screen item is the menu, which is a selection of fields. Usually one field on the menu is highlighted in some way. Pressing Enter selects the highlighted field. Using the cursor keys moves the highlight to another field. Typing the first letter of one of the fields immediately selects the field, without having to move the cursor.

### Listing 16.13 Menu Function

```
#include <terminal.h>

int menu_in(pfield, size, first_selection)
/* Displays a menu and inputs a selection */
struct sfield *pfield;          /* Points to array of fields */
int size;                       /* Number of fields */
int first_selection;            /* First field to select */
        {
        int number_choice;         /* Number in menu */
        int selection;             /* Current selection */
        struct sfield *pf;         /* Pointer to current field */
        int ret;                   /* Return value */
        int old_selection;         /* Previous selection */
        int done;                  /* Flag when done with menu */
        int chr;                   /* Input character */

        /* Display the choices */
        set_attribute(NORMAL);
        pf = pfield;
        number_choice = size;
        while (number_choice--)
                {
                field_out(pf++);
                }

        selection = first_selection;
        old_selection = selection;
```

```
        done = FALSE;
        set_attribute(HIGHLIGHT);
        /* Output the current field */
        field_out(&pfield[selection]);

        while (!done)
            {
            in_cursor(pfield[selection].line, pfield[selection].column);
            chr = charin();
            switch (chr)
                {
            case C_UP_CURSOR:
            case C_LEFT_CURSOR:                /* Decrement selection counter */
                selection--;
                if (selection < 0)
                    selection = size - 1;
                break;
            case C_DOWN_CURSOR:
            case C_RIGHT_CURSOR:               /* Increment selection counter */
                selection++;
                if (selection == size)
                    selection = 0;
                break;
            case C_CARRIAGE_RETURN:
                ret = selection;
                done = TRUE;
                break;
            case C_ESCAPE:
                ret = END_ESCAPE;
                done = TRUE;
                break;
            case C_ACCEPT:
                ret = selection;
                done = TRUE;
                break;
            default:                           /* Check whether character matches
                                                        1st letter of choice */
                pf = pfield + size;
                number_choice = size;
                while (number_choice--)
                    {
                    pf--;
                    chr = toupper(chr);
                    if (chr == pf->string[0])
                        {
                        ret = number_choice;
                        done = TRUE;
```

```
                          }
                      }
                  }                   /* End of switch */
              }
          if (selection != old_selection)
              {
              /* Set highlight off for old selection, on for new */
              set_attribute(NORMAL);
              field_out(&pfield[old_selection]);
              set_attribute(HIGHLIGHT);
              field_out(&pfield[selection]);
              old_selection = selection;
              }
          }                           /* End of while on !done */

    /* Write selection out as normal */
    set_attribute(NORMAL);
    field_out(&pfield[selection]);

    return ret;
    }
```

---

## SAMPLE PROGRAM—GRADES

Listing 16.14 presents the student grade program from Chapter 13, rewritten using the functions described in this chapter. Notice that the main_menu now simply calls the menu function in the terminal package. Input is performed using the screen_in function. The display on the terminal is now screen oriented, rather than scrolling as on a teletype display.

### Listing 16.14 Grades Program with Field Function

```
#include <stdio.h>
#define OKAY 1                    /* Value for good return */
#define NOT_OKAY 0                /* Value for bad return */
#define FALSE 0
#define TRUE 1

/* Structure of the student record */
#define SIZE_NAME 20              /* Size of name */

struct s_student
    {
    char name[SIZE_NAME + 1]; /* Name of student with space for NUL char */
```

```
        int grade;                    /* Grade */
        };

#define RECORD_SIZE sizeof(struct s_student)
                               /* Size of a record */

#define ADD_NAME 0              /* Menu value for adding a name */
#define FIND_NAME 1            /* Menu value for finding a name */
#define PRINT_NAME 2          /* Menu value for printing names */
#define END_PROGRAM 3         /* Menu value for ending program */


/***************************** MAIN PROGRAM *****************************/

#include <terminal.h>

int main()
/* This program keeps track of student's grades */
    {
    int ret;                    /* Return values */
    int main_select;            /* Main menu option */
    static struct sfield error_message_file =
        {24,1, 10,"File error"};
    static struct sfield error_message_close =
        {24,1, 20,"File error in closing"};
    static struct sfield error_message_close =
        {24,1, 20,"File error in opening"};
    /* Open the data file */
    ret = init_file();
    if (ret == OKAY)
        {
        do
            {
            main_select = main_menu();
            switch (main_select)
                {
            case ADD_NAME:
                ret = add_name();
                break;
            case FIND_NAME:
                ret = find_name();
                break;
            case PRINT_NAME:
                ret = print_name();
                break;
                }
            if (ret != OKAY)
```

```
                           {
                           screen_out(&error_message_file, 1);
                           break;
                           }
                        }
                   while (main_select != END_PROGRAM);

              ret = end_file();
              if (ret != OKAY)
                   screen_out(&error_message_close, 1);
              }
         else
              screen_out(&error_message_close, 1);

         exit(0);
         }

/***************************** MAIN MENU *****************************/

int main_menu()
/* This displays the choices for the main menu */
      /* Returns one of the choices
              ADD_NAME            Menu value for adding a name
              FIND_NAME           Menu value for finding a name
              PRINT_NAME          Menu value for printing names
              END_PROGRAM         Menu value for ending program
      */
      {
      int chr;               /* For input character */
      int done;              /* Flag for while loop */
      int ret;               /* Return value */

      static struct sfield background[]=
            {
            {5, 5, 30," What would you like to do?"},
            {6, 5, 30," Type the first letter of your choice"}
            };
      #define SIZE_BACKGROUND sizeof(background)/sizeof(struct sfield)

      static struct sfield mainmenu[]=
            {
            {10, 5, 30, "Add a name"},
            {12, 5, 30, "Print the names"},
            {14, 5, 30, "Find a name"},
            {16, 5, 30, "End the program"},
            };
      #define SIZE_MAINMENU sizeof(mainmenu)/sizeof(struct sfield)
```

```
        done = FALSE;
        clear_screen();
        screen_out(background, SIZE_BACKGROUND);
        ret = menu_in(mainmenu, SIZE_MAINMENU,0);

        return ret;
        }

/*************************** EXTERNAL VARIABLES ***************************/

/* These are used by the add, find, and print routines */

static int current_record;      /* Current record in the file */
static int last_record;         /* Last record in the file */
                                /* The first record contains this number */
                                /* Data records start with the 2nd record */
static FILE *data_file;          /* Pointer to data file */
#define FILENAME "student.dat"  /* Name of data file */

static FILE *print_file;         /* File pointer for print file */
#define PRINT_FILE "PRINTER"    /* Printer file */

/*************************** INITIALIZE FILE ***************************/

int init_file()
/* Opens the data file */
    {
    int ret;                /* Return value */
    int count;              /* Count of bytes read */
    char buffer[RECORD_SIZE]; /* Buffer for read */

    data_file = fopen(FILENAME, "r+");
    if (data_file == NULL)
        {
        /* Open a new file */
        data_file = fopen(FILENAME, "w+");
        if (data_file == NULL)
            ret = NOT_OKAY;
        else
            {
            /* Write record count on new file */
            sprintf(buffer, "%d", last_record);
            count = fwrite(buffer, RECORD_SIZE, 1, data_file);
            if (count != 1)
                ret = NOT_OKAY;
            else
                ret = OKAY;
```

```
                        }
                  }
            else
                  {
                  /* Read record count from file */
                  count = fread(buffer, RECORD_SIZE, 1, data_file);
                  if (count != 1)
                        ret = NOT_OKAY;
                  else
                        {
                        ret = OKAY;
                        sscanf(buffer, "%d", &last_record);
                        }
                  }
            if (ret == OKAY)
                  printf("\n File contains %d students", last_record);

            return ret;
            }


/*************************** TERMINATE FILE ***************************/

int end_file()
/* Ends the data file */
      {
      int ret;                      /* Return value */
      int count;                    /* Count of bytes read */
      char buffer[RECORD_SIZE];     /* Buffer for read */
      int ret_seek;                 /* Return from seek */

      /* Write the record count on the first record */
      sprintf(buffer, "%d", last_record);

      ret_seek = fseek(data_file, (long) 0, SEEK_SET);
      if (ret_seek != 0)
            ret = NOT_OKAY;
      else
            {
            count = fwrite(buffer, RECORD_SIZE, 1, data_file);
            if (count != 1)
                  ret = NOT_OKAY;
            else
                  {
                  ret = OKAY;
                  printf("\n File now contains %d students", last_record);
                  }
            }
      }
```

```
        fclose(data_file);
        return ret;
        }

/*************************** ADD NAME TO FILE ****************************/

#define SIZE_BUFFER 3              /* Buffer size for grade */

int add_name()
/* Add a name to the file */
    {
    int ret;                       /* Return value */
    int count;                     /* Write count */
    char buffer[SIZE_BUFFER + 1];  /* Buffer for integer input*/
    struct s_student student;      /* Buffer for record */
    int ret_seek;                  /* Return from seek */
    static struct sfield background[]=
        {
        {5, 5, 30," Adding a name"},
        {7, 5, 20," Name:"}
        {9, 5, 20," Grade:"},
        };
    #define SIZE_BACKGROUND sizeof(background)/sizeof(struct sfield)

    static struct sfield input[]
        {
        {7, 25, SIZE_NAME, student.name},
        {9, 25, SIZE_BUFFER, buffer},
        };
    #define SIZE_INPUT sizeof(input)/sizeof(struct sfield)

    clear_screen();
    screen_out(background, SIZE_BACKGROUND);
    /* Input the name and grade */
    screen_in(input, SIZE_INPUT);


    sscanf(buffer, "%d", &student.grade);

    /* Record the name and grade */
    last_record++;
    current_record = last_record;
    ret = OKAY;

    ret_seek = fseek(data_file, (long) last_record * RECORD_SIZE, SEEK_SET);
    if (ret_seek != 0)
        ret = NOT_OKAY;
    else
```

```
            {
            count = fwrite(&student, RECORD_SIZE, 1, data_file);
            if (count != 1)
                  ret = NOT_OKAY;
            else
                  printf("\n Students on file %d", last_record);
            }

      return ret;
      }

/*************************** FIND NAME IN FILE *************************/

int find_name()
/* Find a name in the file */
      {
      int ret;                 /* Return value */
      int count;               /* Read/write count */
      struct s_student match;    /* Buffer for matching values */
      struct s_student student;  /* Buffer for record */
      char buffer[SIZE_BUFFER + 1];
                               /* Buffer for grade */
      int found;               /* Flag for found */
      int ret_seek;            /* Return from seek */

      static struct sfield background[]=
            {
            {5, 5, 30," Finding a name"},
            {7, 5, 20," Name:"}
            };
      #define SIZE_BACKGROUND sizeof(background)/sizeof(struct sfield)

      static struct sfield input[]
            {
            {7, 25, SIZE_NAME, match.name},
            };
      #define SIZE_INPUT sizeof(input)/sizeof(struct sfield)

      static struct sfield background1[]=
            {
            {5, 5, 30," NAME WAS FOUND"},
            {7, 5, 20," Name:"}
            {7, 25, SIZE_NAME, match.name},
            {9, 5, 20," New grade:"}
            };
      #define SIZE_BACKGROUND1 sizeof(background1)/sizeof(struct sfield)
```

```
static struct sfield input1[]=
    {
    {5, 25, SIZE_BUFFER, buffer},
    };
#define SIZE_INPUT sizeof(input1)/sizeof(struct sfield)
/* Input the name to find */

clear_screen();
screen_out(background, SIZE_BACKGROUND);
/* Input the name */
screen_in(input, SIZE_INPUT);

found = FALSE;
ret = OKAY;
/* Rewind file and look for matching name in the file */
ret_seek = fseek(data_file, (long) RECORD_SIZE, SEEK_SET);
if (ret_seek != 0)
    ret = NOT_OKAY;
else
    {
    for (current_record = 1; current_record <= last_record;
        current_record++)
        {
        count = fread(&student, RECORD_SIZE, 1, data_file);
        if (count != 1)
            ret = NOT_OKAY;
        else
            {
            if (strncmp(match.name, student.name, SIZE_NAME) == 0)
                {
                clear_screen();
                screen_out(background1, SIZE_BACKGROUND1);
                screen_in(input1, SIZE_INPUT1);
                /* If buffer is blank, grade will not be changed */
                sscanf(buffer, "%d", &student.grade);

                /* Rewrite the record */
                ret_seek = fseek(data_file,
                    (long) current_record * RECORD_SIZE, SEEK_SET);
                if (ret_seek != 0)
                    ret = NOT_OKAY;
                else
                    {
                    count = fwrite(&student, RECORD_SIZE, 1,
                        data_file);
                if (count != 1)
                    {
```

```
                                    ret = NOT_OKAY;
                                    }
                        else
                            found = TRUE;
                        break;
                            }
                        }
                    }
                }
            }
        if (!found)
            printf("\n Student not found");

        return;
        }

/************************ PRINT NAMES IN FILE ************************/

int print_name()
/* Print all the names in the file */
    {
    int ret;                /* Return value */
    int count;              /* Read count */
    struct s_student student;  /* Buffer for record */
    int ret_seek;           /* Return from seek */
    printf("\n Printing the names on %s", PRINT_FILE);

    ret = OKAY;
    print_file = fopen(PRINT_FILE, "w");
    if (print_file == NULL)
        {
        printf("\n Unable to open printer");
        ret = NOT_OKAY;
        }
    else
        {
        /* Rewind the file and print the records */
        ret_seek = fseek(data_file, (long) RECORD_SIZE, SEEK_SET);
        if (ret_seek != 0)
            ret = NOT_OKAY;
        else
            {
            for (current_record = 1; current_record <=
                last_record; current_record++)
                {
                count = fread(&student, RECORD_SIZE, 1, data_file);
                if (count != 1)
```

```
                              ret = NOT_OKAY;
                    else
                         {
                         fprintf(print_file,
                               "\n Student %30.30s Grade %5d", student.name,
                               student.grade);
                         }
                    }
               }
          fclose(print_file);
          }

     return ret;
     }
```

## SUMMARY

- Packages provide sets of useful functions, making it easier to create and test programs.
- Interfaces to packages should be clean and simple.
- Structures should be used if possible for parameters.
- Objects are structures whose internal details need not be known by the user.

## SELF-TEST

1. Why should you create packages?
2. What do header files provide?
3. What is the advantage of abstraction?
4. What are two ways of implementing the different I/O terminal handlers (such as MS-DOS and UNIX)?

## ANSWERS

1. Packages help you avoid rewriting the same code over and over.
2. They provide the interface specification for a package.
3. You do not need to worry about the details. There is little or no change required on your part if the package changes.
4. They could reside in separate libraries and the appropriate one linked. They could be in the same source file and #ifdefs could choose which one was compiled.

## PROBLEMS

1. Write additions to the complex number package for subtracting and dividing complex numbers.
2. Write a package of general list handling routines, using pointers either to structures or objects.
3. Write a screen handling package for your particular terminal, if it does not have ANSI standard sequences. Test it with code like the following:

```c
#include "terminal.h"

int main()
/* Test of the standard I/O package */
    {
    int row;
    int col;
    int chr;

    init_terminal();

    /* Put various characters at various positions */
    for (row = 0; row < 25; row++)
        {
        col = row + 40;
        cursor(row, col);
        charout(row + 'A');
        }

    charin();
    clear_screen();
    charin();

    /* Fill up the screen */
    for (row = 1; row <= 24; row++)
        {
        cursor(row, 1);
        for (col = 0; col < 80; col++)
            {
            charout(col + row + ' ');
            }
        }

    charin();
    /*Clear the screen */
    clear_screen();
```

```
        charin();

        /* Input characters */
        for (row = 1; row <= 24; row++)
            {
            col = row + 10;
            cursor(row, col);
            chr = charin();
            charout(chr);
            }

        /* Try the highlight */
        for (row = 1; row <= 24; row++)
            {
            col = row + 10;
            cursor(row, col);
            if (row % 2)
                set_attribute(NORMAL);
            else
                set_attribute(HIGHLIGHT);
            charout(row + 'A');
            }

        end_terminal();
        exit(0);
        }
```

4. If you were writing a routine called day_of_week, what should it return—an integer, an enumerated variable, or a character string pointer?

5. Write the code for subtract_dates and day_number.

6. Write routines for inputting and outputting dates in several formats:

   a. Simple string, in the form MMDDYYYY.
   b. String with slashes, in the form MM/DD/YYYY.
   c. String with alphabetic month, in the form MMM DD,YYYY.

   Be sure to validate the input dates.

7. Write a routine to add a number of days to a date.

8. Write a package of time functions. These could include functions as check_time and subtract_times. What other functions might you want to include in your package?

9. Write a function to add a number of seconds to a structure of type TIME.

10. Should you create a typedef BOOLEAN for functions that only return True or False (or Good/Nogood) values? What are the advantages and disadvantages of this?

11. Write a package that provides for unlimited precision arithmetic. The user would supply character strings and the functions would add, subtract, multiply, and divide these strings and produce a string with the result.

12. If the field structure in `terminal.h` was used extensively, how could you save data space with only a few changes in it?

13. What are two ways of implementing the different I/O terminal handlers (MS-DOS and UNIX)?

14. Change Listing 16.2 so that the initial and final calls are not needed. (Hint: Use an initialize flag.)

# Appendix A

# Bibliography

## BOOKS AND PERIODICAL ARTICLES

American National Standards Institute, American National Standard for Information Systems. *Programming Language C.* (In preparation.)

Bell Laboratories. *UNIX Programmer's Manual.* 2 vols. New York: Holt, Rinehart and Winston, 1983.

Bentley, Jon. *Programming Pearls.* Reading, Mass.: Addison-Wesley, 1986.

Dahl, O. J.; Dijkstra, E. W.; and Hoare, C. A. R. *Structured Programming.* New York: Academic Press, 1972.

Gries, David. *The Science of Programming.* Springer-Verlag, 1981.

Hoare, C. Anthony R., "Quicksort," *Computer Journal* 5, no. 1 (1962), pp. 10–15.

Kernighan, B. W., and Plauger, P. J. *Software Tools in Pascal.* Reading, Mass.: Addison-Wesley, 1981.

Kernighan, B. W., and Ritchie, D. M. *The C Programming Language.* Englewood Cliffs, N.J.: Prentice-Hall, 1978.

Knuth, Donald E. *The Art of Computer Programming: Fundamental Algorithms.* Vol 1. Reading, Mass.: Addison-Wesley, 1968.

Knuth, Donald E. *The Art of Computer Programming: Seminumerical Algorithms.* Vol 2. Reading, Mass.: Addison-Wesley, 1969.

Knuth, Donald E. *The Art of Computer Programming: Searching and Sorting.* Vol 3. Reading, Mass.: Addison-Wesley, 1973.

Koenig, A. *C Traps and Pitfalls*, AT&T Bell Laboratories Computing Science Technical Report No. 123, July 1, 1986.

Press, William H.; Flannery, Brian P.; Teukolsky, Saul A.; and Vetterling, William T. *Numerical Recipes, The Art of Scientific Computing.* New York: Cambridge University Press, 1986.

Pugh, Kenneth H. *C Language for Programmers.* Glenview, Ill.: Scott Foresman, 1985.

Schneider, G. M., and Bruell, S. C. *Advanced Programming and Problem Solving with Pascal.* New York: John Wiley and Sons, 1981.

Strawberry Software. *Applied C.* Van Nostrand Reinhold, 1986.

Ward, Robert. *Debugging C.* Lawrence, Kans.: R & P Publications, 1988.

Wirth, Niklaus. *Algorithm and Data Structures.* Englewood Cliffs, N.J.: Prentice-Hall, 1986.

Yourdon, Edward, and Constantine, Larry. *Structured Design.* Englewood Cliffs, N.J.: Prentice-Hall.

## USER GROUPS

C User's Group
2120 W. 25th St., Suite B.
Lawrence, KS 66046
(913) 841 – 1631

Software Tools Users Group
1259 El Camino Real #242
Menlo Park, CA 94025

## MAGAZINES

*C Journal*
2120 W. 25th St. Suite B.
Lawrence, KS 66046

*Computer Language*
CL Publications
650 Fifth Street, Suite 311
San Francisco, CA 94107

*Communications of the ACM*
Association for Computing Machinery
11 West 42nd Street
New York, NY 10036

*Dr. Dobb's Journal*
M&T Publishing
2464 Embarcadara Way
Palo Alto, CA 94303

IEEE Computer Society
Institute of Electrical and Electronic Engineers
345 E. 47th Street
New York, NY 10017

*SIGPLAN* (Special Interest Group on Programming Languages)
11 West 42nd Street
New York, NY 10036

# To Suit Your Computer

The compiler you use may not yet support all the features of ANSI C. It may not have all the new types or it may lack some library routines.

## DATA TYPES

The sample programs have been written to minimize dependence on new features in the ANSI standard. However, a few programs will require the following lines to be inserted:

```
typedef size_t int;
typedef char *void_pointer;
#define void /* */
#define const /* */
```

## printf FORMAT

If you are running the programs in a UNIX environment, you may wish to add printf("\n"); immediately prior to the call to exit() in each program. This repositions the cursor to the next line before control returns to the operating system.

The format specifier for printf for pointers is "%p". This specifier may not be available, so you can use either "%x" or "%lx", based on the size of pointers. This program will help you decide which to code:

```
#include <stdio.h>
main()
/* Determine which format specifier to use for pointer */
    {
    char *pc;
```

```
          int i;
          long l;

          if (sizeof(pc)==sizeof(int))
              printf("\n Use %%x for pointer");
          else if (sizeof(pc)==sizeof(long))
              printf("\n Use %%lx");
          else
              /* Can't tell; just print the size */
               printf("\n Pointer size is %d",sizeof(pc));
          }
```

## LIBRARY FUNCTIONS

The compiler library may be missing functions. Two functions that may not be available are rand and srand. Here are a couple of alternative functions you can code.

```
static unsigned long current_random; /* Current random number */

void srandint(seed)
/* Seeds the random number */
int seed;                                  /* Starting value for random number */
     {
     current_random = seed;
     return;
     }

#define IA 1103515245
#define IC 12345
#define IB 32768

unsigned int rand()
/* Returns a random integer */
     {
     unsigned int ret;                     /* Returned integer */

     /* Compute a new random number */
     current_random = current_random * IA + IC;

     /* Use the high order bits and put into the range */
     ret = (unsigned int) (current_random/(2*IB)) % IB;

     return ret;
     }
```

Another function that may be missing is memmove. You could use the following code as a substitute:

```
memmove(destination,source,count)
/* Moves count bytes from source to destination */
char *destination;              /* Where to move to */
char *source;                   /* Where to move from */
int count;                      /* Number of bytes to move */
                                /* NOTE: This works in correct manner
                                          for overlapping locations */
    {
    if (count>0)
        {
        if (destination<source)
            {
            while (count--)
                {
                *destination++=*source++;
                }
            }
        else
            {
            destination += count;
            source += count;
            while (count--)
                {
                *(--destination)=*(--source);
                }
            }
        }
    return;
    }
```

## HEADER FILES

You may be missing header files. If ctype.h is missing, you can either eliminate the #include statement or create a file with that name with nothing in it.[1]

If math.h is missing, you should create a file with that name that has double sqrt();. If stdlib.h is missing, you can make a file with that name that has

```
void *malloc();
unsigned int rand();
```

---

[1] The isdigit function and the other is.. functions are typically #defined in this header to be a lookup into an array. If ctype.h is not provided, these functions are treated as regular library functions.

## STRUCTURES

Older compilers may not support passing entire structures to and from functions. To run the programs in Chapter 7, you need to change calling sequences to pass address of the structures and to change the functions to accept pointers to structures. Chapter 8 on pointers shows how to do this.

## FUNCTION NAMES

If your linker gives you a DUPLICATE NAME error when your function names contain identical characters for the first six or eight characters, you can use a macro to redefine the duplicate names. For example,

```
#define date_check(a) date1(a)
#define date_correct(a) date2(a)
```

You need to include this macro in all source files in which the call appears and in the file in which the function is defined.

## COMPILER OPTIONS

Most compilers support command line values for setting flags and filenames. The most common of these defines a name as if a #define had been in the source file. This usually has a -d flag. For example, invoking the compiler with cc filename.c -dDEBUG makes it act as if there was a #define DEBUG in the file, so all #ifdef DEBUG tests will be true.

Some compilers enable you to give a value for the name. For example,

```
cc filename.c -DDEBUG=5
```

has the same effect as a #define DEBUG 5 in the source file.

# Appendix C

# Changes from K&R

The ANSI C Programming Language Standard committee, X3J11, has made extensions to the language defined in the Kernighan and Ritchie book. Most of these extensions first appeared in the C compiler for the UNIX system and have been adopted by many other compiler makers. Most of the changes have dealt with creating a type-checking mechanism for function parameters and return values, expanding the power of the preprocessor, and deciding on an expanded set of common functions.

Because the ANSI standard is being phased in over the next few years, many compilers meet the K&R standard, but not the ANSI standard. A summary of the changes is given here, in the event you have an older compiler.

## VARIABLES, CONSTANTS, AND EXPRESSIONS

The K&R standard included only octal valued escape sequences, not hexadecimal sequences (\x). Octal sequence with the digits 8 or 9 are no longer valid. The escape sequences \a (alert), \v (vertical tab), and \? (question mark) are additions. Trigraphs (such as ??#) are a new feature.

The float format (such as 3.3F), unsigned int (for example, 455U), and unsigned long int (such as 32UL) constants were not in K&R.

The synonym of long float for double has disappeared. New types added are long double, unsigned short int, unsigned long int, unsigned char, signed char, wide characters (wchar_t and L"" strings).

The word entry was reserved for K&R, but is no longer.

Only 8 characters of a name were significant in the original implementation. For example, abcdefghi and abcdefghz represented the same variable name.

Two new data types were introduced—enum and void. The signed type modifier was added. The concept of storage type modifiers—const and volatile—was not in K&R.

Automatic arrays and structures may now be initialized.

465

Computation involving two float values may be done in single precision, rather than converting to double and back to float.

Regrouping of expressions and ignoring parentheses are no longer accepted.

In K&R, two adjacent string literals were not concatenated. Such a linkage would have been an error.

---

## FUNCTIONS

K&R's implementation permitted programs to redeclare a parameter in the opening declarations of a function. This made the parameter value inaccessible to the function, as in

```
int putc(c)
int c;
    {
    double c;
    ...
    }
```

If a prototype appears in a source file, the default widening of parameters (char to int and float to double) may not occur.

Only one definition of an external variable was allowed.

```
int i;
int i;
```

was not allowed, but

```
extern int i;
int i;
```

was acceptable, because the extern does not define the variable (set aside memory space for it) but simply declares its type.

Only the simple function prototype existed in K&R, and it declared the return type.

A pointer to a function can now be used without an indirection indicator, for example,

```
(*p_function)()
```

and

```
p_function()
```

are both acceptable.

## ARRAYS

K&R allowed a declaration and reference of an array using the comma operator, such as

```
int array[3,4];      Declares a single dimensioned array of 4 elements
array[2,3]=7;        Sets the 3rd element in array to 7
```

The ANSI standard prohibits using the comma operator with constants, so at least this mistake should not occur.

## PREPROCESSOR

The quote operator (#), the token concatenator operator (##), and the defined operator are ANSI inventions. The #error, #pragma, #elif, and the null # are not in K&R. The "#" of a directive had to be the first character in the line, with no intervening spaces. The #asm directive is no longer a keyword. You may redefine a #define without an intervening #undef, if the values are the same. The defined() preprocessor operator has been added, as well as five predefined names (such as __LINE__).

## STRUCTURES AND UNIONS

The only action the K&R system performed with structures and unions was to take their address or to use one of their members. Structures and unions could not be assigned as a whole, passed as a whole to functions, or returned by functions.

The member names of all structures had to be unique, with a few exceptions. Bit fields could only be unsigned ints.

Unions could not be initialized, not even the first member.

## LIBRARY FUNCTIONS

The K&R standard did not explicitly specify library functions to be included with a C compiler. The UNIX C library was implicitly the standard. Compiler manufacturers varied in the number of library functions they supported. In general, the functions listed in Table C.1 were supplied in compiler libraries.

Unbuffered input and output functions were eliminated from the standard. These functions are covered at the end of this appendix with suggestions on how to program these with the standard functions.

The only major changes in the function specifications were in the formatted input and output functions. Several additional format specifiers were added. A

**Table C.1 Library Functions Usually Supplied with C Compilers**

*Buffered Input and Output:*

| *File Operations* | *Character I/O* | *String I/O* | *Formatted I/O* |
|---|---|---|---|
| fopen | getc | gets | scanf |
| freopen | putc | puts | fscanf |
| fclose | fgetc | fgets | sscanf |
| fread | fputc | fputs | printf |
| fwrite | getchar | | fprintf |
| fseek | putchar | | sprintf |
| ftell | ungetc | | |
| rewind | | | |
| ferror | | | |
| clearerr | | | |
| fileno | | | |
| fflush | | | |

*Unbuffered Input and Output:*

| *File Operations* | *File I/O* |
|---|---|
| open | read |
| creat | write |
| close | |
| unlink | |
| lseek | |

*Other Functions:*

| *System Functions* | *Memory Allocation* | *Utility* |
|---|---|---|
| exit | malloc | clearmem |
| | calloc | movmem |
| | free | |

| *Character* | *String* |
|---|---|
| isdigit | strlen |
| isalpha | strcpy |
| islower | strcat |
| isupper | strcmp |
| isspace | |
| toupper | |
| tolower | |

%p specifier was added for outputting and inputting pointer values. A %i specifier was added for inputting and outputting integer values in multiple formats.

Header files have been declared for every function. These are shown in Appendix G. For example, the stdio.h file should be included in every source file that has formatted input and output (such as printf), although programs run without it on most compilers.

## UNBUFFERED INPUT AND OUTPUT FUNCTIONS

These routines use the concept of a file descriptor, which is an integer number. The numbers 0, 1, and 2 are used by most systems to represent standard input, standard output, and standard error output. The open routine returns a file descriptor, which is passed to the other routines to show which file you wish to work with.

```
int open(file_name,mode)
char *file_name;
int mode;
```

This opens a file with the name file_name. The mode determines how the file is opened. Values for mode are

| | |
|---|---|
| 0 | opened for reading only |
| 1 | opened for writing only |
| 2 | opened for reading and writing |

If the file can be opened, it is positioned to the beginning. The function returns a file descriptor, which is a positive integer referenced for other operations on the file. If the file cannot be opened, the function returns a negative value.

```
int creat(file_name, mode)
char *file_name;
int mode;
```

This creates a file with the name file_name. If the file exists, it is deleted. The mode values are system dependent. The function returns a file descriptor, which is a positive integer referenced for other operations on the file. If the file cannot be opened, it returns a negative value.

```
int read(file_descriptor, buffer, count)
int file_descriptor;
char *buffer;
int count;
```

This reads `count` bytes from the file referenced by `file_descriptor` to the address starting at `buffer`. The number of bytes read is returned. The value 0 is returned if end of file was encountered. A negative value is returned if an error occurred.

```
int write(file_descriptor, buffer, count)
int file_descriptor;
char *buffer;
int count;
```

This writes `count` bytes from the address starting at `buffer` to the file referenced by `file_descriptor`. The number of bytes written is returned. A negative value is returned if an error occurred.

```
int close(file_descriptor)
int file_descriptor;
```

This closes the file referenced by `file_descriptor`. It returns 0 if successful, a negative value if an error occurred.

```
long lseek(file_descriptor, long_offset, mode)
int file_descriptor;
long long_offset;
int mode;
```

This positions the file referenced by `file_descriptor` to the position specified by `long_offset` and `mode`. The new file position is returned, if successful. A negative value is returned if an error occurred. Values for `mode` are

| | |
|---|---|
| 0 | `long_offset` relative to beginning of file |
| 1 | `long_offset` relative to current position |
| 2 | `long_offset` relative to end of file |

```
int unlink(file_name)
char *file_name;
```

This removes the file `file_name` from the system. If successful, it returns 0; otherwise, it returns a negative value.

## NEW FUNCTION CALLS

You can replace calls to the old functions by the new calls listed in the right column of the following list.

| **Old Function Call** | **New Function Call** |
|---|---|
| fd=creat(file_name, mode) | fp=open(file_name, "wb+");<br>setbuf(fp, NULL) |
| fd=open(file_name, 0) | fp=open(file_name, "rb");<br>setbuf(fp, NULL) |
| fd=open(file_name, 1) | fp=open(file_name, "wb");<br>setbuf(fp, NULL) |
| fd=open(file_name, 2) | fp=open(file_name, "rb+");<br>setbuf(fp, NULL) |
| ret=read(fd, buffer, count) | ret=fread(buffer, 1, count, fp) |
| ret=write(fd, buffer, count) | ret=fwrite(buffer, 1, count, fp) |
| ret=close(fd) | ret=fclose(fp); |
| ret=lseek(fd, long_offset, mode) | ret=fseek(fp, long_offset, mode) |
| ret=unlink(file_name) | ret=remove(file_name) |

# Appendix D

# Formal Definition

*Backus-Naur Form (BNF)* is a system for describing the rules of a language. The rules state what character or symbol sequences are possible in a language. However, not all sequences may have meaning or may be compilable.

A *production* is a rule that defines what makes up a syntactic category. For example, the category *digit* is made up of the characters 0 through 9. These digits are called *terminals*, because they are not categories but symbols for which there are no further productions. Categories are shown in italics, terminals are shown in roman. For example,

```
digit := 0 | 1 | 2 | 3 | 4 | 5 | 6 | 7 | 8 | 9
```

states that *digit* is a category whose value falls in the range $0\ldots9$. The := means the category consists of what appears on the right side of the =. The vertical bar stands for *or*. If two symbols appear in a production without a vertical bar, then they are simply concatenated. For example,

```
paren_zero := (0)
```

states that *paren_zero* is made of (0). Once a category is defined, you can use it in other productions, such as

```
numeric_constant := digit₁₊
```

The subscript $_{1+}$ states that the symbol must be used at least once. A $_{0+}$ subscript states that the symbol can be used zero or more times. An $_{opt}$ subscript states that it can be used zero or one times.

A pair of angle brackets, <>, group the enclosed symbols. Two additional subscripts are also used. The subscript $_1$ means one choice (separated by the vertical bars) must be used. The subscript $_{1+nr}$ means one or more of the choices may be used without repeating any choice.

The definition of a language can be recursive. A category can be used in the production that defines it. A category can use a second category in its production that has a production that includes the first category. This description of the language is adapted from the ANSI standard.

## TERMINALS

The following are the terminal productions, which define the character categories.

*nondigit* := 
```
_ | a | b | c | d | e | f | g | h | i |
j | k | l | m | n | o | p | q | r | s |
t | u | v | w | x | y | z |
A | B | C | D | E | F | G | H | I |
J | K | L | M | N | O | P | Q | R | S |
T | U | V | W | X | Y | Z
```

*digit* := 
```
0 | 1 | 2 | 3 | 4 | 5 | 6 | 7 | 8 | 9
```

*non_zero_digit* ::= 1 | 2 | 3 | 4 | 5 | 6 | 7 | 8 | 9

*hex_digit* := 
```
0 | 1 | 2 | 3 | 4 | 5 | 6 | 7 | 8 | 9
a | b | c | d | e | f |
A | B | C | D | E | F
```

*octal_digit* := 0 | 1 | 2 | 3 | 4 | 5 | 6 | 7

*punctuator* := 
```
[ | ] | ( | ) | { | } | * | , | : |
= | ; | ... | #
```

*operator* := 
```
[ | ] | ( | ) | . | -> | ++ | -- | & | * | + | - | ~ | ! | sizeof |
/ | % | << |>> | < | > | <= | >= | == | != | ^ | | | && | | | |
? | :
= | *= | /= | %= | += | -= | <<= | >>= | &= | ^ = | | | = | , | # | ##
```

*escape_sequence* := | \' | \" | \? | \\ | \o | \oo | \ooo |
\xh| \xhh | \xhhh |
\a | \b | \f | \n | \r | \t | \v

## IDENTIFIERS

These productions define identifiers as variable names and constants.

*identifier* := nondigit <nondigit | digit>$_{0+}$

## Constants

| | |
|---|---|
| unsigned_suffix:= | u \| U |
| long_suffix := | l \| L |
| integer_suffix := | $\langle$unsigned_suffix \| long_suffix$\rangle_{1+nr}$ |
| sign := | + \| - |
| | |
| octal_constant := | 0 $\langle$octal_digit$\rangle_{0+}$ |
| hex_constant := | $\langle$ 0x \| 0X $\rangle_1$ $\langle$hex_digit$\rangle_{1+}$ |
| decimal_constant := | non_zero_digit $\langle$digit$\rangle_{0+}$ |
| | |
| integer_constant := | $\langle$decimal_constant \| octal_constant \| hex_constant$\rangle_1$ <br> $\langle$integer_suffix$\rangle_{opt}$ |
| | |
| float_suffix := | f \| l \| F \| L |
| | |
| fraction_part := | $\langle$ $\langle$digit$\rangle_{0+}$ . $\langle$digit$\rangle_{1+}$ $\rangle$ \| <br> $\langle$ $\langle$digit$\rangle_{1+}$ . $\rangle$ |
| | |
| exponent_part := | $\langle$ e \| E $\rangle_1$ sign$_{opt}$$\langle$digit$\rangle_{1+}$ |
| | |
| float_constant := | $\langle$fraction_part \| $\langle$digit$\rangle_{1+}$ $\rangle_1$ <br> $\langle$exponent_part$\rangle_{opt}$ $\langle$float_suffix$\rangle_{opt}$ |
| | |
| enum_constant := | identifier |
| | |
| char_constant := | $\langle$any character except single quote, backslash, or newline$\rangle$ \| <br> escape_sequence |
| | |
| character_constant := | ' $\langle$char_constant$\rangle_{1+}$ ' |
| | |
| constant := | float_constant \| integer_constant \| enum_constant <br> \| character_constant |

## String Literals

| | |
|---|---|
| string_char := | $\langle$ any character except double quote, backslash, or newline $\rangle$ \| escape_sequence |
| | |
| string_literal := | $\langle$L$\rangle_{opt}$" $\langle$string_char$\rangle_{0+}$ " |

## OPERATORS

These productions describe the operators.

| | |
|---|---|
| multiplicative_operator := | * \| % \| / |
| additive_operator := | + \| - |
| shift-operator := | >> \| << |
| relational_operator := | < \| > \| <= \| >= |
| equality_operator := | \| == \| != |
| AND_operator := | & |
| OR_operator := | \| |
| XOR_operator := | ^ |
| logical_AND_operator := | && |
| logical_OR_operator := | \|\| |
| assignment_operator := | = \| *= \| /= \| %= \| += \| <<= \| >>=&= \| ^= \| \|= |

## EXPRESSIONS

This is a recursive definition for an expression. The *expression* and *assignment_expression* productions are defined at the end.

| | |
|---|---|
| primary_expression := | identifier \| constant \| string_literal \| (expression) |
| argument_list := | assignment_expression <, assignment_expression>$_{0+}$ |
| post_fix := | [ expression ] \| (argument_list$_{opt}$) \| . identifier \| -> identifier \| ++ \| -- |
| post_fix_expression := | <primary_expression> <post_fix>$_{0+}$ |
| unary_operator := | & \| * \| + \| - \| ! \| ~ |
| pre_fix := | ++ \| -- \| sizeof |
| unary_expression := | <pre_fix>$_{0+}$ post_fix_expression \| unary_operator cast_expression \| sizeof (type_name) |
| cast_expression := | < ( type_name ) >$_{0+}$ unary_expression |

These definitions implicitly describe the precedence of the operators.

| | |
|---|---|
| multiply_expression := | <multiply_expression multiplicative_operator >$_{0+}$ cast_expression |
| additive_expression := | <additive_expression additive_operator >$_{0+}$ multiply_expression |
| shift_expression := | <shift_expression shift_operator>$_{0+}$ additive_expression |
| relational_expression := | <relational_expression relational_operator>$_{0+}$ shift_expression |
| equality_expression := | <equality_expression equality_operator>$_{0+}$ relational_expression |
| AND_expression := | <AND_expression AND_operator>$_{0+}$ equality_expression |
| XOR_expression := | <XOR_expression XOR_operator>$_{0+}$ AND_expression |
| OR_expression := | <OR_expression OR_operator>$_{0+}$ OR_expression |
| logical_AND_expression := | <logical_AND_expression logical_AND_operator>$_{0+}$ OR_expression |
| logical_OR_expression:= | <logical_OR_expression logical_OR_operator>$_{0+}$ logical_AND_expression |
| conditional_expression := | logical_OR_expression \| logical_OR_expression ? expression : conditional_expression |
| assignment_expression := | <unary_expression assignment_operator>$_{0+}$ assignment_expression |
| expression := | <expression ,>$_{0+}$ assignment_expression |
| constant_expression := | conditional_expression |

# DECLARATIONS

There is a bit of recursiveness here. These define the declaration statements.

| | |
|---|---|
| *storage_class* := | typedef \| extern \| static \| auto \|register |
| *typedef_name* := | *identifier* |
| *type_qualifier* := | const \| volatile |
| *type_specifier* := | void \| char \| short \| int \| long \| float \| double \| signed \| unsigned \| *struct_union_specifier* \| *enum_specifier* \| *typedef_name* |
| *initializer* := | *assignment_expression* \| {*initializer_list* } {*initializer_list,* } |
| *initializer_list* := | *initializer* < , *initializer*>$_{0+}$ |
| *declarator_init* := | *declarator* <= *initializer*>$_{opt}$ |
| *declarator_list* := | *declarator_init* <, *declarator_int*>$_{0+}$ |
| *declaration_specifier* := | <*storage_class* \| *type_specifier* \| *type_qualifier*> |
| *declaration* := | *declaration_specifier*$_{1+}$ <*declarator_list*>$_{opt}$ |
| *struct_union* := | struct \| union |
| *struct_declarator* := | *declarator* \| *declarator*$_{opt}$ : *constant_expression* |
| *struct_declarator_list* := | *struct_declarator* <, *struct_declarator*>$_{0+}$ |
| *struct_declaration* := | <*type_specifier* \| *type_qualifier*>$_{1+}$ *struct_declarator_list* ; |
| *struct_union_specifier* := | *struct_union identifier* \| *struct_union identifier*$_{opt}$ { <*struct_declarations*>$_{1+}$ } |

enum_value :=                          enum_constant <=constant_expression >$_{opt}$

enum_list :=                           enum_value <, enum_value>$_{0+}$

enum_specifier :=                      enum identifier |
                                       enum identifier$_{opt}$ { enum_list }

parameter_declaration :=               declaration_specifier$_{0+}$
                                       declarator | abstract_declarator$_{opt}$

parameter_list :=                      <parameter_declaration>$_{0+}$ <,...>$_{opt}$

pointer :=                             * <type_specifier | type_qualifier>$_{0+}$

declarator :=                          pointer$_{opt}$ direct_declarator

post_declare :=                        [constant_expression$_{opt}$]
                                       (parameter_list)
                                       (identifier_list$_{opt}$)

direct_declarator :=                   identifier |
                                       ( declarator ) |
                                       direct_declarator post_declare

abstract_declarator :=                 pointer |
                                       pointer$_{opt}$ direct_abstract_declarator

direct_abstract_declarator :=          (abstract_declarator
                                       direct_abstract_declarator$_{opt}$
                                       <[constant_expression$_{opt}$] |
                                       (parameter_list$_{opt}$)

---

## CONTROL FLOW STATEMENTS

The following are the control flow statements.

jump_statement :=                      goto identifier; |
                                       continue; |
                                       break; |
                                       return expression$_{opt}$ ;

iteration_statement :=                 while (expression) statement |
                                       do statement while (expression); |
                                       for (expression$_{opt}$ ; expression$_{opt}$ ;
                                           expression$_{opt}$ ) statement

| | |
|---|---|
| *selection_statement* := | `if (`*expression*`)` *statement* \| <br> `if (`*expression*`)` *statement* `else` <br>  *statement* \| <br> `switch (`*expression*`)` *statement* |
| *expression_statement* := | *expression*$_{\text{opt}}$`;` |
| *labeled_statement* := | *identifier* `:` *statement* \| <br> `case` *constant_expression* `:` *statement* \| <br> `default :` *statement* |
| *compound_statement* := | `{` *<declaration>*$_{0+}$ *<statement>*$_{0+}$ `}` |
| *statement* := | *labeled_statement* \| <br> *compound_statement* \| <br> *expression_statement* \| <br> *selection_statement* \| <br> *iteration_statement* \| <br> *jump_statement* |

---

# FILE

A source file consists of functions and external declarations, such as

| | |
|---|---|
| *function_definition* := | *declaration_specifier*$_{\text{opt}}$ *declarator* <br>  *declaration_list*$_{\text{opt}}$ <br>  *compound_statement* |

*<declaration* \| *function_definition>*$_{0+}$

---

# PREPROCESSING

These are the preprocessor tokens.

| | |
|---|---|
| *preprocess_token* := | *identifier* \| <br> *constant* \| <br> *string_literal* \| <br> *operator* \| <br> *punctuator* \| <br> *each non-white space not one of the* <br>  *previous* |
| *header_char* := | *any character except new-line and* `>` |

```
header_name :=              < header_char₁₊ >

new_line :=                 new-line character

left_paren :=               left parenthesis with no white space
                               before it

control_line :=             #include <preprocess_token₁₊ |
                               header_name> new_line |
                            #define identifier <preprocess_token>₀₊
                               new_line |
                            #define identifier left_paren
                               identifier_list_opt )
                               <preprocess_token>₀₊ new_line |
                            #undef identifier new_line |
                            #line preprocess_token₁₊ new_line |
                            #error preprocess_token₀₊ new_line |
                            #pragma preprocess_token₀₊ new_line |
                            #new_line

endif_line :=               #endif new_line

else_group :=               #elif constant_expression new_line
                               pp_group_opt

elif_group :=               #else new_line pp_group_opt

if_group :=                 < #if constant_expression |
                            #ifdef identifier |
                            #ifndef identifier >
                            new_line pp_group_opt

if_part :=                  if_group <elif_group>₀₊ else_group_opt
                               endif_line

pp_part :=                  preprocess_token₀₊ new_line |
                            if_part | control_line

pp_group :=                 <pp_part>₁₊
```

   The translation of a source file occurs in several stages. Any problems in how a particular sequence of code might be interpreted can be resolved by examining how these stages operate.

1. Trigraphs are translated.
2. Physical lines are transformed to logical lines by deleting all '\'new-line sequences.

3. The source is broken into tokens and white space. Comments are replaced by one space.
4. The preprocessor directives are executed. Include files are placed in the source. For each one, steps 1 to 3 are executed.
5. Escape sequences (such as `'\t'`) are converted to single characters.
6. Strings that are adjacent are concatenated.

# Summary of C

This summary is adapted from the ANSI C Standard.

## DATA TYPES

### Integer Types

| | |
|---|---|
| char | single character |
| signed char | char that contains negative and positive numbers |
| unsigned char | char that contains only positive numbers |
| short | integer with less or equal range as int |
| signed short int | same as short |
| unsigned short int | short that contains only positive numbers |
| int | integer |
| signed int | same as int |
| unsigned int | int that contains only positive numbers |
| long | integer with equal or greater range than int |
| signed long int | same as long |
| unsigned long int | long that contains only positive numbers |

### Floating Point Types

| | |
|---|---|
| float | floating point |
| double | floating point with equal or extended range over float |
| long double | floating point with equal or extended range over double |

### Void Type

| | |
|---|---|
| void | used for functions that do not return values pointers to void are universal pointers |

### Enumerated Type

enum                        takes on restricted list of values, e.g., enum *tag-type*
                            { *enum-values* };

### Type Modifiers

const                       variable should not change value
volatile                    variable should not be optimized

*Examples*

int const i;                i is constant
int volatile i;             i is volatile

### Aggregates and Derived Types

structure                   struct  *tag-type*
                                {
                                declarations of members
                                };

union                       union *tag-type*
                                {
                                declaration of members
                                };

array                       *data-type* name[*size*]

pointers                    *data-type* *name
                            pointer to *data-type*

*Examples*

int const *name; or
const int *name;            pointer to an int that is constant
int * const name;           variable that is constant points to an int

You can recursively apply these derived types.

## typedef

The `typedef` assigns a new name to a data type. For example,

`typedef data-type TYPE;`

## Usage Types

| | |
|---|---|
| *Integral Types* | integer and enumerated types |
| *Arithmetic Types* | integral and floating point types |
| *Scalar Types* | arithmetic and pointers types |
| *Constants* | |

*Integer-constant:*

| | |
|---|---|
| Decimal | non-zero starting `char` |
| Octal | 0 followed by 0 to 7 |
| Hexadecimal | 0x or 0X followed by 0 to 9, A to F, or a to f |

*Type suffixes:*

| | |
|---|---|
| unsigned | u or U |
| long | l or L (or value cannot fit in `int`) |

*Floating-constant:*

Number with decimal point and optional exponent

*Type suffixes:*

| | |
|---|---|
| double | no suffix |
| float | f or F |
| long double | l or L |

*Enum constant:*

must have been listed in enum declaration

*Char constant:*

surrounded by single quotes.

*Escape characters*
*Sequence and Meaning*        *ASCII Value*

| | |
|---|---|
| \a alert (bell) | 7 |
| \b back-space | 8 |
| \t tab (horizontal) | 9 |
| \n new-line | 10 |
| \v vertical tab | 11 |
| \f form-feed | 12 |
| \r carriage-return | 13 |
| \" quote (in a string) | 34 |
| \' single quote (as a character constant) | 39 |
| \? question mark | 63 |
| \\ backslash (the literal character) | 92 |

*String literals:*

Characters surrounded by double quotes.[1]
\new-line allows you to continue to next line.
Two adjacent string literals are concatenated.

*Comments*

Surrounded by /* */
May not appear within character constant, string literal, or another comment

*Variables storage classes:*

Automatic:
> Inside a function
> No keyword or auto
> Can be initialized with any expression
> Does not retain values between calls to function

Register:
> Inside a function
> Keyword is register
> Can be initialized with any expression
> Cannot take address of register variable
> Does not retain values between calls to function

Static:
> Inside a function
> Keyword is static
> Can be initialized with constant expression
> If no explicit initializer, initialized to zero
> Retains values between calls to function

---

[1] If preceded by an *L,* it is a string literal of wchar_t type. See Appendix I.

External:                    Outside a function with no keyword
                            Outside or inside function with keyword `extern`
                            Can be initialized with constant expression
                            If not explicit initializer, initialized to zero
                            Can be referenced by functions in other files

Static external:             Outside a function with keyword `static`[2]
                            Can be initialized with constant expression
                            If not explicit initializer, initialized to zero

## OPERATORS

Bitwise operators must have integral type operands. The operators are summarized in Table E.1.

## STATEMENTS

Simple              *expression*;

Compound            {
                    *zero-or-more-statements*
                    }

Control
if:                 if (*condition*)
                    *statement*

if-else:            if (*condition*)
                        *statement*
                    else
                        *statement*

while:              while (*condition*)
                        *statement*

do-while:           do
                        *statement*
                    while (*condition*);

---

[2] You can reference static externals from inside a function using the `extern` keyword, but this is usually unnecessary.

## Table E.1 Bitwise Operators

*Precedence and Associativity*

| Operator | Meaning | Associativity | Order of Evaluation |
|---|---|---|---|
| () | function call | left to right | |
| [] | array element | | |
| -> | pointer to structure member | | |
| . | member of structure | | |
| ! | logical negation | right to left | |
| ~ | ones complement | | |
| ++ | increment | | |
| -- | decrement | | |
| - | unary minus | | |
| + | unary plus | | |
| (*type*) | cast | | |
| * | indirection (pointer) | | |
| & | address | | |
| sizeof | size of object | | |
| * | multiplication | left to right | |
| / | division | | |
| % | modulus | | |
| + | addition | left to right | |
| - | subtraction | | |
| << | left shift | left to right | |
| >> | right shift | | |
| < | less than | left to right | |
| <= | less than or equal to | | |
| > | greater than | | |
| >= | greater than or equal to | | |
| == | equality | left to right | |
| != | inequality | | |
| & | bitwise AND | left to right | |
| ^ | bitwise XOR | left to right | |
| \| | bitwise OR | left to right | |
| && | logical AND | left to right | left to right |
| \|\| | logical OR | left to right | left to right |
| ? : | conditional | right to left | left to right |
| = | assignment | right to left | |
| *op*= | shorthand assignment | | |
| , | comma | left to right | left to right |

for:                       for (*expression1*;*expression2*;*expression3*)
                               *statement*

switch:                    switch(*integral_expression*)
                               {
                               case *integral-constant*:
                               . . .
                               default:
                               . . .
                               }

break:                     exits the while, do-while, for loops and the switch
                           statement

continue:                  goes to the test condition in the while and do-while loops
                           goes to *expression3* in the for loop

---

# FUNCTIONS

*data-type function-name(parameter-list)*
*declarations-of-parameters*
        {
        *declaration-of-local-variables*
        *statements*
        }

main() (argc, argv)        command with tokens passed to it.

exit(value)                ends the program and returns to the operating
                               system.

---

# PREPROCESSOR

#define *NAME*             defines a name
#define *NAME*(tokens)     defines a macro
#undef *NAME*              undefines a name or macro
#ifdef                     tests for #define
#ifndef                    tests for no #define
#if *expression*           tests expression

| | |
|---|---|
| #else | other half of test |
| #endif | end of #if, #ifdef, #ifndef |
| #elif | else-if |
| #line | sets up a line number |
| #error | creates an error in compilation |
| #pragma | local feature to a compiler |
| # | null directive |
| \newline | for continuation of preprocessor statements |
| defined(*NAME*) | tests for #define—for use in #if |
| # | quoting operator |
| ## | token pasting operator |

## KEYWORDS

| Keywords | Usage |
|---|---|
| auto | storage type |
| break | control flow (in for, while, do-while, switch) |
| case | control flow (in switch) |
| char | data type |
| const | data type modifier |
| continue | control flow (in for, while, do-while) |
| default | control flow (in switch) |
| do | control flow |
| double | data type |
| else | control flow (with if) |
| enum | data type |
| extern | storage type |
| float | data type |
| for | control flow |
| goto | control flow |
| if | control flow |
| int | data type |
| long | data type modifier |
| register | storage type |
| return | control flow (in function) |
| short | data type modifier |
| signed | data type modifier |
| sizeof | built-in operator |
| static | storage type |
| struct | aggregate data type |
| switch | control flow |
| typedef | data type declarator |

| | |
|---|---|
| union | aggregate data type |
| unsigned | data type modifier |
| void | data type |
| volatile | data type modifier |
| while | control flow |

| *Symbol* | *Meaning* |
|---|---|
| + | addition |
| | (++) auto increment |
| | unary + |
| - | subtraction |
| | negation |
| | (--) auto decrement |
| / | divide |
| | (/*) comment start |
| | (*/) comment end |
| * | multiply |
| | indirection |
| | (/*) comment start |
| | (*/) comment end |
| % | modulus |
| ! | not logical |
| | (!=) not equal |
| \| | or bitwise |
| | (\| \|) logical |
| ~ | ones complement bitwise |
| ^ | exclusive or bitwise |
| & | and bitwise |
| | (&&) and logical |
| | address of (as a unary operator) |
| ( | associativity |
| | function parameter list start |
| ) | associativity |
| | function parameter list end |
| ' | character constant start and end |
| " | string constant start and end |
| ? | conditional operator (with :) |
| , | comma operator |
| | function parameter list separator |
| | data initialization separator |
| < | less than operator |
| | (<=) less than or equal to |
| > | greater than operator |
| | (>=) greater than or equal to |

|   |   |
|---|---|
| = | assignment operator |
|   | (with +, –, and so on) shorthand assignment |
|   | (==) equality operator |
|   | (<=) less than operator |
|   | (>=) greater than operator |
| : | conditional operator (with ?) |
|   | label switch |
|   | label goto |
| # | preprocessor command—quote |
| ## | preprocessor command—token concatenation |
| [ | starts an array index |
| ] | ends an array index |
| { | starts a block (compound statement) |
|   | starts an initialization list |
| } | ends a block (compound statement) |
|   | ends an initialization list |
| \ | escape character |
| ; | statement terminator |

## Scope of Identifiers

program

function

file              if outside of a function or block, extends to end of source
                  file

block             in a block compound statement or in list of function
                  parameters
                  any identifiers redeclared in a block are instances of
                  new identifiers

function prototype   only within the function prototype

## Linkage of Identifiers

External linkage   In a set of files and libraries that make up the pro-
                   gram, the same identifier denotes same object identifi-
                   ers for functions and objects declared outside of
                   functions.

Internal linkage   If the word static precedes the function or object
                   identifier, then it is known only within the source file.

extern
: If the identifier was previously declared as internal linkage (static), extern has no effect. Otherwise, it declares the identifier to have external linkage. If the identifier is not called in the source file, no external reference need be made for it.

## Sequence Points

volatile
: Values must be intact when a sequence point is reached (they cannot be optimized out of a loop and any interrupt must ensure they are intact). Sequence points are function calls, unary + operator, comma operator, logical OR and logical AND, and conditional operator.

# ASCII Code

| DECIMAL | OCTAL | HEXA-DECIMAL | BINARY | CHAR-ACTER | NOTE |
|---|---|---|---|---|---|
| 0 | 000 | 00 | 0000000 | NUL | null character |
| 1 | 001 | 01 | 0000001 | SOH | |
| 2 | 002 | 02 | 0000010 | STX | |
| 3 | 003 | 03 | 0000011 | ETX | |
| 4 | 004 | 04 | 0000100 | EOT | |
| 5 | 005 | 05 | 0000101 | ENQ | |
| 6 | 006 | 06 | 0000110 | ACK | |
| 7 | 007 | 07 | 0000111 | BEL | Produces beep or bell |
| 8 | 010 | 08 | 0001000 | BS | Backspace (\b) |
| 9 | 011 | 09 | 0001001 | HT | Horizontal tab (\t) |
| 10 | 012 | 0A | 0001010 | LF | Line feed (\n) |
| 11 | 013 | 0B | 0001011 | VT | Vertical tab |
| 12 | 014 | 0C | 0001100 | FF | Form feed (\f) |
| 13 | 015 | 0D | 0001101 | CR | Carriage return (\r) |
| 14 | 016 | 0E | 0001110 | SO | |
| 15 | 017 | 0F | 0001111 | SI | |
| 16 | 020 | 10 | 0010000 | DLE | |
| 17 | 021 | 11 | 0010001 | DC1 | |
| 18 | 022 | 12 | 0010010 | DC2 | |
| 19 | 023 | 13 | 0010011 | DC3 | |
| 20 | 024 | 14 | 0010100 | DC4 | |
| 21 | 025 | 15 | 0010101 | NAK | |
| 22 | 026 | 16 | 0010110 | SYN | |
| 23 | 027 | 17 | 0010111 | ETB | |
| 24 | 030 | 18 | 0011000 | CAN | |
| 25 | 031 | 19 | 0011001 | EM | |
| 26 | 032 | 1A | 0011010 | SUB | |
| 27 | 033 | 1B | 0011011 | ESC | Escape |
| 28 | 034 | 1C | 0011100 | FS | |

| DECIMAL | OCTAL | HEXA-DECIMAL | BINARY | CHARACTER | NOTE |
|---------|-------|--------------|--------|-----------|------|
| 29 | 035 | 1D | 0011101 | GS | |
| 30 | 036 | 1E | 0011110 | RS | |
| 31 | 037 | 1F | 0011111 | VS | |
| 32 | 040 | 20 | 0100000 | SP | Space |
| 33 | 041 | 21 | 0100001 | ! | |
| 34 | 042 | 22 | 0100010 | " | |
| 35 | 043 | 23 | 0100011 | # | |
| 36 | 044 | 24 | 0100100 | $ | |
| 37 | 045 | 25 | 0100101 | % | |
| 38 | 046 | 26 | 0100110 | % | |
| 39 | 047 | 27 | 0100111 | ' | Single quote |
| 40 | 050 | 28 | 0101000 | ( | |
| 41 | 051 | 29 | 0101001 | ) | |
| 42 | 052 | 2A | 0101010 | * | |
| 43 | 053 | 2B | 0101011 | + | |
| 44 | 054 | 2C | 0101100 | , | Comma |
| 45 | 055 | 2D | 0101101 | - | Hyphen |
| 46 | 056 | 2E | 0101110 | . | Period |
| 47 | 057 | 2F | 0101111 | / | |
| 48 | 060 | 30 | 0110000 | 0 | |
| 49 | 061 | 31 | 0110001 | 1 | |
| 50 | 062 | 32 | 0110010 | 2 | |
| 51 | 063 | 33 | 0110011 | 3 | |
| 52 | 064 | 34 | 0110100 | 4 | |
| 53 | 065 | 35 | 0110101 | 5 | |
| 54 | 066 | 36 | 0110110 | 6 | |
| 55 | 067 | 37 | 0110111 | 7 | |
| 56 | 070 | 38 | 0111000 | 8 | |
| 57 | 071 | 39 | 0111001 | 9 | |
| 58 | 072 | 3A | 0111010 | : | Colon |
| 59 | 073 | 3B | 0111011 | ; | Semicolon |
| 60 | 074 | 3C | 0111100 | < | |
| 61 | 075 | 3D | 0111101 | = | |
| 62 | 076 | 3E | 0111110 | > | |
| 63 | 077 | 3F | 0111111 | ? | |
| 64 | 100 | 40 | 1000000 | @ | |
| 65 | 101 | 41 | 1000001 | A | |
| 66 | 102 | 42 | 1000010 | B | |
| 67 | 103 | 43 | 1000011 | C | |
| 68 | 104 | 44 | 1000100 | D | |
| 69 | 105 | 45 | 1000101 | E | |
| 70 | 106 | 46 | 1000110 | F | |
| 71 | 107 | 47 | 1000111 | G | |
| 72 | 110 | 48 | 1001000 | H | |

| DECIMAL | OCTAL | HEXA-DECIMAL | BINARY | CHAR-ACTER | NOTE |
|---------|-------|--------------|--------|------------|------|
| 73 | 111 | 49 | 1001001 | I | |
| 74 | 112 | 4A | 1001010 | J | |
| 75 | 113 | 4B | 1001011 | K | |
| 76 | 114 | 4C | 1001100 | L | |
| 77 | 115 | 4D | 1001101 | M | |
| 78 | 116 | 4E | 1001110 | N | |
| 79 | 117 | 4F | 1001111 | O | |
| 80 | 120 | 50 | 1010000 | P | |
| 81 | 121 | 51 | 1010001 | Q | |
| 82 | 122 | 52 | 1010010 | R | |
| 83 | 123 | 53 | 1010011 | S | |
| 84 | 124 | 54 | 1010100 | T | |
| 85 | 125 | 55 | 1010101 | U | |
| 86 | 126 | 56 | 1010110 | V | |
| 87 | 127 | 57 | 1010111 | W | |
| 88 | 130 | 58 | 1011000 | X | |
| 89 | 131 | 59 | 1011001 | Y | |
| 90 | 132 | 5A | 1011010 | Z | |
| 91 | 133 | 5B | 1011011 | [ | |
| 92 | 134 | 5C | 1011100 | \ | |
| 93 | 135 | 5D | 1011101 | ] | |
| 94 | 136 | 5E | 1011110 | ^ | |
| 95 | 137 | 5F | 1011111 | __ | Underline |
| 96 | 104 | 60 | 1100000 | ' | Back quote |
| 97 | 141 | 61 | 1100001 | a | |
| 98 | 142 | 62 | 1100010 | b | |
| 99 | 143 | 63 | 1100011 | c | |
| 100 | 144 | 64 | 1100100 | d | |
| 101 | 145 | 65 | 1100101 | e | |
| 102 | 146 | 66 | 1100110 | f | |
| 103 | 147 | 67 | 1100111 | g | |
| 104 | 150 | 68 | 1101000 | h | |
| 105 | 151 | 69 | 1101001 | i | |
| 106 | 152 | 6A | 1101010 | j | |
| 107 | 153 | 6B | 1101011 | k | |
| 108 | 154 | 6C | 1101100 | l | |
| 109 | 155 | 6D | 1101101 | m | |
| 110 | 156 | 6E | 1101110 | n | |
| 111 | 157 | 6F | 1101111 | o | |
| 112 | 160 | 70 | 1110000 | p | |
| 113 | 161 | 71 | 1110001 | q | |
| 114 | 162 | 72 | 1110010 | r | |
| 115 | 163 | 73 | 1110011 | s | |
| 116 | 164 | 74 | 1110100 | t | |

| DECIMAL | OCTAL | HEXA-DECIMAL | BINARY | CHARACTER | NOTE |
|---------|-------|--------------|--------|-----------|------|
| 117 | 165 | 75 | 1110101 | u | |
| 118 | 166 | 76 | 1110110 | v | |
| 119 | 167 | 77 | 1110111 | w | |
| 120 | 170 | 78 | 1111000 | x | |
| 121 | 171 | 79 | 1111001 | y | |
| 122 | 172 | 7A | 1111010 | z | |
| 123 | 173 | 7B | 1111011 | { | |
| 124 | 174 | 7C | 1111100 | | | |
| 125 | 175 | 7D | 1111101 | } | |
| 126 | 176 | 7E | 1111110 | ~ | |
| 127 | 177 | 7F | 1111111 | DEL | Rubout |

# Function Listing

The C library contains a wide variety of useful functions. Most important are the input and output functions, because the C language itself does not have any input or output commands. Many functions that operate on strings are provided. Common mathematical functions and system interface routines make up the rest of the library.

Table G.1 lists the groups of functions along with the page number of the start of their description in this appendix. The function descriptions are adapted from the ANSI C standard.

**Table G.1 Function Groups**

## LIBRARY NAMES

The functions supplied by the computer are listed in Table G.2. The #defines and typedefs in the header files are listed in Table G.3. All the library function names, all the typedefs, and all #define names are reserved. You should not create a function that has the same name as one in the library.

Additionally, other identifiers may be reserved in the future. They are the following:

1. Function names beginning with *is* and *to* and a lowercase letter may be added for character testing functions.
2. Current function names with a suffix of *f* (for float) or *l* (for long double) may be added.
3. Macros beginning with *SIG* and an uppercase letter may be added for signal handling.
4. Function names beginning with *str* and *mem* may be added to string-handling and memory functions.
5. All external identifiers and macros beginning with an underscore (_) are reserved.
6. Macros beginning with *E* and an uppercase letter may be added for definitions of errors by a compiler.
7. Macros beginning with *LC_* and an uppercase letter may be added for definitions and locale.

**Table G.2 Library Functions in Alphabetical Order**

| Name | Use |
|---|---|
| abort | forces an abnormal termination of a program |
| abs | returns absolute value of an integer |
| acos | returns arccosine |
| asctime | converts a time structure into a string |
| asin | returns arcsine |
| atan | returns arctangent for single argument |
| atan2 | returns arctangent for two arguments |
| atexit | sets a function to be called on program termination |
| atof | converts a string to a double |
| atoi | converts a string to an integer |
| atol | converts a string to a long |
| bsearch | searches an array of objects for a match |
| calloc | allocates memory for number of objects |
| ceil | returns smallest integer (ceiling) |
| clearerr | clears end-of-file and error indicators for a file |
| clock | returns processor time used |
| cos | returns cosine |
| cosh | returns hyperbolic cosine |
| ctime | converts calendar time to string with local time |
| difftime | computes difference between two calendar times |
| div | computes quotient and remainder of an integer division |
| exit | exits a program |
| exp | returns exponential |
| fabs | returns absolute value of double |
| fclose | closes a file |
| feof | tests whether file is at end-of-file |
| ferror | tests whether file has error indicator set |
| fflush | flushes the output buffers of a file |
| fgetc | gets a character from a file |
| fgetpos | gets the current position in a file for use by fsetpos |
| fgets | gets a string of characters from a file |
| floor | returns largest integer (floor) |
| fmod | returns remainder of double divided by double |
| fopen | opens a file |
| fprintf | sends formatted output to a file |
| fputc | puts a character to a file |
| fputs | puts a string of characters to a file |
| fread | reads a number of bytes from a file |
| free | frees allocated memory |
| freopen | reopens a file |
| frexp | breaks double into fraction and power of 2 |

| Name | Use |
|------|-----|
| fscanf | sends formatted input from a file |
| fseek | sets the current position of a file by character count |
| fsetpos | sets the current position of a file from previous fgetpos |
| ftell | gets the current position of a file in characters |
| fwrite | writes a number of bytes to a file |
| getc | gets a character from a file |
| getchar | gets a character from the standard input |
| getenv | gets a value from the program environment |
| gets | gets a string of characters from the standard input |
| gmtime | converts calendar time to string with Greenwich mean time |
| isalnum | tests for alphabetic/numeric character |
| isalpha | tests for alphabetic character |
| iscntrl | test for control character |
| isdigit | tests for digit |
| isgraph | tests for graphic character |
| islower | tests for lowercase character |
| isprint | tests for printable character |
| ispunct | tests for punctuation character |
| isspace | tests for white-space character |
| isupper | tests for uppercase character |
| isxdigit | tests for hexadecimal digit |
| labs | returns absolute value of a long |
| ldexp | multiplies double by power of 2 |
| ldiv | computes quotient and remainder of a long division |
| localtime | converts calendar time to a time structure with local time |
| log | returns natural logarithm |
| log10 | returns logarithm base 10 |
| longjmp | returns execution to where setjmp was called |
| malloc | allocates memory for a given size |
| memchr | finds character in memory |
| memcmp | compares two areas of memory |
| memcpy | copies a number of bytes to another location |
| memmove | moves a number of bytes to another location with checking for overlap |
| memset | sets memory to a value |
| mktime | converts a string into a calendar time |
| modf | breaks double into integer and fraction |
| perror | writes a file error to the standard output |
| pow | returns double raised to a power |
| printf | sends formatted output to standard output |
| putc | puts a character to a file |

| Name | Use |
|------|-----|
| putchar | puts a character to the standard output |
| puts | puts a string of characters to the standard output |
| qsort | sorts an array of objects for a match |
| raise | raises a signal to be handled |
| rand | returns a random number |
| realloc | changes the size of allocated memory |
| remove | removes a file from the system |
| rename | renames a file on the system |
| rewind | sets the current position in a file to zero |
| scanf | sends formatted input from standard input |
| setbuf | sets a buffer for a file |
| setjmp | sets up return for longjmp |
| setlocale | selects program environment |
| setvbuf | sets the type of buffering for a file |
| signal | sets up handling for system signals |
| sin | returns sine |
| sinh | returns hyperbolic sine |
| sprintf | sends formatted conversion to a string |
| sqrt | returns square root |
| srand | sets the seed for rand |
| sscanf | sends formatted conversion from a string |
| strchr | finds character in a string |
| strcmp | compares two strings |
| strcoll | transforms a string with non-ASCII characters |
| strcpy | copies a string to another string |
| strcspn | finds length of string with multiple ending characters |
| strerror | converts a file error to a string |
| strftime | sends formatted conversion of a time structure to a string |
| strlen | computes the length of a string |
| strcat | concatenates two strings |
| strncat | concatenates two strings up to a number of characters |
| strncmp | compares two strings up to a number of characters |
| strncpy | copies a string to another string up to a number of characters |
| strpbrk | finds string within a string |
| strrchr | finds last occurrence of character in a string |
| strspn | finds length of string of selected characters |
| strstr | searches for a string in a string |
| strtod | converts a string to a double with error setting |
| strtok | breaks a string into tokens one at a time |
| strtol | converts a string to a long with error setting |

| Name | Use |
|---|---|
| strtoul | converts a string to a long with error setting |
| strxfrm | transforms a string using the locale setting |
| system | calls the operating system |
| tan | returns tangent |
| tanh | returns hyperbolic tangent |
| time | returns the current calendar time |
| tmpfile | creates a temporary file |
| tmpnam | generates a unique file name |
| tolower | returns lowercase of character |
| toupper | returns uppercase of character |
| ungetc | pushes a character back onto an input file |
| vfprintf | sends formatted output to a file using array of values |
| vprintf | sends formatted output to standard output using array of values |
| vsprintf | sends formatted conversion to a string using array |

**Table G.3 Library Defines and Macros**

| #defines Name[1] | Header File | Use |
|---|---|---|
| __DATE__ | predefined | date of compilation |
| __FILE__ | predefined | source filename |
| __LINE__ | predefined | line number |
| __STDC__ | predefined | standard version |
| __TIME__ | predefined | time of compilation |
| _IOFBF | stdio.h | setvbuf |
| _IOLBF | stdio.h | setvbuf |
| _IONBF | stdio.h | setvbuf |
| assert() | assert.h | |
| BUFSIZ | stdio.h | |
| CHAR_BIT | limit.h | |
| CHAR_MAX | limit.h | |
| CHAR_MIN | limit.h | |
| CLOCK_TICK | time.h | number of seconds for a clock tick |
| DBL_DIG | float.h | |
| DBL_EPSILON | float.h | |
| DBL_MANT_DIG | float.h | |
| DBL_MAX | float.h | |
| DBL_MAX_EXP | float.h | |
| DBL_MAX_10_EXP | float.h | |

[1] All names beginning with an underscore are reserved.

| #defines Name | Header File | Use |
|---|---|---|
| DBL_MIN | float.h | |
| DBL_MIN_EXP | float.h | |
| DBL_MIN_10_EXP | float.h | |
| errno | errno.h | global variable for errors |
| EDOM | errno.h | floating point error |
| EOF | stdio.h | end-of-file value |
| ERANGE | errno.h | floating point error |
| EXIT_FAILURE | stdlib.h | |
| EXIT_SUCCESS | stdlib.h | |
| FILE | stdio.h | file type |
| FILENAME_MAX | stdio.h | length of filename |
| FLT_DIG | float.h | |
| FLT_EPSILON | float.h | |
| FLT_MANT_DIG | float.h | |
| FLT_MAX | float.h | |
| FLT_MAX_EXP | float.h | |
| FLT_MAX_10_EXP | float.h | |
| FLT_MIN | float.h | |
| FLT_MIN_EXP | float.h | |
| FLT_MIN_10_EXP | float.h | |
| FLT_RADIX | float.h | |
| FLT_ROUNDS | float.h | |
| FOPEN_MAX | stdio.h | number of possible open files |
| HUGE_VAL | math.h | floating point error |
| INT_MAX | limit.h | arithmetic limit |
| INT_MIN | limit.h | arithmetic limit |
| L_tmpnam | stdio.h | tmpnam |
| LC_ALL | locale.h | |
| LC_COLLATE | locale.h | |
| LC_CTYPE | locale.h | |
| LC_NUMERIC | locale.h | |
| LC_MONETARY | locale.h | |
| LC_TIME | locale.h | |
| LDBL_DIG | float.h | |
| LDBL_EPSILON | float.h | |
| LDBL_MANT_DIG | float.h | |
| LDBL_MAX | float.h | |
| LDBL_MAX_EXP | float.h | |
| LDBL_MAX_10_EXP | float.h | |
| LDBL_MIN | float.h | |
| LDBL_MIN_EXP | float.h | |
| LDBL_MIN_10_EXP | float.h | |
| LONG_MAX | limit.h | |
| LONG_MIN | limit.h | |
| MB_CUR_MAX | stdlib.h | |

| *#defines Name* | *Header File* | *Use* |
|---|---|---|
| MB_LEN_MAX | limit.h | |
| NDEBUG | | not defined, used in assert.h |
| NULL | stddef.h | null pointer value (also in stdio.h and string.h) |
| offsetof | stddef.h | offset in structure |
| RAND_MAX | stdlib.h | |
| SCHAR_MAX | limit.h | |
| SCHAR_MIN | limit.h | |
| SEEK_CUR | stdio.h | fseek |
| SEEK_END | stdio.h | fseek |
| SEEK_SET | stdio.h | fseek |
| SHRT_MAX | limit.h | |
| SHRT_MIN | limit.h | |
| stderr | stdio.h | standard error |
| stdin | stdio.h | standard input |
| stdout | stdio.h | standard output |
| SIG_DFL | signal.h | |
| SIG_ERR | signal.h | |
| SIG_IGN | signal.h | |
| SIGABRT | signal.h | |
| SIGFPE | signal.h | |
| SIGILL | signal.h | |
| SIGINT | signal.h | |
| SIGSEGV | signal.h | |
| SIGTERM | signal.h | |
| TMP_MAX | stdio.h | tmpnam |
| UCHAR_MAX | limit.h | |
| UINT_MAX | limit.h | |
| ULONG_MAX | limit.h | |
| USHRT_MAX | limit.h | |
| va_start() | stdarg.h | |
| va_arg() | stdarg.h | |
| va_end() | stdarg.h | |

## Typedefs:

| *Name* | *Header File* | *Use* |
|---|---|---|
| clock_t | time.h | time |
| div_t | stdlib.h | div() |
| fpos_t | stdio.h | file position |
| jmp_buf | setjmp.h | setjmp/longjmp |
| ldiv_t | stdlib.h | ldiv() |
| prtdiff_t | stddef.h | difference in two pointers |
| sig_atomic_t | signal.h | variables for signals |

| Name | Header File | Use |
|---|---|---|
| size_t | stddef.h | result of sizeof (also in stdio.h) |
| time_t | time.h | time |
| va_list | stdarg.h | variable parameter list |

**Structure Tags:**

| | | |
|---|---|---|
| tm | time.h | structure for time |

---

## LIBRARY USAGE

There is *no* error checking on values passed to standard functions. Functions may be macros or actual functions. Using #undef on a function name or surrounding the name with parentheses ensures the actual function is called, if one exists. For example, with the standard header alone:

```
#include <stdlib.h>
...
i = func();
```

func may be a macro. However, if you code either

```
#include <stdlib.h>
#undef func
...
i = func();
```

or

```
i = (func)();
```

or

```
i = (func)();
```

func is forced to be a call to a function, even if it was a macro. Note that the parentheses inhibit the preprocessor from expanding func. You can explicitly declare a function prototype or allow the compiler to implicitly determine it. Using the header files for the prototypes saves work.

```
extern int func(parm_list);   explicit declaration
i = func();                   implicit declaration
```

## HEADER FILES

Each library function has an associated header file that accompanies it. You should include the file if you use the function. The file includes typedefs, #defines, and function prototypes. The header files are shown in Table 11.2.

### stddef.h

There is a standard header file called "stddef.h". This file contains some common typedefs and #defines that are useful in writing a program. They are

| | |
|---|---|
| ptrdiff_t | difference between two pointers (typedef) |
| size_t | result of sizeof (typedef) |
| NULL | null pointer (define) |
| offsetof(struct_type, member) (define) | offset in bytes of member of a structure of struct_type |

### errno.h

This file contains three definitions for error handling.

| | |
|---|---|
| errno | external error value for some library functions |
| EDOM | define domain error value |
| ERANGE | define range error value |

### float.h

Two header files contain the limits of numbers for a particular compiler. If you represent a floating point number as

$$\text{sign} * \text{base}^{exp} * \text{mantissa}$$
$$\text{exponent min} <= \text{exponent} <= \text{exponent max}$$

then the values in this header file give the limits for this representation. They are for float (FLT), double (DBL), and long double (LDBL).

| | |
|---|---|
| FLT_RADIX | base of exponent, defined as 2 |
| FLT_ROUNDS | type of addition |
| | > 0 rounds |
| | = 0 chops |
| | − 1 indeterminate |

| | |
|---|---|
| `FLT_MANT_DIG` | number of bits in mantissa |
| `DBL_MANT_DIG` | |
| `LDBL_MANT_DIG` | |
| `FLT_EPSILON` | smallest number such that 1.0 + epsilon does not equal 1.0 |
| `DBL_EPSILON` | |
| `LDBL_EPSILON` | |
| `FLT_DIG` | number of decimal digits in mantissa |
| `DBL_DIG` | |
| `LDBL_DIG` | |
| `FLT_MIN_EXP` | smallest negative power of 2 that can be expressed |
| `DBL_MIN_EXP` | |
| `LDBL_MIN_EXP` | |
| `FLT_MIN` | smallest positive floating point number |
| `DBL_MIN` | |
| `LDBL_MIN` | |
| `FLT_MIN_10_EXP` | smallest negative power of 10 that can be expressed |
| `DBL_MIN_10_EXP` | |
| `LDBL_MIN_10_EXP` | |
| `FLT_MAX_EXP` | largest power of 2 that can be expressed |
| `DBL_MAX_EXP` | |
| `LDBL_MAX_EXP` | |
| `FLT_MAX` | largest number |
| `DBL_MAX` | |
| `LDBL_MAX` | |
| `FLT_MAX_10_EXP` | largest power of 10 that can be expressed |
| `DBL_MAX_10_EXP` | |
| `LDBL_MAX_10_EXP` | |

### limits.h

This file gives the limits for integer data types.

| | |
|---|---|
| `CHAR_BIT` | number of bits in a `char` |
| `SCHAR_MIN` | minimum value for `signed char` |
| `SCHAR_MAX` | maximum value for `signed char` |
| `UCHAR_MAX` | maximum value for `unsigned char` |
| `CHAR_MIN` | minimum value for a plain `char` |
| `CHAR_MAX` | maximum value for a plain `char` if sign extension `CHAR_MIN==SCHAR_MIN` and `CHAR_MAX==SCHAR_MAX` if no sign extension `CHAR_MIN=0` and `CHAR_MAX==UCHAR_MAX` |
| `SHRT_MIN` | minimum value for a `short` |
| `SHRT_MAX` | maximum value for a `short` |

| | |
|---|---|
| USHRT_MAX | maximum value for an unsigned short |
| INT_MIN | minimum value for an int |
| INT_MAX | maximum value for an int |
| UINT_MAX | maximum value for an unsigned int |
| LONG_MIN | minimum value for a long |
| LONG_MAX | maximum value for a long |
| ULONG_MAX | maximum value for an unsigned long |

## MATHEMATICAL FUNCTIONS

These functions share a common way of reporting errors. If there is an error, a value of either EDOM or ERANGE is placed in errno.

| | |
|---|---|
| EDOM | returned if input argument is outside of the domain for which the function is valid. Return value is undefined. |
| ERANGE | returned if result cannot be represented as a double. |
| HUGE_VAL | returned if the magnitude is too big. 0 is returned if the magnitude underflows. |

For example,

| | |
|---|---|
| sqrt(-1.0) | places EDOM in errno; return value is undefined. |
| pow(10., 10000.) | places ERANGE in errno; returns HUGE_VAL as result. |

### math.h

This file contains the prototypes for all the mathematical functions and the following definitions:

| | |
|---|---|
| EDOM | value for errno for domain errors |
| ERANGE | value for errno for range errors |
| HUGE_VAL | value for a return if result overflows |

### Trigonometric Functions

The trigonometric functions include the regular functions, the arc functions, and the hyperbolic functions. Many of them return a domain error if the parameters are out of a given range.

## Regular Functions

These are the regular trigonometric functions.

```
double cos(angle)                /* #include <math.h> */
double angle;                    /* Angle in radians */
```

The cos function returns the cosine of angle. If angle is large, the result may be imprecise, so you should use fmod(angle, (2*PI)) as the argument.

```
double sin(angle)                /* #include <math.h> */
double angle;                    /* Angle in radians */
```

The sin function returns the sine of angle. If angle is large, the result may be imprecise, so use fmod(angle, (2*PI)) as the argument.

```
double tan(angle)                /* #include <math.h> */
double angle;                    /* Angle in radians */
```

The tan function returns the tangent of angle. If angle is large, the result may be imprecise, so use fmod(angle, (2*PI)) as the argument.

## Arc Functions

These are the inverse trigonometric functions.

```
double acos(value)               /* #include <math.h> */
double value;
```

The acos function computes the arccosine of value. It returns an angle from 0.0 to PI. If value is not between –1.0 and 1.0, errno is set to EDOM.

```
double asin(value)               /* #include <math.h> */
double value;
```

The asin function computes the arcsine of value. It returns an angle from –PI/2 to PI/2. If value is not between –1.0 and 1.0, errno is set to EDOM.

```
double atan(value)               /* #include <math.h> */
double value;
```

The atan function computes the arctangent of value. It returns an angle between –PI/2 and PI/2.

```
double atan2(opposite, adjacent) /* #include <math.h> */
double opposite;
double adjacent;
```

The atan2 function computes the arctangent of opposite/adjacent. It returns an angle between –PI and PI, based on the signs of opposite and adjacent. If both opposite and adjacent are 0.0, errno is set to EDOM.

### Hyperbolic Functions

These are the hyperbolic trigonometric functions.

```
double cosh(value)              /* #include <math.h> */
double value;
```

The cosh function returns the hyperbolic cosine of value. If value is too large, errno is set to ERANGE.

```
double sinh (value)             /* #include <math.h> */
double value;
```

The sinh function returns the hyperbolic sine of value. If value is too large, errno is set to ERANGE.

```
double tanh(value)              /* #include <math.h> */
double value;
```

The tanh function returns the hyperbolic tangent of value. If value is too large, errno is set to ERANGE.

### Exponential Functions

These functions return various powers and logarithms of numbers.

```
double exp(power)               /* #include <math.h> */
double power;
```

The exp function returns e raised to power. If power is too large, errno is set to ERANGE.

```
double log(value)               /* #include <math.h> */
double value;
```

The log function returns the natural logarithm of value. If value is negative, errno is set to EDOM. If value is 0.0, errno is set to ERANGE.

```
double log10(value)             /* #include <math.h> */
double value;
```

The log10 function returns the logarithm base 10 of value. If value is negative, errno is set to EDOM. If value is 0.0, errno is set to ERANGE.

```
double pow(base, exponent)      /* #include <math.h> */
double base;
double exponent;
```

The pow function returns base raised to the exponent power. If the base is 0.0 and exponent is less than or equal to 0.0 or if base is less than 0.0 and exponent is not an integer, errno is set to EDOM. For some pairs of parameters, errno may be set to ERANGE.

```
double ldexp(number, exponent) /* #include <math.h> */
double number;
int exponent;
```

The ldexp function returns the value of number * $2^{exponent}$. If the result is too large, errno is set to ERANGE.

```
double sqrt(value)              /* #include <math.h> */
double value;
```

The sqrt function returns the square root of value. If value is less than 0.0, errno is set to EDOM.

## Floating Point Numbers

These functions look at a floating point value in different ways.

```
double frexp(number, pexponent)/* #include <math.h> */
double number;
int *pexponent;
```

The frexp function breaks number into a normalized fraction and a power of 2. The return value is between 0.5 and 1.0. *pexponent is set such that number = return_value * $2^{(*pexponent)}$. If number is 0.0, both the return value and *pexponent are set to 0.

```
double modf(number, pinteger)   /* #include <math.h> */
double number;
double *pinteger;
```

This breaks number into an integer part and a fractional part. The return value is the fractional part. The integer part is placed where pinteger points.

## Miscellaneous

These compute the ceiling (ceil) and floor values and find absolute and modulus values.

```
double ceil(value)          /* #include <math.h> */
double value;
```

This returns the smallest integer not less than value. This is the ceiling.

```
double floor(value)         /* #include <math.h> */
double value;
```

This returns the largest integer not greater than value. If ceil(value) equals floor(value), value is an integer.

```
double fabs(number)         /* #include <math.h> */
double number;
```

This returns the absolute value of number.

```
double fmod(number, mod)    /* #include <math.h> */
double number;
double mod;
```

This returns the floating point remainder of number/mod. If mod is zero, zero is returned. The remainder has the same sign as number.

---

## INPUT/OUTPUT

Input and output functions operate on *data streams* (series of characters read from or output to files or devices). There is basically no difference in operation whether these functions refer to a disk file or an input/output device. The exception is whether a particular device can support a particular operation (for example, a keyboard cannot be rewound).

There are two types of streams—text and binary. *Text streams* contain new-line characters, which terminate lines. Text streams assume that both printable characters and white space characters are being written to it. If you write out control characters to a text stream and attempt to read the stream, you may not input equivalent characters. Spaces just before new-lines may not be written out. New-line characters may be converted on output to a sequence of characters (such as carriage return, line feed). When this sequence is read in, it is converted back to a single new-line character. There is usually one character, called the *end-of-file character,* which terminates the stream and forces functions to return the end-of-file indicator (EOF).

*Binary streams* are simple sets of characters. There are no conversions and what is output to a stream matches what is input later from the stream. An input binary stream may have NUL characters appended to it.

You associate a stream with a file or device by opening the stream. The open functions return a pointer to a typedef FILE. This pointer is used by subsequent calls to other functions on the stream. When a stream is opened, it is positioned to the first character. It may be created and opened at the same time. If a prior file exists with the same name, its contents are erased. The type of stream—text or binary—is specified when the stream is opened by fopen or freopen.

A stream may be buffered in three ways: block, line, or none. In *block buffering*, a block of characters is transmitted to or from the file whenever the corresponding buffer is full. Line buffering forces the characters to be transmitted when a newline character is encountered or when the buffer is full. No buffering (that is, use of unbuffered mode) causes the characters to be sent as soon as possible. setbuf and setvbuf permit you to set the buffering for a particular stream. This buffering is performed by the library functions. The operating system may have its own internal buffers that are unaffected by setvbuf and setbuf.

Closing a stream disassociates it from the particular file or device. If there is anything remaining in an output stream buffer, it is written out before closing. The exit function (or equivalently, ending the main function) forces a close on all open files. Use of the abort function or an abnormal program termination may not close files properly.

Three streams are opened when the main function starts: the standard input (stdin), standard output (stdout), and standard error (stderr) streams. They are normally associated with the keyboard (stdin) and the terminal screen (stdout and stderr). stdin and stdout can be redirected on the command line to other files or devices on operating systems that support redirection.

Each stream has a file position value that is an indication where the next characters will be read from or written to. The ftell and fgetpos functions return the current file position. The fseek and fsetpos set the current file position.

### stdio.h

This includes several definitions used by the input and output functions and function prototypes. In the following, the first two items are typedefs, and the remainder are macros.

| | |
|---|---|
| FILE | structure that holds stream information (typedef) |
| fpos_t | File position type for fgetpos and fsetpos (typedef) |
| _IOFBF | Used by setvbuf (macro) |
| _IOLBF | (macro) |
| _IONBF | (macro) |
| BUFSIZE | size of buffer used by setbuf (macro) |

```
EOF                 end-of-file indicator (macro)
```

L_tmpnam            size of array required to hold name returned by tmpnam (macro)

FOPEN_MAX           number of files that can be opened simultaneously (macro)

FILENAME_MAX        maximum length for a filename (macro)

SEEK_CUR            Used by fseek (macro)
SEEK_END            (macro)
SEEK_SET            (macro)

TMP_MAX             Number of unique filenames tmpnam can generate. (macro)

stdin               point to structures of type FILE
stdout              for standard input, standard output,
stderr              and standard error

In the future, for fprintf use of a leading 0 to specify padding with zeros may
not be supported. Other lowercase letters may be added to the format specifiers
for fprintf and fscanf.

## File Manipulations

```
FILE *fopen(file_name, open_mode)              /* #include <stdio.h> */
char *file_name;
char *open_mode;
```

The fopen function opens a file or device whose name is pointed to by file_name.
The value pointed to by open_mode states how to open the file and whether to
create it.

A file can be opened for reading, writing, or appending. An attempt to open a
file that does not exist in order to read it will fail. Opening a file for appending forces
all writes to the file to be at the current end-of-file. Both reading and writing can
be performed on a file opened for updating. However, calls to input and output
functions must be separated by a call to fflush or a file-positioning function (fseek,
fsetpos, or rewind). The stream is fully buffered, unless it refers to an interactive
device. The characters pointed to by file_name and open_mode are not modified.

Values for open_mode are given in Table G.4. fopen returns a pointer to a type
FILE for subsequent function calls on the stream. It returns NULL if an error occurs.
If the mode is updating, a call to fflush, fseek, fsetpos, or rewind must occur
between calls to input functions and calls to output functions.

```
FILE *freopen(file_name, open_mode, stream)    /* #include <stdio.h> */
char *file_name;
char *open_mode;
FILE *file_pointer;
```

**Table G.4 Modes for fopen**

| *Text Streams* | *Binary Streams* | |
|---|---|---|
| "r" | "rb" | open stream for reading |
| "w" | "wb" | create stream for writing |
| "a" | "ab" | open stream or create stream for appending (writes appended to end of file) |
| "r+" | "r+b" or "rb+" | open stream for updating |
| "w+" | "w+b" or "wb+" | create stream for updating |
| "a+" | "a+b" or "ab+" | open stream or create stream for updating (writes appended to end of file) |

The `freopen` function opens a file or device whose name is pointed to by `file_name`. The value pointed to by `open_mode` states how to open the file and whether to create it. The values for `open_mode` are the same as for `fopen`. The function first closes the file specified by `file_pointer`.

The `freopen` function returns a pointer to a type `FILE` for subsequent function calls on the stream. It returns `NULL` if an error occurs. The primary use of `freopen` is to reassign the file associated with `stdin`, `stdout`, or `stderr`. The characters pointed to by both `file_name` and `open_mode` are not modified.

```
fflush(file_pointer)          /* #include <stdio.h> */
FILE *file_pointer;
```

The `fflush` function flushes the output buffer to the operating system. If `file_pointer` is an input stream, it undoes the effect of any preceding `ungetc` calls. It returns zero if there is no error or nonzero if any write error occurs.

```
int fclose(file_pointer)      /* #include <stdio.h> */
FILE *file_pointer;
```

The `fclose` function closes the stream pointed to by `file_pointer`. The stream is disassociated from the file specified in the `fopen` or `freopen` function. The output buffer, if any, is flushed before the close. If successful, it returns zero. If an error occurs or the stream is already closed, it returns a nonzero value.

```
int remove(file_name)         /* #include <stdio.h> */
char *file_name;
```

The `remove` removes the file whose name is pointed to by `file_name` from the operating system. The file should not be open when `remove` is called. If the operation is successful, `remove` returns zero. If unsuccessful, it returns a nonzero value. The characters pointed to by `file_name` are not modified.

```
int rename(old_name, new_name) /* #include <stdio.h> */
char *old_name;
char *new_name;
```

The `rename` function renames the file whose name is pointed to by `old_name` to the name pointed to by `new_name`. If there is already a file with the name `new_name`, the result is uncertain. If the operation is successful, the function returns zero. If unsuccessful, it returns a nonzero value. The characters pointed to by `old_name` and `new_name` are not modified.

```
FILE *tmpfile();                  /* #include <stdio.h> */
```

The `tmpfile` function creates a temporary binary stream, opened for update. The stream disappears when the stream is closed or the program terminates. The line returns a pointer to the temporary stream. It returns NULL if it cannot create a temporary stream.

```
char *tmpnam(name)                /* #include <stdio.h> */
char *name;
```

The `tmpnam` function generates a string that is not the same as an existing filename. It returns a pointer to the string. If name is not NULL, `tmpnam` places the string into the location and returns the value of name.

The value of name should be an array of at least L_tmpnam characters. The function can be called at least TMP_MAX (minimum of 25) times, each time generating a new name. This function is useful for creating filenames that might be used for interprogram files.

### File Errors

There are two flags for each file you can set using the input/output functions. They are the end-of-file flag and the error indication flag. The end-of-file flag is set if an end-of-file is read on input. The error flag is set if an error occurs while the system is reading or writing. Both flags are reset when a file is opened and when `clearerr` or `rewind` is called.

```
int ferror(file_pointer)          /* #include <stdio.h> */
FILE *file_pointer;
```

The `ferror` code tests the error flag for the file pointed to by `file_pointer`. It returns zero if no error occurs or nonzero if an error occurs.

```
void clearerr(file_pointer)       /* #include <stdio.h> */
FILE *file_pointer;
```

The `clearerr` function clears the error and end-of-file flags for the file pointed to by `file_pointer`.

```
int feof(file_pointer)                          /* #include <stdio.h> */
FILE *file_pointer;
```

This tests the end-of-file flag for the file pointed to by file_pointer. It returns zero if end-of-file has not been reached or nonzero if it has.

### File Buffering

```
int setvbuf(file_pointer, buffer, mode, size)  /* #include <stdio.h> */
FILE *file_pointer;
char *buffer;
int type;
size_t size;
```

The setvbuf function sets the type of buffering on a file. If you use it, you must call it after the file pointed to by file_pointer is opened and before you read from or write to the file. The type of buffering is specified by type. The values are

| | |
|---|---|
| _IOFBF | fully buffered |
| _IOLBF | line buffered (new-line written, buffer is full, or input is requested) |
| _IONBF | completely unbuffered |

If buffer is not NULL, it is used as a buffer. One will not be allocated by the fopen function. The value of size should be the length of buffer. The function returns nonzero if mode or size is invalid or if the file cannot be buffered in the requested type. It returns zero if successful.

```
void setbuf(file_pointer, buffer)               /* #include <stdio.h> */
FILE *file_pointer;
char *buffer;
```

The setbuf function is the equivalent of calling setvbuf(file_pointer, buffer, _IOFBF, BUFSIZE). If buffer has a value of NULL, it is the equivalent of calling setvbuf(file_pointer, buffer, _IONBF, 0).

### File Positioning

```
long int ftell(file_pointer)                    /* #include <stdio.h> */
FILE *file_pointer;
```

The ftell function returns the current file position for the file pointed to by file_pointer. If there is a failure, it returns −1L and sets the value of errno. For a binary file, the position is the number of characters from the beginning of the file. For a text file, the position may not be the number of characters. However, in either case the value returned may be used in a call to fseek to position the file to the same place.

```
fseek(file_pointer,offset,mode)                /* #include <stdio.h> */
FILE *file_pointer;
long offset;
int mode;
```

The fseek function changes the current file position for the file pointed to by file_pointer. For a binary file, the mode may be one of three values that return how offset is used. These are

| | |
|---|---|
| SEEK_SET | offset from beginning of file |
| SEEK_END | offset from end-of-file |
| SEEK_CUR | offset from current position |

For a text file, the mode must be SEEK_SET and offset a value returned by a call to ftell or offset must be 0. The function returns a nonzero if an error occurs.

```
int fgetpos(file_pointer, pposition)           /* #include <stdio.h> */
FILE *file_pointer;
fpost_t *pposition;
```

The fgetpos function returns the current file position for the file pointed to by file_pointer in the location pointed to by pposition. If there is a failure, fgetpos returns a nonzero value and sets the value of errno. This value may be passed to fsetpos to set the position of the file. This function and fsetpos are for files that may have more bytes than can be represented in the long offset value used by fseek and ftell.

```
int fsetpos(file_pointer, position)            /* #include <stdio.h> */
FILE *file_pointer;
fpos_t *position;
```

The fsetpos function sets the current file position for the file pointed to by file_pointer to the value in the location pointed to by pposition. If there is a failure, fsetpos returns a nonzero value and sets the value of errno. This value must be one returned by fgetpos. The value pointed to by position is not modified.

```
void rewind(file_pointer)                      /* #include <stdio.h> */
FILE *file_pointer;
```

The rewind function sets the current file position for the file pointed to by file_pointer to 0. No errors can occur. It is equivalent to fseek(file_pointer, 0L, SEEK_SET);.

```
int ungetc(chr, file_pointer)                  /* #include <stdio.h> */
int chr;
FILE *file_pointer;
```

The ungetc function "ungets" the value of chr in the input file pointed to by file_pointer. This value is returned by the next read from the file. If a file positioning function or fflush is called before the character is read, it is thrown away. If the value of chr is EOF, nothing occurs; ungetc returns the value of chr or EOF if it fails.

For a binary file, the file position is decremented by a call to ungetc. For a text file, the file position is indeterminate. When all characters that have been "ungotten" have been read, the file position is the same as prior to any ungetc calls. Some compilers allow stacking of "ungotten" characters.

**Formatted I/O**

```
int fprintf(file_pointer, format, values)   /* #include <stdio.h> */
FILE *file_pointer;
char *format;
values
```

The fprintf function outputs characters to the file pointed to by file_pointer. The format is a string of characters that specifies what is to be written. The string consists of

- ordinary characters, written as is
- format specifiers

The specifiers begin with % and tell fprintf that a corresponding value is being passed and to convert it and output it. If you pass fewer values than you have conversion specifiers, the output characters are undefined. The string pointed to by format is not modified.

A format specifier consists of

%
flags—characters (optional)
width—a number (optional)
precision—decimal point followed by a number (optional)
data width—a character (optional)
conversion type—a character

Flag characters are

| | |
|---|---|
| - | left justify |
| + | begin a signed conversion with a + or - |
| (space) | begin a signed conversion with a space (for positive values) or - |
| # | convert to an alternate form for conversion types: |
| | c, d, i, s, and u no effect |
| o | nonzero will begin with 0 |
| x or X | nonzero will begin with 0x or 0X |

|  |  |  |
|---|---|---|
| | e, E, f, g, G | decimal point is included even if not needed for g and G; do not remove trailing zeros |
| 0 | | pad left side with leading zeros |

*Width* denotes the minimum field width. If more characters are required, they are output. If fewer characters are required, the field is right-justified (padded on the left with spaces). If the - flag is included, it will be left-justified (padded on the right with spaces). If the width starts with a zero digit, the padding will be zero characters.[1] If the width is specified by a *, the width will be taken from the corresponding *values*.

*Precision* is a decimal point followed by a value. The value is interpreted differently depending on the conversion type.

| | |
|---|---|
| d, i, o, u, x, X | specifies the minimum number of digits to be output. If the value can be represented in fewer digits, leading zeros are appended. |
| e, E, F | specifies the number of digits after the decimal point. |
| g, G | specifies the maximum number of significant digits. |
| s | specifies the maximum number of characters. |

If the precision is specified by a *, it is taken from the value supplied in *values*. *Data width* is an optional modifier on the conversion type. The values are

| | |
|---|---|
| h | For d, i, o, u, x, X. The value is converted to a short or unsigned short int before outputting. |
| l | For d, i, o, u, x, X. The corresponding value is a long int or long unsigned int. |
| L | For e, E, f, g, G. The corresponding value is a long double. |

*Conversion types* are as follows:

| | |
|---|---|
| d or i | value output as signed int (decimal) |
| o | value output as octal |
| u | value output as unsigned int |
| x | value output as hexadecimal with lowercase digits |
| X | value output as hexadecimal with uppercase digits |

For all of the above, the default precision is one.

If precision is zero, and value is zero, no characters are output. The value should be of type int or unsigned int.

---

[1] This method of specifying zero padding characters is being replaced by the use of precision.

e,E    value output as (-)d.dddddde(+/- )dd. There is one nonzero digit before the decimal point. The precision specifies the number of digits after the decimal point. If the precision is zero, no decimal point appears. The default precision is six. The value is rounded to the number of digits. For E, the number will contain E, rather than e. The value should be of type float or double.

f    value output as (-)ddd.dddddd. The precision specifies the number of digits after the decimal point. The default precision is six. If the precision is zero, no decimal point appears. The value is rounded to the number of digits. The value should be of type float or double.

g, G    value output as f or e, depending on whichever takes fewer characters. The value should be of type float or double.

c    value output as a character. The value should be of type char or int.

s    value must be a pointer to a string. Characters are output up to, but not including the terminating NUL. If the precision is specified, then it is the maximum number of characters output.

p    value is a pointer to void. The value is output as a sequence of characters which is compiler defined.

%    A % is output. No value is converted.

n    The corresponding value is a pointer to an int. The number of characters output so far by fprintf is written to the location.

The function returns the number of characters output, as Table G.5 shows. It returns a negative value if an error occurred. fprintf is able to output at least 509 characters with each call.

```
int printf(format, values)                /* #include <stdio.h> */
char *format;
values
```

The printf function acts just like fprintf, but all output goes to the standard output file. The printf function is just like a call fprintf(stdout, format, values). It returns the number of characters output or a negative number if there is an error.

```
int sprintf(string, format, values)       /* #include <stdio.h> */
char *string;
char *format;
values
```

The sprintf function acts just like fprintf, but all output goes to the string specified. A NUL character is written at the end of the string. It returns the number of characters written to string or a negative number if there is an error.

```
int fscanf(file_pointer, format, addresses)   /* #include <stdio.h> */
FILE *file_pointer;
char *format;
addresses
```

**Table G.5 Characters Output by fprintf**

| Value | Format | Output[1] |
| --- | --- | --- |
| | | Column |
| | | 0              1 |
| | | 1234567890123 |
| | | |
| "abc" | %s | abc_ |
| "abc" | %10s |        abc_ |
| "abc" | %.2s | ab_ |
| "abc" | %-10s | ab       _ |
| | | |
| 354 | %d | 354_ |
| 354 | %5d |   354_ |
| 354 | %0.5d | 00354_ |
| 354 | %+d | +354_ |
| | | |
| 3.5 | %f | 3.500000_ |
| 3.5 | %10.2f |      3.50_ |
| 3.0 | %.0f | 3_ |
| 3.1 | %.1f | 3.1_ |
| 3.2 | %.2f | 3.20_ |

[1] The _ character shows where next char may be output.

This inputs characters from the file pointed to by file_pointer. It scans the input characters for values to be converted. The format is a string of characters specifying what is to be read. This string consists of ordinary characters and format specifiers. Ordinary characters are read as is. Format specifiers, which begin with %, tell fscanf that a corresponding address is being passed. It converts the input and places the resulting value at the address. If you pass fewer addresses than you have conversion specifiers, the function places the resulting values at garbage locations. The string pointed to by format will not be modified.

The function stops scanning the input whenever there is no more input or the input is not appropriate for the type of value being converted (a matching failure). The function returns the number of values converted and assigned or EOF if there is an error before any values are assigned.

If the ordinary character is a space or white space (tabs and other such characters), the input characters are read until a nonwhite space is encountered. This character is unread (it is "pushed back" onto the input). If there are no white-space characters, then the scanning fails.

If the ordinary character is not a format specifier, the input character must match it. If they do not match, the character is unread, and the scanning fails.

If the format is a specifier, the input characters are read until either the value to be converted is input or the scanning fails. Except for c,n, and [, leading spaces are read and ignored. The characters are then read until a character that could not be part of the value is input. That character is "unread," and the characters up to that point are converted. If the number of characters read for an item is zero, then there is a matching failure and the scanning stops.

A format specifier consists of

%

flag—assignment suppression (optional)
width—a number (optional)
precision—decimal point followed by a number (optional)
data width—a character (optional)
conversion type—a character

The *flag character* is *, which converts the input, but does not place the result anywhere.

*Width* is the maximum field width, the most number of characters that are read for an input value. If the width is specified, the scanning stops after that many characters or when a character is read that cannot be part of the converted type, whichever comes first. If the width is not specified, the scan continues until a non-convertible character is read.

*Data width* is an optional modifier on the conversion type. The values are

| | |
|---|---|
| h | For d, i, n, o, x, the address points to a short int. |
| | For u, the address points to an unsigned short int. |
| l | For d, i, n, o, X, the address points to a long int. |
| | For u, the address points to an unsigned long int. |
| | For e, f, g, the address points to a double, rather than a float. |
| L | For e, f, g, the address points to a long double. |

*Conversion types* include

| | |
|---|---|
| d | Input value is an integer. |
| i | Input value is an integer with decimal, octal, or hexadecimal representation. |
| o | Input value is an octal number. |
| u | Input value is unsigned integer. |
| x | Input value is a hexadecimal number. |

For all of the previous, the address should point to an int or unsigned int.

| | |
|---|---|
| e, f, g | Input value is of the form (-)ddd.ddd(E+/- dd), that is, a valid floating point number. The address should point to a float. |
| c | Input one or more characters. The field width states how many characters are acceptable, with a default of 1. The address should point to a character array large enough to hold the |

|     |     |
|-----|-----|
|     | width. No NUL character is placed on the end of this array. |
| s   | Input a string of nonwhite-space characters. The address should point to an array of characters large enough to hold the characters. A NUL character is placed on the end. |
| p   | Input value is a sequence of characters that represents a pointer value produced by fprintf using the p type. This is compiler-defined. The address should point to a pointer to void. |
| %   | A % is expected. No conversion takes place. |
| n   | The corresponding address is a pointer to an int. The number of characters input so far by fscanf is written to the location. |
| [   | Starts a series of characters expected in the input string. The series terminates with a right bracket, ]. Characters that match a value in this series are read. The address should point to an array of characters. The characters read are placed in this array, and a NUL is added to the end.<br><br>If the first character after the [ is ], the ] is included in the series, and the next ] terminates the series.<br><br>If the first character after the bracket is ^, then the values in the series are all characters except those listed. If the first character after the ^ is ], ] is included in characters to be excepted, and the next ] terminates the series. For example, |
| "%[abcdefghijklmnopqrstuvwxyz]" | reads characters until a nonlowercase character is read. |
| "%[^0123456789]" | reads characters until a digit is read. |

The function returns the number of input items assigned values. It returns EOF if an error occurred.

Table G.6 illustrates the values converted for these conversion types given these variables:

```
int i;
float f;
char string[100];
```

```
int scanf(format, addresses)          /* #include <stdio.h> */
char *format;
addresses
```

**Table G.6 Sample Formats for fscanf**

| Input String | Format and Values | Values Converted |
|---|---|---|
| "123ABC" | "%d%s",&i,string | d = 123 |
| | | s = "ABC" |
| | "%2d%s",&i,string | d = 12 |
| | | s = "3ABC" |
| "ABC DEF" | "%s",string | s = "ABC" |
| | "%5c",string | s = "ABC D" (no NUL) |
| | "%[AB]",string | s = "AB" |
| "ABC DEF\n" | "%[^\n]",string | s = "ABC DEF" |

The scanf function acts just like fscanf, but all input comes from the standard input file. The scanf call is like a call to fscanf(stdin, format, *values*). The function returns the number of input items assigned values. It returns EOF if an error occurs.

```
int sscanf(string, format, values)     /* #include <stdio.h> */
char *string;
FILE *file_pointer;
char *format;
values
```

Here, sscanf acts just like fscanf, except input comes from the specified string. If the NUL character at the end of the string is read, the character acts like an end-of-file. The function returns the number of input items assigned values. It returns EOF if an error occurs.

## Character I/O

These functions input and output a character at a time.

```
int fgetc(file_pointer)                /* #include <stdio.h> */
FILE *file_pointer;
```

The fgetc function reads the next character from the file pointed to by file_pointer. The function returns the character read or EOF if at the end of the file. The function returns EOF and sets the error indicator for the file if an error occurs.

```
int getc(file_pointer)                 /* #include <stdio.h> */
FILE *file_pointer;
```

The getc function is equivalent to fgetc, but it may be a macro, rather than an actual function call.

```
int getchar(void)                          /* #include <stdio.h> */
```

The getchar function is equivalent to getc(stdin). It is usually a macro.

```
int fputc(character,file_pointer)          /* #include <stdio.h> */
int character;
FILE *file_pointer;
```

The fputc function writes character to the file pointed to by file_pointer. The function returns the character written. The function returns EOF and sets an error indicator for the file if an error occurs.

```
int putc(character,file_pointer)           /* #include <stdio.h> */
int character;
FILE *file_pointer;
```

The putc function is equivalent to fputc, but it may be a macro, rather than an actual function call.

```
int putchar(character)                     /* #include <stdio.h> */
int character;
```

The putchar function is equivalent to putc(stdout). It is usually a macro.

```
int ungetc(character,file_pointer)         /* #include <stdio.h> */
int character;
FILE *file_pointer;
```

The ungetc function puts character back onto the input file pointed at by file_pointer. The next time the file is read, this character will be the first one returned. The function does not actually write the character to the file. The function returns the character pushed and resets the end-of- file flag if the operation is successful. The function returns EOF if not successful.

The functions fflush, fseek, and rewind erase the character that was pushed. The "ungetting" of one character is supported by all compilers. Multiple calls to ungetc without reading the file in between may not work.

For binary files, the file position value is decremented by one for each ungetc. For a text file, the file position value is indeterminate. For both types, once all pushed characters are read, the file position value is the same as what it was before any characters were pushed.

### String I/O

```
char *fgets(string,count,file_pointer)    /* #include <stdio.h> */
char *string;
int count;
FILE *file_pointer;
```

The fgets function reads a line of characters (up to a new-line character) from the file pointed to by file_pointer. The characters are placed into the array pointed to by string. The new-line character and a terminating NUL are placed at the end. If count −1 characters have been read without a new-line being input, the function stops inputting and places a NUL at the end.

The function returns the value of string if successful. If the end-of-file comes before any characters are read, no characters are placed in string, and it returns the NULL pointer. The function returns a NULL pointer if an error occurs.

```
char *gets(string)                        /* #include <stdio.h> */
char *string;
```

The gets function reads a line of characters (up to a new-line character or end-of-file) from the standard input file, stdin. The characters are placed into the array pointed to by string. A terminating NUL character is placed at the end. The new-line character is not placed in the array.

The function returns the value of string if successful. If the end-of-file comes before any characters are read, no characters are placed in string, and the function returns the NULL pointer. The function returns a NULL pointer if an error occurs.

```
int fputs(string,file_pointer)            /* #include <stdio.h> */
char *string;
FILE *file_pointer;
```

The fputs function writes the characters in the array pointed to by string to the file pointed to by file_pointer. The writing does not include the terminating NUL. A new-line character is then written to the file. The function returns zero if successful or nonzero if an error occurs.

```
int puts(string)                          /* #include <stdio.h> */
char *string;
```

This writes the characters in the array, pointed to by string, up to the NUL character, to the standard output file, stdout. A new-line character is then written to the file. The function returns zero if successful or nonzero if an error occurs.

### Direct I/O

These functions read one or more characters from a file without interpreting the meaning of the characters.

```
int fread(buffer, element_size, number_elements, file_pointer)
                                        /* #include <stdio.h> */
void *buffer;
size_t element_size;
size_t number_elements;
FILE *file_pointer;
```

The fread function reads a number of characters from the file pointed to by file_pointer. The characters are placed in the array starting at buffer. The number of characters read is element_size * number_elements. The function returns the number of elements read. If an error or end-of-file occurs, this number may be less than number_elements. If either element_size or number_elements is zero, the function does not read characters, and the contents of buffer are unchanged.

```
int fwrite(buffer, element_size, number_elements, file_pointer)
                                        /* #include <stdio.h> */
void *buffer;
size_t element_size;
size_t number_elements;
FILE *file_pointer;
```

The fwrite function stores a number of characters in the file pointed to by file_pointer. The characters are obtained from the array starting at buffer. The number of characters written is element_size * number_elements. The function returns the number of elements written. If an error occurs, this number may be less than number_elements.

## GENERAL UTILITY FUNCTIONS

The functions described in this section perform various conversions.

### stdlib.h

The stdlib.h header file is required by the general utility functions.

| | |
|---|---|
| `div_t` | type returned by `div` |
| `ldiv_t` | type returned by `ldiv` |
| `RAND_MAX` | maximum value returned by `rand` |
| `EXIT_FAILURE` | values for exit |
| `EXIT_SUCCESS` | values for exit |

### String-to-Number Conversions

These routines convert character strings into numeric values. The strings should follow the form of a `double` or `signed int` constant.

```
double atof(string)                   /* #include <stdio.h> */
char *string;
```

The `atof` function returns the value of `string` converted to a double. If the result is out of range, there is no value that is returned as unspecified. `string` is not modified.

```
int atoi(string)                      /* #include <stdio.h> */
char *string;
```

The `atoi` function returns the value of `string` converted to an integer. If the value is out of range, there is no specified error return. The `string` is not modified.

```
long atol(string)                     /* #include <stdio.h> */
char *string;
```

The `atol` function returns the value of `string` converted to a long integer. If the value is out of range, there is no specified error return. The `string` is not modified.

```
double strtod(string, rest_of_string) /* #include <stdio.h> */
char *string;
char **rest_of_string;
```

The `strtod` function returns the result of converting the characters in `string` to a double. If no conversion could be performed, it returns 0.0. If the converted value overflows, `HUGE_VAL` is returned and `errno` is set to `ERANGE`. If the converted value underflows, 0.0 is returned and `errno` is set to `ERANGE`.

If `rest_of_string` is not NULL, it is set to point to the place in `string` where conversion stopped. Conversion stops due to reaching the terminating NUL or a character that cannot be part of a double constant. The `string` is not modified.

```
long strtol(string, rest_of_string, conversion_base)
                                      /* #include <stdio.h> */
char *string;
char **rest_of_string;
int conversion_base;
```

The `strtol` function returns `string` converted to a long with base `conversion_base`. If no conversion can be performed, the function returns 0. If the converted value may overflow, `LONG_MAX` or `LONG_MIN` is returned and `errno` is set to `ERANGE`. The `string` is not modified.

If `rest_of_string` is not `NULL`, it is set to point to the place in the string where conversion stopped. Conversion stops due to reaching the terminating `NUL` or a character that cannot be part of a long constant of the `conversion_base`. The digits for a given `conversion_base` run from 0 to 9, then *A* to *Z*. Lowercase letters are converted to uppercase. If the base is 16, the constant may be preceded by `0x` or `0X`.

For example, for base 2, the only allowable digits are 0 and 1. For base 20, they are 0 to 9 and *A* to *J* and *a* to *j*.

```
unsigned long strtoul(string, rest_of_string, conversion_base)
/* #include <stdio.h> */
char *string;
char **rest_of_string;
int conversion_base;
```

The `strtoul` function returns `string` converted to an `unsigned long` with base `conversion_base`. If no conversion can be performed, the function returns 0. If the converted value may overflow, `ULONG_MAX` is returned and `errno` is set to `ERANGE`. `string` will not be modified.

The conversion works as for `strtol`, except the conversion also stops when a character that cannot be part of an `unsigned long` is reached.

## Random Number

These functions provide random integer numbers, either within a set sequence or randomly.

```
int rand();                              /* #include <stdlib.h> */
```

The `rand` function returns a random number from 0 to `RAND_MAX`. The random number is computed using a random number generator. Unless `srand()` is called, `rand()` returns the same sequence of random numbers each time it is repetitively called.

```
void srand(seed)                         /* #include <stdlib.h> */
unsigned int seed;
```

The `srand` function sets the seed for a sequence of random numbers returned by `rand()`. The default value for the `seed` is 1. If `srand` is called with the same value for `seed`, each time the same sequence of random numbers is returned.

## Memory Management

These functions allocate memory for the use of a program. The memory values that these functions return are suitable for storing any data as long as the `sizeof` the object was requested.

```
void *malloc(size)                      /* #include <stdlib.h> */
size_t size;
```

The `malloc` function allocates space of `size` bytes. The function returns a pointer to the first memory location of that space. If space cannot be allocated, it returns `NULL`. If `size` is zero, the function may return either `NULL` or a unique pointer value.

```
void *calloc(number_element, sizeof_element)
/* #include <stdlib.h> */
size_t number_element;
size_t sizeof_element;
```

The `calloc` function allocates space for an array of `number_elements`. Each element is `sizeof_element` bytes. The allocated space is set to zero. The function returns a pointer to the first memory location of the space. If space cannot be allocated, `calloc` returns `NULL`. If either `number_element` or `sizeof_element` is zero, the function returns either `NULL` or a unique pointer value.

```
void free(pointer)                      /* #include <stdlib.h> */
void *pointer;
```

The `free` function deallocates space pointed to by `pointer`. The space is returned to the free memory pool for future allocation. If `pointer` has the value `NULL`, nothing occurs. If `pointer` has a value other than one returned by `malloc`, `calloc`, or `realloc`, or if the space has been freed, the results are indefinite. If you try to reference the space pointed to by `pointer` after `free` is called, then the results of that operator are indefinite.

```
void *realloc(pointer, new_size)        /* #include <stdlib.h> */
void *pointer;
size_t new_size;
```

The `realloc` function changes the size of an allocated space without altering the contents. The space pointed at by `pointer` is increased or decreased to the `new_size`. `pointer` must be a value returned by a previous call to `calloc`, `malloc`, or `realloc`. If `pointer` is `NULL`, the call is equivalent to calling `malloc` with `new_size`. If `new_size` is zero, the call is equivalent to `free(pointer)`.

## Sorting and Searching

These sort arrays and search arrays for a value. They both require a pointer to a user-supplied function that performs a comparison. It is passed pointers to two values and must return less than zero, zero, or greater than zero if the first value is less than, equal to, or greater than the second. The prototype for this function might look like int pcompfunc(void *, void *);. For example, a typical comparison function for unsigned integers could look like

```
int comp_int(pelement1, pelement2)
/* Compares two unsigned integer values that are pointed to */
unsigned int *pelement1;
unsigned int *pelement2;
    {
    int ret;
    ret = (*pelement1 - *pelement2);
    return ret;
    }
```

The functions call the supplied function every time a comparison is required.

```
void *bsearch(key, base, number_el, size_el, pcompfunc)
                                        /* #include <stdlib.h> */
void *key;
void *base;
size_t number_el;
size_t size_el;
int (*pcompfunc)();
```

The bsearch function searches an array for a matching value. The array begins at base and has number_el elements. The size of each element is size_el. The key points to the value to search for. The function pointed at by pcompfunc must point to a function that compares two pointers to elements. The array must be in ascending sorted order (based on pcompfunc). The key and the array at base are not modified. The function returns a pointer to the matching value or the NULL pointer if no match is found.

```
void qsort(base, number_el, size_el, pcompfunc)
                                        /* #include <stdlib.h> */
void *base;
size_t number_el;
size_t size_el;
int (*pcompfunc)();
```

The qsort function sorts an array. The array begins at base and has number_el elements. The size of each element is size_el. The function pointed at by pcompfunc must point to a function that compares two elements. You should call qsort for an array before using bsearch on the same array. The array at base is not modified.

### Integer Arithmetic Functions

These functions compute absolute values and division remainders for integers.

```
int abs(number)                        /* #include <stdlib.h> */
int number;
```

   The abs function returns the absolute value of number. If INT_MAX is less than the absolute value of INT_MIN, abs(INT_MIN) returns an undefined value.

```
div_t div(numerator, denominator)      /* #include <stdlib.h> */
int numerator;
int denominator;
```

   The div function computes the quotient and the remainder of numerator divided by denominator. The function returns a structure with these two values. The structure includes these members:

```
int quot;                              /* Quotient */
int rem;                               /* Remainder */
```

The order of these in the structure is not specified.

```
long labs(number)                      /* #include <stdlib.h> */
long number;
```

   The labs function returns the absolute value of number. If LONG_MAX is less than the absolute value of LONG_MIN, abs(LONG_MIN) returns an undefined value.

```
ldiv_t ldiv(numerator, denominator)    /* #include <stdlib.h> */
long numerator;
long denominator;
```

   This computes the quotient and the remainder of numerator divided by denominator. The function returns a structure with these two values. The structure includes these members:

```
long quot;                             /* Quotient */
long rem;                              /* Remainder */
```

## STRING HANDLING

   These functions operate on strings. If the destination is not big enough to hold the values transferred, errors may result.

### string.h

This header file contains the prototypes for these functions.

### Copying

```
char *strcpy(destination, source)      /* #include <string.h> */
char *destination;
char *source;
```

The strcpy function copies the string from source to destination. If these overlap in memory, the copy may not be correct. The function returns the value of
destination. source is not modified, unless it overlaps destination.

```
char *strncpy(destination, source, max_number)
                                       /* #include <string.h> */
char *destination;
char *source;
size_t max_number;
```

This copies up to max_number characters from string in source to destination.
If these overlap in memory, the copy may not be correct. If the string length in
source is less than max_number of characters, NUL characters are added to the end
of the string in destination. If the NUL character in the string in source comes after
max_number of characters, then no NUL character is copied into destination. The function returns the value of destination. source is not modified, unless it overlaps
destination.

### Concatenation

```
char *strcat(destination, source)      /* #include <string.h> */
char *destination;
char *source;
```

The strcat function concatenates a copy of the string from source to the string
at destination. The NUL character of destination is overwritten by the first character copied from source. The NUL character from source is copied. The function
returns the value of destination. The source is not modified, unless it overlaps
destination.

```
char *strncat(destination, source, max_number)
                                       /* #include <string.h> */
char *destination;
char *source;
size_t max_number;
```

The strncat function concatenates up to max_number of characters of the string from source to the string at destination. The NUL character of destination is overwritten by the first character copied from source. If the NUL character from source is not in max_number of characters in source, a NUL character is added to destination anyway. The function returns the value of destination. The source is not modified, unless it overlaps destination.

## String Comparison

The corresponding characters in each string are compared. The result is based on the first two characters that are not equal. If the high-order bit is set in a character being compared, the result may be erroneous.

```
int strcmp(string1, string2)          /* #include <string.h> */
char *string1;
char *string2;
```

The strcmp function compares string1 to string2. The function returns a value less than zero, zero, or greater than zero, depending on whether string1 is less than, equal to, or greater than string2. Neither string1 nor string2 is modified.

```
int strncmp(string1, string2, max_number)
                                       /* #include <string.h> */
char *string1;
char *string2;
size_t max_number;
```

The strncmp function compares up to max_number of characters in string1 to string2. The function returns a value less than zero, zero, or greater than zero, depending on whether string1 is less than, equal to, or greater than string2. Neither string1 nor string2 is modified.

## String Search

```
char *strchr(string, character)       /* #include <string.h> */
char *string;
int character;
```

The strchr function searches string for the first occurrence of the character. The function returns a pointer to the location containing character or NULL, if the character is not found. The string is not modified.

```
char *strrchr(string, character)      /* #include <string.h> */
char *string;
int character;
```

The strrchr function searches string for the last occurrence of the character. The function returns a pointer to the location containing character or NULL, if it is not found. The string is not modified.

```
char *strpbrk(string, match_chars)      /* #include <string.h> */
char *string;
char *match_chars;
```

The strpbrk function searches string for the first occurrence of a set of characters. The match_chars parameter consists of an array of characters, terminated with the NUL character. The function returns a pointer to the first character in string that matches any of the characters in match_chars (except for the NUL) or NULL if no characters in match_chars are in string. Neither string nor match_chars is modified.

```
size_t strspn(string, match_chars)      /* #include <string.h> */
char *string;
char *match_chars;
```

The strspn function computes the number of contiguous characters in string, starting at the beginning, that are all in the set of characters in match_chars. The function returns this number. Neither string nor match_chars is modified.

```
size_t strcspn(string, match_chars)     /* #include <string.h> */
char *string;
char *match_chars;
```

The strcspn function computes the number of contiguous characters in string, starting at the beginning, that are not in the set of characters in match_chars. The function returns this number. Neither string nor match_chars is modified.

```
char *strstr(string, match_string)      /* #include <string.h> */
char *string;
char *match_string;
```

The strstr function searches string for the first occurrence of match_string (ignoring the NUL character). The function returns a pointer to the starting location of the matched string or NULL, if it is not found. Neither string nor match_char is modified.

```
char *strtok(string, delimited_chars)   /* #include <string.h> */
char *string;
char *delimited_chars;
```

The strtok function breaks a string into tokens. The delimited_chars parameter consists of an array of characters, terminated with the NUL character. It searches string for the first character not in delimited_chars. If none is found, there is no token. The function then searches from that character for a character in delimited_chars. If one is found, it is replaced by a NUL character. If none is found, the token ends at the NUL character at the end of string. The delimited_chars parameter is not modified.

The function returns a pointer to the first character of a token or NULL if no token is found.

The strtok function keeps an internal pointer to the next character after the NUL character. To obtain the next token, a NULL value should be passed for string. strtok uses this internal pointer as the starting place for the search. For each call, the set of delimiting characters may be different. For example,

```
#include <string.h>
static char string[]="*abc*d, e";
static char delimiter1[]="*";
static char delimiter2[]="*, "
char *token;
```

```
token=strtok(string, delimiter1);        token points to "abc"
token=strtok(NULL, delimiter2);          token points to "d"
token=strtok(NULL, delimiter2);          token points to "e"
token=strtok(NULL, delimiter2);          token is NULL
```

## Miscellaneous

```
char *strerror(error_number)          /* #include <string.h> */
int error_number;
```

The strerror function converts error_number to a pointer to a string. The contents of the string are system dependent.

```
void perror(string)                    /* #include <stdio.h> */
char *string;
```

The perror function writes a line to the standard error file. The line consists of the string, a colon and a space, and a compiler-defined error message based on the contents of errno. The error message is equivalent to that returned by strerror(errno). If string is NULL or has zero length, only the error message is written. The string is not modified.

```
size_t strlen(string)                  /* #include <string.h> */
char *string;
```

The strlen function returns the length of string, the number of characters before the NUL character. The string is not modified.

```
strcoll()
```

See Appendix I for information about this function.

```
strxfrm()
```

See Appendix I for information about this function.

## MEMORY FUNCTIONS

These functions operate on arrays of bytes (or characters). The NUL character, which terminates string functions, has no effect on these functions. The result is based on the first two bytes that are not equal. If the high-order bit is set in a byte being compared, the result may be erroneous.

```
void *memcpy(destination, source, number) /* #include <string.h> */
void *destination;
void *source;
size_t number;
```

The memcpy function copies up to number bytes from source to destination. If these overlap in memory, the copy may not be correct. The function returns the value of destination. The source parameter is not modified, unless it overlaps destination.

```
void *memmove(destination, source, number) /* #include <string.h> */
void *destination;
void *source;
size_t number;
```

The memmove function copies up to number bytes from source to destination. Even if these overlap in memory, the copy is correct. The function returns the value of destination. The source is not modified, unless it overlaps destination.

```
int memcmp(memory1, memory2, number)   /* #include <string.h> */
void *memory1;
void *memory2;
size_t number;
```

The memcmp function compares up to number bytes at memory1 to memory2. The function returns a value less than zero, zero, or greater than zero, depending on whether memory1 is less than, equal to, or greater than memory2. If two structures are being compared, any holes caused by alignment may cause an erroneous result, unless the structures were implicitly set to zero (external or static) or explicitly set once to zero (such as by memset). Neither memory1 nor memory2 is modified.

```
void *memchr(memory, byte, number)      /* #include <string.h> */
void *memory;
int byte;
size_t number;
```

The memchr function searches for the first occurrence of the value of byte starting at memory. Only number of locations are searched. The function returns a pointer to the location containing byte or NULL, if byte is not found. The memory parameter is not modified.

```
void *memset(memory, byte, number)      /* #include <string.h> */
void *memory;
int byte;
size_t number;
```

The memset function sets number of locations starting at memory to the value of byte. The byte is converted to an unsigned char. The function returns the value of memory.

---

## DATE AND TIME

These functions deal with *clock time,* which is the processor time, and *calendar time,* which is the current date. *Local time* is the calendar time for a specific time zone. *Daylight saving time (DST)* is the local time changed, if required, when DST is in effect.

The time.h header file contains the prototypes and the following:

| | |
|---|---|
| CLOCK_TICK | macro conversion factor for clock_t value into seconds |
| clock_t | typedef represents the processor ticks returned by clock |
| time_t | typedef represents a time value |
| struct tm | structure tag contains these time members: |

```
struct tm
    {
    int tm_sec;      seconds (0 to 59)
    int tm_min;      minutes (0 to 59)
    int tm_hour;     hours (0 to 23)
    int tm_mday;     day of the month (1, 31)
    int tm_mon;      month since January (0, 11)
    int tm_year;     years since 1900
    int tm_wday;     weekday (0, 6); 0 is Sunday
```

```
int tm_yday;        days since January 1 (0, 365)
int tm_isdst;       flag for DST
tm_isdat            is positive if DST in effect, zero if not, or negative if
                    unknown.
};
```

## Timing

```
clock_t clock(void);                /* #include <time.h> */
```

   The `clock` function returns processor time used since the beginning of the program execution. It is only an approximate time, given in units of clock ticks. The number of seconds is `clock()/CLOCK_TICK`. The function returns a −1 if processor time is not available.

```
time_t time(time_pointer)           /* #include <time.h> */
time_t *time_pointer;
```

   The `time` function returns the current calendar time. If `time_pointer` is not NULL, this value is also stored at the location pointed to. The function returns –1 if calendar time is not available.

```
double difftime(time1, time2)       /* #include <time.h> */
time_t time1;
time_t time2;
```

   The `difftime` function returns the difference between two calendar times (`time1` - `time2`) in seconds.

## Time Conversion

```
struct tm *localtime(time_pointer)   /* #include <time.h> */
time_t *time_pointer;
```

   The `localtime` function converts the calendar time pointed to by `time_pointer` into a time structure, using local time. The function returns a pointer to this structure. The `time_pointer` argument is not modified.

```
struct tm *gmtime(time_pointer)      /* #include <time.h> */
time_t *time_pointer;
```

   The `gmtime` function converts the calendar time pointed to by `time_pointer` into a time structure, using Greenwich mean time (GMT). The function returns a pointer to this structure. If the conversion to GMT is not available, the function returns NULL. The `time_pointer` argument is not modified.

```
time_t mktime(time_pointer)              /* #include <time.h> */
struct tm *time_pointer;
```

The `mktime` function converts the values in the structure pointed to by `time_pointer` to a calendar time. The initial values for `tm_yday` and `tm_wday` are ignored. If the conversion is successful, they are set to the proper values. The function returns the calendar time if the values of the time structure can be converted, or the value $-1$ if they cannot.

```
char *asctime(time_pointer)              /* #include <time.h> */
struct tm *time_pointer;
```

The `asctime` function converts the values in the time structure pointed to with `time_pointer` into a string of the form

*WWW MMM DD HH:MM:SS YYYY*

where

*WWW* is the day of the week (using the first three characters)
*MMM* is the month (using the first three characters)
*DD* is the day of the month
*HH* is the hour
*MM* is the minute
*SS* is the second
*YYYY* is the year

A new-line and a NUL character terminate the string. The function returns a pointer to this string.

```
char *ctime(time_pointer)                /* #include <time.h> */
time_t *time_pointer;
```

The `ctime` function converts the calendar time pointed to by `time_pointer` to a string. The function returns a pointer to the string. The function is the equivalent of `asctime(localtime(time_pointer));`. The `time_pointer` argument is not modified.

```
strftime()
```

See Appendix I for information about this function.

## CHARACTER HANDLING

These functions test character values to determine whether they are particular types; if they are, the functions convert alphabetic characters from one case to another.

Even though these functions take int arguments, the values of the characters tested must be representable by an unsigned char or have the value of EOF.

*Printing characters* are ones that have graphic representations (including the space character). *Control characters* are all other characters.

The ctype.h header file contains the prototypes and the macros, if any, for these functions.

## Character Conversion

```
int toupper(character)              /* #include <ctype.h> */
int character;
```

The toupper function returns the uppercase value for character. If character is not a letter or is already uppercase, the function returns the value of character.

```
int tolower(character)              /* #include <ctype.h> */
int character;
```

The tolower function returns the lowercase value for character. If character is not a letter or is already lowercase, the function returns the value of character.

## Character Testing

The following functions are all passed an integer. They return nonzero (true) if the value represents a character of the particular type or zero if it does not. They all have the form

```
int is_____(character)
int character;
```

The set of characters is divided into several groups. These are dependent on the computer and the locale. The groups for standard ASCII are given in Table G.7. For other values, the type of the character is implementation-defined.

**Table G.7 Groups for Character Test Functions**

| Group | ASCII Values |
| --- | --- |
| Control characters | 0 to 8, 14 to 31, and 127 |
| Punctuation characters | 33 to 47, 57 to 64, 91 to 96, and 123 to 126 |
| White-space characters | (' '), '\f', '\n', '\r', '\t', '\v' |
| Digits | 0 to 9 |
| Lowercase letters | a to z |
| Uppercase letters | A to Z |
| Implementation defined | values greater than 127 |

```
int isdigit(character)                    /* #include <ctype.h> */
int character;
```

The isdigit function tests character to see whether it is a digit.

```
int isxhdigit(character)                  /* #include <ctype.h> */
int character;
```

The isxhdigit function tests character to see whether it is a hexadecimal digit (0 to 9, *a* to *f*, or *A* to *F*).

```
int isupper(character)                    /* #include <ctype.h> */
int character;
```

The isupper function tests character to see whether it is an uppercase letter.

```
int islower(character)                    /* #include <ctype.h> */
int character;
```

The islower function tests character to see whether it is a lowercase letter.

```
int isalpha(character)                    /* #include <ctype.h> */
int character;
```

The isalpha function tests character to see whether it is a letter, upper- or lowercase.

```
int isalnum(character)                    /* #include <ctype.h> */
int character;
```

The isalnum function tests character to see whether it is a letter, upper- or lowercase, or a digit.

```
int iscntrl(character)                    /* #include <ctype.h> */
int character;
```

The iscntrl function tests character to see whether it is a control character.

```
int isprint(character)                    /* #include <ctype.h> */
int character;
```

The isprint function tests character to see whether it is a printable character (a noncontrol character).

```
int isgraph(character)                    /* #include <ctype.h> */
int character;
```

The `isgraph` function tests `character` to see whether it is a printable character (a noncontrol character) and not the space character ( ).

```
int ispunct(character)              /* #include <ctype.h> */
int character;
```

The `ispunct` function tests `character` to see whether it is a punctuation character or a white-space character except the space character ( ).

```
int isspace(character)              /* #include <ctype.h> */
int character;
```

The `isspace` function tests `character` to see whether it is a white-space character.

---

## ENVIRONMENT

The environment functions terminate programs and communicate with the operating system to perform operations.

The `stdlib.h` header file contains the prototypes for environment functions and the following definitions:

```
EXIT_FAILURE                              failure value for exit
EXIT_SUCCESS                              success value for exit
```

```
void abort();                       /* #include <stdlib.h> */
```

The `abort` function forces the program to terminate abnormally. Open files may not be closed, depending on the system. This function signals the equivalent of `raise(SIGABRT)`. The function never returns to the caller.

```
int at_exit(pfunc)                  /* #include <stdlib.h> */
int (*pfunc)();
```

The `at_exit` function sets up a list of functions to execute when the `exit` function is called. Each time it is called, the function pointed at by `pfunc` is added to the list.

```
void exit(status)                   /* #include <stdlib.h> */
int status;
```

The `exit` function normally terminates a program. Any functions passed to `atexit` are called. The last function added is called first. All output streams are flushed, all open streams are closed, and all temporary files are removed. The value of `status` is returned to the operating system.

If `status` is zero or `EXIT_SUCCESS`, a successful termination value is returned. If `status` is `EXIT_FAILURE`, an unsuccessful termination value is returned.

```
char *getenv(name)                      /* #include <stdlib.h> */
char *name;
```

The getenv function returns a pointer to a string associated with name. The value of name must appear in the "environment" of the operating system. If it does not, NULL is returned.

```
int system(string)                      /* #include <stdlib.h> */
char *string;
```

The system function passes string to the operating system. The operating system executes string as if it were a command typed directly to the system. The return value is system dependent. If string has the value NULL, the function returns zero if there is no command processor, nonzero otherwise.

## DIAGNOSTIC

The assert.h header file contains a macro that looks like a function called assert that enables you to insert diagnostics into a program for debugging purposes.

```
void assert(expression)                 /* #include <assert.h> */
int expression;
```

If the expression is false, information on name of source file and line number (__FILE__)and (__LINE__) is written to stderr, and abort is called. If the expression is true, no action is taken. If NDEBUG has been defined in the source file (before the #include <assert.h>), this macro has no effect.

## NONLOCAL JUMPS

The two functions described here enable you to set a spot in a program to which you wish to return. When you use them you can go back to that spot from anywhere in the program. They are like a goto that can go to a label in any function.

Limit your use of these routines to handling error conditions that occur in deeply nested, low-level routines. They can avoid having each level of functions check for errors. As with all programming constructs that substitute speed or decreased code for readability, they should be used with care.

The setjmp.h header file contains the prototypes and this definition:

```
jmp_buf        type of variable passed to setjmp and longjmp
```

```
int setjmp(environment)                 /* #include <setjmp.h> */
jmp_buf environment;
```

The setjmp function sets a "place holder" at the location where a subsequent call to longjmp will go. It saves the current status in environment, which is later used by longjmp. Part of what is saved in environment is the value of the program counter of the call itself. The longjmp uses this value to return to this place. Call longjmp in a routine that is called (or ultimately called) from the routine in which the corresponding setjmp appears. All objects in this routine should be declared volatile to ensure that they retain the proper values. When setjmp is called directly from a function, it returns a zero value. If the function returns via a longjmp call, it returns a nonzero value.

```
void longjmp(environment, value)        /* #include <setjmp.h> */
jmp_buf environment;
int value;
```

The longjmp function executes a jump to the last setjmp called with the corresponding environment. The value argument is the numeric value returned to the setjmp call.

If there is no setjmp with the environment or if the function containing the setjmp has executed a return, undefined behavior occurs. Variables not typed volatile may not have their proper values when control returns to setjmp.

If longjmp tries to return zero, the return from setjmp is forced to 1. Here is an example of how to use setjmp / longjmp.

```
#include <setjmp.h>
jmp_buf save_env;
int ret;
...
ret=setjmp(save_env)
if (ret==0)
    {
    /* Do normal processing */
    }
else {
    /* This is a return from longjmp */
    /* Do appropriate processing */
    if (ret==3)
        /* This is a return from the example of longjmp */
    }
```

In this or another file, you can now do a long jump back to the setjmp just shown with

```
extern jmp_buf save_env;
...
longjmp(save_env, 3);
```

## SIGNAL HANDLING

*Signals* are interrupts that occur during program execution. These interrupts occur from an action in the program, such as attempting to divide by zero, or they can be external to the program, such as a user pressing a break key on the keyboard. Signals may also be generated by a call to raise.

Functions that handle signals may be called at any time the program is executing. They are usually called by the operating system, rather than the program itself. They must be written carefully to ensure that the program will continue to run after they return. Writing interrupt handlers is beyond the scope of this text. The routines are presented here for completeness.

The signal.h header file supplies #defines for various signals. These #defines are used by both signal and raise. They are

| | |
|---|---|
| sig_atomic_t | types of variable used by function that handles a signal |
| SIG_DFL | default action for a signal |
| SIG_IGN | ignore a signal |
| SIG_ERR | return value of signal if an error |
| SIGABRT | abnormal termination signal |
| SIGFPE | floating point error signal |
| SIGILL | invalid program in core |
| SIGINT | user has pressed an interrupt signal |
| SIGSEGV | segment violation (invalid storage access) signal |
| SIGTERM | termination request signal |

```
void (*signal (int signal_type,
void (*function_pointer)(int))) (int);   /* #include <signal.h> */
```

The signal function designates a handler for a signal. The signal_type is one of the #defines listed in signal.h. function_pointer is the address of the function to be called when signal_type occurs. If SIG_DFL is passed for function_pointer, the default handler for the operating system is called. If SIG_IGN is passed, signal_type is ignored.

The function returns the address of the function previously handling the signal. If an error occurs, the function returns SIG_ERR.

When the signal occurs, the signal handler is first reset to the default handler. Then the function addressed by function_pointer is called. It may call abort, exit, or longjmp to end. If the function uses a return to end and the value of the signal was not SIGFPE, the program executes normally. With SIGFPE, the result of the computation is unknown, so the program may not execute properly. The standard library functions should not be called by a signal handler, because they are not guaranteed to be reentrant. The function may assign values to variables of type sig_atomic_t.

```
int raise(signal_type);                /* #include <signal.h> */
int signal_type;
```

This raises a signal of `signal_type`. If successful, it returns zero, otherwise it returns a nonzero value.

---

## VARIABLE ARGUMENTS

These macros and functions go through lists of arguments whose type and number can be variable. The library functions—`fprintf` and `fscanf`—and their related functions use these macros to allow them to be written in C.

Using functions with a variable number of arguments can be a source of errors. You can write most functions that might require a variable number with a fixed number by using an array of objects and a count as the parameters. These functions are only presented in this section for completeness.

The `va_list` item is a `typedef` for an object that holds information for these functions. You need to declare an object with this type. You then call `va_start` to initialize the variable list. Each argument is accessed using `va_arg`. Before control returns from the variable argument function, `va_end` should be called.

### stdarg.h

The `stdarg.h` header file contains the prototypes, macro definitions, and the following:

`va_list`        typedef for object for holding variable parameters

`void va_start(va_list argument_list, last_parameter)`

The `va_start` macro initializes `argument_list` for use by `va_arg` and `va_end`. The `last_parameter` is the name of the rightmost parameter in the list (the one just before the variable parameters).

`type va_arg(va_list argument_list, type)`   /* #include <stdarg.h> */

This returns the next value in the parameter list converted to the value `type`. If the value cannot be converted to `type`, the result is undefined. The first time this is called, it returns the first value after the `last_parameter` in the call. Each subsequent call returns the next value.

`void va_end(va_list argument_list);`        /* #include <stdarg.h> */

This sets up the function for a normal return. It should be called after all the arguments have been accessed with `va_arg` and before control returns from the function.

```
vfprintf(file_pointer,format,argument_list)    /* #include <stdio.h> */
                                                /* #include <stdarg.h> */
FILE *file_pointer;
char *format;
va_list argument_list;
```

The vfprintf function is the equivalent to calling fprintf where the variable argument list (*values*) has been initialized by a call to va_start. The function returns the number of characters output or a negative number if an error occurs. format is not modified.

```
vprintf(format,argument_list)                   /* #include <stdio.h> */
                                                /* #include <stdarg.h> */
char *format;
va_list argument_list;
```

The vprintf function is the equivalent to calling printf where the variable argument list (*values*) has been initialized by a call to va_start. The function returns the number of characters output or a negative number if an error occurs.

```
vsprintf(string,format,argument_list)           /* #include <stdio.h> */
                                                /* #include <stdarg.h> */
char *string;
char *format;
va_list argument_list;
```

The vsprintf function is the equivalent to calling sprintf where the variable argument list (*values*) has been initialized by a call to va_start. The function returns the number of characters placed in string or a negative number if an error occurs.

# Portability

One reason for using C is to be able to write efficient code that is easily ported from one type of computer or operating environment to another. If you follow a few guidelines and do not attempt to write "tricky code," your programs should be portable.

The ANSI standard provides a formal agreement about how the C language works. Its goal is to enable programmers to create code that is portable for a wide range of computers and operating systems.

You can write a program that follows the standard that may not be portable. There are certain areas in which the standard allows alternative behavior (such as logical or arithmetic shifts for right shifts). This looseness in some rules was part of C's heritage. However, if your program obeys all the numerical limits and does not assume any particular behavior, it should be portable.

In the description of the C language, there are three descriptions of behavior of a particular feature that should be noted. The first is *unspecified behavior,* for which the feature may work one way or another, such as the right shift. The second is *implementation-defined behavior.* The compiler developer had to choose how something would work. The compiler manual should document which choice the developer made. The third is *undefined behavior.* For a program that contains an error that has undefined behavior, the compiler may ignore the problem, output an error message, or abort when it executes.

Each compiler has limitations on how complex a program it can translate. These limits include the number of #include files that can be nested and the number of dimensions in an array. Each computer has limits on the sizes of numbers it can represent. Though you will seldom exceed the compiler's limits, the numerical limits should be considered carefully.

## GENERAL GUIDELINES

Use only those features that are standard ANSI. Some compilers have extensions to the standard. These include additional library routines and use of other characters (such as accepting the character $) in names.

Avoid developing any code that assumes a particular binary representation of values. For example, on some computers, the least significant byte of a two-byte int comes first; on other systems that byte comes second.

Use the lint program or equivalent commercial software to ensure that parameter and return value types in function match those in the function definition. A program may function perfectly on one computer, but may not run at all on another, because the sizes of the data types differ.

## ANSI STANDARDS

Keep the names of external variables less than or equal to the limit of significance (six characters). Use the extern declaration for all externals not defined in a source file.

The sizes of data types vary among computers and compilers. Use a type that has a range that matches your expected values. If you are trying to keep the data compact, you could use code like

```
#include <limits.h>
#define MAX_VALUE 40000
        /* Maximum value in the program */
#if INT_MAX < MAX_VALUE
        typedef INTEGER long
#else
        typedef INTEGER int
#endif
```

## DATA REPRESENTATION

Use the sizeof operator to determine the size of variables, especially structures. If you need to find the offset of a member in a structure, use the offsetof macro.

Use the escape sequences for character values (such as '\t') instead of numeric values (such as '\011').

Use plain char variables only to store ASCII characters. Otherwise, use either signed char or unsigned char, depending on your purpose.

The sign extension on right shifts varies. Cast the value to be shifted to an unsigned int, and the shift will always be logical.

To create a bit mask that has the high order bits set to one, use ~0x3, rather than 0xFFFC. The latter would have to change to 0xFFFFFFFC for compilers with four-byte integers.

Do not write expressions that are dependent on the order of evaluation. These involve expressions that have side-effects. The lint program can pinpoint most of these expressions.

Porting binary data among different types of computers is difficult, as binary representations vary. Convert all binary data to text data using the `fprintf` function or its equivalent. Read it in using `fscanf` on the other computer.

If you must write code that depends on the particular computer you are using, isolate it to a few functions. Only those few will require change when you convert the application to another machine.

## DATA TYPES

Differences in the sizes of data types among computers can be a source of problems, especially if you do not use a program to check for data type agreement. For example, suppose you wrote a function that returns a pointer used by other functions. This code might look like:

Source file one:

```
int *new_pointer();
/* Returns a pointer to be used by other functions in this package */


...
do_something(pointer)
/* Does something with the pointer returned by new_pointer */
int *pointer;
...
```

Suppose that in another source file a variable is declared to hold this return value. Assume that you declare it as an integer, rather than a pointer to an integer.

Source file two:

```
int pointer;
...
pointer=new_pointer();
...
do_something(pointer);
...
```

When you compile this on a computer where the size of an `int` was the same as the size of a pointer, the program runs correctly. However, when you transfer it to a computer where a pointer is larger than an `int`, the code often does not run correctly. If you run `lint` on these two source files, you get a message regarding the mismatch.

# Internationalization Issues

To make C an international language, additional features have been added to the language. These include provisions for characters that cannot fit in a byte and multiple forms for displaying time. The descriptions here are adapted from the ANSI standard.

## CHARACTERS

A single char may be multiple characters. For example, 'AB' may produce a single character that represents a foreign language character. There is a type wchar_t that represents the size of a multibyte (wide) character. Strings may be prefixed with an *L* to make them strings of multibyte characters, each of type wchar_t.

*Trigraphs* are sets of three characters representing a single character. These have been created so terminals that do not have keys for some C punctuation can still produce C programs.

| Sequence | Character |
|----------|-----------|
| ??= | # |
| ??( | [ |
| ??/ | \ |
| ??) | ] |
| ??' | ^ |
| ??< | { |
| ??! | \| |
| ??> | } |
| ??- | ~ |

---

# FUNCTIONS

Some functions in the standard library help you create programs that work with a number of different character sets. These are concerned with the ordering of characters as viewed by the string functions. The "locale" is the foreign language environment (or custom environment) under which the C program is operating.

A set of functions for operating on multibyte characters and transforming regular strings to multibyte strings has been added.

### Header File

The header file "locale.h" contains several macros for use with these international functions.

| Name | Used by |
|------|---------|
| LC_ALL | setlocale |
| LC_COLLATE | setlocale |
| LC_CTYPE | setlocale |
| LC_MONETARY | setlocale |
| LC_NUMERIC | setlocale |
| LC_TIME | setlocale |
| MB_CUR_MAX | wide characters |
| MB_LEN_MAX | wide characters |

It also describes one structure tag, struct lconv. This structure tag is described in localeconv:.

### Locale

```
char *setlocale(category,setting)
int category;
char *setting;
```

The setlocale function sets the program's functions that are dependent on the area of the world in which the program may be running. The value of category states which functions are to be altered:

| | |
|------|---------|
| LC_ALL | entire set of functions |
| LC_COLLATE | collation sequence for strcoll and strxfrm |
| LC_CTYPE | character handling functions |
| LC_MONETARY | monetary information |
| LC_NUMERIC | decimal point character |
| LC_TIME | for strftime function |

The value of setting tells how the functions are altered. The standard value is "C" for a standard C environment. The null string ("") and all other values are for implementation-defined environments. The function returns a pointer to a string referencing the current locale or NULL, if there is no matching locale. If the value of setting is the NULL pointer, a pointer to the current locale is returned. The setting is not modified.

### Collation Sequence

```
int strcoll(string1, string2)
char *string1;
char *string2;
```

The strcoll function compares string1 to string2. It returns a value less than zero, zero, or greater than zero, depending on whether string1 is less than, equal to, or greater than string2. The comparison is based on the strings after transformation according to the program's locale. The strings string1 and string2 are not modified.

```
size_t strxfrm(destination, source, max_number)
char *destination;
char *source;
size_t max_number;
```

The strxfrm function transforms strings that may not be in the computer's normal sorting sequence (that sequence used for strcmp). This transformation is based on the locale. Two transformed strings can be compared using strcmp. Transformed strings may be twice as long as source strings. The source is not modified.
The string in source is transformed into a string in destination. No more than max_number of characters is placed in destination, including the NUL. If the transformed source cannot fit in max_number of characters, the contents of destination are undetermined. The function returns the number of characters in destination or zero, if the transformed string could not fit.

### Time Transformation

```
size_t strftime(string,size,format,time)
char *string;
size_t size;
char *format;
struct tm *time;
```

The strftime function converts time into a string under format control. The format works much like sprintf, with the values placed in the string coming from the time structure. No more than size characters are placed in string, including the terminating NUL. The format and the structure pointed to by time are not modified. The format specifiers are

| | |
|---|---|
| a | Abbreviated weekday name |
| A | Full weekday name |
| b | Abbreviated month name |
| B | Full month name |
| c | Locale's date and time |
| d | Day of the month (01–31) |
| H | Hour (00–23) |
| I | Hour (01–12) Twelve-hour clock |
| j | Day of year (001–366) |
| m | Month (01–012) |
| M | Minute (00–59) |
| p | Locale's A.M. or P.M. |
| S | Second (00–59) |
| U | Week number of year (00–52) Sunday is first day |
| w | Weekday (0–6) Sunday is 0 |
| W | Week number of year (00–52) Monday is first day |
| x | Locale's date |
| X | Locale's time |
| y | Year (00–99) |
| Y | Year with century (0000–9999) |
| Z | Timezone name (if any) |
| % | The character % |

The function returns the number of characters converted. If the converted string cannot fit in size characters, it returns zero.

## Monetary Information

```
struct lconv *localeconv();
```

The localeconv function returns a pointer to a structure of type lconv. The information could be used to format monetary quantities. That structure contains the following.

```
struct lconv
    {
    char *decimal_point;        /* Decimal point character for nonmonetary */
    char *thousands_sep;        /* Thousand separator for nonmonetary */
    char *grouping;             /* Size of groups that are separated */
    char *int_curr_symbol;      /* International currency symbol */
    char *currency_symbol;      /* Local currency symbol */
    char *mon_decimal_point;    /* Decimal point character for monetary */
    char *mon_thousands_sep;    /* Thousand separator for monetary */
```

```
char *mon_grouping;        /* Size of groups that are separated */
char *positive_sign;       /* Positive sign */
char *negative_sign;       /* Negative sign */
char *int_frac_digits;     /* Number of fractional digits for
                              international */
char *frac_digits;         /* Number of fractional digits for local */
char p_cs_precedes;        /* True if positive sign precedes value */
char p_sep_by_space;       /* True if positive sign is separated by a
                              space from value */
char n_cs_precedes;        /* True if negative sign precedes value */
char n_sep_by_space;       /* True if negative sign is separated by a
                              space from value */
char p_sign_posn;          /* Indicates position of positive sign */
char n_sign_posn;          /* Indicates position of negative sign */
}
```

## String Operations

Some multibyte strings depend on a shift state. Each call to these functions has its own shift state memory. The internal shift state is altered if a shift character appears in the string passed to the function. If the string passed to a function is NULL, the function returns a nonzero if multibyte strings have shift states. Arrays of type wchar_t store multibyte codes. Each multibyte code has a regular character (char) string representation, which uses multiple characters to represent the same code. These functions convert between the wchar_t and char representations.

```
int mblen(multi_pointer, size)
wchar_t *multi_pointer;
size_t size;
```

The mblen function computes the number of bytes in the multibyte string that is passed. The function returns –1 if the string contains invalid multibyte codes.

```
int mbtowc(multi_pointer, string, size)
wchar_t *multi_pointer;
char *string;
size_t size;
```

The mbtowc function computes the number of bytes in the multibyte character representation that is pointed to by string. If multi_pointer is not NULL, it stores the code for that character at that address. The function returns the number of bytes of string that were used for the multibyte character, 0 if the character was NUL, or –1 if there was not a valid multibyte character.

```
int wctomb(string, multi_char)
char *string;
wchar_t multi_char;
```

   The wctomb function computes the number of bytes needed to represent the code stored in multi_char. If string is not NULL, it stores the character representation at that address.

```
size_t mbstowcs(multi_pointer, string, size)
wchar_t multi_pointer;
char *string;
size_t size;
```

   The mbstowcs function converts the characters in string to a sequence of codes in multi_pointer. At most, size codes will be stored. The function returns the number of codes stored or –1 if there was an invalid character representation.

```
size_t wcstombs(string, multi_pointer, size)
char *string;
wchar_t *multi_pointer;
size_t size;
```

   The wcstombs function converts the sequence of codes in multi_pointer into a sequence of characters stored at string. At most, size bytes are stored in string. The function returns the number of bytes stored or –1 if there was an invalid multibyte code.

# Expanded Function Prototypes

To give some examples of expanded function prototypes and the corresponding functions' headers, here are a few functions from Chapter 7 rewritten with these headers.

**Listing J.1 Rewrite of Listing 7.3**

```
#include "date.h"
#define FIRST_YEAR 50          /* First year for day number calculations */
char daymonth[2][12] =
    {
    {31, 28, 31, 30, 31, 30, 31, 31, 30, 31, 30, 31},     /* Nonleap year*/
    {31, 29, 31, 30, 31, 30, 31, 31, 30, 31, 30, 31}      /* Leap year */
    };

int date_number(struct s_date date)
/* Computes the number of days since January 1, 1950 */
/* Date is date to determine number */
                            /* Returns
                                    date number if date is valid
                                    INVALID_DATE if date is invalid
                            */
    {
    int leap;               /* Leap year flag */
    int m;                  /* Month index */
    int year_count;         /* Years from 1950 */
    int day_number;         /* Returned value */
    int leap_years;         /* Number of leap years to account for */

    if (check_date(date))
        {
        leap = is_leap_year(date.year);
        /* Determine the count */
```

```
            year_count = date.year - FIRST_YEAR;
            if (year_count >= 0)
                {
                /* Add up number of days in previous years */
                day_number = year_count * 365;

                /* Add up the extra leap years */
                leap_years = (year_count + 1) / 4;
                day_number = day_number + leap_years;

                /* Add up the number of days in prior months */
                for (m = 0; m < date.month - 1; m++)
                    {
                    day_number = day_number + daymonth[leap][m];
                    }

                /* Add the day of the month */
                day_number = day_number + date.day - 1;
                }
            else
                {
                /* Number of days in years till FIRST_YEAR */
                day_number = (year_count + 1) * 365;

                /* Add in the extra leap years */
                leap_years = (year_count - 1) / 4;
                day_number = day_number + leap_years;

                /* Add in the number of days in ending months of current year */
                for (m = 11; m > date.month - 1; m--)
                    {
                    day_number = day_number - daymonth[leap][m];
                    }
                    /* Add in the number of days in rest of month */
                    day_number = day_number - (daymonth[leap][date.month - 1] -
                        date.day) - 1;
                }
            }
        else
            day_number = INVALID_DATE;

        return day_number;
        }

#define FALSE 0
#define TRUE 1
```

```
int is_leap_year(int year)
/* Determines whether year is a leap year */
/* int year;                      Year to check */
                                  /* Returns
                                       TRUE if leap year
                                       FALSE if not leap year
                                  */
    {
    int ret;                      /*Return value */

    if (year % 4)
        ret = FALSE;
    else
        ret = TRUE;

    return ret;
    }
```

### Listing J.2 Rewrite of Listing 7.4

```
#include "date.h"

int date_compare(struct s_date first_date, struct s_date second_date)
/* Compares two dates */
/* first_date First date to compare */
/* second_date Second date to compare */
                              /* Returns -1 if first < second */
                                   /* 0 if first == second */
                                   /* 1 if first > second */
                                   /* INVALID_DATE if either date is bad */
    {
    int first_test;           /* Date number of first date */
    int second_test;          /* Date number of second date */
    int ret;                  /* Return value */

    first_test = date_number(first_date);
    second_test = date_number(second_date);

    if (first_test != INVALID_DATE && second_test != INVALID_DATE)
        {
        if (first_test < second_test)
            ret = -1;
        else if (first_test == second_test)
            ret = 0;
        else
```

```
                              ret = 1;
                      }
              else
                  ret = INVALID_DATE;

      return ret;
      }
```

## Listing J.3 Rewrite of Listing 7.5

```
#include "date.h"
#define DAYS_IN_WEEK 7                  /* Number of days in a week */
#define FIRST_DAY 0                     /* Day of week of January 1, 1950 */

int day_of_week(struct s_date date)
/* Determines the day of the week */
/* date Date to determine day of week of */
                                        /* Returns
                                              0 (SUNDAY) to 6 (SATURDAY)
                                              INVALID_DATE if date is invalid
                                        */
      {
      int day_century;                 /* Day of century */
      int ret;                         /* Return value */

      day_century = date_number(date);
      if (day_century >= 0)
          ret = day_century % DAYS_IN_WEEK + FIRST_DAY;
      else
              {
              ret = (-day_century) % DAYS_IN_WEEK;
              ret = (-ret) + FIRST_DAY;
              if (ret < 0)
                  ret = ret + DAYS_IN_WEEK;
              }

      return ret;
      }
```

## Listing J.4 Rewrite of Listing 7.6

```
#include "date.h"

struct s_date next_month(struct s_date date_in)
/* Adds one to month and returns the next date */
/* date_in Date to increment by a month */
      {
      struct s_date date_out;              /* Return value */
```

```
/* Set the return date and increment the month */
date_out = date_in;
date_out.month++;
if (date_out.month > 12)
     {
     date_out.month = 1;
     date_out.year++;
     }

/* See whether the date is invalid--greater than last day of new month */
if (check_date(date_out))
     {
     if (is_leap_year(date_out.year))
          date_out.day = daymonth[1][date_out.month-1];
else
          date_out.day = daymonth[1][date_out.month-1];
     }
return date_out;
}
```

To use these functions, you would include the header file called "date.h". The file contains these headers and expanded function prototypes:

```
#define INVALID_DATE -32767              /* Return value for invalid date */
int date_number(struct s_date date);
int date_compare(struct s_date first_date, struct s_date second_date);
int day_of_week(struct s_date date);
struct s_date next_month(struct s_date date_in);
```

# Bits, Bytes, and Numbers

## BIT VALUES[1]

A *bit* (short for binary digit) can have the value of 0 or 1. A string of bits has an arithmetic value. Each bit position has a value that is equal to twice that of the bit position to the right. If there is a 1 in a bit position, that value is included in the total for the string.

For example, the arithmetic value of the bit string 01101010 is determined by

| Bit position | 7 | 6 | 5 | 4 | 3 | 2 | 1 | 0 |
|---|---|---|---|---|---|---|---|---|
| Value of bit position | 128 | 64 | 32 | 16 | 8 | 4 | 2 | 1 |
| Sample bit string | 0 | 1 | 1 | 0 | 1 | 0 | 1 | 0 |

$$
\begin{array}{r}
64 \\
32 \\
8 \\
\underline{2} \\
100
\end{array}
$$
Decimal value of the bit string

In a typical computer, strings of 8, 16, or 32 bits are used to store numbers. The leftmost bit (called the *most significant bit* or *MSB*) may be used to store the sign of the number. Typically, the sign is 0 for a positive number and 1 for a negative number. The bit string for a negative number can be the complement of the positive number, where each bit is negated (0 for 1 and 1 for 0). This is called *one's complement*. Alternatively, a value of 1 may be added to negative numbers. This is called *two's complement*.

---

[1] This appendix is adapted from *C Language for Programmers* by Kenneth Pugh (Glenview, Ill.: Scott, Foresman, 1985) and is used by permission.

|  |  | Negative Value |
| --- | --- | --- |
| Positive Value | One's Complement | Two's Complement |
| 00000001 | 11111110 | 11111111 |
| 01111111 | 10000000 | 10000001 |

Note that char values may be treated as either signed or unsigned, depending on the compiler. The int values are signed by default. The unsigned data type modifier makes the compiler treat the MSB of the variable as a value bit, so that it holds only positive numbers.

## SIGN EXTENSION

If a string of bits is expanded to a longer string, the leftmost bits in the expanded string may either be set to 0 or may depend on the sign bit in the smaller string. The latter case is called *sign extension*. If the sign bit of the small string is a 1, the leftmost bits in the expanded string will be set to 1.

|  | 16 Bit-String | |
| --- | --- | --- |
| 8-Bit String | Without Sign Extension | With Sign Extension |
| 01101110 | 00000000 01101110 | 00000000 01101110 |
| 10010000 | 00000000 10010000 | 11111111 10010000 |

Notice that the difference in the result occurs only if the original string had a negative sign. There is no sign extension for unsigned integer types. There is sign extension for signed integer types. char variables are signed extended if they are treated as signed variables by the compiler.

## SHIFTS

A bit string can be shifted left or right. If the string is shifted left, the rightmost bit (*least significant bit* or *LSB*) is set to 0. If the string is shifted right, the sign bit (MSB) may be set to either 0 (termed a *logical shift*) or it may keep its starting value (an *arithmetic shift*). These two types of shifts differ if the sign bit is a 1.

|  | Logical Shift | | Arithmetic Shift |
| --- | --- | --- | --- |
| 8 Bit string | Left | Right | Right |
| 01001001 | 10010010 | 00100100 | 00100100 |
| 10011000 | 00110000 | 00001100 | 11001100 |

Shifts of unsigned integer values are always logical shifts. Shifts of signed values may be either arithmetic or logical, depending on the compiler.

# MEMORY LOCATIONS

A memory location has two numeric values associated with it: its address and the value that contains the address. In a typical computer, each memory location contains one byte (eight bits) of information. The address uniquely identifies a memory location. Addresses typically start at zero and go up to one less than the number of bytes in the computer.

The `char` values occupy one memory location, or one byte. `int` values occupy two or four bytes, depending on the computer. The low-order byte (the one with the LSB) or the most significant byte (the one with the MSB) may occupy the first memory location. The order in which the bytes are stored is computer dependent. The `double` values occupy eight or more bytes, depending on the computer. Representation of floating point values (exponent and mantissa) is dependent on the processor.

When a variable is allocated memory, it is given successive memory locations. Addresses of the memory locations for `static` and external variables are fixed while the program is executing. Memory locations for automatic variables are assigned when a function is entered. When the function returns, those memory locations may be reused by automatic variables in other functions. The address operator applied to a variable name computes the address of the first memory location where the variable is stored.

Elements in an array are stored in successive bytes. So, the second element in an array of `char` is stored in a memory location whose address is one greater than the first element. The third element is stored at an address one greater than the second. For an `int` array, each element is stored at an address either two or four greater than the previous element, depending on the size of an `int`.

A pointer variable occupies two or four bytes, depending on the computer. The value it contains does not appear any different than values stored in other variables, such as `int`s. If a reference to a pointer variable is made without any operators, the value at the pointer's memory location is accessed. If an indirection operator is applied to a pointer variable, the contents of the pointer's memory location are first retrieved. That value is then treated as an address of another variable. The content at that address is then accessed.

# Quick Reference

The main reference for each element in C is given by the page number.

## OPERATORS

| Operator | | Associativity | Page |
|---|---|---|---|
| ( ) | function call | left to right | 57 |
| [ ] | array element | | 100 |
| -> | pointer to structure member | | 178 |
| . | member of structure | | 130 |
| ! | logical negation | right to left | 35 |
| ~ | one's complement | | 203 |
| ++ | increment | | 50, 210 |
| -- | decrement | | 50, 210 |
| - | unary minus | | 17 |
| + | unary plus | | 17 |
| (type) | cast | | 194 |
| * | indirection (pointer) | | 158 |
| & | address | | 157 |
| sizeof | size of object | | 102, 132 |
| * | multiplication | left to right | 17 |
| / | division | | 216 |
| % | modulus | | 17 |
| + | addition | left to right | 17 |
| - | subtraction | | 17 |
| << | left shift | left to right | 204 |
| >> | right shift | | 204 |

| Operator | | Associativity | Page |
|---|---|---|---|
| < | less than | left to right | 31 |
| <= | less than or equal to | | 31 |
| > | greater than | | 31 |
| >= | greater than or equal to | | 31 |
| == | equality | left to right | 31 |
| != | inequality | | 31 |
| & | bitwise AND | left to right | 203 |
| ^ | bitwise XOR | left to right | 203 |
| \| | bitwise OR | left to right | 203 |
| && | logical AND | left to right | 35 |
| \|\| | logical OR | left to right | 35 |
| ? : | conditional | right to left | 212 |
| = | assignment | right to left | 16, 214 |
| op= | shorthand assignment | | 216 |
| , | comma | left to right | 213 |

## KEYWORDS

| Keyword | Page |
|---|---|
| Storage types: | |
| auto | 15 |
| extern | 69 |
| register | 199 |
| static | 16 |
| Data types: | |
| char | 12 |
| double | 12, 189 |
| enum | 195 |
| float | 189 |
| int | 12, 189 |
| void | 64, 241 |

| *Keyword* | *Page* |
|---|---|
| **Data type modifiers:** | |
| const | 199 |
| long | 189 |
| short | 189 |
| signed | 191 |
| unsigned | 189 |
| volatile | 200 |
| | |
| **Aggregate data types:** | |
| struct | 150 |
| union | 148 |
| | |
| **Data type declarator:** | |
| typedef | 197 |
| | |
| **Built-in operator:** | |
| sizeof | 102, 132 |
| | |
| **Control flow:** | |
| break | 46, 230 |
| case | 228 |
| continue | 233 |
| default | 228 |
| do | 45 |
| else | 32 |
| for | 48, 224 |
| goto | 226 |
| if | 30 |
| return | 61 |
| switch | 228 |
| while | 41 |

*Elements in Following Sample Program:*

Comment
Include file
#define
Function prototype;
Enumeration list
Structure tag-type
Array
Data type modifiers
Enumerated variable
Float variable
External variable

*Keywords in Following Sample Program:*

Main function
Main function parameters
Function open
Local declarations
Integer variable
Float variable
Structure variable
Array
Pointer
Static variable
File pointer
Output function
Input function
For loop
Compound statement
Function call
Array element
End of compound statement
Open file
If statement
else statement
Structure assignment
While loop
Decrement operator
File write
If
Break from while
Increment
Close file
Exit function
Function header
Parameter declarations
Function body
Local variable declarations
Conditional compilation
Switch statement
case statement
break in switch
default statement

*Page Numbers Referring to C Concepts Shown*                    *Page*

```
return statement
/* This is a working program that includes most of the features of C.
It is not the best solution to the problem */
```
19

*Page*

```
#include <stdio.h>                                              270
#define SIZE_NAME 20            /* Size of person's name */      22
#define SIZE_FILENAME 20        /* Size of file name to write to */
#define PAY_RATE 18.2           /* Rate of pay for all persons */
#define NUMBER_PERSONS 50       /* Maximum number of persons */
double compute_pay(unsigned int, double, enum e_weekday );      240
enum e_weekday {sunday, monday, tuesday,                        195
    wednesday, thursday, friday, saturday};
struct s_person                                                 131
    {
    char name[SIZE_NAME];       /* Name of person */            100
    unsigned int hours_worked;  /* How long worked */           189
    enum e_weekday day_worked;  /* Day worked */                195
    double pay;                 /* Pay for work */               12
    };
int number_people;             /* Number of people to input */   69
main(argc, argv)                                                 73
/* This program determines pay for a person */
int argc;                       /* How many arguments */         284
char *argv[];                   /* Pointers to arguments */
    {                                                            57
    int i;                      /* Counter for people */         58
    int ret;                    /* Return value from functions */ 12
    double pay_rate = PAY_RATE;  /* Rate of pay */               12
    struct s_person person;     /* One person */                131
    static struct s_person persons_all[NUMBER_PERSONS];         100
                                /* Table for all people */
    struct s_person *pperson;    /* Pointer to structure of persons */ 158
    static char filename[SIZE_FILENAME];
                                /* Name of file */               16
    FILE *file;                 /* File pointer */              327
    /* Get number of people and where to write data */
    printf("\n How many people?");                               83
    scanf("%d", &number_people);
    printf("\n Name of file to write to ");                      83
    scanf("%s",filename);
    /* Input each person */
    for (i = 0; i < number_people; i++)                          48
        {                                                        32
        printf("\n Name of person?");
        scanf("%s", person.name);
        printf("\n Hours worked?");
        scanf("%lf", &person.hours_worked);
        printf("\n Day of week (0 = Sun, 6 = Sat)?");
        scanf("%u",&person.day_worked);
```

```
        person.pay = compute_pay(person.hours_worked, pay_rate,     59
             person.day_worked);
        persons_all[i] = person;                                    100
        }                                                           32
/* Write out all the data */
file = fopen(filename,"wb");                                        327
if (file == NULL)                                                   30
        {
        printf("\n Unable to open file");
        }
else                                                                32
        {
        pperson = persons_all;                                      132
        while (number_people--)                                     41
             {                                                      50
             ret = fwrite(pperson, sizeof(struct s_person), 1, file); 330
             if (ret != 1)                                          30
                  {
                  printf("\n Error in writing");
                  break;                                            46
                  }
             pperson++;                                             50
             }
        fclose(file);                                               327
        }
    exit (0);                                                       73
    }
double compute_pay(hours_worked, pay_rate, day_worked)              57
/* Computes pay for a person */
unsigned int hours_worked;          /* How long worked */           58
double pay_rate;                    /* Rate of pay */
enum e_weekday day_worked;          /* Day of work */
    {                                                               57
    double rate_multiplier = 1.0;   /* For overtime rates */
    double pay;                     /* Computed pay */
#ifdef DEBUG                                                        271
    printf("\n Compute pay hours %u rate %lf",hours_worked, pay_rate);
#endif
    switch(day_worked)                                             228
        {
    case sunday:                                                   228
        rate_multiplier = 2.0;
        break;
    case saturday:
        rate_multiplier = 1.5;
```

# Index